"Since the latter half of the 20th century, regional organisations have emerged in many of the world's regions. Much focus has been devoted to the success story that is the European Union, yet another regional organisation deserves our recognition: ASEAN. It is hard to overstate ASEAN's contributions to peace, prosperity and transnational cooperation across South East Asia. Its positive impact is felt by millions of peoples in what has traditionally been one of the more complex and divided regions of the world. This book is a timely reminder that regional organisations, and ASEAN in particular, are a vital feature of modern international architecture."

—*Kofi Annan*, former Secretary-General of the United Nations

"This book on ASEAN explains well how the pragmatic Indonesian philosophy of *musyawarah* and *mufakat* has been critical for ASEAN's success. Indonesian leadership has led to the creation and development of one of the world's most successful regional organizations, which has fundamentally transformed the geopolitics and geoeconomics of Southeast Asia. As ASEAN begins a new, possibly perilous, journey into the next fifty years, we should read this book as an indispensable guide to ASEAN's future. We cannot take our success for granted. We have to work even harder to strengthen and, if necessary, reinvent ASEAN. This book explains how."

—*Dr. Susilo Bambang Yudhoyono*, sixth President of Indonesia

"ASEAN has successfully maintained regional peace and security for almost five decades. I would attribute ASEAN's unlikely success to two key factors. First, the founding leaders held firm to a shared vision to resolve differences among Southeast Asian countries quietly and face common threats together in order to secure and improve the livelihood of their peoples. However, in the early years following ASEAN's founding, Summits were held infrequently—in fact, ASEAN leaders met only three times up to 1990, the year I became Prime Minister. Second, succeeding generations of ASEAN leaders were able to work closely together for the common good of the region. We institutionalised annual ASEAN Summits, which became more structured. The increased opportunities for interaction bred familiarity among ASEAN leaders and made our interactions less formal. A slew of initiatives followed, starting with the ASEAN Free Trade Area which later led to the ASEAN Common Market, and the ASEAN + 3 and other Dialogues.

Nonetheless, ASEAN is not a frictionless, perfect organisation. There is much more ASEAN member states can do together, particularly to strengthen our cohesion in addressing regional challenges. Kishore and

Jeffery's book makes concrete proposals for ASEAN's way forward: it's a good read for those concerned with geopolitics and regional cooperation."
—*Goh Chok Tong*, Emeritus Senior Minister, Singapore

"ASEAN was born in Bangkok. Thailand can take great pride in the fact that this Thai baby has emerged as a world success story. Indeed, many significant ASEAN achievements were initiated by Thailand, including AFTA and ASEM. Kishore and Jeffery have done the world a huge favour in documenting this success story and in making concrete proposals to strengthen ASEAN further. This is a must-read for all who have interest in ASEAN affairs."
—*Anand Panyarachun*, former Prime Minister of Thailand

"Kishore and I have written that the world is coming together in a Fusion of Civilizations. This book documents beautifully how ASEAN has achieved this fusion. The ASEAN story is hugely instructive and this book tells it very well."
—*Lawrence W. Summers*, President Emeritus of Harvard University and former US Secretary of the Treasury

"We live in turbulent times. The global consensus in favour of open trade is eroding. Few of us speak up strongly and eloquently about the need to resist protectionism. This is why this volume on ASEAN is so timely. It describes how a Third World region has emerged as a dynamic economic powerhouse, thanks to open trade and economic integration. ASEAN, on track to become the fourth-largest economy in the world by 2050, can serve as a model. The authors also describe how ASEAN can be further strengthened institutionally. Its Secretariat clearly needs more resources. This book is a must-read for policymakers all around the world."
—*Pascal Lamy*, former Director-General, World Trade Organization

"ASEAN is an under-rated regional organization. Its progress year by year may seem slow. Sometimes, it appears even to go backwards. However, looking at Southeast Asia against the sweep of Cold War and post-Cold War history, ASEAN has been a remarkable success. Most importantly, it has kept relations among member-states harmonious despite occasional disputes. The integration of war-torn Vietnam, Cambodia and Laos into ASEAN has been relatively smooth. The peaceful transition of Myanmar from a military government to a democracy is a miracle which ASEAN made possible. ASEAN economies are now all benefiting from being increasingly integrated into an expanding Chinese economy which is on track to becoming the biggest in the world. The growth of India will be an added boost. Provided there is a larger peace, which will be a continuing test of ASEAN's indispensable diplomacy, the prospect for ASEAN in the 21st century is bright. This is an excellent book by Kishore and Jeffery. It explains, in clear and simple terms, how and why ASEAN has become one of the most successful regional organizations in the world. Based on his long experience in ASEAN diplomacy, without making light of ASEAN's weaknesses and mistakes, Kishore corrects a wrong view prevalent in Western writings that ASEAN is little more than a talk shop. Indeed, it is 'a catalyst for peace in Asia'."

—*George Yeo*, former Foreign Minister of Singapore

"At a time when Western internationalism is in retreat, *The ASEAN Miracle* from Kishore Mahbubani and Jeffery Sng is a refreshingly hopeful reminder of how a group of small and developing countries can lead the way in building peace and progress. A powerful and passionate account of how, against all odds, ASEAN transformed the region and why Asia and the world need it even more today."

—*Amitav Acharya*, Professor of International Relations at the School of International Service, American University

"Two thousand years ago, an Indian wave swept through Southeast Asia. Today, India is about to take off again and resume its historical ties with the region. It has much to learn from ASEAN's success, and this fine book is a good place to start."

—*Gurcharan Das*, best-selling author of *India Unbound* and other books

"Over the years, Kishore Mahbubani has been as eloquent and visionary as he has been tireless in championing Asia's growing role in world affairs. In this impressive volume, Mahbubani and Sng tell the story of Southeast Asia's ascent and the often underappreciated role of ASEAN as a regional provider of peace and stability. As the book makes clear, it is an unfinished story—ASEAN is uniquely situated to work with regional and global great powers in the search for common ground, but ASEAN is also vulnerable to neglect and decline. In the end, the authors offer a powerful argument for a new era of ASEAN leadership."

—*G. John Ikenberry*, Albert G. Milbank Professor of Politics and International Affairs, Princeton University

The ASEAN Miracle

The ASEAN Miracle

A Catalyst for Peace

Kishore Mahbubani and Jeffery Sng

OXFORD
UNIVERSITY PRESS

OXFORD
UNIVERSITY PRESS

Oxford University Press is a department of the University of Oxford.
It furthers the University's objective of excellence in research, scholarship,
and education by publishing worldwide. Oxford is a registered trademark of
Oxford University Press in the UK and in certain other countries.

Published in India by
Oxford University Press
2/11 Ground Floor, Ansari Road, Daryaganj, New Delhi 110 002, India

ISBN-13: 978-0-19-948525-3
ISBN-10: 0-19-948525-9

Printed in India by Replika Press Pvt. Ltd

The edition is for sale only in India, Bangladesh, Pakistan, Sri Lanka,
Nepal, Bhutan, and Maldives

To
Anne and Pim

Contents

Acknowledgements   xiii
Preface   xv

Introduction   1

1. The Four Waves   15
      The Indian Wave   18
      The Chinese Wave   25
      The Muslim Wave   29
      The Western Wave   35

2. The ASEAN Ecosystem of Peace   48
      First Factor: The Fear of Communism   51
      Second Factor: The Role of Strong Leaders   59
      Third Factor: Geopolitical Luck   65
      Fourth Factor: Market-Oriented Economic Policies   68
      Fifth Factor: ASEAN-Based Regional Networks   74

3. ASEAN and the Great Powers   76
      ASEAN and America   82
      ASEAN and China   97
      ASEAN and the EU   112
      ASEAN and India   121
      ASEAN and Japan   127

4. Pen Sketches   137
      Brunei   139
      Cambodia   141
      Indonesia   144
      Laos   148
      Malaysia   150
      Myanmar   155
      The Philippines   159
      Singapore   165
      Thailand   168
      Vietnam   172

5. ASEAN: Strengths and Weaknesses   177
        Strengths   179
        Weaknesses   184
        Threats   190
        Opportunities   197
        Conclusion   206

6. ASEAN's Peace Prize   207
        Three Bold Recommendations   221

Bibliography   233
Index   251

Acknowledgements

Both of us are blessed that we were able to get interviews with two truly insightful observers of Southeast Asia before they passed away in August 2016 and December 2015 respectively. The first was the former president of Singapore Mr S.R. Nathan. Indeed, he was present in Bangkok at the signing of the ASEAN Declaration on 8 August 1967 and was directly involved in the negotiations on the document. The second was the eminent scholar on Southeast Asia Dr Ben Anderson. Jeffery got to know Ben well when he studied at Cornell University. Few can match the profound insights that Ben shared with the world in his classic work *Imagined Communities: Reflections on the Origin and Spread of Nationalism*.

We also learned a lot from the personal interviews we had with other eminent policy makers and scholars in ASEAN. None of them should be held responsible for the contents of the book. Nonetheless, we would like to thank the following individuals for being so generous to us with their time and wisdom. In alphabetical order, they are Sanchita Basu Das, Suchit Bunbongkarn, Tej Bunnag, Termsak Chalermpalanupap, Barry Desker, S. Dhanabalan, Rebecca Fatima Sta Maria, S. Jayakumar, Hong Jukhee, Bilahari Kausikan, Tommy Koh, Sulaimah Mahmood, Vanu Gopala Menon, Mohamed Jawhar Hassan, Bunn Nagara, Narongchai Akrasanee, Ong Keng Yong, Ravidran Palaniappan, Pradap Pibulsonggram, Chitriya Pinthong, Pushpanathan Sundram, Andrew Tan, Fraser Thompson, Wang Gungwu, Wong Kan Seng, Walter Woon and George Yeo.

We also want to thank the several eminent personalities who agreed to provide generous blurbs for this book, namely, Amitav Acharya, Kofi Annan, Gurcharan Das, Goh Chok Tong, John Ikenberry, Pascal Lamy, Anand Panyarachun, Larry Summers, George Yeo and Susilo Bambang Yudhoyono.

Both of us would also like to thank our research assistants for the excellent work they have done. Amrita Vijayakumar Nair and Kristen Tang have been working on the book since August 2014. They also travelled to Bangkok and Kuala Lumpur to do additional research on this volume. Before Amrita and Kristen joined us, we were helped by Rhoda Severino and Vandana Prakash Nair. We are glad that Rhoda was able to receive an autographed copy of *Imagined Communities* from Ben Anderson. The A-team from Kishore's office, especially Carol Chan, Esther Lee and Amirah Binte Mohamed Fadali, also played a key role in completing this book.

It was not easy to get a publisher for this book. Kishore's literary contacts in New York told him that Western publishers had no interest in the ASEAN story, despite its global significance. We were therefore happy that NUS Press made the brave decision to publish this book. The editors, Peter Schoppert, Paul Kratoska and Sunandini Arora Lal, have done a brilliant job of polishing the manuscript.

The choice of NUS Press proved to be a brilliant decision because of an exceptionally generous gift by the Lee Foundation of Singapore. As we explain in this book, one weakness of ASEAN is that the 600 million people who live in Southeast Asia do not feel a sense of ownership of ASEAN. Indeed, they know little about the organization. To remedy this ignorance, the Lee Foundation gave us a generous gift to have this book translated into all the major languages of the ASEAN countries. Hence, this book will be translated into Bahasa Melayu, Bahasa Indonesia, Burmese, Khmer, Lao, Tagalog, Thai and Vietnamese. The strong associations NUS has in Southeast Asia will facilitate these translations. For this generous gift, we would like to thank from the bottom of our hearts the Lee Foundation, especially its chairman, Dr Lee Seng Tee, who personally experienced the turbulence of Southeast Asia when he was beaten up by Japanese soldiers in World War II.

Finally, both of us would also like to thank our numerous friends in various Southeast Asian capitals. The warm friendship and deep insights they shared with us over several decades gave us the confidence to write this book on Southeast Asia. We cannot name them all, but we hope that when they read this book they will find some of the gems of wisdom they have shared with us over the years.

Preface

It has taken almost six decades of friendship between Jeffery and me to finally produce a book together. It has also taken us almost six decades of living in Southeast Asia to get under its skin.

Southeast Asia is, in civilizational terms, the most diverse corner of planet Earth. No other region even comes close. Hence, it is a difficult region to understand and describe well. Fortunately, Jeffery and I have had the good fortune of getting to know several Southeast Asian societies well.

We were born and brought up in Singapore, a Chinese-majority state. We got to know each other as children as we lived in the poor neighbourhood of Onan Road. Jeffery is ethnically Chinese (of Hokkien/Hakka descent). I am Indian (of Sindhi descent). Yet, in school both of us learned Malay—the language of a plurality of Southeast Asia.

Both of us studied philosophy in NUS. Then our paths diverged. Jeffery went on to obtain a master's degree in Southeast Asian studies in 1982 from Cornell University, where he met several eminent Southeast Asian scholars, including George Kahin and Ben Anderson. In Cornell, Jeffery also met his Thai wife, Pimpraphai Bisalputra. He has been living in Bangkok since the early 1980s and speaks Thai fluently. Pim and Jeff have produced two excellent books on Thailand: one on Thai Bencharong pottery[1] and the other on the Thai Chinese.[2]

Jeffery has also gotten to know Indonesia well. When he worked for the Quakers, he got to know several Indonesian leaders, including the late Indonesian President Abdurrahman Wahid (affectionately known as Gus Dur). Indeed, Gus Dur used Jeffery as a special envoy to develop close links with Thailand when he was president.

Jeffery also got to know ordinary folk well. Once, when he was visiting a poor Lao village, the villagers felt that Jeffery deserved a

---

1. Jeffery Sng and Pimpraphai Bisalputra, *Bencharong & Chinawares in the Court of Siam* (Bangkok: Chawpipope Osathanugrah, 2011).
2. Jeffery Sng and Pimpraphai Bisalputra, *A History of the Thai-Chinese* (Singapore: Editions Didier Millet, 2015).

special treat as a VIP visitor. Hence, they vigorously thrashed the earth mounds in the rice fields to get the rats to jump out. When the rats did so, they were bludgeoned by the villagers. Jeffery was then given a royal feast with rat meat as the dish of honour. I have not had this experience.

But I have lived in other Southeast Asian societies. I lived for a year in Phnom Penh, Cambodia, from July 1973 to June 1974. As far as I can recall, the city, which was under siege from the Khmer Rouge, was shelled every day while I was there. Sadly, the Khmer Rouge took over nine months after I left. I lost many friends to the Cambodian killing fields. From 1976 to 1979, I served as the deputy chief of mission in the Singapore High Commission in Kuala Lumpur, Malaysia. I learned at first hand that the bitterness of the separation between Malaysia and Singapore in 1965 had still not evaporated.

Both Jeffery and I have therefore experienced the turbulence of Southeast Asia in the second half of the 20th century. We can speak with great confidence about the "miracle" ASEAN has brought to Southeast Asia, because we know how different the outcomes could have been for several Southeast Asian societies in the absence of ASEAN. Many American social scientists on Southeast Asia who seem to rely primarily on *New York Times* press clippings for raw information on the region do not really understand well the societies of Southeast Asia.

This is what has motivated us to produce this book together. We hope that it captures our years of study and close understanding of Southeast Asia. We also hope that the lessons from Southeast Asia's exceptional success will be shared and emulated in other corners of the world. A world in which other developing regions emulate Southeast Asia's success in producing peace and prosperity will be a happy world.

Kishore Mahbubani

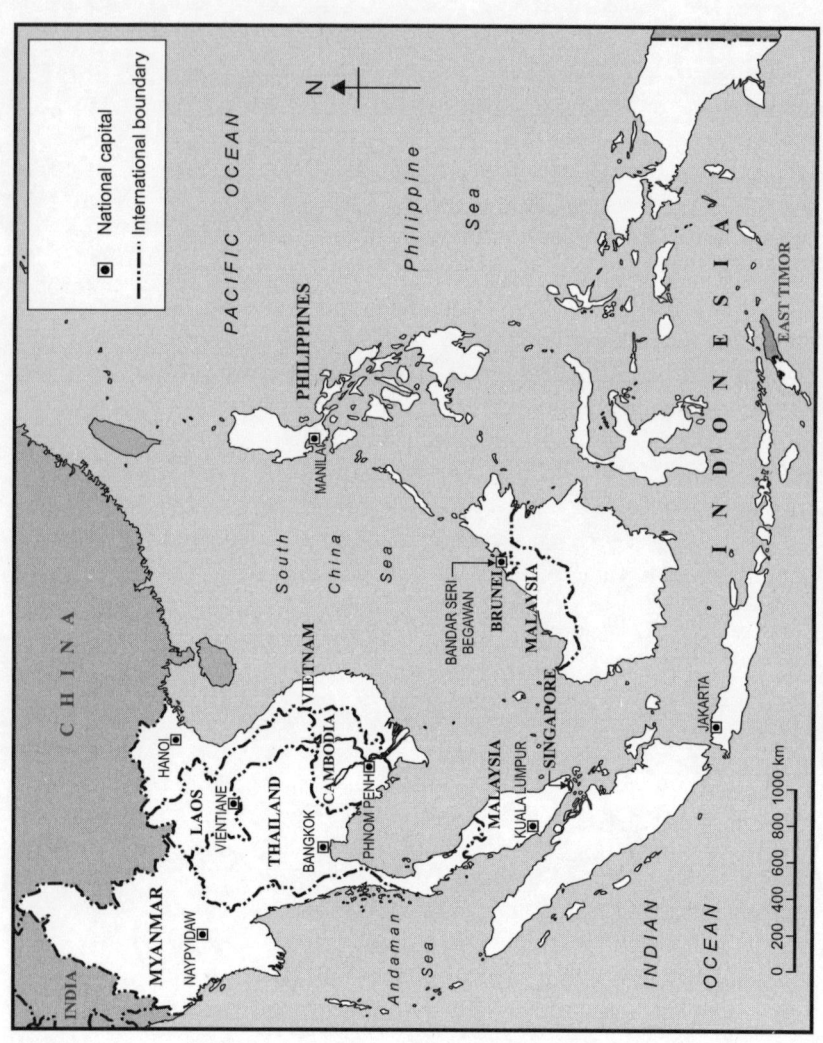

The Association of Southeast Asian Nations (ASEAN)

Introduction

ASEAN is a living and breathing modern miracle. Why? No other regional organization has done as much as the Association of Southeast Asian Nations (ASEAN) to improve the living conditions of a broad swath of humanity. The more than 600 million people living in the region have seen remarkable progress in the 50 years since the formation of the association. ASEAN has brought peace and prosperity to a troubled region, generated inter-civilizational harmony in the most diverse corner of the earth and brought hope to many people. It may have also acted as a critical catalyst for China's peaceful rise. ASEAN is therefore more deserving of the next Nobel Peace Prize than any other person or institution today.

It is no secret that our global discourse is dominated today by pessimistic voices. In many areas, however, ASEAN has generated optimistic narratives. In an era of growing cultural pessimism, where many thoughtful and influential individuals believe that different civilizations—especially Islam and the West—cannot live together in peace, ASEAN provides a living laboratory of peaceful civilizational coexistence. Few are aware that Southeast Asia has become a microcosm of our global condition. In the past, different civilizations existed in separate geopolitical compartments. Today, our shrinking world means they are coming closer together. Southeast Asia is the only region where so many civilizations live together cheek by jowl. And they live together in peace. This miracle was delivered by ASEAN.

Second, in an era of growing economic pessimism, where many young people, especially in America and Europe, believe that their lives will get worse in coming decades, Southeast Asia bubbles with optimism. This once-impoverished region has experienced a remarkable economic miracle. World Bank President Jim Yong Kim observed, "In just 30 years, Vietnam has reduced extreme poverty from 50 per cent to roughly 3 per cent—an astounding accomplishment."[1] Indonesia, once a metaphor for continuing and persistent poverty, has one of the most optimistic youthful populations in the world.

---

1. Kim, Jim Yong, "Lessons from Vietnam in a Slowing Global Economy", *Straits Times*, 24 Feb. 2016, http://www.straitstimes.com/opinion/lessons-from-vietnam-in-a-slowing-global-economy, accessed 14 Oct. 2016.

According to Nielsen in May 2015, Indonesian consumer confidence was the "2nd highest globally".[2] How did such a poor country become so optimistic? ASEAN has generated economic optimism.

Third, in an era of growing geopolitical pessimism, when many leading geopolitical thinkers predict rising competition and tension between great powers—especially between America and China—ASEAN has created an indispensable diplomatic platform that regularly brings all the great powers together. Moreover, ASEAN has created conducive environments for the great powers to talk to each other. Within ASEAN, a culture of peace has evolved as a result of imbibing the Indonesian custom of *musyawarah* and *mufakat* (consultation and consensus). Now ASEAN has begun to share this culture of peace with the larger Asia-Pacific region. When tensions rise between China and Japan and their leaders find it difficult to speak to each other, ASEAN provides a face-saving platform and the right setting to restart the conversation. ASEAN has especially facilitated China's peaceful rise by generating an ecosystem of peace that moderated aggressive impulses.

Does this mean that ASEAN is the perfect regional organization? Absolutely not. It is hugely imperfect. This is precisely why the world has not understood the ASEAN story. Its many imperfections have been well documented, especially in the Anglo-Saxon media. For example, *The Economist* observed on 2 January 2016:

> Grandiose statements from the Association of South-East Asian Nations (ASEAN) are the region's Christmas crackers: they appear at regular intervals, create a commotion but contain little of substance … Perhaps inevitably, the commitment of such a diverse bunch to regional integration, and the pooling of sovereignty it implies, is not as strong as ASEAN's triumphant statements suggest. There is no mechanism to enforce the group's many agreements and treaties. Regional banking systems and capital markets remain unintegrated. Tariffs may vanish, but non-tariff barriers pop up in their place. Members continue to

---

2.　Mila Lubis, "Indonesia Remains the 2nd Most Optimistic Country Globally", *Nielsen*, 30 May 2015, http://www.nielsen.com/id/en/press-room/2015/indonesia-remains-the-2nd-most-optimistic-country-globally.html/, accessed 12 Oct. 2016.

set their own intellectual-property, land-use and immigration policies.[3]

Any reader who doubts this should do an online search for "ASEAN". He or she will drown in a flood of articles documenting the many imperfections of ASEAN.

These stories are not wrong. ASEAN never progresses in a linear fashion. It often moves like a crab: it takes two steps forward, one step backwards and one step sideways. Viewed over a short period, progress is hard to see. Yet miraculously, when one takes a longer view, analyzing progress decade by decade, ASEAN's forward progress becomes visible. Despite its many imperfections, it keeps moving forward. This book hopes to explain the great mystery of how this happens.

One essential paradox about ASEAN needs to be observed at the very beginning of this volume: ASEAN's strength can be found in its weakness. The reason ASEAN has emerged as the indispensable platform for great-power engagement in the Asia-Pacific region is that it is too weak to be a threat to anyone. So all the great powers instinctively trust it. As George Yeo, the brilliant former Singapore foreign minister, said:

> In the end, everybody came to the conclusion that however ungainly, however inefficient, however elliptical ASEAN's ways are, it's still better than not having an ASEAN. That is the genius of ASEAN foreign policy. In the end, almost with a sneer, they accepted that ASEAN should be in the driving seat. Yes, ASEAN's leadership is the most preferred because no other driver would be trusted by the others.[4]

Another essential fact about ASEAN needs to be absorbed at the outset: It was born to fail, not to succeed. Indeed, when ASEAN was founded on 8 August 1967 in Bangkok, it would have been difficult to find a more troubled region than Southeast Asia. This is how a veteran Singaporean diplomat, Bilahari Kausikan, described the regional environment in that year:

> Consider the situation in 1967. All five ASEAN countries faced Chinese-inspired, if not directly backed, internal Communist

---

3. "More Hat than Cattle", *The Economist*, 2 Jan. 2016, http://www.economist. com/news/finance-and-economics/21684811-seamless-regional-economic-bloc-just-around-corneras-always-more-hat/, accessed 12 Oct. 2016.
4. Authors' interview with George Yeo, 5 Feb. 2016.

insurgencies. China itself was seized with the revolutionary madness of the Cultural Revolution. On mainland Southeast Asia, the war in Indochina was one of the hottest frontlines of the Cold War. Three years earlier, the Vietnam War had escalated with direct American bombing of North Vietnam. At the same time, almost every member of the five original ASEAN members was at the other's throat. Malaysia and Singapore had recently separated, and relations were fraught with racial tensions. Indonesia, which had undergone the agony of a bloody abortive Communist coup, had just ended an undeclared war against Singapore and Malaysia: Konfrontasi. The Philippines laid claim to a large chunk of East Malaysia, known as Sabah. Proto-irredentist movements on their porous borders, where the writ of the centre was at best tenuous, plagued relations between Malaysia and Thailand and between Indonesia and the Philippines. Almost all Southeast Asian states were artificial entities, whose boundaries were established only during the colonial era, still imperfectly integrated, and therefore subject to fits of insecurely insistent nationalism.[5]

Many contemporary observers shared this pessimistic view of Southeast Asia's prospects. Several distinguished American scholars predicted doom and gloom for Southeast Asia. Philip W. Thayer, then dean of the School of Advanced International Studies at Johns Hopkins University, quotes Justice William Douglas in the winter 1954 issue of *World Affairs* as saying that Southeast Asia, "confronted with staggering problems … rich in people and in resources and a prize for the Soviet empire builders—will long be turbulent and uneasy".[6] Columbia University professor Nathaniel Peffer was dismissive of the potential benefits of a Southeast Asian regional organization:

> For practical purposes, having regard to the situation that confronts us in Southeast Asia in 1954, what would a Southeast Asia organization amount to? The situation is clear enough; Indo-China falling partly under communist domination at the best, wholly under communist domination at the worst, and Thailand first and then Burma falling under the red shadow.[7]

---

5. Bilahari Kausikan, "The Ages of ASEAN", in *The Inclusive Regionalist: A Festschrift Dedicated to Jusuf Wanandi*, ed. Hadi Soesastro and Clara Joewono (Jakarta: Centre for Strategic and International Studies, 2007).
6. Philip Warren Thayer, ed., *Southeast Asia in the Coming World* (Baltimore: Johns Hopkins Press, 1971).
7. Nathaniel Peffer, "Regional Security in Southeast Asia", *International Organization* 8, 3 (1954): 311–5.

Another key point needs to be emphasized at the beginning of this volume: Even if politics had not troubled the region in 1967, Southeast Asia would still have been unsuitable ground for an exercise in regional cooperation. No other region on our planet is as diverse as Southeast Asia.

We live on a planet with over seven billion human beings who identify with different human civilizations: Judaeo-Christian, Chinese-Confucianist, Islamic, Hindu and Buddhist, just to mention a few of the more dominant ones. In most of the world, these civilizations live largely apart in different geographical compartments. Christians live in Europe and the Americas, Chinese-Confucianists live in China and East Asia, and Muslims live in an arc from Morocco to Indonesia. Hindus live mostly in India, and Buddhists are found sprinkled from Sri Lanka to China, Korea and Japan.

Only in Southeast Asia do all these different cultures and civilizations meet. No other region in the world can match its cultural, religious, linguistic and ethnic diversity. In a relatively small geographical space, we find 240 million Muslims, 130 million Christians, 140 million Buddhists and 7 million Hindus. This range of religious diversity is remarkable in itself. But it actually masks a deeper cultural diversity. In Indonesia, the Acehnese and most Javanese are Muslim. Yet, culturally they could not be more different. And this is one reason why the Acehnese fought a bitter war of separation from Indonesia for several decades. Many historians and scholars have noted the extraordinary diversity of Southeast Asia. One well-known British historian, C.A. Fisher, described the region as the "Balkans of Asia",[8] adding that the Balkans of Asia were even more diverse than the Balkans of Europe. He predicted trouble for Southeast Asia. Similarly, one of the five founding fathers of ASEAN, Thanat Khoman, wrote in a 1964 *Foreign Affairs* article: "In terms of power politics, Southeast Asia became more or less Balkanized, as Eastern Europe had been on the eve of World War I. Each nation, following its own destiny, spoke a political language of its own, which was not generally understood. There was neither unison nor a *lingua franca*."[9]

This is what makes ASEAN so extraordinary. If one were looking around the world to find the most promising region for international

---

8.　Charles A. Fisher, "Southeast Asia: The Balkans of the Orient? A Study in Continuity and Change", *Geography* 47, 4 (1962).
9.　Thanat Khoman, "Which Road for Southeast Asia?" *Foreign Affairs* 42, 4 (1964): 629.

cooperation, Southeast Asia would have been at the bottom of the list. Europe would have looked promising because the vast majority of people belonged to one civilization. So too the people of Latin America. Similarly, African and Arab peoples could claim to live in culturally coherent universes, as could the people of Northeast Asia. But 50 years ago, no one would have looked to Southeast Asia to provide a test bed for successful regional cooperation.

Indeed, regional cooperation succeeded in Europe. The European Union (EU) is the world's most successful regional organization. This is not surprising, because the Europeans had a huge incentive to put their violent rivalries behind them. But it is surprising that the world's second-most successful regional organization is ASEAN, emerging from the world's least promising region. What makes ASEAN truly remarkable is not just that it was born in unpromising times and nurtured on unpromising soil. If ASEAN had been a human baby, it might not have reached full term. Instead, the precarious baby became a world star.

There is one more pressing reason why the world needs to understand ASEAN. ASEAN's success stories can bring hope to many difficult regions and lighten our planet's problems. Try imagining a world where the Middle East is at peace. The thought seems almost inconceivable. Imagine a world where Israel and Palestine, two nations splintered from one piece of territory, live harmoniously. Impossible? This is what Malaysia and Singapore accomplished. After an acrimonious divorce in 1965, they live together in peace. Imagine a world where Egypt, the most populous Islamic country in the Middle East, emerges as a stable and prosperous democracy. Impossible? Then ask yourself how it is that Indonesia, the most populous Islamic country in Southeast Asia (with a population more than four times that of Egypt) has emerged as a beacon of democracy. Egypt and Indonesia have many other parallels. Both suffered from corruption. Both experienced decades of military rule under strong military rulers—Suharto (1967–98) and Mubarak (1981–2011). Yet, Egypt remains a troubled country still under military rule while Indonesia has emerged as the leading democracy in the Islamic world. What explains the difference? The one-word answer is ASEAN.

The obvious retort to this is that the Middle East has long been a region of war while Southeast Asia has been a region of peace. Certainly, the Middle East has experienced many wars: the 1967 and 1973 Arab-Israeli wars, the 1980–88 Iran-Iraq War, the 1990 Iraqi invasion of Kuwait, and the 2003 American invasion of Iraq. Yet, more bombs have been dropped in Southeast Asia than in any other region of the world since World War II. Southeast Asia has experienced larger and longer wars than the Middle East. The Vietnam War, which spilled over into Laos and Cambodia, lasted from the fall of Dien Bien Phu in 1954 until the fall of Saigon in April 1975, when American diplomats and soldiers beat an ignominious retreat. This was followed by the Vietnamese invasion of Cambodia in December 1978, which in turn triggered a decade-long struggle between China and Vietnam. In simple numerical terms, the number of military casualties in Southeast Asia since World War II, from 1946 to 2008 (estimates range from 1.87 million to 7.35 million), has exceeded the military casualties in the Middle East during the same period (estimates range from 530,000 to 2.43 million). When then President Barack Obama visited Laos in September 2016, he reminded us that America had

> dropped more than two million tons of bombs here in Laos— more than we dropped on Germany and Japan combined during all of World War II. It made Laos, per person, the most heavily bombed country in history. As one Laotian said, the 'bombs fell like rain.' Villages and entire valleys were obliterated. The ancient Plain of Jars was devastated. Countless civilians were killed.[10]

This is precisely why it cannot be denied that ASEAN is a miracle. It has brought durable peace to a region that experienced great conflicts. As the conclusion of this book will stress, a Nobel Peace Prize for ASEAN is long overdue.

It is no secret that the West is deeply pessimistic about the prospects for the Islamic world. Deep pessimism and fear of the Islamic world seem almost hard-wired into the body politic of the Western world. Donald Trump exploited this to the hilt when he called for "a total and complete shutdown of Muslims entering the United States".[11] Even though Trump was roundly condemned for this, he still won the presidential election. He had tapped into a deep lode of anxiety about Islam in the American psyche.

---

10. "Remarks of President Obama to the People of Laos", White House, 6 Sept. 2016, https://www.whitehouse.gov/the-press-office/2016/09/06/remarks-president-obama-people-laos, accessed 21 Nov. 2016.
11. "Donald J. Trump Statement on Preventing Muslim Immigration", Donald J. Trump for President, 7 Dec. 2015, https://www.donaldjtrump.com/press-releases/donald-j.-trump-statement-on-preventing-muslim-immigration/, accessed 12 Oct. 2016.

Those looking for hope in the Islamic world, and for a narrative that can counter such dark views, should look no farther than Southeast Asia. About 25,000 young people from all over the world, including the West, have joined the Islamic State in Iraq and Syria (ISIS). Yet, should we focus on these 25,000 Muslims or on the 8,000-times-larger number of 205 million Muslims who live peacefully in Indonesia, the world's most populous Islamic country? As the most successful democracy in the Islamic world, Indonesia reinforces Southeast Asia's status as a haven of peace, in contrast to the troubled countries at the heart of the Arab world, including Libya and Syria, Iraq and Yemen, which will remain in conflict for some time.

There are more Muslims in Southeast Asia, as a percentage, than any other region outside the Middle East. If the large Muslim population of Southeast Asia—almost as numerous as the entire population of the Arab world—can live in peace with their non-Muslim neighbours and also continue to progress economically, they provide hope that the world is not destined for a clash of civilizations.

The influx of almost a million Syrian refugees into Europe in 2015 has made Europe acutely aware that its fate is closely linked to the Islamic world. Europe seems particularly troubled by the emergence of radical Islamism within its borders. The Paris attacks of 13 November 2015 were carried out mostly by young Muslims who were born and brought up in Europe, not in the Middle East.

Few of today's European intellectuals see a way for Europe to work out a peaceful coexistence with Muslims within and just outside its borders. The impulse today in Europe is to build walls and put up border controls. Trump demonstrates that even within the relatively open society of America, there is this impulse to build walls and bar Muslims. The American and European intelligentsia need to make an intellectual pilgrimage to Southeast Asia. They need to immerse themselves in a region of hope and experience a world where different civilizations live in peace and progress together.

Europe has been the most successful continent for the past four centuries, especially in economic and social development. Europeans can barely conceive of the possibility that they could learn important lessons from other parts of the world. That is one reason for this volume on ASEAN, to stimulate the hitherto closed European mind to explore the possibility of learning lessons from other regions.

Similarly, the American intelligentsia could also learn lessons from this volume. The United States has emerged as the most successful society in human history. No other society can match America's track record of economic productivity and cultural creativity (or its exceptional military power). Yet despite being the world's most successful society, the American middle class is falling prey to a European-style pessimism. Suicide rates among white middle-class males have grown significantly. Fareed Zakaria has written about this: "The main causes of death are as striking as the fact itself: suicide, alcoholism, and overdoses of prescription and illegal drugs. 'People seem to be killing themselves, slowly or quickly,' [Angus] Deaton told me. These circumstances are usually caused by stress, depression and despair ..."[12] Rising suicide rates represent the most extreme expression of growing pessimism.

The ongoing politics of pessimism in America and Europe is dangerous. There is no doubt that this pessimism is killing the prospect of sensible centrist leaders. The destruction of Jeb Bush in the 2016 Republican presidential primaries and the even more stunning defeat of Hillary Clinton in November 2016 demonstrated this clearly. It would be far too alarmist to remind the West that such political pessimism provided fertile soil for the emergence of Adolf Hitler in Germany in the 1930s, although Martin Wolf hinted at this danger in a March 2016 column for the *Financial Times*.[13]

So does pessimism mean that we cannot produce positive transformational leaders? Here again the story of ASEAN can bring some hope to our troubled times. This chapter has already documented how dark and gloomy Southeast Asia looked in the 1960s. Yet, in these dark times, five men stepped in to provide the leadership for the birth of ASEAN. What is truly amazing is how different these five men were in their cultural and political backgrounds.

Following are introductions to the five brave men who came together to sign the founding ASEAN declaration on 8 August 1967.

Thanat Khoman, a Buddhist, was born in Thailand in 1914 and educated in France. As a result of his French education, he was more familiar with European wines, literature and cuisine than he was with

---

12. Fareed Zakaria, "America's Self-destructive Whites", *Washington Post*, 31 Dec. 2015, https://www.washingtonpost.com/opinions/americas-self-destructive-whites/2015/12/31/5017f958-afdc-11e5-9ab0-884d1cc4b33e_story.html/, accessed 12 Oct. 2016.
13. Martin Wolf, "Donald Trump Embodies How Great Republics Meet Their End", *Financial Times*, 2 Mar. 2016, http://www.ft.com/cms/s/2/743d91b8-df8d-11e5-b67f-a61732c1d025.html#axzz4Kxj87a3R/, accessed 12 Oct. 2016.

Southeast Asian history or literature. Yet, he was also a fervent anti-colonialist. He wrote:

> On 8 August 1967 the "Bangkok Declaration" gave birth to ASEAN, the Association of Southeast Asian Nations, an organization that would unite five countries in a joint effort to promote economic co-operation and the welfare of their peoples. After repeated unsuccessful attempts in the past, this event was a unique achievement, ending the separation and aloofness of the countries of this region that had resulted from colonial times when they were forced by the colonial masters to live in *cloisons etanches*, shunning contact with the neighbouring countries.[14]

Narciso Ramos, a Christian, the Filipino signatory, was born in the Philippines in 1900 and studied in Manila. He probably knew more about American history and the American founding fathers than he did of Southeast Asia.

Adam Malik, a Muslim, was born in Sumatra, Indonesia, in 1917 and studied in Indonesia. He was fluent in Bahasa Indonesia and Dutch, and he spoke some English. His worldview had been conditioned by the anti-colonial struggle against the Dutch and Sukarno's nationalist speeches. Even though he was working towards creating a regional organization involving two immediate neighbours, Malaysia and Singapore, he likely shared Sukarno's view that they were artificial neocolonial creations. Rightfully, they should have belonged to a greater Indonesian nation, the Nusantara. He suppressed these nationalist instincts in the face of the Communist threat.

Abdul Razak, a Muslim, was born in Pahang, Malaysia, in 1922 and educated at Raffles College in Singapore before furthering his studies in London in 1947–50, at Lincoln's Inn. It was in London that he got to know many Singaporean leaders, especially Lee Kuan Yew, Dr Goh Keng Swee and S. Rajaratnam, as they had come together to fight against British colonial rule. Razak knew Singapore well. In theory, as Adam Malik and Abdul Razak were both Malay-speaking Muslims, they should have felt a greater cultural affinity with each other. In practice, Abdul Razak felt a greater cultural affinity with his Singaporean counterpart, Rajaratnam, since both had spent their key formative years in London. Both probably drank beer together in London pubs.

---

14. Thanat Khoman, "ASEAN Conception and Evolution", ASEAN, 1 Sept. 1992, http://asean.org/?static_post=asean-conception-and-evolution-by-thanat-khoman/, accessed 12 Oct. 2016.

S. Rajaratnam was born into a Sri Lankan Tamil Hindu family in 1915 in Jaffna, Sri Lanka. He moved to Singapore, which was also under British colonial rule, in 1915 (when he was three months old) before going to London to study from 1937 to 1948. Even though he never formally graduated from any university, he wielded a powerful pen and wrote eloquently and passionately to drum up nationalist sentiment against colonial rule.

In short, when these five men—one Buddhist Thai, one Christian Filipino, two Muslims and a lapsed Hindu—came together to sign the ASEAN declaration, they could not have come from more diverse cultural universes. Only Razak and Rajaratnam shared a common British educational experience. However, Razak's Malay Muslim identity was important to him, while Rajaratnam had no interest in religious life. If one had to put together a cast of characters to launch the second-most successful regional organization in the world, one would not have started with this cast of five characters from five countries.

Now imagine a world where Donald Trump (a Christian), Xi Jinping (a Confucian Communist), Vladimir Putin (an Orthodox Christian), Ayatollah Khamenei (a Muslim) and Narendra Modi (a Hindu) came together to sign a declaration for peaceful collaboration. Given the many political divisions among these five leaders, it seems clearly inconceivable. Yet the political divisions among the five founding fathers of ASEAN were equally great, if not greater. Chapter 2, "The ASEAN Ecosystem of Peace", tries to explain how the miraculous peace story of ASEAN emerged and succeeded.

Still, one cannot understand the Southeast Asian story just by looking at the past 50 years. There are deeper cultural roots that drive the character and identity of ASEAN. This is why this book will begin from the very beginning.

It will first try to explain how the extraordinary diversity of Southeast Asia came about. In all the many interpretations of the region's history, there is one undeniable fact: Southeast Asia has served as the crossroads of the world for over 2,000 years. The remarkable cultural diversity of Southeast Asia is also a result of this. At least four major cultural waves have swept through Southeast Asia: the Indian, Chinese, Muslim and Western waves. The diversity of Southeast Asia cannot be properly understood without an understanding of how each wave left behind historical ripples that continue to influence the behaviour of Southeast Asian societies today and provide the basis for the rich cultural diversity of the region.

One surprising feature of these four waves is that three of them arrived relatively peacefully. Only the Western wave arrived on a tide of violence. A brief description of how Portuguese Admiral Vasco da Gama treated the women and children of a Muslim vessel ferrying pilgrims to Mecca illustrates well the violence Western colonialists unleashed in Asia:

> As [Tomé] Lopes describes the matter evocatively, the women on board waved their gold and silver jewellery and precious stones, crying out to the Admiral that they were willing to give him all that for their lives; some of the women picked up their infants and pointed at them, "making signs with their hands, so far as we could make out, that we should have pity on their innocence".[15]

However, in the end, "the Admiral had the said ship burnt with the men who were on it, very cruelly and without any pity". Of the 200 people on the ship, "everyone on board was killed save seventeen children ... and a hunchback who was the pilot".

Chapter 2 explains how peace emerged in an unpromising region of the world in most unpromising times. Indeed, ASEAN has developed a resilient ecosystem of peace. No two ASEAN states have gone to war with each since the organization's founding in 1967. There have been quarrels, even minor military skirmishes (as between Cambodia and Thailand), but a war like those which the world saw in the Middle East and Balkans of Europe has not broken out in Southeast Asia. One key assumption of this book is that this ecosystem of peace can be replicated in other unpromising regions of the world. ASEAN will serve as a beacon of hope for the world. A better understanding of the ASEAN experience can lead to a more peaceful world.

Chapter 3 emphasizes that ASEAN will still need the support and cooperation of the great powers for this happy scenario to continue. The previous chapter explained how ASEAN benefited from favourable geopolitical winds coming out of the Cold War. The strong strategic alliance between the US and China in the 1980s played a critical role in reinforcing the cohesion of the ASEAN states. Indeed, the 1980s were perhaps most critical in developing a strong sense of ASEAN identity among the five founding member states.

---

15. Sanjay Subrahmanyam, *The Career and Legend of Vasco Da Gama* (Cambridge: Cambridge University Press 1997), pp. 206–7.

Yet, if favourable geopolitical trends helped ASEAN build its identity, ASEAN must now prepare itself for unfavourable geopolitical winds. The most important strategic relationship is always that between the world's greatest power (today, the US) and the world's greatest emerging power (China). Both worked closely together to thwart the Soviet Union in the 1980s. This helped ASEAN. Today, even though there is a remarkable degree of cooperation between the US and China, there is also a rising degree of competition. If this competition gets out of hand, ASEAN could be split apart. This is why a key message of this chapter is that all the great powers, including America, China, India, Japan and the EU, have a stake in keeping ASEAN together. No great power is benign. No appeal is being made here to benevolent instincts. Instead, this chapter appeals to the naked self-interests of each great power.

The current situation of the ten Southeast Asian member states of ASEAN is covered in Chapter 4, in a series of brief pen sketches. Each of the ten countries has a rich and complex history, and the pen sketches cannot do justice to these complex identities. However, we hope that the reader will get sufficient insight into the ASEAN states, their current challenges, their geopolitical postures and their relationship to the regional organization.

Chapter 5 attempts an assessment of ASEAN as a regional organization today, by looking at its strengths and weaknesses as well as the opportunities and threats it faces (the well-known SWOT analysis). Like a complex living organism, ASEAN can die, as a result of either neglect or wilful efforts. The current leaders of ASEAN bear an enormous responsibility. They cannot allow the work of ASEAN's founding fathers to go to waste. They must see it as their responsibility to sustain ASEAN as a strong regional organization that can continue to serve as a beacon of hope for humanity. If the current leaders of ASEAN succeed in sustaining and strengthening the organization (and so the region), they will bring benefits to the region's 625 million people. But we argue here that they will also benefit the remaining 6.7 billion citizens of planet Earth, who will have a second beacon of hope (besides the US) that they can look up to.

Finally, Chapter 6 looks at ASEAN's future prospects. It also suggests some concrete steps ASEAN can take to strengthen itself. Fortunately, none of these steps will be very difficult. Some will be eminently affordable. Clearly, ASEAN needs to strengthen its secretariat. In contrast to the budget of the EU Secretariat, which is US$154 billion, the annual budget of the ASEAN Secretariat is US$19 million. Since the combined ASEAN GDP rose from US$95 billion in 1970 to US$2.5 trillion in 2014, it would be penny wise and pound foolish to starve the ASEAN Secretariat of badly needed funds. Once the ASEAN leaders recognize what a treasure the association has become, they should see it to be in their national interests to provide more funding.

One important outcome of a stronger ASEAN Secretariat and a better-performing ASEAN organization should be to build over time a greater sense of ownership of ASEAN among the people of the region. In the first 50 years of its existence, ASEAN was owned and managed by its governments. They have done a marvellous job, despite the many flaws and weaknesses of ASEAN. However, if we are to ensure the region's continuing growth and success, then ownership of ASEAN must pass from governments to the people. When it does, ASEAN may actually become the world's number one regional organization.

Right now, this may seem like a wild prospect. But if we remember the organization's 1967 starting point, ASEAN's achievements are nothing less than spectacular. If ASEAN can keep up its current momentum, there is no limit. The higher it soars, the brighter it will become as a beacon for humanity.

Chapter

1

The Four Waves

Why is Southeast Asia the most culturally diverse region on our planet?

One simple answer could be that it is the only region to have felt the impact of four distinct waves of cultural influence. Southeast Asia has been intimately associated and involved with four of the great universalist cultures and civilizations of the world: India, China, Islam and the West. It may be an understatement to view these encounters as waves. Given their long-lasting impact, they should be called tsunamis. However, the word "wave" may be more appropriate because, with the exception of the Western wave, these interactions were mostly peaceful. It is important to develop a good understanding here because, as George Yeo told us, "ASEAN is but the continuing expression of historical Southeast Asia".[1]

We should also emphasize at the outset that the term "wave" is used metaphorically. The arrival and impact of these four distinct civilizations into Southeast Asia could not have been more different. Yet, what makes Southeast Asia truly unique is that it is the only region to have absorbed so many different and distinct civilizations. The expression "four waves" highlights this distinctiveness. This also makes Southeast Asia a unique human laboratory for historical study. The goal of this chapter is to give a glimpse into why this region is so fascinating in historical terms.

The big question that needs to be answered at the outset is what existed in Southeast Asia before these four waves. At the beginning of the 20th century, historians were likely to say "not very much". The

---

1. Authors' interview with George Yeo, 5 Feb. 2016.

15

Indian nationalist historian R.C. Majumdar proclaimed, "The Hindu colonists brought with them the whole framework of their culture and civilization and this was transplanted in its entirety among the people who had not yet emerged from their primitive barbarism."[2] He wrote this in 1941. The French scholar George Coedés would write similar words around the same period.

More recent historians have thoroughly revised the old picture painted by Majumdar and Coedés. Among other revisions, new research shows just how active Southeast Asians were in the long-distance maritime trade across Asia,[3] with Southeast Asian ships carrying out trade across the Indian Ocean[4] some 500 years before the Hindu religion and the Sanskrit language came into common currency.

In recent years, historians have emphasized the commonalities across the region that underlie the impact of big ideas from outside, religions, court rituals and so on. The eminent historian Anthony Reid looks at it this way:

> The bewildering variety of language, culture and religion in Southeast Asia, together with its historic openness to waterborne commerce from outside the region, appear at first glance to defy any attempts at generalizations. Yet as our attention shifts from court politics and religious "great traditions" to the popular beliefs and social practices of ordinary Southeast Asians, the common ground becomes increasingly apparent.[5]

Southeast Asia's deep cultural diversity is reflected in its linguistic map: it is among the most linguistically diverse regions in the world. However, the hundreds of Southeast Asian languages and dialects can be subsumed under several language families that comprise broad groupings of related languages with a common root. These language families are the Austronesian (including most of the languages of Indonesia, Malaysia and the Philippines, as well as the subgroup

---

2.   Pierre Yves Manguin, A. Mani and Geoff Wade, eds, *Early Interactions between South and Southeast Asia: Reflections on Cross-cultural Exchange* (Singapore: Institute of Southeast Asian Studies, 2011), p. xv.

3.   Craig A. Lockard, *Southeast Asia in World History* (Oxford: Oxford University Press, 2009), p. 15.

4.   Kenneth R. Hall, "Review: 'Borderless' Southeast Asia Historiography: New Scholarship on the Interactions between Southeast Asia and Its South Asian and Chinese Neighbours in the Pre-1500 Era", *Bijdragen tot de Taal-, Land- en Volkenkunde* 167, 4 (2011): 527–42.

5.   Anthony Reid, *Southeast Asia in the Age of Commerce: 1450–1680* (New Haven: Yale University Press), p. 3.

of Polynesian languages spoken in Hawaii and New Zealand); the Austroasiatic (including Khmer and Vietnamese); the Tai (Thai and Lao); and the Tibeto-Burman (Burmese).[6] The alignment of geography and culture tends to reinforce the fundamental division of the region into mainland Southeast Asia—dominated by Austroasiatic, Tai and Burmese speakers—and the maritime archipelago—dominated by Austronesian speakers. All of these languages have changed and adapted under the impact of the four waves, taking words from Sanskrit and other Indian languages, from Arabic, Chinese, Portuguese, Dutch and English.

In the centuries before the Common Era, Austronesian speakers were masters of the seashores and oceans, with a culture oriented to water. Austronesian speakers were the pioneering seafaring traders, explorers and settlers of Eastern Asia, the Indian Ocean and even the Pacific. Their exploits more than rival those of the legendary Phoenicians of the Mediterranean Basin. Skilled navigators who were fearless in confronting the dangers of the open sea, Austronesian speakers populated shores from Madagascar—off the coast of Africa— to New Zealand and Hawaii—deep in the Pacific Ocean.

In later centuries, a group of Austronesian speakers around the Straits of Malacca and the Java Sea took advantage of their location at what Chinese travellers described as the end of the monsoons. The early Indonesians benefited from occupying a strategic position for maritime commerce on a wide scale. Situated at the junction between the Northeast and Southwest Monsoon winds, the Straits of Malacca served as the commercial crossroads through which people, ideas and trade goods passed. The prevailing wind patterns in the South China Sea and Indian Ocean allowed ships sailing southwest from China and southeast from India or Persia to meet in the straits and on the Malay Peninsula, where they exchanged goods. They sailed back home when the winds reversed. From their strategic location at the Straits of Malacca, early Malay-Indonesian seafarers dominated both the China trade and the Indian Ocean trade. The Indonesians "traded with India by 500 BCE and China by 400 BCE, and around the beginning of the Common Era, they carried goods between China and India".[7] A Chinese observer in the 3rd century CE was impressed by the large

---

6. Lockard, *Southeast Asia*, p. 13.
7. Ibid., p. 15.

multi-masted ships that were more than 50 metres in length and able to carry 600–700 people and up to 600 tons of cargo.[8]

With China and India once again set to resume their traditional places as the world's two largest economies, it is only natural that the close connections between Southeast Asia and China and India, which were disrupted by centuries of Western colonial occupation, will once again resume. This is another reason why modern Southeast Asia should make a greater effort to understand the deep history of the region's links with Europe, South Asia, the Middle East and East Asia. Even as we try to understand the impact of these waves, we should bear in mind that Southeast Asians were not just passive recipients of foreign influences. They explored outwards and made use of outside ideas for their own purposes. This may explain Rabindranath Tagore's cryptic remark during his visit to Southeast Asia in 1927. He said that he saw India everywhere in Southeast Asia but did not recognize it.

The Indian Wave

It is not surprising that Tagore saw India everywhere. Some records place the contact between India and Southeast Asia as far back as 3,000 years. The millennia of cultural contact clearly left a deep impression on Southeast Asia.

It is significant that Indian cultural influences penetrated both mainland and maritime Southeast Asia. Anyone who doubts this should visit the magnificent monuments of Angkor Wat in Cambodia and Borobudur in Java. The British historian William Dalrymple describes the Ta Prohm temple, part of the Angkor complex:

> Tree trunks spiral out of the vaults of the shingled Buddhist temple roofs like the flying buttresses of a Gothic cathedral; branches knot over Sanskrit inscriptions composed in perfect orthography and grammar, before curving around the reliefs of Indic lions and elephants, gods and godlings, sprites and tree spirits. The trees' roots fan out like fused spiderwebs and grip crumbling friezes of bare-breasted *apsarasas* (heavenly dancing girls) and dreadlocked *sadhus* (wandering holy men).[9]

---

8. *"Nan-fang Ts'ao-mu Chuang"* [A Fourth Century Flora of South-East Asia], trans. Li Hui-Lin (Hong Kong: Chinese University Press, 1979).
9. William Dalrymple, "The Great & Beautiful Lost Kingdoms", *New York Review of Books*, 21 May 2015, http://www.nybooks.com/articles/2015/05/21/great-and-beautiful-lost-kingdoms/, accessed 12 Oct. 2016.

Traces of the region's contact with the high cultures of India are not preserved only in dead monuments. Indian influences remain alive and well in the rituals of Southeast Asia's royal courts. To this day, for example, Brahmins have a special role in Thai court ritual.

The Chinese presence is also deep-seated in Thailand. The founder of the Chakri dynasty, King Rama I (who began his reign in 1782), was of Chinese descent. Indeed, one of his successors, King Mongkut (r. 1851–68), was very proud to proclaim his Chinese lineage. Today, Chinese have assimilated so completely into Thai culture that it is hard to tell who is Thai and who is Chinese in Thai society. But when the Chinese assimilated into Thai society, they accepted the Indian cultural legacy that was embedded in the arts, philosophy, writing system and religion of Thailand. A Thai of Chinese origin can therefore feel comfortable in both Chinese and Indian cultures.

This ability of Thailand to comfortably assimilate both the Indian and Chinese cultural waves may well demonstrate a secret cultural genius of Southeast Asian societies: the ability to accept and live with differences. This may be why the Indian and Chinese cultural waves were able to overlap comfortably with each other as Southeast Asia began to interact with both civilizations around the same time.

In the early years of the new millennium, trading activity across the Indian Ocean intensified. Societies began to become more stratified, with ruling groups entrenching their power into institutions of kingship and royal courts. And at a certain point, they adopted ideas and a new language from India. Sheldon Pollock's magisterial *The Language of the Gods in the World of Men* shows how the Sanskrit language became the language of power across the Indian Ocean world, being adopted by kings and princes "from Kashmir to Kelantan".[10] Hinduism and Buddhism were nurtured and promoted by courts around the same time, and across a broad area of Asia, in what Pollock calls a Sanskrit cosmopolis.

Hindu ideas of kingship and Sanskrit as the sacred language of court and religious rituals could soon be found across Southeast Asia.[11] Especially in mainland Southeast Asia, local elites who spoke radically different languages—such as Mon-Khmer, Tai and Malay—

---

10. Sheldon I. Pollock, *The Language of the Gods in the World of Men: Sanskrit, Culture, and Power in Premodern India* (Berkeley: University of California Press, 2006), p. 257.

11. George Cœdès, *The Indianized States of Southeast Asia* (Honolulu: East-West Center Press, 1968), p. 15.

and lived in different cultural worlds suddenly adopted Sanskrit and its attendant political philosophy and literary aesthetic.[12] (This process was occurring across different regions of India at roughly the same time.) Societies in the plains and deltas of mainland Southeast Asia became more and more organized, with rituals and great temples and palaces. And the symbolism and the names and texts were Indian. Travellers from India—craftsmen, Brahmins, experts—were certainly part of the cosmopolitan scene in these courts, just as Southeast Asians were present in India, though historians continue to find it difficult to reconstruct their numbers, roles and exact place in Southeast Asian societies.[13]

One of the earliest Khmer inscriptions records how a 5th-century ruler in what is now Laos took the Indic name Devanika and the Sanskrit title Maharaj Adhiraja (King of Kings) during a ceremony in which he installed a Shiva *lingam*—the phallic symbol representing the Hindu deity Shiva—under a phallic-shaped mountain that overlooked his capital city of Champasak. In addition, he consecrated a water tank with the name Kurukshetra after the plain in India where the great battle of the Sanskrit epic *Mahabharata* was fought.[14]

Even though the ardent converts to Indian civilization were largely elites, Indian influence also enriched local Southeast Asian folk culture, through the introduction of new religious ideas, mythology and folklore that interacted with older stories and ideas. Through the Indian connection, Hinduism and Buddhism both spread to these early states and for many centuries existed there in a complex interaction. Eventually, the states of the mainland became predominantly Buddhist.

Significantly, this Indianization was felt in both mainland and insular Southeast Asia. The earliest Indianized states appeared on the mainland, along the lower reaches of the Mekong River and on the southern coasts of Cambodia and Vietnam, where they benefited from maritime trade with India and China. Prior to the rise of the Indonesian port polities, they were the most prosperous states. The first of these Indianized states to achieve historical prominence was Funan, located on the Mekong near present-day Phnom Penh, and in the Mekong delta. Local inhabitants of Funan are likely to have spoken

---

12. Pollock, *Language of the Gods*, p. 124.
13. Charles Higham, "The Long and Winding Road That Leads to Angkor", *Cambridge Archaeological Journal* 22, 2 (2012): 265.
14. Dalrymple, "The Great & Beautiful Lost Kingdoms".

the Khmer language like today's ethnic Cambodians. In fact, the people of present-day Cambodia trace their descent to the people of the kingdom of Funan. The Hindu-Khmer empire of Funan flourished for about 500 years.

The rise of Funan reveals something about the relationship between the Indian and Chinese waves. It occurred during the first great period of global trade, when the Silk Road was opened, linking Han China and the Roman empire across Asia. The overland Silk Road excites our imagination, with its caravans and oases, but in recent years we have learned more of the maritime routes that passed through Southeast Asian seas. In its heyday, Funan carried on a lucrative trade with both India during the Murunda dynasty and China in the period of the Three Kingdoms.

It seems that in the earliest days of this trade, rather than passing through the Straits of Malacca, cargoes from Chinese junks plying the South China Sea were transported overland across the narrow Isthmus of Kra in Southern Thailand. Upon reaching the coast of the Andaman Sea, for example at the port of Kedah, the cargoes were reloaded on ships sailing across the Bay of Bengal to India and the Persian Gulf, where they rejoined the overland routes on the way to Europe. Goods coming in the opposite direction were transshipped overland across the isthmus to the shores of the South China Sea. Merchants then boarded other vessels sailing along the Gulf of Thailand until they reached Funan.

Funan's domination of the trade networks was eventually challenged by rival trading powers emerging in maritime Southeast Asia, especially around the Straits of Malacca. This was possibly also a result of changes at both ends of the Silk Road, with the Roman empire in decline and the Han no longer able to keep the overland Silk Road open. The decline of Funan heralded the end of the initial phase of Indianization in Southeast Asia. With the passing of Funan power on the Indochinese mainland, the locus of Indianization shifted away from mainland Southeast Asia towards the maritime archipelago of Indonesia.

Borobudur became the embodiment of Mahayana Buddhism, which spread from India to Southeast Asia, China and Japan after the 7th century. It must have been a time of great intellectual and religious ferment, as Buddhism and Brahmanist cults existed side by side and intertwined, sometimes mobilized by rival political clans. Both Hinduism and Buddhism flourished in central Java, witnessed by the monumental architectural legacies of Prambanan and Borobudur respectively, a few dozen kilometres apart.

Soon a new Buddhist kingdom emerged in Sumatra, centred on Palembang. With a fine natural harbour accessible even to the largest ocean-going vessels, and located strategically in the Straits of Malacca, the new kingdom of Srivijaya became a more competitive port of call as trade between the South China Sea and the Indian Ocean flowed through the straits. Srivijaya prospered rapidly and was able to maintain a commercial hegemony over the smaller ports of the Indonesian archipelago, dominating seaborne commerce from the 7th to the 11th centuries. Srivijaya was the first in a succession of great seaports (Malacca, Aceh, Batavia, Penang and Singapore) that were to derive their strength from occupying a prominent location alongside the Straits of Malacca.

As with Funan, the fortunes of Southeast Asia's ports were linked with global trading patterns. The rise of Srivijaya also coincided with a revival of the maritime and overland Silk Road under the resurgent Tang dynasty in China. Palembang soon became the favoured port for ships sailing from China with the Northeast Monsoon. But Srivijaya's prominence was not just related to trade: the monk Atisa, born to a princely Bengali family, travelled to Srivijaya to study with a famous teacher of Buddhism. After 12 years in Sumatra, Atisa returned to South Asia, eventually travelling in 1043 to Tibet, where he is still remembered as the founder of the Kadampa school of Buddhism.[15]

By the 11th century, after the fall of the Tang and as the rise of the Song dynasty led to new demand from China, Srivijaya's dominance of Southeast Asia was challenged from an unusual quarter, India. The Cholas of Tanjore, in southern India, were developing a powerful navy and began extending their commercial influence along the sea route eastwards towards the Straits of Malacca. Chola and Srivijaya seemed to have had friendly relations for a time. Srivijaya built a Buddhist temple at Nagapattinam on the Coromandel Coast in c.1005.[16]

15. John N. Miksic, *Historical Dictionaries of Ancient Civilizations and Historical Eras, No. 18* (Lanham: Scarecrow Press, 2007), p. 33; Damien Keown, *A Dictionary of Buddhism* (Oxford: Oxford University Press, 2004).
16. Brian Harrison, *South-East Asia, a Short History* (London: Macmillan, 1963), p. 30.

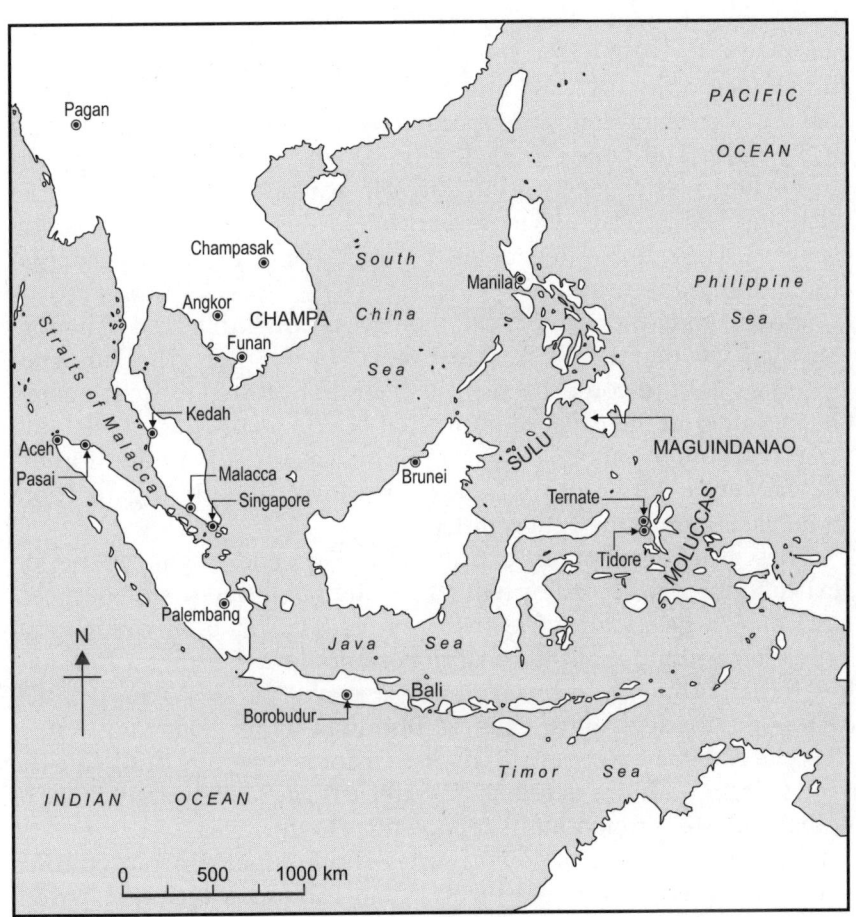

Historical Southeast Asia

But commercial rivalry between the two powers developed soon afterwards. Srivijaya may have attempted to restrict or impede Chola commerce on its way through the Straits of Malacca, or the former may have made exorbitant demands for transit and port dues. After all, commercial monopoly has a long history in the Straits of Malacca. In its eagerness to corner the China trade, Srivijaya may have indelicately overplayed its hand by presenting itself as a regional hegemon of the Indian Ocean. In 1017, a Tamil tributary mission to China reported that the Chola kingdom was regarded by the Chinese as a dependency of Srivijaya. The young King Rajendra, who had just ascended the throne and was eager to prove himself, was in no mood to tolerate such an insult.[17] This led to several battles between the Cholas and Srivijaya. The number of tributes to China sent by Srivijaya decreased dramatically thereafter.

While Srivijaya receded, another powerful Indianized kingdom emerged on mainland Southeast Asia, in Angkor. The influence of Indian culture could be seen in the burst of architectural energy that resulted in the great monumental buildings of Angkor Wat and Angkor Thom. Angkor Wat was built by King Suryavarman II in the first half of the 12th century. King Jayavarman VII built Angkor Thom in the later part of the 12th century.

These brief descriptions of Funan, Srivijaya and Angkor do not do justice to the rich record of centuries of Indian influence in Southeast Asia and India's interaction with the region. This brief chapter can only offer a glimpse of the Sanskrit cosmopolis in Southeast Asia and the Indian influence in the region in different periods. Almost 1,400 years ago, the legendary Chinese Buddhist monk Xuanzang wrote: "People of distant places with diverse customs generally designate the land that they admire as India."[18] Southeast Asia's ready acceptance of Indian culture throughout history testifies to this.

We see this history as explaining why Southeast Asian cultures are "soft" in contrast to Northeast Asian cultures, which are "hard". This is admittedly a personal and subjective view of cultures, yet it is based on long experience. If one were to look for proof, one should do a cultural comparison of two societies, Thailand and Korea. Both

---

17. Arthur Cotterell, *A History of Southeast Asia* (Singapore: Marshall Cavendish, 2014), p. 114.
18. Xuanzang, *The Great Tang Dynasty Record of the Western Regions*, trans. Li Rongxi (Berkeley: Numata Center for Buddhist Translation and Research, 1995), p. 49.

were influenced by Chinese culture—indeed, many in the Thai establishment have Chinese ancestry. Yet, because Thailand had over a millennium of Indian cultural influence while Korea did not, Thai society has a "soft" dimension to it while Korean society has a "hard" one. This framing helps explain for us the underlying cultural logic of Southeast Asian societies.

The Chinese Wave

During all these centuries of deep Indian cultural penetration of Southeast Asia, China's presence in Southeast Asia could be felt equally strongly. Yet, while Southeast Asia was part of the Sanskrit cultural cosmopolis, China's impact was greater in the political and economic realms.

The land border between China and Southeast Asia is mountainous and difficult: today's borderlands have long been dominated by small polities, hill tribes, and a diversity of ethnic groups who value their autonomy. The seas and the monsoon trading routes were an easier route for trade, and for sojourners and settlers, but during many periods of history China's coasts and their trading potential were considered peripheral and unimportant.

But one feature remained constant in China-Southeast Asia relations. For centuries, the Indianized kingdoms of Southeast Asia paid tribute to the emperors of China. We do not know exactly how and when this tributary system started. But we do know that the Funan kingdom was sending tributes to China as early as AD 500, about 1,500 years ago.

One might expect that China's exaction of tributes demonstrated a desire to assert hegemony over Southeast Asia. In reality, the rulers of Southeast Asia were keen to send tributes to China because they found it to be immensely profitable. The Chinese regarded all relationships with foreign missions as "tributary".[19] The Chinese performed investiture ceremonies, which they considered to be the political acknowledgement of and a symbolic submission to Chinese hegemony.[20] When Southeast Asian rulers sent tribute missions to China, the tributes they offered would be returned with even more

---

19. Martin Stuart-Fox, *A Short History of China and Southeast Asia: Tribute, Trade and Influence* (Crows Nest: Allen & Unwin, 2003), p. 30.
20. Ibid., p. 31.

valuable gifts. Foreign missions were also able to sell their goods at commercial value in Chinese markets. Hence, Southeast Asian kingdoms derived great benefits from their tributary relationships with the Chinese.

By paying tribute, these kingdoms could in turn engage in profitable trade with China. They exported tin, spice and a variety of forest products to China while importing much-coveted Chinese luxury goods (such as ceramics, tea and silk) and metals (such as iron and copper). The shrewd Chinese leaders understood that withholding market access to, or restricting the supply of, coveted Chinese luxury products could provide Beijing with leverage over foreign kingdoms. Occasionally, Chinese rulers introduced sanctions to regulate or limit private trade in order to achieve foreign policy goals.

The nature of the tribute trade changed over time, but D. Mitchell and C. McGiffert see a long-term pattern that "China usually gave much more than it received from these missions, reflecting the court's attitude that its smaller neighbours had little to offer their great nation, and demonstrating Chinese generosity".[21] These "lavish gifts" from China did not carry a strong cultural charge: the tribute missions were more focussed on practicalities:

> In the end, the system primarily served the practical purpose of facilitating trade for the tributary states ... While flawed, the tributary system offered mutual benefit from both economic and security standpoints to the tributary states and China alike. Tributary states received trade benefits and, in some cases, security guarantees, while China got strategic peace of mind, reaffirmation of its self-regard, and an effective means of saving the cost of maintaining a large standing army to patrol all its borders.[22]

The mutual benefits of two-way trade, and the willingness of Southeast Asian rulers to submit, at least symbolically, to China may also explain the relative lack of military conflict between China and

21. Derek Mitchell and Carola McGiffert, "Expanding the 'Strategic Periphery': A History of China's Interaction with the Developing World", in *China and the Developing World: Beijing's Strategy for the Twenty-first Century*, ed. Joshua Eisenman, Eric Heginbotham and Derek Mitchell (Armonk: M.E. Sharpe, 2007), pp. 3–28.
22. Joshua Eisenman, Eric Heginbotham and Derek Mitchell, eds, *China and the Developing World: Beijing's Strategy for the Twenty-first Century* (Armonk: M.E. Sharpe, 2007), pp. 8–9.

Southeast Asia over the centuries. The main exception to this pattern was Vietnam, occupied by China for almost 1,000 years—from 111 BC, when Chinese Emperor Wudi conquered the southern kingdom of Nanyue (which includes present-day Guangzhou province and parts of northern Vietnam), until about AD 963–979, when Dinh Bo Linh established a kingdom in northern Vietnam that was independent of Chinese rule. Burma too suffered Chinese incursions, but not the same sort of long-term existential threat faced by Vietnam: the Mongols sacked Pagan at the end of the 13th century, and the Qing dynasty's attempt to invade Burma in the middle of the 18th century more or less settled today's borders.

Yet, even though Vietnam gained independence from China over 1,000 years ago, it remains deeply influenced by Chinese culture. The Chinese who assimilated into Thailand gave up Confucianism and ancestor worship and adopted Indian court rituals. By contrast, even though the Vietnamese fought hard to gain and retain political independence from China, they became culturally Sinicized and adopted Confucianism, Chinese political philosophy and a centralized form of government on the Chinese model. Vietnamese identity was formed in its opposition to China, but based on a deep familiarity.

The payment of tributes and the requests for protection from the Imperial Court did not always result in China's will holding sway. Professor Wang Gungwu describes Champa, for example, as "Vietnam's perennial enemy and a loyal vassal of China which depended on China to hold the Vietnamese back … China's authority was backed by its enormous military potential which the Vietnamese had no wish to test. An admonition from the Ming emperor was a useful deterrent."[23] Sadly, "when the Ming armies failed again and again to crush the Vietnamese 'rebels,' that authority lost its deterrent force". This led to Champa's eventual destruction at the hands of Vietnam.

The story of the largest naval expedition ever sent to Southeast Asia illustrates the mostly unrealized potential of a more active southwards engagement by China. This was the famous series of naval expeditions of Admiral Zheng He, a Muslim Chinese who first appeared in Southeast Asia in 1405 on an imperial mission from the Ming dynasty, with over 300 ships, carrying over 27,000 men. As many as 62 of these

---

23. Wang Gungwu, "Ming Foreign Relations: Southeast Asia", in *The Cambridge History of China*, ed. Denis Twitchett (Cambridge: Cambridge University Press, 1998), pp. 317–8.

ships were huge "treasure ships", or *baochuan*, which could have measured up to 122 metres in length and 52 metres across the beam.[24] Zheng He was involved in seven voyages from 1405 to 1433. Wang Gungwu writes, "Zheng He's voyages were an aberration in China's maritime history. The voyages showed capacity but no ambitions to dominate the seas or build maritime empires. The voyages were stopped when they proved that there were no enemies that threatened China from the seas."[25]

As part of the diplomatic efforts of the Zheng He expeditions, the Yongle Emperor gave special recognition to the trading port of Malacca, established by princes fleeing the sacking of Singapore at the very end of the 14th century, and used by Zheng He as a base. In November 1405, the Emperor granted Malacca an inscription for its western mountain, which was designated the Grand Mountain of the State. Wang Gungwu points out:

> What is outstanding is the fact that Malacca was the first foreign nation to receive the emperor's inscription. Only three other nations went through the same ceremony, Japan in 1406 (three months after Malacca), Brunei in 1408, and Cochin in 1416. But Malacca was the only one to receive this inscription with its very *first* mission to China.[26]

With such a blessing from China, and later, with its ruler's conversion to Islam, Malacca's role as the leading emporium of Asia was firmly established.

The millennia of neighbouring states maintaining profitable relations with China explains why it was wise for China's President Xi Jinping to launch his One Belt One Road initiative. The goal of this initiative was to resuscitate the famous Silk Road trade that China carried out with the rest of Asia, over land and sea. In his September 2013 speech at Nazarbayev University, in which he proposed the Silk Road economic belt project, President Xi said:

---

24. Frank Viviano, "China's Great Armada, Admiral Zheng He", *National Geographic*, July 2005, http://ngm.nationalgeographic.com/features/world/asia/china/zheng-he-text/, accessed 12 Oct. 2016.

25. Wang Gungwu, "Singapore's 'Chinese Dilemma' as China Rises", *Straits Times*, 1 June 2015.

26. Wang Gungwu, "The Opening of Relations between China and Malacca, 1403–05", in *Admiral Zheng He & Southeast Asia*, ed. Leo Suryadinata (Singapore: Institute of Southeast Asian Studies, 2005).

Throughout the millennia, the people of various countries along the ancient Silk Road have jointly written a chapter of friendship that has been passed on to this very day. The over 2,000-year history of exchanges demonstrates that on the basis of solidarity, mutual trust, equality, inclusiveness, mutual learning and win-win cooperation, countries of different races, beliefs and cultural backgrounds are fully capable of sharing peace and development. This is the valuable inspiration we have drawn from the ancient Silk Road.[27]

As China re-emerges as a great power, one big question that Southeast Asian states face is whether relations between the two will return to the age-old pattern of Southeast Asian countries paying tribute to China. In the modern era, it is hard to imagine a resuscitation of the old feudal pattern of kowtowing. Still, it would be unwise to believe that the pattern of relations between China and Southeast Asia established over millennia is without some symbolic power. This is why Southeast Asian states need to develop a deep understanding of how China views the long-term impact of the Chinese wave.

The Muslim Wave

We learned in school that Islam came to Southeast Asia peacefully through traders. Historians today write about the cosmopolitan world of Islam, linked by traders, travellers, pilgrims and teachers, stretching from Al-Andalus in Spain to Quanzhou in China, from the 7th to the 16th centuries. In addition to Arabs and Indians, Chinese Muslims were important to this picture and so are part of the story of Islam's introduction to Southeast Asia.

But more than the question of who, there is the question of how and why. Islam's entry to Southeast Asia remains a puzzle. There existed a small colony of foreign Muslims on the west coast of Sumatra by 674 CE, and other Muslim settlements began to appear after 878 CE. But it was not until the 12th or 13th century that we start to see evidence of conversions.

What was it that increased interest in Islam, starting in the 12th and 13th centuries and accelerating over the next few centuries? As with

---

27. Xi Jinping, "Promote Friendship between Our People and Work Together to Build a Bright Future", 7 Sept. 2013, http://www.fmprc.gov.cn/ce/cebel/eng/zxxx/t1078088.htm, accessed 9 Nov. 2016.

Indianization centuries earlier, we know that it had something to do with politics, power and trade. One common pattern was for a ruler or chief to adopt Islam—perhaps because of a desire to attract traders; or to be associated with powerful Muslim kingdoms like Mamluk Egypt, and later Ottoman Turkey and Mughal India; or because of the attraction of Muslim teaching. Mystical Islam (Sufism), which aimed at direct contact with Allah with the help of a teacher using techniques such as meditation and trance, was very appealing to rulers seeking to enhance their charisma.

The acceleration of the impact of Islam took place in a Southeast Asia on the threshold of revolutionary change. Southeast Asian trade began to expand rapidly from the late 14th century through to the middle of the 17th. A new factor on the scene was demand for Southeast Asian products from Europe, with the "spice orgy" which began after the Crusades and the opening of the Red Sea–Suez route to the Mediterranean.

Thus, the period when many Southeast Asians began to accept Islam coincided with economic and social change driven by a revolutionary transformation of the international trading environment. It was also during this period that cities began to develop with astonishing rapidity. Malacca, Grisek, Makassar, Aceh, Banten and Patani all grew during this period. These cities were markets for ideas as well as merchandise.

Gujerat, Bengal, and the Muslim areas of South India all had strong trading ties to Southeast Asia. According to the 16th-century Portuguese trader and writer Tomé Pires, Bengali traders had long frequented the port city of Pasai in north Sumatra; and in the latter part of the 13th century they had been responsible for placing "a Moorish king of the Bengali caste" on the throne of Pasai.[28] From Pasai, Islam spread to neighbouring Aceh. Aceh adopted Islam in the mid-14th century and quickly developed into a centre for Muslim trade. Acehnese rulers became renowned for their patronage of Islam, and their campaigns carried the faith along both the east and west coasts of Sumatra.

---

28. Tomé Pires, *Suma Oriental of Tomé Pires: An Account of the East, from the Red Sea to China, Written in Malacca and India in 1512–1515*, ed. and trans. Armando Cortesao (New Delhi: Asian Educational Services, 2005), p. 143.

A turning point came with the adoption of Islam by the ruler of Malacca. In his great chronicle, Tomé Pires claimed that the rulers of Malacca were inspired by the way Muslim Pasai benefited from the patronage of Indian Muslim traders. Pires (a Christian) maintained that Islam's success was due to pragmatic rather than spiritual motives.

In the 15th century, Muslim merchant networks dominated world trade and controlled the East-West trade routes stretching from Europe to China as well as Maluku in East Indonesia's spice archipelago.[29] Zheng He, the leader of the great Chinese fleet that had dominated Southeast Asia's seas in the first 30 years of the century, was a Muslim, as were many of his key lieutenants.[30] A contradiction had developed between politics and commerce: a situation was emerging in the port cities of island Southeast Asia in which the king was pagan whilst the merchants were Moors.

Conversion to Islam resolved the contradiction between political authority and commercial power. Melaka would have all to gain by joining the Muslim orbit. Moreover, Islam presented Melaka with a political instrument of great potential value. By officially adopting Islam, Melaka secured admittance to what the Dutch scholar Jacob Cornelis van Leur has described as the "unity of Islam", with its promise of powerful allies.[31]

The pace of Islamization across the region accelerated only in the 16th and 17th centuries. Several factors combined to help quicken the pace of Islamization after 1500 CE, not least the influence of princes and traders fleeing the fall of Malacca to the Portuguese.

Another important port in the spread of Islam was Brunei, in Borneo. Brunei's ruling family converted to Islam around 1520, though there are intriguing records of Muslim princes ruling Brunei 200 years earlier.[32] Brunei quickly achieved a reputation for sponsoring Islamic missionary activity in the Philippines archipelago. By the time the Spaniards arrived in the Philippines in 1565, the courts of Sulu

---

29. D.G.E. Hall, *A History of South-East Asia* (London: Macmillan, 1955), p. 180.
30. For a discussion of the Chinese factor in the Islamization of Malacca and Southeast Asia, see Geoff Wade, "Early Muslim Expansion in South-East Asia, Eighth to Fifteenth Centuries", in *The New Cambridge History of Islam*, Vol. 3: *The Eastern Islamic World, Eleventh to Eighteenth Centuries*, ed. David O. Morgan and Anthony Reid (Cambridge: Cambridge University Press, 2010), pp. 395–7.
31. Jacob Cornelis van Leur, *Indonesian Trade and Society: Essays in Asian Social and Economic History* (The Hague: W. Van Horve, 1967).
32. Wade, "Early Muslim Expansion", p. 369.

and Magindanao were already under Muslim rulers. Manila was controlled by relatives of the Sultan of Brunei.[33]

Although the maritime world of the Malay-Indonesian archipelago eventually came to be dominated by Muslim traders and Koranic scholars, there was also resistance to the Muslim advance. While most ports along the major trade routes between Melaka and the Spice Islands had a community of Muslim traders, by no means had all coastal rulers accepted the faith, despite a long exposure to the Muslim presence.

Moreover, the spread of Islam was largely contained within island Southeast Asia and made few successful inroads into mainland Southeast Asia, with the exception of Champa. Even within island Southeast Asia, the faith advanced slowly and took many centuries to percolate into the eastern reaches of Java and the spice archipelago. When the Dutch first arrived in Java around 1597, most of the interior was still "infidel".

Bali successfully repulsed all attempts to introduce Islam, even when Holy War was proclaimed against its princes and people by Sultan Agung of Mataram in the 1630s. Bali continued to maintain close links with the Hindu-Buddhist states of East Java and became a repository of old Javanese culture and literature when the advance of Islam caused them to disappear from Java and elsewhere.

Finally, Islam's entry into Southeast Asia was matched by the tenacious persistence of strong local animist and Hindu-Buddhist cultural traditions. In many parts of island Southeast Asia, the strong loyalty of the populace to their *adat* (customary law) meant they were not interested in the more austere and doctrinaire sides of Islam. Not surprisingly, it was an unorthodox and mystical variant of Islam that enjoyed considerable acceptance and success in Southeast Asia— Sufism.

As anthropologists such as Clifford Geertz have documented, Islam in Southeast Asia is highly diverse, varying from place to place and even between different people in the same district or village. Aceh, the northernmost province of Sumatra, has long been famous for its strong Islamic identity, and even today it has the most conservative Islamic laws in the region. It has implemented Sharia law, which includes severe penalties.

---

33. Nicholas Tarling, ed., *The Cambridge History of Southeast Asia*, Vol. 1: *From Early Times to c. 1800* (Cambridge: Cambridge University Press, 1992), p. 519.

By contrast, Islam is less central to Javanese identity.[34] Geertz notes that in Java, for centuries,

> The gentry, deprived of Indic ritualism but not of Indic pantheism, became increasingly subjectivist, cultivating an essentially illuminationist approach to the divine, a kind of Far Eastern gnosticism, complete with cabalistic speculations and metapsychic exercises. The peasantry absorbed Islamic concepts and practices, so far as it understood them, into the same general Southeast Asian folk religion into which it had previously absorbed Indian ones, locking ghosts, gods, jinns, and prophets together into a strikingly contemplative, even philosophical, animism. And the trading classes, relying more and more heavily upon the Meccan pilgrimage as their lifeline to the wider Islamic world, developed a compromise between what flowed into them along this line (and from their plainer colleagues in the Outer Islands) and what they confronted in Java to produce a religious system not quite doctrinal enough to be Middle Eastern and not quite ethereal enough to be South Asian.[35]

Anyone who needs proof that Islam rested gently on Javanese soil need go no farther than the major traffic roundabout near the Indonesian Independence Monument in Jakarta. At this roundabout, one encounters a major sculpture, several times life size, of a chariot with warriors being pulled by a string of horses—the Arjuna Wijaya chariot sculpture. The sculpture depicts a scene from the *Mahabharata*.

This sculpture was erected in 1987, four decades after Indonesia became independent in 1945. In short, this testimonial to a major Hindu epic was erected centuries after the Javanese population had converted to Islam. President Suharto, who must have approved this massive sculpture, was Muslim. Yet, he believed that this dramatic concrete rendition of a scene from a major Hindu epic would move the hearts and minds of the people of Java.

Hindu legends continue to live on in the consciousness of the Javanese population in other ways, too. Javanese culture is well known for its traditional shadow-puppet theatre (*wayang kulit*). Many of the scenes performed in *wayang kulit* come from Hindu epics. The stories are usually drawn from the Hindu epics the *Ramayana* and *Mahabharata* or from the *Serat Menak*. One particularly adored creature is the famous Hindu monkey god, Hanuman.

---

34. Clifford Geertz, *Islam Observed: Religious Development in Morocco and Indonesia* (Chicago: University of Chicago Press, 1971), p. 15.
35. Ibid., p. 13.

This culture of coexistence between Islamic religion and Hindu myths is part of the culture of tolerance of difference that Indonesian society has developed. President Sukarno's five principles of Pancasila captured well this culture of tolerance. The five principles are: belief in the one and only God, just and civilized humanity, the unity of Indonesia, democracy, and social justice. This culture of tolerance may also explain the resilience of the Indonesian nation after independence. Indonesia, given its geography, history and culture, is one of the most diverse countries in the world, much more diverse than the former Yugoslavia was.

Yet even though Indonesia has experienced worse crises than the former Yugoslavia did, such as the Asian Financial Crisis of 1997–98 or the terrible violence of 1965, it never fell apart as a nation. The culture of tolerance has not always prevented inter-ethnic violence, but it has prevailed. Such a culture cannot be created overnight; it takes centuries. The centuries of coexistence of different strains of Islam in Java are part of this culture of tolerance.

This culture of tolerance may also explain the endurance of Bali. It is somewhat unusual for Bali to have survived as a small isolated island of Hindu culture amidst a sea of Islamic neighbours. History has few examples of this. For example, the inability of the supposedly advanced Christian societies in Europe to tolerate the relatively culturally similar societies of Jews in their midst indicates the general difficulty for human society to tolerate people of different cultures. Interestingly, just as Islamic societies in Indonesia were able to tolerate and protect a pocket of Hinduism in Bali, Islamic societies in Spain and Turkey were also able to protect pockets of Jewish enclaves comprising Jews who had fled Christian persecution in Europe.

Since many Christian societies today believe that Islamic societies are inherently intolerant, they should remind themselves of this longer history of tolerance in many Islamic societies around the world. Mughal Emperor Akbar, who reigned in India from 1556 to 1605, was one of the most enlightened rulers of all time. As Amartya Sen writes in *The Argumentative Indian*, "Akbar's overarching thesis that 'the pursuit of reason' rather than 'reliance on tradition' is the way to address difficult problems of social harmony included a robust celebration of reasoned dialogue." He adds:

> It is worth recalling that in Akbar's pronouncements of four hundred years ago on the need for religious neutrality on the part of the state, we can identify the foundations of a non-denominational, secular state which was yet to be born in

India or for that matter anywhere else. Thus, Akbar's reasoned conclusions, codified during 1591 and 1592, had universal implications.[36]

By contrast, while India was enjoying the rule of a tolerant and open-minded Islamic ruler, Spain was suffering the trials of the Inquisition (1478–1834).

The Western Wave

The great paradox of the impact of the Western wave on Southeast Asia is that it completely transformed the region in some ways and left it untouched in others. Especially in the last 150 years, the region's political and economic systems were completely transformed. However, with the exception of the Philippines—which was Christianized under Spanish colonial rule—religion, the underlying cultural fabric of the region, was left untouched by the Western wave.

Why was all of Southeast Asia not Christianized like the Philippines? Definitive answers may be difficult, but it should be noted that the Western wave had two key traits associated with it: commercialism and violence. It would be fair to say that missionary goals were far down on the priority list for the first Europeans to arrive in Southeast Asia, even though the Portuguese used the Crusades to justify their killing of Muslims. Europeans were lured to Southeast Asia in the 16th and 17th centuries by that period's equivalent of a "gold rush": the search for direct access to the valuable spices of Southeast Asia. Before the Industrial Revolution in the mid- to late 19th century, demand for goods such as tea, spices, porcelain and silk drove European imperialism.

The search for spices was the main goal of the Portuguese, who were the first to arrive in Southeast Asia. Indeed, quite remarkably, they landed in Southeast Asia over 500 years ago. Changes in the Middle East in the 14th and 15th centuries had disrupted the spice trade between Southeast Asia and Europe. To overcome this, the Portuguese set out to find an alternative route. The breakthrough happened in 1497, when a fleet of ships led by Vasco da Gama managed to sail around the difficult Cape of Good Hope, at the southern tip of Africa.

---

36. Amartya Sen, *The Argumentative Indian: Writings on Indian History, Culture, and Identity* (New York: Farrar, Straus and Giroux, 2005).

As a result, da Gama was able to reach the Malabar Coast of India in May 1498.

From India, it was inevitable that the Portuguese would aim to get to Malacca, the most thriving port of that time. On 1 July 1511, as the town was celebrating the wedding of the Sultan of Malacca's daughter, Viceroy Afonso de Albuquerque "appeared in the roads with the entire force of Portuguese India, —nineteen ships, 800 European soldiers and 600 native sepoys, —with trumpets sounding, banners waving, guns firing, and every demonstration that might be expected to create a panic among the junks in the harbour and the warriors in the town".[37] By 24 August 1511, Malacca was in Portuguese hands. According to Reid, inter alia, "The Portuguese were able to seize the city because they concentrated on it an intensity of firepower unprecedented below the winds."[38]

The excessive violence the Portuguese used to conquer Malacca was to become a hallmark of the Western wave and its impact on Southeast Asia. Over time, the Western wave would bring many benefits to the region. Indeed, the modernization of the region could not have occurred without it. Yet, since many Western historians tend to emphasize the supposedly civilizing aspects of Western influence, it is vital to emphasize that the first Westerners to appear in Southeast Asia had no desire to civilize. Instead, they came in search of pure profit and were prepared to use any means to secure their commercial goals. There was no restraint in their use of violent means.

Brian Harrison puts it well:

> The peculiar combination of commercial war and religious crusade that the Portuguese introduced was something with which the region had not been confronted before. For Portugal, the advance to the East was not simply an invasion along the main highway of Asian trade but also a great forward outflanking movement in the holy war between Christianity and Islam. Her commercial aims, and the means of achieving them—deeds of violence against Moslems, or the plunder of Moslem shipping— were therefore conveniently sanctified.[39]

In other words, the purpose of Christianity was to sanctify the violence.

---

37. R.J. Wilkinson, "The Capture of Malacca, A.D. 1511", *Journal of the Straits Branch of the Royal Asiatic Society* 61 (1912): 71–6.

38. Anthony Reid, *Southeast Asia in the Age of Commerce 1450–1680*, Vol. 2: *Expansion and Crisis* (New Haven and London: Yale University Press, 1993), p. 271.

39. Harrison, *South-East Asia*, p. 70.

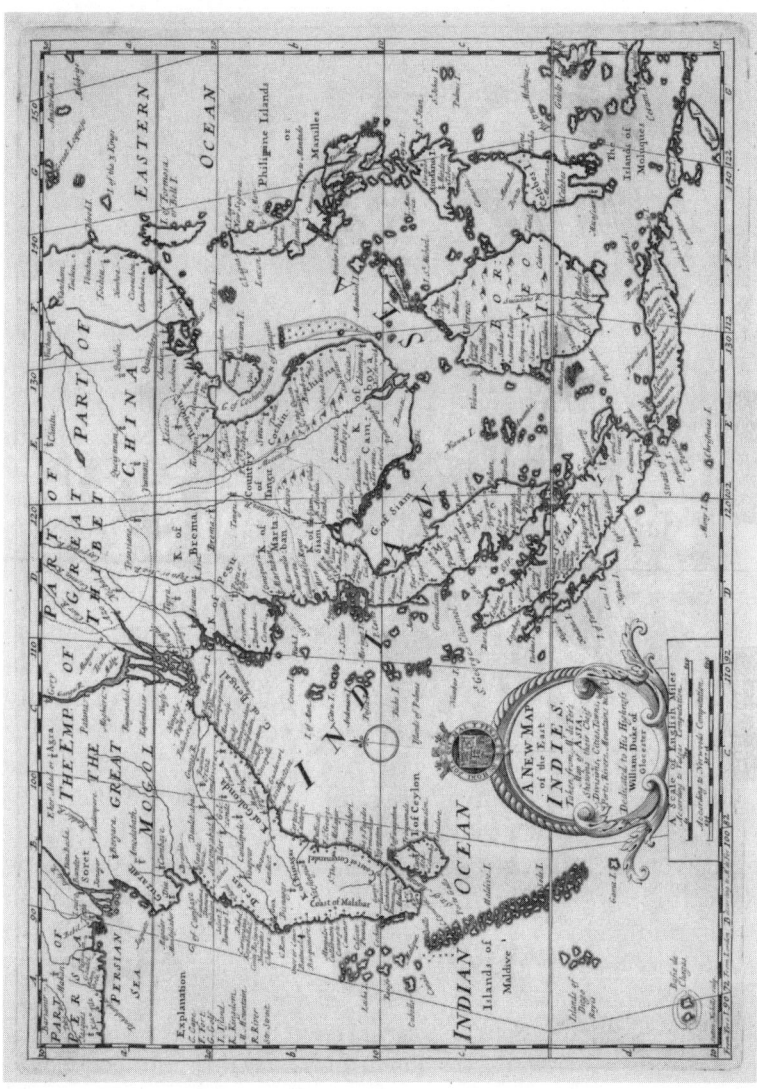

Lionel Pincus and Princess Firyal Map Division, The New York Public Library. "A new map o East Indies, taken from Mr. de Fer's Map of Asia, shewing their chief divisions, cities, towns, ports, rivers, mountains &c." New York Public Library Digital Collections.

Seen from the perspective of local rulers and traders, the violence and the superior weaponry of the Europeans did not change the basic shape of Southeast Asia's world, even of the trading regime. The Europeans were simply spread too thin. Asians quickly learned how to use and then to make better weaponry, minimizing the Europeans' military advantage, until the 19th century at any rate.[40] When the Europeans had an advantage, they did not hesitate to use it. The Portuguese and Spanish, as well as the British, Dutch and French, were equally unrestrained in their use of violent methods. But it is significant that the Western wave started slowly and built up over time. Europeans were of little more than marginal importance to Asia for the first nearly 300 years of their presence: they made little effort to control territory in Southeast Asia during this period.

Since the colonizers' main aims were commercial, the goal of each colonizer was to conquer and retain control of key commercial nodes. The colonizers fought each other over control of these nodes perhaps even more than they did Asian trading powers. The rivalries among the colonial powers in Southeast Asia were basically extensions of their wars and rivalries in Europe. The Portuguese conquered Malacca in 1511, but they lost it to superior Dutch forces in 1641. The Dutch ruled Malacca for almost two centuries before ceding control to the British as part of the Anglo-Dutch Treaty of 1824.

Similarly, the Portuguese and the Spanish fought over control of the famous Spice Islands, the Moluccas. They were helped by the fact that the rulers of two key islands, Tidore and Ternate, were permanently feuding. Significantly, the Spanish and Portuguese arrived in the Spice Islands by vastly different routes. The Spanish travelled west via the Atlantic and past South America, while the Portuguese travelled east via the Indian Ocean and past Africa. In the early 16th century, the Portuguese won the struggle. The Spanish were expelled from the Spice Islands in 1527. This led the Spanish to focus on the colonization of the Philippines, and four centuries of steady expansion of Spanish colonial rule followed, leading to its deep imprint on the soul of the Filipino people.

None of the other emergent colonizers tried to establish a territorial empire in Southeast Asia. The Portuguese could only aspire to control a few commercial nodes: Malacca, Timor, New Guinea and the Maluku Islands. Similarly, when the Dutch arrived, they followed

---

40. Tonio Andrade, *The Gunpowder Age: China, Military Innovation, and the Rise of the West in World History* (Princeton: Princeton University Press, 2016).

the same pattern of focussing on a few strategic points from which to gain control of the spice trade. Only slowly, over 400 years, did they come to control larger territories in Java, parts of Sumatra, Borneo, the Lesser Sunda Islands, Sulawesi, parts of Maluku, and Papua.

The British and French came relatively late to Southeast Asia. The British were preoccupied with India in the 17th and 18th centuries and did not establish any kind of physical presence in Southeast Asia until they occupied Manila for two years, from 1762 to 1764. The Sultan of Johor, in an effort to get British support against regional rivals, had offered Singapore 60 years earlier, in 1703, to an English trader named Alexander Hamilton. Hamilton explained his decision to turn down the Johor offer:

> In Anno 1703 I called at Johor on my way to China, and he [Sultan 'Abdu'l Jalil Ri'ayat Shah] treated me very kindly, and made me a present of the Island of Sincapure [*sic*], but I told him it could be of no use to a private person, tho' a proper place for a Company to settle a colony on, lying in the centre of trade, and being accommodated with good rivers and safe harbours, so conveniently situated, that all winds served shipping both to go out and come into those rivers. The soil is black and fat; and the woods abound in good masts for shipping, and timber for building. I have seen large beans growing wild in the woods, not inferior to the best in Europe for taste and beauty; and sugar cane five or six inches round growing wild also.[41]

The British had made a play for the Spice Islands during the 1600s, but they were rebuffed by the Dutch, who massacred the British in Ambon in 1623. The real contest was to come over 150 years later. The British declared war on the Dutch in December 1780 because they discovered that the latter were colluding with the American colonies then in rebellion. A Dutch factory in Padang, Sumatra, was seized by the British in 1781. Interestingly, Britain's eventual loss of the American colonies contributed to its having a stronger presence in Asia, including Southeast Asia.

Everything changed with the advent of the Industrial Revolution. European demand for raw materials dramatically increased. New modes of organizing agriculture into plantations—for sugar, indigo, cotton and coffee—demanded access to labour and control of populations as well as the violent means to enforce it. In the 18th

---

41. Alexander Hamilton, *A New Account of the East Indies*, Vol. 2 (Edinburgh: John Mosman, 1727), p. 97.

century Europeans were focussed on the New World, but by the 19th century the British, French and Dutch began to bring this economy to Southeast Asia. The Western wave had fully arrived now, with a vengeance. This stage of colonialism was to last for about 100 years, from the mid-19th century to the mid-20th.

The modern map of Southeast Asia shows the result of geopolitical clashes and conflicts among the European powers in Europe. That Sumatra remained Dutch and the Malay Peninsula British was purely a result of an Anglo-Dutch agreement of 1824, following their collaboration against the French in the Napoleonic Wars. Since the colonial powers determined the modern boundaries of Southeast Asia, driven by external geopolitical development and not indigenous trends, Southeast Asia could have ended up with messy and politically unworkable borders.

It is a geopolitical miracle that modern Southeast Asia has ended up with workable borders. An obvious contrast might help to drive home the point. In the Middle East, the British diplomat Sir Mark Sykes and French diplomat François Georges-Picot drew completely artificial boundaries in the desert in 1916. Their artificial maps have cursed the region for over a century. Robin Wright states: "The Sykes-Picot Agreement launched a nine-year process—and other deals, declarations, and treaties—that created the modern Middle East states out of the Ottoman carcass. The new borders ultimately bore little resemblance to the original Sykes-Picot map, but their map is still viewed as the root cause of much that has happened ever since."[42] He also writes, "The colonial carve-up was always vulnerable. Its map ignored local identities and political preferences. Borders were determined with a ruler—arbitrarily." Several modern commentators have confirmed the damage done by the Sykes-Picot Agreement. Nawzad Hadi Mawlood, the governor of Iraq's Erbil province, told Wright: "Hundreds of thousands have been killed because of Sykes-Picot and all the problems it created. It changed the course of history—and nature." Zikri Mosa, an adviser to Kurdistan's President Masoud Barzani, said, "Sykes-Picot was a mistake, for sure. It was like a forced marriage. It was doomed from the start. It was immoral, because it decided people's future without asking them."[43]

---

42. Robin Wright, "How the Curse of Sykes-Picot Still Haunts the Middle East", *New Yorker*, 20 Apr. 2016, http://www.newyorker.com/news/news-desk/how-the-curse-of-sykes-picot-still-haunts-the-middle-east/, accessed 12 Oct. 2016.
43. Ibid.

Southeast Asia could have ended up with several artificial and unnatural political borders like the Sykes-Picot map of the Middle East. Amazingly, mainland Southeast Asia ended up with national boundaries which reflected well the traditional historical entities. The British domination of Burma (modern Myanmar) and the French domination of Indochina (which includes modern Vietnam, Laos and Cambodia) resulted in viable states emerging after decolonization. Thailand was never colonized, but it was able to preserve most of its territory by cleverly playing off the French against the British. Luck also helped the Thais.

Western influence also helped to preserve some small or more vulnerable states. Cambodia could have disappeared as an independent state in the face of Vietnamese expansion. French rule saved Cambodia from Vietnam and Thailand. Indeed, the only current hotly contested boundary dispute in Southeast Asia is the one between Cambodia and Thailand over the Preah Vihear temple. The Thais and Cambodians almost came to full-scale military warfare as recently as 2011. That incident was troubling, but its exceptional occurrence also demonstrated that most of the borders in Southeast Asia are settled.

While the borders of mainland Southeast Asia formed around the relatively stable state entities of Burma, Thailand, Laos, Cambodia and Vietnam, the borders of maritime Southeast Asia are not quite so easy to justify, as alluded to earlier. For most of the first and second millennia in the contemporary era, the kingdoms and empires that emerged in the region straddled the Straits of Malacca.

The post-Western division of maritime Southeast Asia into two separate "Malay" entities, Malaysia and Indonesia (or three if Brunei is included), is a somewhat artificial division. Yet it has worked quite well and has been peacefully adopted, at least after the brief period of "Confrontation" by President Sukarno against Malaysia from 1963 to 1966. The then prime minister of Malaysia, Tunku Abdul Rahman, has explained in his memoirs that President Sukarno was worried that the creation of an independent Malaysia could lead to Sumatra declaring independence from Indonesia and joining Malaysia. He wrote:

> Sukarno was difficult because at the back of his mind he always wanted to crush us, because I think, chiefly, he was suspicious of the strong Malay feeling which existed between us and the Sumatrans. No doubt there was strong feeling for us in Sumatra. He felt that the people of Sumatra were closer to us than they

were to Java. Most of the Malays in Sumatra felt they should be
linked with us ...[44]

Although it would not be accurate to characterize European colonial
rule of Southeast Asia as benign, it is fair to say that in the last century
preceding their departure from their colonies, the European colonial
rulers did bring various aspects of modernization to the region.
The opening of the Suez Canal in 1869

> facilitated a speedy increase in the number of steamships
> operating in Southeast Asia, rapidly ushering in a new
> mechanised age of sea transportation in the region ... This new
> route, linking the Mediterranean and Indian Ocean via the
> Red Sea, reduced the length of time it took for steam vessels
> from Europe to reach Asia by one-third ... The benefits were
> immediately felt in Singapore as its trade figures jumped from
> just over £58 million in 1868 to nearly £90 million in 1873.[45]

The significant increase of rubber production in the region in the
late 20th century is a good illustration of this trade expansion and the
West's new hunger for the natural resources of the region. In 1905
Southeast Asia exported 200 tons of rubber. By 1920 the number had
increased to 196,000 tons, and by 1948 the amount had reached 700,000
tons.[46]

This significant increase of economic activity and resource exports
from Southeast Asia during European colonial rule in the late 19th and
early 20th centuries led to another development that can also be listed
as a major impact of the Western wave on Southeast Asia: the arrival
of economic immigrants from China and India. They came in massive
numbers and changed the political and economic chemistry of several
Southeast Asian states.

Since the British ruled both India and Burma, large numbers of
Indian immigrants came to Burma in the mid-19th century. They came
to work in

> all fields: unskilled and skilled labourers, clerks, teachers,
> engineers, and the like. Workers for the railroads, river shipping,
> post offices, rice mills, mines, oil fields, banks, and for the shops

---

44. Tan Sri Abdullah Ahmad, *Conversations with Tunku Abdul Rahman* (Singapore:
    Marshall Cavendish, 2016), p. 68.
45. S. Dobbs, *The Singapore River: A Social History, 1819–2002* (Singapore: Singapore
    University Press, 2003), p. 10.
46. Harrison, *South-East Asia*, p. 212.

were especially needed. No new public, army, police, or civilian administrative office was established in Burma without Indians. Following them came others whose services were required by both Europeans and Indians. These were servants, launderers (a special caste in India: dhobis), shoemakers, watchmen (also a special caste), money-changers, restaurant owners, hoteliers, men of every profession hitherto completely unknown in Burma.[47]

Similarly, many Indians went to Malaya to work in the rubber plantations from 1907 to 1957. Due to the "kangani" system, in which recruitment from India and supervision on the plantations in Malaya were in the hands of Tamil headmen, large groups of Tamils emigrated to Malaya. Tamils worked also in the cities of Malaya and Burma in various capacities. Later in the 20th century, the Japanese advances in Southeast Asia had disastrous consequences for Tamil plantation workers. Around 100,000 of them were conscripted by the Japanese to construct the "death railway" between Thailand and Myanmar.[48]

After the war Indian plantation workers in Malaya did not face the level of opposition from the "sons of the soil" that their counterparts in other Southeast Asian countries did, especially in Burma, from which ethnic Indians were expelled in 1962. Indian communities in Malaysia and Singapore have flourished, with ethnic Indians working in a diverse range of fields including law, business and politics. A striking example of the success of ethnic Indians in Malaya is S.R. Nathan, former president of Singapore. His father emigrated to Malaya when he was posted as a clerk in a law firm that catered to rubber plantations. Similarly, V.T. Sambanathan, one of the founding fathers of Malaysia along with Tunku Abdul Rahman and Tan Cheng Lock, was the son of a pioneer rubber planter in Sungai Siput.

The Chinese came in far larger numbers and had a far greater impact on the economy and society of Southeast Asia. The country that absorbed the largest number was Thailand, which has accepted Chinese émigrés for centuries. For the most part, they have been

---

47. Moshe Yegar, *The Muslims of Burma: A Study of a Minority Group* (Wiesbaden: Otto Harrassowitz, 1972).
48. Ravindra K. Jain, *South Indians on the Plantation Frontier in Malaya* (New Haven and London: Yale University Press, 1970), in Christophe Z. Guilmoto, "The Tamil Migration Cycle, 1830–1950", *Economic and Political Weekly* (16–23 Jan. 1993): 111–20.

happily assimilated into Thailand. Jeffery and his wife, Pim, have written a book[49] that documents this well.

Indonesia, Malaysia and the Philippines also attracted large numbers of Chinese migrants in the 19th and early 20th centuries. While the Chinese were enormously successful in economic terms in these three countries during this time, their political reception was often less than welcoming.

The Philippines, as a Christian country, found it easier to assimilate its recent Chinese migrants, many of whom converted to Catholicism or adopted Hispanized names. Perhaps a history of Chinese migration to the Philippines that dates back as far as the 10th century helped. In 1879 the Spanish writer Carlos Recur wrote, "from the commercial point of view, the Philippines is an Anglo-Chinese colony with a Spanish Flag."[50] European colonial forces favoured the Chinese as middlemen, and there were many Chinese Filipino entrepreneurs in the country. Many of the largest conglomerates in the Philippines are owned by Chinese Filipinos and grew from small businesses.

By contrast, Chinese have not easily been assimilated into Malaysian or Indonesian societies. In both places, the Chinese thrived economically in the 20th century but had to deal with serious political challenges. In relative terms, Malaysia took in far larger numbers of Chinese. The Chinese arrived mainly in the 19th century, initially to work in the tin mines and later to work on plantations as well. As Charles Hirschman describes it:

> The 1840s and 1850s marked the beginning of a decisive demographic and economic break with the past. The expansion of trade, especially as the industrial revolution took hold in the West, stimulated a quantum leap in economic activity and labour migration. The demand for tin was the initial factor, but subsequent commerce forays in agriculture (coffee, sugar, etc.) also required larger amounts of cheap labour for the growing export sector. Malaya was sparsely settled and labour in short supply. Malay peasants were understandably reluctant to enter into the almost slavelike conditions of employment in the early

---

49. Sng and Bisalputra, *A History of the Thai-Chinese.*
50. Carlos Recur y Carazo, *Filipinas: estudios administrativos y comerciales* (Madrid: Imprenta de Ramón Moreno y Richardo Rojas, 1879), in E. Wichberg, *Early Chinese Economic Influence in the Philippines, 1850–1898* (Lawrence: Center for East Asian Studies, University of Kansas, 1962), p. 110.

mines and plantations. Other Asian peoples had fewer options and were induced to come to Malaya as contract labourers.[51]

By the time Malaya achieved independence in 1957, the number of Chinese had gone up to 38 per cent of the total population. The Malays, initially in Malaya and later in Malaysia, feared losing control of their political destiny and worked hard to restrain Chinese political rights. Even Tunku Abdul Rahman, the relatively tolerant and open-minded first prime minister of Malaya and Malaysia, expressed this concern. He said that the decision to separate Singapore was "entirely mine and if there is any blame, I accept it. But in my mind, deep in my heart, that was the correct policy. Otherwise the Chinese would dominate our country, completely dominate this country of ours with their population of two million more than the Malays." Many years before that, when he was a student, he had written: "In the end, if Malaya becomes independent, it has got to be separated. We can't have it as one country because the Chinese would be predominant and would be in a very much stronger position than the Malays. And so there was no choice; like a bad leg it had to be amputated."[52]

As in the Philippines, Chinese migration to Indonesia has a long history. But the migration that started in the 19th century was of a different order of magnitude. Dewi Susanti makes the following observation:

> After Indonesian independence in 1945 and up until 1998, the position and identity of the Chinese Indonesians as fabricated by the Dutch were maintained for political reasons. During the New Order (1966–1998), Chinese Indonesians were politically and culturally alienated. They were 'designated' to run businesses because of their business acumen and because they posed no political threat to the government. Socially and residentially, they often chose to segregate themselves from other Indonesians.[53]

51. Charles Hirschman, "The Meaning and Measurement of Ethnicity in Malaysia: An Analysis of Census Classifications", *Journal of Asian Studies* 46, 3 (1987): 555–82.
52. Tan Sri Abdullah Ahmad, *Conversations with Tunku Abdul Rahman*.
53. Dewi Susanti, "Paradoxes of Discriminatory Policies and Educational Attainment: Chinese Indonesians in Contemporary Indonesia", in *Equity, Opportunity and Education in Postcolonial Southeast Asia*, ed. C. Joseph and J. Matthews (New York: Routledge, 2014), p. 135.

Given their economic presence, and the social distance Susanti describes, in times of unrest the Chinese found themselves the targets of violent pogroms: in Tangerang in 1946, in Sumatra in the 1950s, as part of the wider killings across Indonesia in 1965, and during the May 1998 riots.

Chinese migrated to all of the ASEAN countries. However, except for the countries mentioned above, and Singapore, their numbers were not significant. Nevertheless, these small Chinese communities played a key role in fostering intra-Southeast Asian trade, creating a "bamboo network". According to Murray Weidenbaum, "The 'bamboo network' transcends existing national boundaries. It is comprised of key locations where business executives, traders, and financiers of Chinese backgrounds make most of the day-to-day economic decisions."[54]

There is no question that the Western wave had a profound impact on the course of Southeast Asian history. Nick Knight says:

> The impact of European colonialism on East and Southeast Asia was uneven and sporadic, but cumulatively very great. Local histories and cultures remained important in shaping local historical outcomes. But the West, through the agency of colonialism, unleashed alien forces in East and Southeast Asia—an international trading system based on capitalism, industrialisation and commercialised agricultural production, the nation-state and nationalism—which were to have dramatic consequences for the peoples and societies of the region.[55]

The drawing of modern borders for Southeast Asia was a result of the Western wave. Reid points out:

> The failure of Southeast Asian attempts to vary imperial boundaries in the name of historical, cultural or ideological claims illustrates the power of the [imperial] alchemy. Thailand's wartime annexation of western Cambodia, some of eastern Burma, and northern Malaya (1941–5), Indonesia's annexation of (Portuguese) East Timor in 1975–99, the division of Vietnam in 1954–75 (even though coinciding with its precolonial history of division), the regional rebellions in Indonesia (1956–62), Cambodia's probing of its south-eastern border in 1978 and

---

54. Murray Weidenbaum, *One-Armed Economist: On the Intersection of Business and Government* (New Brunswick and London: Transaction Publishers, 2005), pp. 264–5.
55. Nick Knight, *Understanding Australia's Neighbours: An Introduction to East and Southeast Asia* (New York: Cambridge University Press, 2011), pp. 61–2.

Vietnam's subsequent invasion of Cambodia, all failed in the long run to dethrone the power of imperial boundaries. The succession of Malaysia to Britain's untidy empire in the Malay World was fought by Indonesia in 1962–6 and opposed by the Philippines (which laid a claim to Sabah in 1962), yet in the long run it was only the departure of tiny Brunei (1962) and Singapore (1965) that diminished the imperial heritage.[56]

Fortunately, these borders fitted in well with the underlying political and social fabric of Southeast Asian societies, or at any rate were less of a shock to local societies than were the lines on the map drawn in the Middle East or between India and Pakistan.

Much of the modern infrastructure that can be found in Southeast Asia—roads and railways, schools and hospitals (to name a few)— was started in the colonial era and fortunately sustained. Apart from Cambodia's brief experience with Pol Pot's genocidal rule from 1975 to 1978, no Southeast Asian state has come close to outright failure. The various modern administrative systems left behind by the colonial era, including in the non-colonized Thailand, have endured and continue to provide the administrative backbone of many Southeast Asian states. Singapore's exceptional success after independence was due to many factors, including its ability to build on and strengthen the many institutions of governance left behind by the British.

None of this means that the Western colonizers deserve a thank-you note from the modern Southeast Asian states. There is an equally strong negative legacy left behind by European colonial rule: the brutal violence used against militarily weaker societies and the ruthless exploitation of peasant and urban labour. In the 1840s, for example, the Dutch Cultivation System (*cultuurstelsel*) led to famines and epidemics across Java, as the Dutch made excessive demands of corvée labour from villages to grow cash crops such as coffee, sugar cane and indigo.[57] Even after formal independence, it took decades for Southeast Asians to shrug off mental colonization. This delayed the rejuvenation of Southeast Asian societies. In short, the impact of the Western wave on modern Southeast Asia is a mixed one that deserves deeper study by future generations of Southeast Asian historians.

---

56. Anthony Reid, *Imperial Alchemy: Nationalism and Political Identity in Southeast Asia* (Cambridge: Cambridge University Press, 2010), p. 2.
57. Siddharth Chandra and Timothy Vogelsang, "Change and Involution in Sugar Production in Cultivation System Java, 1840–1870", *Journal of Economic History* 59, 4 (1998): 885–911.

2

The ASEAN Ecosystem of Peace

No other region on our planet has been so open to such very distinct and different waves of history. This may also explain why no other region on our planet is as diverse and as differentiated as Southeast Asia. In short, no region on our planet should be more inhospitable than Southeast Asia as a place to launch an ambitious exercise in regional cooperation.

The logic of history should have dictated the failure of ASEAN. It is a true miracle that ASEAN succeeded and produced peace and prosperity in an inhospitable region. So why and how did ASEAN bring peace to the Balkans of Asia? Some wise soul once remarked that for every thousand books written on the causes of war, one is written on the causes of peace. Indeed, when war breaks out, whether it be in Kosovo or Georgia, Syria or Libya, we notice it immediately. Thousands of articles pour forth to explain the reasons for conflict. Yet when a durable ecosystem of peace settles in, few notice. Even fewer try to explain. Here in ASEAN, a once-troubled region of the globe has achieved durable peace. This is the great mystery that no one has tried to explain.

Sadly, Western international relations scholars are not likely to fill the gap. Such scholars rely on news clippings and reports of "events" (such as the bombing of Kosovo) as the empirical data for their scholarly analyses. But peace is a non-event. No one reports on it. Years of peace can go unreported, but every small event of conflict is news. This helps explain why peace within ASEAN does not attract much scholarly attention.

The goal of this chapter, then, is to solve that major historical mystery: how a durable ecosystem of peace came to develop in one of the most improbable and unpromising corners of earth—Southeast

Asia. The story is a complex one, involving many twists and turns. As is normal with most living processes, good fortune and misfortune intervened from time to time to influence the course of ASEAN's development.

Before spelling out the factors that led to the development of this ecosystem, it is essential to understand the chronology. The first and most critical phase of ASEAN's development took place during the Cold War, from 1967 to 1990. But this critical phase had two parts. From 1967 to 1975, when Communism overran Indochina, the founding members of ASEAN (Indonesia, Malaysia, the Philippines, Singapore, Thailand) lived in fear of the Communist tide overwhelming them. However, soon after, when it became evident that the Communist world had split into two—with deep schisms between the Soviet Union and China (paralleled by those between Vietnam and Cambodia)— ASEAN's fear receded. Indeed, ASEAN's solidarity in responding to the Vietnamese invasion of Cambodia in December 1978 and its concerted global campaign to reverse the Vietnamese occupation of Cambodia led to the creation of a deep sense of community among the five and then six ASEAN member states (Brunei joined in 1984). Without this decade of close collaboration against the Vietnamese occupation of Cambodia, it is possible that ASEAN may not have succeeded in creating this durable ecosystem of peace.

Phase 2 lasted through most of the 1990s. It began with the end of the Cold War and ended with the disastrous impact of the Asian Financial Crisis on several ASEAN states in 1997–98. During this decade, ASEAN lived on the political capital of solidarity it had accumulated over the previous two decades, with key leaders such as Lee Kuan Yew, Mahathir and Suharto continuing habits of ASEAN cooperation. At the same time, the nature of the ASEAN community changed with the entry of Vietnam (1995), Laos (1997), Myanmar (1997) and Cambodia (1999). Amazingly, many erstwhile adversaries joined ASEAN in quick succession. A more inclusive Southeast Asian community emerged as a result.

Phase 3 began in the early years of the 21st century. In this phase, ASEAN significantly enhanced its institutional development. The ASEAN Free Trade Area (AFTA), whose implementation had begun in 1993, was slated to fully come into force by 2003 (2006 for Vietnam, 2008 for Laos and Myanmar, and 2010 for Cambodia). Most significantly, the ASEAN Charter was negotiated and concluded in a record 11 months, from January to November 2007. This phase of institutional development, building upon the solid foundation of political solidarity accumulated in the previous three decades, led to the creation of the strong regional organization that the world sees in ASEAN today.

The big question we will try to answer in this chapter is: What were the key factors that led to the creation of the ecosystem of peace that ASEAN now enjoys? Any list would include the following. First, the main impulse that drew together the five founding members of ASEAN was fear. The founding countries feared that they would become falling "dominoes" as Communism expanded. Second, the ASEAN countries were blessed with relatively good leaders. Leadership is always a critical factor in international affairs. Third, luck was also a factor. ASEAN ended up on the winning side in the major geopolitical contest of the late 20th century, the Cold War between the United States and the Soviet Union. There were also other geopolitical accidents, such as the Sino-Soviet split of 1969, which helped ASEAN. Fourth, the ASEAN countries successfully wove themselves into the thriving East Asian economic ecosystem, at a time when world trade was expanding. They set this in motion by learning economic lessons from Japan and the "Four Tigers" and emulating the best practices of these successful East Asian countries in their national development policies. The decision to embrace free trade and open markets was not preordained. All the ASEAN countries were members of the Group of 77 in the UN, which advocated nationalist and protectionist policies inspired by the nationalist ideology of Raúl Prebisch.[1] The ASEAN countries rejected these conventional Third World policies. Fifth, as the ASEAN dynamic gained momentum and ASEAN moved towards creating hundreds of multilateral meetings a year, the Southeast Asian region became more closely connected, with several spiderwebs of networks in different areas. The role of these networks in delivering peace has not been well analyzed.

One more factor was important. Kishore has often said—only half in jest—that Southeast Asia is at peace because of a four-letter word. This four-letter word is golf. Kishore resolved many thorny issues with his ASEAN colleagues after a happy round of golf that generated friendship and camaraderie. Former Foreign Minister of Singapore Wong Kan Seng agreed that "Golf was an important factor. It helped to break down barriers and promote camaraderie. We even had an

---

1. "Establishment of the Group of 77", *G77*, http://www.g77.org/paris/history/establishment-of-g77.html/, accessed 12 Oct. 2016.

ASEAN golf game at a weekend when we attended the annual UN General Assembly."[2] He added:

> The annual ASEAN dinner in the UN was a show of unity. Ministers' wives would come and shake people's hands— that was not seen in other regional organizations. There were memorable but simple gifts as well. Orchids would be given at the end of receptions. A lot of people would turn up, including the UN secretary-general.

In short, the whole world could see at first hand at the UN ASEAN's model of peaceful cooperation. This ecosystem of peace that ASEAN created became self-reinforcing when it also brought benefits to many of ASEAN's neighbours. Several of ASEAN's dialogue partners, including Japan and South Korea, Australia and New Zealand, found value in participating in ASEAN meetings and benefiting from this ASEAN ecosystem, which spread its ethos of cooperation around the larger East Asian and Asia-Pacific regions.

First Factor: The Fear of Communism

Let us begin with the beginning of ASEAN. The key factor that brought ASEAN together was a naked fear of Communism. This raw fear cannot be understood today without a deep understanding of the political context of the 1960s. Today, the victory of the non-Communist world, led by the United States, against the Communist world, led by the Soviet Union, seems to have been inevitable, something easily predicted. However, as we grew up in Southeast Asia in the 1960s, we know that victory seemed far from inevitable at the time. Indeed, Communism seemed to be the irresistible tide.

The five founding ASEAN countries also feared Communism because each had experienced Communist insurgencies at home. Malaysia and Singapore had suffered terrorist attacks carried out by the Communist Party of Malaya in the 1940s and 1950s. The Indonesian government led by President Suharto was traumatized by the attempted coup of 1965 inspired by the Communist Party of Indonesia (PKI). The plotters killed several Indonesian generals and had targeted Suharto, then commander of the Strategic Reserve. Thailand worried about both the domestic Communist insurgency led by the Communist Party of Thailand as well as becoming a frontline

---

2.   Authors' interview with Wong Kan Seng, 24 July 2015.

state if Indochina fell to the Communists. The Philippines experienced the Hukbalahap insurgency from 1942 to 1954.

After China fell to Communist rule in 1949, the two subsequent battles against Communist expansion took place in Korea and Indochina. The situation in Korea stabilized when the war ended with the Korean Armistice Agreement of 27 July 1953. The guns fell silent, but the Korean peninsula was divided. However, the guns began firing with greater intensity, initially in Vietnam and Laos and subsequently in Cambodia, especially after the CIA deposed Sihanouk on 18 March 1970. Kishore lived for a year in Phnom Penh, Cambodia, from July 1973 to June 1974 and experienced at first hand the daily shelling of the city by Khmer Rouge forces. He will never forget the experience of being at home when bomb shrapnel blasted and smashed all the glass windows of his house. The determination of the Communist parties of Vietnam, Laos and Cambodia was formidable. They were convinced that history was on their side.

By contrast, the non-Communist leaders of the five founding countries of ASEAN feared for their lives and for their countries. James Lay, then executive secretary of the US National Security Council, had predicted in a 1952 report that

> The loss of any of the countries of Southeast Asia to communist control as a consequence of overt or covert Chinese Communist aggression would have critical psychological, political and economic consequences. In the absence of effective and timely counteraction, the loss of any single country would probably lead to relatively swift submission to or an alignment with communism by the remaining countries of this group.[3]

This idea gained traction. In 1954 American President Dwight Eisenhower said that Indochina was of strategic importance because "You have a row of dominoes set up, you knock over the first one, and what will happen to the last one is the certainty that it will go over very quickly. So you could have a beginning of a disintegration that would have the most profound influences."[4]

---

3. "Report to the National Security Council by the Executive Secretary (Lay)", 25 June 1952, *Foreign Relations of the United States, 1952–1954. East Asia and the Pacific (in two parts)* Vol. 12, part 1, https://history.state.gov/historicaldocuments/frus1952-54v12p1/d36/, accessed 12 Oct. 2016.
4. "President Eisenhower's News Conference, April 7, 1954", *The Pentagon Papers*, Gravel Edition, Vol. 1 (Boston: Beacon Press, 1971), pp. 597–8, https://www.mtholyoke.edu/acad/intrel/pentagon/ps11.htm/, accessed 13 Oct. 2016.

The psychological impact of this theory cannot be overstated. In May 1975, Malaysian Minister of Home Affairs Ghazali Shafie said that while "the domino theory is patently suspect in terms of not only theoretical but also empirical validity ... current events appear like so many portents of a dark and uncertain future. In a climate of despondency the domino theory could well become—ironically—a self-fulfilling prophecy."[5] Given this prevailing climate of fear, at the founding meeting of ASEAN in Bangkok in August 1967, Singapore Foreign Minister S. Rajaratnam could tell his ASEAN colleagues with deep conviction, "if we do not hang together, we of the ASEAN nations will hang separately." The meaning of this is well understood by most English-language speakers, but it led to a humorous misunderstanding by the Thai delegation. After Rajaratnam uttered the words, a Thai delegate said, "As Buddhists, we object to hanging. Why are you only giving us two different ways to be hanged?" Fortunately, the Thai delegation agreed with Rajaratnam after the meaning of the sentence was explained to them.

This is why the fear factor is important. It was the critical glue that held the five countries together. This fear became more and more pronounced as the ASEAN countries watched Communist forces steadily gain ground in Cambodia, Laos and South Vietnam. Indeed, when Kishore lived in Phnom Penh the city was completely under siege. It was not possible to reach the countryside by road. At the same time, the 1972 Watergate political crisis and Richard Nixon's resignation on 9 August 1974 showed the ASEAN countries that the United States, on whom they relied for their security, was preoccupied and distracted by events at home. Over time, this grew into a deeper realization that ASEAN would have—to use Rajaratnam's words—to "hang together or hang separately". On 7 August 1968, then Malaysian Deputy Prime Minister Abdul Razak presciently warned the ASEAN delegates that "it must be our common concern to do nothing—and ensure that nothing is done—which could jeopardise the future of ASEAN".[6]

The darkest moment in the minds of the ASEAN leaders occurred when Saigon fell on 30 April 1975. The dramatic scenes of American

---

5. "Vietnam: The End of the War. Broadcast by Malaysia's Minister of Home Affairs, Tan Sri M. Ghazali Shafie 6 May 1975", *Survival* 17, 4 (1975): 186–8.
6. Tun Razak, "Our Destiny", *Straits Times*, 7 Aug. 1968, http://eresources. nlb.gov.sg/newspapers/Digitised/Article/straitstimes19680807-1.2.3.aspx/, accessed 12 Oct. 2016.

diplomats and soldiers being evacuated from the rooftops of the American Embassy in Saigon only reinforced the leaders' fears that the Communist tide was going to overwhelm all of Southeast Asia. Eight years earlier, on 19 October 1967, Lee Kuan Yew had told American Vice President Hubert Humphrey that if America were to withdraw from Vietnam, "there would be fighting in Thailand within one and a half to two years, in Malaysia shortly thereafter, and within three years, I would be hanging in the public square".[7] When Saigon fell, this dark day must have seemed imminent. Lee told Gerald Ford on 8 May 1975, "My immediate reaction is one of astonishment and alarm at the rapidity with which the situation fell apart."[8] Describing the chaos in Southeast Asia, Lee reported that the Thais believed "the US has no morals. The press is having a carnival ... Laos is a goner. Cambodia is a struggle between China and Hanoi."

This fear of Communist expansion led to the first summit meeting of ASEAN leaders being held in Bali on 23–24 February 1976, one year after the fall of Indochina. Kishore participated in this meeting. As Donald Weatherbee describes it:

> The communist victories in Indochina in 1975 catalyzed the ASEAN states into urgent efforts for greater security cooperation. In February 1976, the ASEAN heads of government met in Bali, Indonesia, for the first ASEAN Summit. There, they laid the foundations for stronger political and economic collaboration within ASEAN without closing the door for reconciliation with the Indochinese states.[9]

In contrast to the fear that predominated in the minds of the leaders meeting in Bali, the leaders of Vietnam were feeling very arrogant. They were confident that history was on their side in Southeast Asia. The former president of Singapore S.R. Nathan got a glimpse of this overweening Vietnamese confidence when he went as a delegate to a meeting of the Non-Aligned Movement Summit meeting in Sri

7. "Foreign Relations 1964–1968, Volume XXVI, Indonesia; Malaysia-Singapore; Philippines", U.S. Department of State Archive, 10 Dec. 1966, http://2001-2009. state.gov/r/pa/ho/frus/johnsonlb/xxvi/4432.htm, accessed 12 Oct. 2016.
8. "Memorandum of Conversation, Washington, May 8, 1975, noon–1 p.m.", *Foreign Relations of the United States, 1969–1976, Volume E–12, Documents on East and Southeast Asia, 1973–1976*, 8 May 1975, https://history.state.gov/historicaldocuments/frus1969-76ve12/d297/, accessed 12 Oct. 2016.
9. Donald Weatherbee, *International Relations in Southeast Asia: The Struggle for Autonomy*, 2nd ed. (Plymouth: Rowman & Littlefield, 2009), p. 76.

Lanka in August 1976. Nathan happened to read a note that the PM of Vietnam, Pham Van Dong, had written to Sirimavo Bandaranaike. In this note, Pham Van Dong said, "following the defeat of the Americans and the unification of Vietnam, the revolution had begun. The communists would sweep across Southeast Asia."[10]

This arrogance of the Vietnamese leadership led to them making one of the strategically most disastrous decisions in Vietnam's history. When the Communists took over Indochina in 1975, it was generally assumed that the Communist parties of Cambodia, Laos and Vietnam would work as a cohesive block, since they had fought together against the American-supported forces in the three countries. However, the opposite happened. Traditional rivalries between Cambodia and Vietnam, which go back several centuries, surfaced soon after the three Communist parties took over. The Cambodian Khmer Rouge regime, led by the genocidal dictator Pol Pot, broke off from Vietnam. Pol Pot began to side with China to counterbalance Vietnam's close alliance with the Soviet Union. The Sino-Soviet split had surfaced in Indochina.

With the split, Vietnam began to make plans to invade and occupy Cambodia. Since the Vietnamese leaders were still feeling very confident after defeating a world superpower, and as they believed that they could rely on the military power of the Soviet Union to protect Vietnam from China, they ignored China's warnings and proceeded to invade and occupy Cambodia in December 1978.

In so doing, Vietnam made several major miscalculations. First, in response, China launched a major invasion of Vietnam in February 1979. Hundreds of thousands of Chinese and Vietnamese fought against each other. Even though the Vietnamese soldiers fought valiantly and won many battles, in the end they had to concede Vietnamese territory to the invading Chinese forces. After having taught Vietnam a "lesson", the Chinese leaders wisely withdrew their soldiers back into Chinese territory. However, they had sent Vietnam a clear signal that they would relentlessly oppose the Vietnamese occupation of Cambodia. In the memorable words of the pithy Deng Xiaoping, if you take a small stone and a large stone and rub them together, the small stone eventually disappears.

The second major miscalculation that Vietnam made was to underestimate the opposition of ASEAN. Having defeated non-

---

10. Timothy Auger, *S.R. Nathan in Conversation* (Singapore: Editions Didier Millet, 2015), pp. 72–3.

Communist forces in Indochina, the Vietnamese leaders assumed that the non-Communist leaders of the ASEAN countries were equally feckless and weak. They were not completely unjustified in this belief. One reason why Thailand had never been colonized in the European colonial era was that Thais had developed a culture of accommodation of the new powers that appeared at their doorstep. Hence, when Vietnamese tanks swiftly crossed Cambodia and arrived at the Thai-Cambodian border, there was a natural tendency on the part of some Thai politicians to accommodate and accept the Vietnamese occupation of Cambodia. One wag commented that the only force that could prevent a Vietnamese takeover of Thailand was the Bangkok traffic jam that would halt the Vietnamese tanks in their tracks.

To the absolute surprise of the Vietnamese, the ASEAN leaders took a firm and united stand opposing the Vietnamese occupation of Cambodia. As Rajaratnam explained in a 1992 essay, "It was not belief in regionalism but resolution, born out of common fear, that eventually brought about the collapse of communist Vietnam."[11] When the full history of ASEAN is written, this will be recorded as one of the most significant decisions taken by ASEAN. It was the decade-long ASEAN struggle against Vietnamese occupation of Cambodia that helped to generate and build a high degree of ASEAN solidarity. As Lee Kuan Yew said, "The seriousness of purpose came only with the shock of the terrible alternatives. There is urgency for greater economic cooperation, to accelerate growth, to reduce poverty and lessen recruits for communist guerrilla bands. The political will has been found to get together to meet the new problems."[12]

Since a large part of this ASEAN struggle against the Vietnamese occupation took place in multilateral fora, especially in the United Nations, Kishore experienced this at first hand when he served as Singapore's ambassador to the UN from 1984 to 1989. The close personal friendships he forged with leading ASEAN diplomats, including Ali Alatas of Indonesia, Zain Azraai of Malaysia, and Nitya

11. S. Rajaratnam, "ASEAN: The Way Ahead", ASEAN, 1 Sept. 1992, http://asean. org/?static_post=asean-the-way-ahead-by-s-rajaratnam/, accessed 12 Oct. 2016.

12. Lee Kuan Yew, "Speech by the Prime Minister, Mr. Lee Kuan Yew, at the Commonwealth Heads of Government Meeting in London on Wednesday, 8 June 1977: Changing Power Relations", National Archives of Singapore, 8 June 1977, http://www.nas.gov.sg/archivesonline/data/pdfdoc/lky19770608. pdf/, accessed 12 Oct. 2016.

Pibulsonggram of Thailand, lasted for many years after the struggle against Vietnam ended. Collaboration and cooperation produced deep reservoirs of social and political capital. This store of capital would hold ASEAN together as ASEAN unity went through inevitable stresses and strains in subsequent decades. Significantly, even though ASEAN's camaraderie was forged in the 1980s and 1990s, the positive effects carried through to the early years of the 21st century, when the ASEAN countries worked together to create an ASEAN Charter. Professor S. Jayakumar, a member of the Eminent Persons Group (EPG) formed to frame the ASEAN Charter, said:

> Although we had various issues, the EPG members were able to arrive at a unanimous report. An important reason for this was that most of the members in the EPG had known each other over many years of interaction in the ASEAN circuit. I had known Malaysia's Musa Hitam, the EPG Chairman, from Students' Union days. I was well acquainted with Indonesia's representative, Ali Alatas, their Foreign Minister. Similarly, the members from Thailand and Vietnam were also former Foreign Ministers. Philippines former President Fidel Ramos and Brunei Representative Lim Jock Seng were also well known to me. This personal chemistry between most EPG members helped to iron out some of the divergence of views among us.[13]

More amazingly, the country that would benefit the most from this store of social and political capital within ASEAN was the country that had inadvertently and unintentionally generated this capital—namely, Vietnam. After the Cold War ended and the Soviet Union imploded, Vietnamese leaders realized that they had lost their protector and had to find new friends and allies to enhance their national sense of security, especially against their traditional adversary, China. In looking around for new ways to enhance their security in the 1990s, the Vietnamese leaders realized that ASEAN could be a viable security partner. Yet the only reason ASEAN could perform this role for Vietnam was that it had developed a close sense of solidarity as a result of opposing Vietnam for a decade. The decision by Vietnam to join ASEAN in July 1995 will go down as one of the biggest ironies of history.

To understand how remarkable this Vietnamese decision to join ASEAN in 1995 was, just look at the statements that Vietnam had been making against ASEAN barely a decade earlier. The Vietnamese were

---

13. S. Jayakumar, *Be at the Table or Be on the Menu: A Singapore Memoir* (Singapore: Straits Times Press, 2015), p. 90.

ferocious in denouncing ASEAN. At the end of 1977, Prime Minister Pham Van Dong said, "The policy of setting up such military blocs as ASEAN in Southeast Asia has failed and passed forever." Alice Ba documents the moment:

> In its many references to "genuine neutrality" and "true independence," for example, Hanoi continued to suggest that ASEAN was neither truly neutral nor truly independent. In the same vein, around the time of ASEAN's Bali Summit in February 1976, both Vietnamese and Lao leaderships continued to accuse ASEAN of being just another imperialist-backed creation like SEATO; ... In their call on NAM to support "the struggle of the people of Southeast Asia against neo-colonialism," they not only questioned the legitimacy of ASEAN governments but also suggested Vietnam's continued political, if not material, support for insurgent activity in the ASEAN countries. In fact, despite overtures to individual ASEAN members, Hanoi continued to resist dealing with ASEAN as an organisation, thus denying ASEAN and its goals recognition and legitimacy.
>
> ... As Thanat Khoman, speaking as a civilian, described the situation in 1976: "[W]hile ASEAN nations have repeatedly extended the hand of friendship to Vietnam and the other new Indochinese regimes, the leaders of these countries have responded by shaking their fists at them."[14]

Despite the recent memory of these fierce denunciations, ASEAN decided to admit Vietnam as a member in July 1995. This decision demonstrated the inherent geopolitical wisdom that ASEAN had gained over the years. The best way to understand this is to compare ASEAN's approach with Europe's record in overcoming its Cold War divisions with Russia, its own erstwhile adversary. Initially, the EU showed great wisdom in embracing Russia in the 1990s. The admission of Russia to the Council of Europe in February 1996 and the G8 in June 1997 seemed to demonstrate the EU's ability to embrace a former adversary. Yet the leading EU members, especially the UK, France and Germany, demonstrated a singular lack of wisdom in pushing NATO towards the borders of Russia. Even more shockingly, these EU members endorsed a NATO statement promoted by the George W. Bush administration in 2008, which called for Ukraine to be admitted to NATO. This deliberate provocation of Russia was clearly

---

14. Alice Ba, *(Re)Negotiating East and Southeast Asia: Region, Regionalism, and the Association of Southeast Asian Nations* (Singapore: NUS Press, 2009), pp. 84–5.

akin to waving a red flag in front of a bull. The EU member states demonstrated a lack of geopolitical wisdom, in contrast to ASEAN, which succeeded in admitting its erstwhile adversary, Vietnam, into the fold.

This is why the story of ASEAN is an amazing one. It was fear that first generated ASEAN cohesion and solidarity. Fear is a negative emotion. Yet, this negative emotion generated positive energy and drive in ASEAN over the years. Instead of being terrified by the advances made by the Communist countries in the 1970s, the ASEAN countries worked hard together to solve their region's challenges and gradually enhance ASEAN solidarity and cohesiveness, especially in the 1980s.

Second Factor: The Role of Strong Leaders

All this could happen because ASEAN was blessed with strong leaders in the 1980s, the most formative period of its history. President Suharto of Indonesia, Prime Minister Lee Kuan Yew of Singapore, Prime Minister Mahathir Mohamad of Malaysia, and Foreign Minister Siddhi Savetsila of Thailand were particularly notable. In terms of character and personality, they could not have been more different. They sprang from very different cultural roots, reflecting the unique cultural diversity of ASEAN. Yet, they shared one strong critical attribute: they had strong spines.

One of Rajaratnam's favourite sayings was the famous remark attributed to Lenin: "Probe with a bayonet. If you meet steel, stop. If you meet mush, then push." The Vietnamese leaders had learned many lessons from Lenin. When they invaded Cambodia in December 1978, they expected to encounter "mush" from the ASEAN leaders. They were truly surprised to discover spines of steel.

Brief pen notes on each of these four key ASEAN leaders will illustrate the spines of steel that they had. Equally important, they had hidden reserves of political wisdom. The most important leader in the early history of ASEAN was clearly President Suharto. More than any other ASEAN leader, he deserves the credit for bringing ASEAN together. Former Singapore Foreign Minister Wong Kan Seng said, "A key part of ASEAN's success was that Suharto was big enough and willing to support ASEAN."[15]

---

15. Authors' interview with Wong Kan Seng, 24 July 2015.

To understand why Suharto's leadership was critical, look at the problems of other regional organizations similar to ASEAN, like the Organization of American States and the South Asian Association for Regional Cooperation. The former failed because its most powerful member state, the United States, always tried to dominate it. By dominating it, the US prevented the emergence of a regional sense of community. Similarly, the South Asian Association for Regional Cooperation failed because India, by far the most powerful member, also tried to dominate it. This prevented any real sense of regional cohesion. Like the US and India, Indonesia is by far the largest and most powerful member state of ASEAN. Unlike the US and India, Indonesia showed extraordinary wisdom in not trying to dominate ASEAN. Instead, Suharto allowed the smaller member states— Thailand, Malaysia and Singapore—to exercise leadership within ASEAN. President S.R. Nathan said in his interview with us, "Suharto's maturity lies in the fact that he decided to play a backroom role in ASEAN, and allow the other member states to carry out their own relations."[16] This helped ASEAN to develop a real and organic sense of community.

Suharto's willingness to step aside and allow others to run ASEAN was truly remarkable because at home he was known to be a strong and dominant leader; he was no shrinking violet. Even though he was perhaps an unlikely candidate for leader of Indonesia, he had emerged as Indonesia's strongman. His predecessor, President Sukarno, was a charismatic leader who could mesmerize the Indonesian population with his brilliant speeches. There is no doubt that the "soul" of the diverse Indonesian population was forged by the extraordinary charisma of Sukarno, even though his economic leadership was disastrous.

Suharto could not have been more different from Sukarno. Suharto could barely manage public speaking. There was no way he could rally the nation together. The only training and education he ever had was military. His rule of Indonesia could have been as disastrous as that of other strong military leaders, such as Saddam Hussein of Iraq, Hafez al-Assad of Syria, or General Ne Win of Myanmar. Quite amazingly, Suharto achieved the opposite. The Indonesian economy thrived under his leadership. The size of the Indonesian economy grew from US$26 billion in 1965 (when he took office) to US$202 billion in 1995

---

16. Authors' interview with the late President Nathan, 27 June 2015.

(three years before he stepped down). More important, the poor in Indonesia benefited from his leadership. The Food and Agriculture Organization of the United Nations awarded him the Gold Medal in 1985 for Indonesia's achievement of rice self-sufficiency. Adam Schwarz has described well the contributions of Suharto:

> During Suharto's tenure, tens of millions of Indonesians have been rescued from poverty. A burgeoning middle class in the cities of Jakarta, Surabaya, and Medan lives in fancy new apartments and shops in gleaming malls. Foreign investors pour billions every year into new factories, putting the sons and daughters of poor farmers to work making everything from Reebok sneakers to Sony televisions. A stable and increasingly prosperous Indonesia provides ballast and leadership to the Association of Southeast Asian Nations, with Suharto playing the role of the region's elder statesman.[17]

There is no doubt that there was corruption during his rule. His immediate family became rich. Yet, the people of Indonesia also benefited a great deal. Similarly, the people of ASEAN also benefited. Suharto showed extraordinary geopolitical wisdom in not trying to dominate or stifle ASEAN. He listened to the wishes of his ASEAN neighbours. For example, he deferred to the other ASEAN countries on the opposition to Vietnam's occupation of Cambodia. What made this truly remarkable was that Suharto was deeply suspicious of China. The Communist Party of China had supported the PKI, which had targeted Suharto in its deadly 1965 coup attempt. Influential voices within his government, including his then chief national security adviser, Benny Moerdani, wanted Suharto to support Vietnam against China.

Jusuf Wanandi, one of Indonesia's most famous public intellectuals, has documented the struggle that took place within the Indonesian government between the pro-Vietnamese forces, led by Benny Moerdani, and the anti-Vietnamese forces, led by then Foreign Minister Professor Mochtar Kusumaatmadja. This is how Jusuf Wanandi describes the outcome:

> In the end it came down to Soeharto. And he said yes to Mochtar. ASEAN was our priority, and that was it. Benny was forced to withdraw a little because of the public support he

---

17. Adam Schwarz, "Indonesia after Suharto", *Foreign Affairs*, July/Aug. 1997, https://www.foreignaffairs.com/articles/asia/1997-07-01/indonesia-after-suharto/, accessed 12 Oct. 2016.

had given Vietnam, and that had confused ASEAN. The whole international community was against Vietnam's invasion of Cambodia. In this diplomatic effort, there was no other way.[18]

All those who take ASEAN unity and cooperation for granted should realize it was the result of decisions made at critical points in ASEAN's history. Given his strong suspicion of China, it would have been perfectly understandable for Suharto to have sided with Benny over Mochtar. This could have destroyed ASEAN unity. The fate of Southeast Asia could have been very different if Suharto had turned Indonesia in the opposite direction. This is why the role of leaders is critical to understanding ASEAN's success.

Another surprising development in the history of ASEAN was the rather unusual deep friendship that developed between Suharto and Lee Kuan Yew in the 1980s. The mental universes of these two leaders could not have been more different. Suharto was trained only in military matters. He was steeped in traditional Javanese culture. Lee Kuan Yew was trained as a British lawyer. Of Chinese and Peranakan cultural heritage, he was educated in English, and his cultural universe was heavily influenced by the Anglo-Saxon vision of the modern world. It is difficult to imagine a pair more unlikely to forge a close collaboration.

Yet this is what they were able to achieve in the 1980s. The two leaders met regularly. In his memoirs, Lee Kuan Yew writes, "Throughout the 1970s and '80s, we met almost every year to keep in touch, exchange views and discuss matters that cropped up."[19] When they met, they would have private "four-eyes" conversations. Through these private meetings, they were able to build trust and confidence in each other. This trust and confidence between two key leaders helped to provide the foundation for ASEAN to come together. Lee Kuan Yew said of Suharto, "I found him to be a man of his word. He made few promises, but delivered whatever he had promised. His forte was his consistency." In 1986, Lee told the Australian press:

> In retrospect, no event has had a more profound influence on the development of the region than the character and outlook of President Suharto of Indonesia. Indonesia's concentration, during the past twenty years, on economic development and

---

18. Jusuf Wanandi, *Shades of Grey: A Political Memoir of Modern Indonesia 1965–1998* (Singapore: Equinox Publishing, 2012), p. 139.
19. Lee Kuan Yew, *From Third World to First: The Singapore Story, 1965–2000*, Vol. 2 (Singapore: Marshall Cavendish, 2000), p. 306.

social upliftment, would not have been, had he not succeeded Sukarno. His policies made it possible for ASEAN [Association of Southeast Asian Nations] to become an organisation for constructive and cooperative relationships between members, and for the solidarity of its members in meeting external problems. If in the 1990s, a man of a similar cut, equally devoted to the development and social advancement of Indonesia, succeeds President Suharto, ASEAN's progress will be assured for the years beyond the year 2000.[20]

Another unexpected partnership within ASEAN was the one forged between Lee Kuan Yew and Mahathir Mohamad. The two men had become bitter political adversaries when Singapore was part of Malaysia between 1963 and 1965. Lee had advocated equal treatment for all races in Malaysia, while Mahathir had advocated special treatment for the Malays. On 26 May 1965, Mahathir dismissed Lee Kuan Yew's position as "the mad ambition of one man to see himself as the first Chinese Prime Minister of Malaysia", saying that he was a good example of an "insular, selfish and arrogant" Chinese chauvinist.[21] Meanwhile, Lee Kuan Yew said, "Well, let me tell [Mahathir] this: when we joined Malaysia, we never agreed to Malay rule; we agreed to Malaysian rule; never Malay rule. This is all bunkum. Somebody has made a grave error of judgment if they believe that we agreed to Malay rule."[22] However, when Mahathir was appointed Malaysia's deputy prime minister on 5 March 1976, both men decided to overcome past conflicts and try to work together. Kishore was present when Mahathir and Lee Kuan Yew met each other for the first time after Mahathir became DPM. This was at a small dinner in Kuala Lumpur hosted by Wee Kim Wee, then Singapore high commissioner to Malaysia. Both men were careful and cautious in their first interaction with each other, but there was no overt animosity.

---

20. "Speech by Prime Minister Lee Kuan Yew to the National Press Club in Canberra, Australia, on 16 Apr. 86", National Archives of Singapore, 16 Apr. 1986, http://www.nas.gov.sg/archivesonline/data/pdfdoc/lky19860416a.pdf/, accessed 12 Oct. 2016.
21. Parliamentary Debates, Malaysia, 26 May 1965, cited in Khoo Boo Teik, *Paradoxes of Mahathirism: An Intellectual Biography of Mahathir Mohamad* (Kuala Lumpur: Oxford University Press, 1995), p. 20.
22. "Transcript of Speech by the Prime Minister, Mr. Lee Kuan Yew, on 30th May, 1965, at the Delta Community Centre on the Occasion of Its 4th Anniversary Celebrations", National Archives of Singapore, 30 May 1965, http://www.nas.gov.sg/archivesonline/data/pdfdoc/lky19650530a.pdf/, accessed 12 Oct. 2016.

In the 1980s, despite their previous political acrimony, both men were able to work with each other. Both sides agreed to bilateral army exercises, which were "initially resisted because they might allow the 'territorial familiarisation' of the host nation by the security forces of the guest country".[23] These were the Semangat Bersatu army exercise started in 1989 and the Malapura naval exercise started in 1984. There were also joint military training programmes. Singapore was the largest investor in Johor state from 1981 to 1990 (although Japan was the largest investor in Malaysia as a whole). Recognizing the growing economic potential of the region, Singapore's then DPM Goh Chok Tong mooted the Singapore-Johor-Riau Growth Triangle to further strengthen economic links and complementarity between the three areas in 1989. It later became the Indonesia-Malaysia-Singapore Growth Triangle as more Indonesian and Malaysian states signed on.

The fourth leader who demonstrated a strong spine and resolve at key moments in the 1980s, in the face of the Vietnamese occupation of Cambodia, was Air Chief Marshall Siddhi Savetsila. From 1975 to 1991, Thailand had, as is its pattern, several prime ministers, including Seni Pramoj, Kukrit Pramoj, Thanin Kraivichien, General Kriangsak Chomanan, Prem Tinsulanonda, Chatichai Choonhavan and Anand Panyarachun. Fortunately, Siddhi Savetsila was able to remain the foreign minister of Thailand for several years, from 1980 to 1990. He enjoyed the confidence of the King of Thailand and key members of the Bangkok establishment. He provided continuity and helped to ensure that Thai policy towards the Vietnamese occupation of Cambodia did not waver, even though there were, as usual, influential voices within the Thai establishment calling for the accommodation of Vietnam.

Since the Philippines is geographically detached from mainland Southeast Asia, its leaders did not share the same level of concern over the Vietnamese occupation of Cambodia. Nonetheless, the Philippines actively joined in the ASEAN campaign against this occupation. It helped that the foreign minister of the Philippines from 1968 to 1984 was the legendary Carlos Rómulo. By the 1980s he was one of the few living signatories of the 1945 UN Charter. He was also enormously charming and charismatic, telling wonderful jokes each time he spoke. He played a critical role in mobilizing international support against the Vietnamese occupation.

---

23. Amitav Acharya, *Constructing a Security Community in Southeast Asia: ASEAN and the Problem of Regional Order* (London: Routledge, 2001), p. 147.

Looking back at the 1980s, it is clear that ASEAN was blessed with many outstanding diplomats at different levels who built up a strong image of ASEAN in the eyes of the international community. Some of the diplomats who deserve special mention are Professor Tommy Koh from Singapore, Ali Alatas from Indonesia, Zain Azraai from Malaysia, and Nitya Pibulsonggram from Thailand. Many of the foreign ministers at the time were also strong political leaders. They included, in addition to Siddhi Savetsila and Carlos Rómulo, S. Rajaratnam from Singapore and Mochtar Kusumaatmadja from Indonesia. Without the contributions of this stellar cast of characters, ASEAN would not have succeeded in forging a critical sense of unity in the 1980s.

If anyone had predicted in 1967, at the founding of ASEAN, that 20 years later a deep sense of friendship and camaraderie would develop between the leaders of Muslim Malaysia and Indonesia, Buddhist Thailand, Christian Philippines, and the secular state of Singapore, this person would have been dismissed as a fool. Yet, the wildly improbable happened. A deep sense of fear combined with the emergence of strong leaders led to the development of this sense of ASEAN fraternity.

Third Factor: Geopolitical Luck

Leadership matters. Luck does too. ASEAN was lucky that a series of geopolitical accidents worked in its favour in the 1980s. First, ASEAN happened to be on the winning side of the Cold War between the US and the Soviet Union. It also benefited from the Sino-Soviet split—the total breakdown in trust and cooperation between the two leading Communist powers of the world. Indeed, if this split had not happened, it is conceivable that the whole of Southeast Asia could have been controlled by Communist or pro-Communist regimes.

ASEAN also benefited from the timing of events in China. The counter-revolution in China—when Deng Xiaoping's pragmatic governance came to replace Mao Zedong's doctrinaire and ideological rule—had a benign influence on the development of ASEAN. When ASEAN was created in August 1967, Mao's government denounced it as a "neo-imperialist" creation. The *Peking Review* called the founding members of ASEAN "the handful of US imperialism's running dogs in Southeast Asia" and denounced ASEAN as "an out-and-out counter-revolutionary alliance rigged up to oppose China, communism and the people, another instrument fashioned by US imperialism and

Soviet revisionism for pursuing neo-colonialist ends in Asia".[24] By contrast, when Deng emerged as China's leader, one of the first things he did was to visit three ASEAN capitals, in November 1978. These visits made him aware of how backward China had become relative to even the ASEAN countries. In 1992, during a tour of southern China, Deng said, "Singapore's social order is rather good. Its leaders exercise strict management. We should learn from their experience, and we should do a better job than they do." Deng also explicitly called upon Guangdong province to catch up with the "four dragons" over the next two decades, "not only catching up with them in terms of economic prosperity but also in terms of social order and public conduct".[25] As a result, instead of denouncing ASEAN, the Chinese government soon came to learn from it.

As students of Marxist thought, we noticed that Marxist leaders were fond of speaking of the "correlation of forces", the implication being that history is on the side of revolution, as the revolutionary masses in different countries were expected to rise up together to remove their few capitalist exploiters. The ironic result of the Sino-Soviet split was that the correlation of forces tilted in favour of the non-Communist ASEAN against Communist Vietnam.

Vietnam's isolation was not a given. In the late 1970s, Vietnam continued to enjoy a positive glow in the eyes of many recently decolonized Third World countries in Asia, Africa and Latin America. After all, it had defeated the United States—the most powerful Western country—in a spectacular fashion. Hence, when Vietnam invaded Cambodia in December 1978, its leaders fully expected the majority of Third World countries to sympathize with them. Instead, to their surprise, Vietnam became isolated in the Third World.

Kishore was present in Havana, Cuba, in August 1979 when Vietnam and its patron, the Soviet Union, used the Cuban chairmanship of the Non-Aligned Movement (NAM) Summit meeting to engineer a result favourable to Vietnam by preventing the previous Khmer Rouge regime from claiming its rightful seat in the NAM forum. The Cubans did this by breaking every procedural rule. To

---

24. Derek McDougall, *The International Politics of the New Asia Pacific* (Singapore: Institute of Southeast Asian Studies, 1997), p. 221.
25. Nicholas D. Kristof, "China Sees Singapore as a Model for Progress", *New York Times*, 9 Aug. 1992, http://www.nytimes.com/1992/08/09/weekinreview/the-world-china-sees-singapore-as-a-model-for-progress.html/, accessed 12 Oct. 2016.

engineer a result favourable to the pro-Soviet group, Fidel Castro convened a small meeting of countries to decide who would represent Cambodia in NAM: the previous "legal" government of Pol Pot's or the quisling government installed by Vietnam. The small room was filled with various heads of government positively disposed to the Soviet Union: Fidel Castro (Cuba), Saddam Hussein (Iraq), Hafez al-Assad (Syria) and so on. The sole dissenting vote in the room was provided by Singapore Foreign Minister Rajaratnam. In the face of this overwhelming pressure, he could have wilted. Instead, he fought back like a lion, demonstrating the mettle of the founding generation of Singapore leaders.

The crude Cuban attempt to hijack Third World sentiment completely backfired. A month after the meeting, a majority of Third World countries rebuked Cuba by voting in favour of a resolution calling on Vietnam to leave Cambodia. This strong rebuke by the UN General Assembly proved to be the beginning of the end for the Vietnamese occupation of Cambodia. ASEAN diplomacy kept gaining ground as the General Assembly votes in favour of the resolution increased over time, from 91 in 1979 to 124 in 1989. Skillful ASEAN diplomacy was one important reason why Vietnam became isolated.

An equally important reason was that two great powers, the US and China, supported ASEAN in this cause. In theory, they were supporting ASEAN because its position aligned with international law. In practice, the US and China had only one overriding goal: to embarrass and humiliate the Soviet Union. ASEAN discovered this inadvertently when an international conference on Cambodia was held in the UN in July 1981. The Soviet Union and its friends boycotted this conference. A key question that this conference had to resolve was which government would take over in Cambodia when the Vietnamese occupation ended.

The Chinese government took the correct position under international law and insisted that the previous Pol Pot government had the right to reassume power. The ASEAN countries opposed China on this. They said that given Pol Pot's horrible genocidal record from 1975 to 1978, the international community would not endorse any call to return Pol Pot to power. When the dispute between ASEAN and China became somewhat heated, the US delegation decided to intervene. Given the sterling record of the US as a defender of human rights, the ASEAN countries fully expected the US to support their moral position. To the absolute shock of the ASEAN countries, the US decided to support China and even tried to bully ASEAN into accepting the Chinese position. In short, the human rights beacon of the world, the US, joined China in calling for the return of the genocidal Pol Pot regime. Kishore says that if he had not personally been present to witness this episode at first hand, he may not have believed that this could actually have happened.

But happen it did. And this just confirmed one of the oldest rules of geopolitics. The United States and China, as great powers, were not working with ASEAN because ASEAN was right on international law or because it represented friendly non-Communist regimes. Instead, the US and China saw ASEAN as a valuable instrument to use in their primary battle to both embarrass and undermine the Soviet Union. ASEAN was clearly being used by two great powers. Despite this unavoidable reality, ASEAN was still "lucky" that it was being used. The support of the two powers ensured that ASEAN eventually succeeded in reversing the Vietnamese occupation of Cambodia. This success in turn boosted the global standing of ASEAN and, equally important, boosted the self-confidence of the ASEAN countries. All the members realized that they were members of a winning team. Their commitment to each other was reinforced. The events of the 1980s provided the foundation for ASEAN to become an even more successful regional organization in future years.

The strong US support for ASEAN also led to ASEAN being embraced by many key allies of the US, including the European Union, Japan, South Korea, Canada, Australia and New Zealand. Indeed, all of them became dialogue partners of ASEAN. Australia became ASEAN's dialogue partner in 1974; New Zealand in 1975; Canada, Japan, the EU and the US in 1977; and South Korea in 1991. Since ASEAN was then in good odour, each felt obliged to bring goodies to the table when they came for ASEAN meetings.

Fourth Factor: Market-Oriented Economic Policies

The foreign aid that many pro-Western developed countries brought to the table for the ASEAN countries was helpful, but it was hardly the main reason for the relative economic success of ASEAN in the 1980s and 1990s. More important, ASEAN learned the best practices of economic development from the leading East Asian economies, especially Japan and the four tigers (South Korea, Taiwan, Hong Kong and Singapore). In short, the ASEAN founders—Indonesia, Malaysia, Singapore, Thailand and the Philippines—wove themselves into the thriving economic ecosystem that was developing across East Asia, taking advantage of (and helping drive) the expansion in global trade. The Philippines was held back by internal political turbulence, but Indonesia, Malaysia, Singapore and Thailand enjoyed rapid economic growth in the 1980s. From 1980 to 1990, the weighted average growth of the ASEAN-5 economies was 6.1 per cent, with Indonesia growing at 6.6 per cent, Malaysia at 6.2 per cent, Singapore at 7.6 per cent, and Thailand at 7.7 per cent. (Unfortunately, the Philippines had a growth rate of only 2.1 per cent during this period.[26])

Dr Mahathir, who became prime minister of Malaysia on 16 July 1981, captured well the spirit of the times with his "Look East" policy. He said:

> Malaysia identified what we believed to be the factors which contributed towards Japan's success. They are the patriotism, discipline, good work ethics, competent management system and above all the close cooperation between the Government and the private sector. And so we tried to adopt these practices and instil these cultures in our people. And everyone now acknowledges that Malaysia has made better progress than most other developing countries. The fastest pace of Malaysia's progress and development took place in the last two decades coinciding with Malaysia's Look East policy.[27]

In the process of the gradual integration of ASEAN with the East Asian economic ecosystem, the chemistry of the region was also gradually transformed. From the outbreak of World War II in the 1940s to the Communist insurgencies of the 1950s, from the devastating warfare in Indochina, leading to the fall of Saigon in 1975, to the Sino-Vietnamese War of 1979, the region had experienced continuous conflict for four decades. It would have been perfectly normal for this continuous pattern of war and conflict to continue. Instead, the abnormal arrived on the scene. The logic of war was replaced by the logic of economic development and growth.

The decision of the five founding members of ASEAN to join the American-led free market ecosystem could have gone the other way.

---

26. Teofilo C. Daquila, *The Economies of Southeast Asia: Indonesia, Malaysia, Philippines, Singapore, and Thailand* (New York: Nova Publishers, 2005), p. 5.
27. Mahathir bin Mohamad, "Look East Policy: The Challenges for Japan in a Globalized World", *Ministry of Foreign Affairs of Japan*, 12 Dec. 2002, http://www.mofa.go.jp/region/asia-paci/malaysia/pmv0212/speech.html/, accessed 12 Oct. 2016.

In the 1970s and 1980s, all five were members of the "Group of 77" (G77), the developing countries bloc. The dominant ideology of the G77 bloc was anti-capitalist and anti-free market. Foreign investment was spurned. Indeed, foreign investors were often portrayed as capitalist leeches sucking the blood of poor Third World peasants and workers.

Kishore experienced this G77 ideology at first hand when he served as the Singapore ambassador to the UN from 1984 to 1989. The Second Committee of the UN saw ferocious debates between the American-led free marketeers and those opposed, led by the Latin Americans. Major Third World economies, including India, Nigeria and Egypt, would sing the anti-free market tune. In this context, Singapore was often a lone voice. Fortunately, we were brave enough to walk into the lion's den of G77 meetings and defend the virtues of foreign investment, often alone. Kishore remembers vividly episodes when his colleague Lim Kheng Hua was attacked in G77 meetings for her speeches in favour of free enterprise.

Singapore's bold and early decision to swim against the dominant Third World current—and its early success with that strategy—may have had a catalytic effect on its neighbouring ASEAN countries. The economic benefits of Singapore's pro-foreign investment policies and drive for exports soon became clear. Singapore's economy grew steadily, at an average rate of around 8 per cent in the 1970s and 1980s. This might help explain why Malaysia, despite its lingering acrimony towards Singapore after the bitter separation of 1965, decided to emulate Singapore's policies. One of the wisest things that Malaysian civil servants did was to completely replicate brochures produced by the Economic Development Board of Singapore on "Why you should invest in Singapore". As a consequence, foreign investment surged into Malaysia too. In Malaysia, foreign direct investment inflows increased from US$94 million in 1970 to US$2.6 billion in 1990. In Singapore, foreign direct investment inflows increased from US$93 million in 1970 to US$5.6 billion in 1990.[28] By 1990, foreign direct investment made up 23 per cent of Malaysia's GDP and 83 per cent of Singapore's.[29]

Around the same time, Thailand decided to open up its economy, benefiting in particular from Japanese investment. No one has as

---

28. United Nations Conference on Trade and Development Statistics, http://unctadstat.unctad.org/, accessed 9 Apr. 2015.
29. Ian Coxhead, ed., *Routledge Handbook of Southeast Asian Economics* (Abingdon: Routledge, 2015).

yet found a good explanation for why the Japanese so favoured Thailand. Certainly, Thailand was cost-competitive. Kishore recalls one Japanese scholar explaining that the Japanese favoured Thailand because it had "the sweet smell of culture". Thailand's dominant Buddhist culture as well as the relative cultural openness of Thai society made the Japanese feel welcome there. Since the Japanese had already begun to invest in Thailand in the 1970s, it was not surprising that when Japanese manufacturers were forced to shift their production operations overseas after the yen surged following the Plaza Accord of 1985, many stepped up their investments in Thailand. Dr K. Techakanont writes:

> Automobile production and sales grew significantly in the 1990s due to two major reasons. On the one hand, the appreciation of the Japanese yen in 1985 encouraged Japanese and [*sic*] part makers to expand their production in Thailand. On the other hand, the Thai government committed to liberalize the auto industry, e.g. the deregulation of the Local Content Requirement regulation in 2000.[30]

Indonesia and the Philippines did not open up to foreign investment as much as Singapore, Malaysia and Thailand did. Fredrik Sjöholm points to the differences in timing and approach between the ASEAN countries: "for instance, Malaysia [was] making changes already in the 1970s, Indonesia in the late 1980s and early 1990s, and the (formerly) centrally planned countries even later."[31] In Indonesia, President Suharto was advised by a well-known "Berkeley Mafia" group of economic advisers. However, Suharto oscillated between liberal and more nationalist camps. He appears to have listened to the Berkeley Mafia and pushed for liberalization and deregulation in the late 1960s and mid-1980s, when the Indonesian economy was facing downturns. However, he listened to the economic nationalists and protectionists in the mid-1970s, when the economy

30. Kriengkrai Techakanont, "Thailand Automotive Parts Industry", in *Intermediate Goods Trade in East Asia: Economic Deepening through FTAs/EPAs, BRC Research Report No. 5*, ed. M. Kagami (Bangkok: Bangkok Research Centre, IDE-JETRO, 2011).
31. Fredrik Sjöholm, "Foreign Direct Investments in Southeast Asia", IFN Working Paper No. 987 (Stockholm: Research Institute of Industrial Economics, 2013).

was booming.[32] The Berkeley Mafia was constrained by a strong nationalist streak in Indonesian thinking. Many Indonesian policy makers believed then (and many continue to believe now) that as Indonesia had a large domestic market, it did not need to open its market as much as Singapore, Malaysia and Thailand had done.

One observer, John Page, described well the forces contributing to ASEAN's economic success. He looked at what he called "common policy threads" linking Singapore, Malaysia, Thailand and Indonesia:

> Macroeconomic management was unusually good and macroeconomic performance unusually stable, providing the essential framework for private investment. Policies to increase the integrity of the banking system, and to make it more accessible to non-traditional savers, increased the levels of financial savings. Education policies that focused on primary and secondary education generated rapid increases in labour force skills. Agricultural policies stressed productivity change and did not tax the rural economy excessively.[33]

Sadly, the Philippines was held back in the 1980s by the increasingly corrupt rule of President Ferdinand Marcos. Although Marcos had started off well when he became president of the Philippines in 1965, he and his wife became greedier and greedier as the years went by. One commentator describes the system at work:

> They had amassed their wealth through bribe-taking and kickbacks from crony monopolies; through the diversion of government loans and contracts; through the profits from over-priced goods and construction; through unaudited government revenue, usually raised from taxes; and through the expedient of taking over businesses by decree and the diversion of yet more funds from government-controlled entities. Nothing was spared. Even payments for fresh flowers delivered daily to the homes of Imee, Irene, and Ferdinand Marcos, Jr., were disbursed from government funds. Imelda and Marcos and their cronies seemed to have devised every conceivable way of making

---

32. Cassey Lee and Thee Kian Wie, "Southeast Asia: Indonesia and Malaysia", in *Routledge Handbook of the History of Global Economic Thought*, ed. Vincent Barnett (Abingdon: Routledge, 2014), pp. 310–1.

33. J. Page, "The East Asian Miracle", in *NBER Macroeconomics Annual 1994*, Vol. 9, ed. Stanley Fischer and Julio J. Rotemberg (Cambridge: MIT Press, 1994).

money through the use of absolute power since the declaration of martial law in 1972.[34]

Another observer, William Overholt, spells out the factors deterring FDI flows into the Philippines:

> Despite impressive paper revisions of the foreign investment laws, red tape and corruption continued to hamper foreign investment … Although the Philippines had previously been a focus of foreign investment in Pacific Asia, during the Marcos years the Philippines became the least favoured site for foreign investment among the market-oriented economies of Pacific Asia. Foreign investment incentives were offset by dozens of presidential decrees and restrictive practices that created monopolies and near-monopolies in nearly every imaginable corner of the economy … Efficient producers with export potential were driven out of business to protect inefficient friends of the President with no export potential. Multibillion dollar corruption constituted a prohibitive tax that fell disproportionately on importers (thereby raising exporters' input costs), exporters, and foreign investors.[35]

The Philippines suffered a crippling disadvantage from the fact that its economy, especially its landownership, was dominated by a few families who were closed and protectionist in their economic attitudes. It was popularly said that the Philippines was a piece of Latin America in Asia.

Yet, even though Indonesia and the Philippines opened up their economies to a lesser degree, they still benefited from an East Asian economic ecosystem that grew in strength in the 1970s and 1980s. This growth stemmed from several factors: the openness of the huge consumer market of the United States; dynamic and competitive manufacturers in Japan, South Korea and Taiwan always looking for new suppliers; the decision by China to open up its economy; the growing policy consensus among key East Asian and ASEAN policy makers that "open" economies did better than "closed" ones; and the willingness of most ASEAN countries to integrate their economies with East Asia. (By contrast, the unwillingness of India to do so led to its falling significantly behind.) To this should be added the growth of networks of businessmen and policy makers across Asia, including

---

34. Carmen Navarro Pedrosa, *Imelda Marcos: The Rise and Fall of One of the World's Most Powerful Women* (New York: St. Martin's Press, 1987).
35. William H. Overholt, "The Rise and Fall of Ferdinand Marcos", *Asian Survey* 26, 11 (1986): 1137–63.

those of Chinese background and those who had studied together in American universities.

As a result, and without any master plan or any single visionary leader (like Jean Monnet) driving the process, the entire East Asian region became increasingly integrated within itself (as well as strongly dependent on the American economy as an engine of growth). Integration into this larger economic ecosystem was a key reason for ASEAN's successful development. An organization that was set up in fear that it would be overcome by a hostile Communist tide unexpectedly found itself in a remarkably benign environment that enabled the five founding members of ASEAN to grow and prosper.

Fifth Factor: ASEAN-Based Regional Networks

The previous section highlighted how ASEAN benefited economically from its integration into the larger East Asian region. This section will highlight how ASEAN reciprocated this generosity by developing a series of regional and extra-regional networks that in turn have benefited the larger East Asian region politically.

"ASEAN centrality" is a phrase one often hears in discussions of ASEAN's diplomatic role. What does it mean? It is a simple way to describe how the larger East Asian region, and the wider Asia-Pacific region, has been integrated over the years. A lot of it has happened because ASEAN has initiated, inspired or provided the platform for regional collaboration efforts. There is now a veritable alphabet soup of terms to describe the regional cooperation processes involving East Asia. ASEAN has been responsible, directly or indirectly, for the success of these processes. This is why ASEAN needs to be nominated for the Nobel Peace Prize someday. It has done more to bring about regional peace than any other regional organization.

It all began innocuously enough in 1978, when ASEAN started the tradition of inviting its dialogue partners and friends to its annual ministerial meeting (AMM). Each AMM was followed by a post-ministerial conference (PMC). The early PMCs were attended by the foreign ministers of the United States and its Cold War allies Australia, New Zealand, Canada, the EU and Japan. The PMCs were followed by what would be termed the ASEAN Plus One meetings. China and India joined these PMCs much later, in 1991 and 1996 respectively.

Over time, the PMC processes led to the development of a much larger community that replicated, to a lesser extent, the sense of community developing among the ASEAN member states. In the 1980s, all the participants were united because they were on the same side in the Cold War and in opposing the Vietnamese occupation of Cambodia. This incipient sense of community that developed among AMM and PMC participants provided the necessary foundation for the subsequent extra-region-wide initiatives. These initiatives included APEC (Asia Pacific Economic Cooperation, 1989); ARF (ASEAN Regional Forum, 1994); ASEM (Asia-Europe Meeting, 1996); and eventually the meetings of the ASEAN Plus Three (China, Japan and South Korea, 1997), ASEAN Plus Six (the ASEAN+3 plus Australia, New Zealand and India, 2005); and the EAS (East Asia Summit, 2005), which began with the ASEAN Plus Six countries and expanded to include the US and Russia in 2011.

In short, to give credit where it is due, ASEAN's success in creating a functioning regional organization (and an ecosystem of peace) in turn led to the spawning of many other regional processes and organizations that built on an ethos of cooperation (and the method of consultation and consensus) that ASEAN had developed. None of these extra-regional processes is perfect. Each of them has had its fair share of ups and downs. However, they should all be judged against one major and overriding criterion: have these extra-regional processes spawned by ASEAN helped to prevent the occurrence of a major war between any two states in the region? The simple and categorical answer is: Yes, they have.

The ecosystem of peace that ASEAN created within Southeast Asia has influenced the wider region, changing its chemistry and moving it in more positive directions. Almost half the world's population lives in the region influenced by ASEAN's ethos. The benefits of ASEAN's peace-generating efforts have influenced the course of world history. This is precisely why the world needs to understand and appreciate ASEAN more.

3

ASEAN and the Great Powers

Asean's future will depend primarily on internal ASEAN decisions. But it will also depend on the external decisions of the great powers. Indeed, the greatest threat to ASEAN as a regional organization comes from outside forces. ASEAN leaders and policy makers have no choice but to develop a deep understanding of the dynamics that drive ASEAN's relations with the great powers. This is what this chapter will try to outline.

As earlier chapters have made clear, ASEAN benefited from favourable geopolitical winds, especially during the Cold War when ASEAN was conceived and created. Looking back, it is clear that ASEAN's growth in the 1980s was positively influenced by the close collaboration between America and China against the Soviet Union and against the Vietnamese invasion of Cambodia. The common American and Chinese interest in supporting ASEAN gave it a major boost.

Geopolitical winds, like the Southeast Asian monsoons, shift directions. ASEAN should therefore prepare itself to deal with unfavourable as well as favourable winds. Just as American-Chinese cooperation gave ASEAN a boost, growing American-Chinese competition in the coming decades will prove to be a real challenge.

The main purpose of this chapter is to encourage policy makers and thought leaders in the capitals of the great powers to reflect deeply and carefully on their long-term interests vis-à-vis ASEAN. Each of these great powers, especially America and China, needs to consider carefully whether it is in its long-term interest to see ASEAN weakened or strengthened.

In theory, great power policies are driven by careful consideration of long-term interests. In practice, the desire to win short-term advantage often trumps long-term thinking. Both China and America have shown a clear lack of wisdom in their dealings with ASEAN in recent years. China was unwise in being unnecessarily assertive in the South China Sea. Its actions in blocking the annual ASEAN joint communiqué in Phnom Penh in 2012 represented one of the lowest points of Chinese diplomacy. Similarly, America's decision to exploit the differences between ASEAN and China on the South China Sea was unwise. That decision may have gained for America some short-term dividends, but it also caused divisions among ASEAN countries. If these divisions lead eventually to the collapse and destruction of ASEAN, America would have made short-term gains at the expense of its long-term interests. To use a well-known expression, it would have cut off its nose to spite its face.

Persuading the great powers to behave wisely is never easy. All too often, short-term political interests, especially short-term electoral interests, trump long-term interests. Many EU politicians, for example, wanted to look good to their home constituents on Myanmar. Hence, they called on the EU to suspend its relations with ASEAN because ASEAN had admitted Myanmar as a member in 1997. Yet, it was precisely because ASEAN engaged with the military regime in Myanmar that Myanmar began its peaceful transition away from military rule. By contrast, in Syria, EU and American sanctions led to war. This is why the section on ASEAN-EU relations advocates an EU apology to ASEAN over its handling of the Myanmar issue.

It would also be a mistake for ASEAN to underestimate the complexity of managing the great powers in the 21st century. As this century progresses, it is clear that we are moving away from the unipolar world that emerged after the end of the Cold War to a much more multipolar world. Eventually, a multipolar world is likely to lead to a more stable balance of power arrangement. Each power will experience different kinds of checks and balances. But it will also mean a more complex game.

It would therefore be useful for each ASEAN leaders' retreat, where the ASEAN heads of government meet only amongst themselves, to have a constant agenda item for discussion: the state of great power relations and their implications for ASEAN. Since many of the ASEAN leaders are shrewd and sophisticated, they would be able to look behind the public statements of great power leaders and discern their real intentions. Quite often in the newspapers, we read about overt competition among great powers. What we do not see is the silent collusion. It was, for example, quite remarkable that America

managed to persuade China to vote in favour of all the UN Security
Council resolutions imposing stiff sanctions on Iran. Since America's
and China's interests on Iran are clearly divergent, how did America
succeed in its persuasion? What were the trade-offs? Were Southeast
Asian interests sacrificed in the process of the complex trade-offs?
Both sides will, of course, deny that any such collusion happens. Any
ASEAN official who believes such denials should have his or her
head examined.

To state the obvious, geopolitics can be a nasty game. Many
small and medium-sized countries can experience grief as a result
of geopolitical manoeuvres by larger powers. ASEAN countries are
equally vulnerable. A contemporary example may drive home this
point. During the Cold War, America was comfortable working with
military regimes in Thailand. Today, with the growing perception in
Washington that the Thai military regime is drifting closer to China,
America will find various ways of distancing itself from Thailand.
George Yeo told us a funny story of how American diplomats tried to
rearrange the standing order of ASEAN foreign ministers to ensure
that the photographs did not show Condoleezza Rice standing next to
the Thai foreign minister. Geopolitics can go down to this petty level.

Given the heavy stakes involved in the geopolitical games
swirling around the region, ASEAN also needs to build up its own
deep institutional knowledge of its long-term relations with the
great powers. Memories matter. For example, during the Cold War,
successive Indian governments kept their distance from ASEAN as it
was perceived to be pro-American. When the Cold War ended and
India saw value in moving closer to ASEAN, Singapore facilitated
India's entry as an ASEAN dialogue partner. Years have passed,
but India remains grateful to Singapore and ASEAN. Reservoirs of
goodwill matter.

We intended to write about ASEAN's relations with each great
power using the same format. However, this proved to be impossible
because each great power is so different. The key considerations that
drive their dealings with ASEAN are each quite different. They also
behave very differently. China has long and deep memories and often
acts on the basis of long-term considerations. By contrast, America is
often driven by short-term considerations. It can also be forgetful. At
the end of the Cold War, when America began to distance itself from
ASEAN, it unwisely abandoned the valuable reservoirs of goodwill it
had accumulated in the organization. Fortunately, not all this goodwill
has dissipated in the face of American amnesia.

With each great power, ASEAN also faces challenges. These will be discussed. It is unnatural in international affairs to have a smooth ride all the time. Bumpy roads are the norm, and indeed ASEAN has hit various kinds of road bumps in its relations with the great powers. The good news is that there has never been a complete break between ASEAN and any of the great powers. The EU-Russian relationship was severely damaged by the events in Ukraine in 2014. ASEAN has not experienced a similar shock with any of its great power relationships. Hopefully, at least part of the reason for this is the wisdom that ASEAN diplomats and leaders have accumulated over the years. Yet, to be honest, it could just be down to luck.

In each of the sections, we suggest some prescriptions to improve ASEAN's relations with each great power. Sometimes the prescription can be as simple as turning up for annual ASEAN ministerial meetings (AMMs). Colin Powell generated goodwill in ASEAN by turning up for each AMM. Condoleezza Rice sent a negative signal by not turning up for her first AMM as secretary of state in 2005. This puzzled the ASEAN countries. As Rodolfo Severino writes: "Long after the event, observers were still trying to figure out why Condoleezza Rice had skipped the Post-Ministerial Conferences and the ASEAN Regional Forum in Vientiane in July 2005. Her staff had stated that her engagement with Middle East events prevented her from going to Asia at that time."[1] In 2007, Rice again missed the AMM and the ARF, and the White House postponed the planned US-ASEAN Summit meeting celebrating the 30th anniversary of ASEAN-US dialogue. George W. Bush then invited ASEAN leaders to a summit meeting at his Texas ranch, but that was also cancelled, this time because of Myanmar's crackdown on dissidents. All these events show that America's long-term interests in maintaining a stable US-ASEAN relationship are often trumped by short-term domestic and international considerations. Several American diplomats whispered to Kishore privately that while they recognized that these would be unwise decisions, they could not influence Rice. This is why institutional memory is so important in long-term relationships. Each great power would benefit from preparing an oral history of its relations with ASEAN. This oral history could then be presented as a gift to the ASEAN Secretariat for those who will write the future histories of the evolution of ASEAN.

---

1. Rodolfo C. Severino, *Southeast Asia in Search of an ASEAN Community: Insights from the former ASEAN Secretary-General* (Singapore: ISEAS Publishing, 2006).

The one great power that will not be discussed in depth here is Russia. Although Russia remains a great power and has a major influence on global developments, its impact and footprint in Southeast Asia have shrunk significantly. In the Cold War, decisions in Moscow had a major influence on Southeast Asia, especially in influencing the Vietnam War and the subsequent Vietnamese invasion of Cambodia. However, after the collapse of the Soviet Union, decisions in Moscow have had little impact on Southeast Asia.

President Putin is a strong and decisive leader. His views matter. However, his major preoccupations are with America, Europe and the Middle East. The Russia-ASEAN relationship is essentially a symbolic one, with little substance. It was good of President Putin to personally host the ASEAN leaders in Sochi in May 2016, the first-ever meeting with ASEAN leaders on Russian soil. Many documents were issued. Yet, they did little to add significantly to the substance of the relationship.

In a perceptive paper,[2] Elena S. Martynova explains well the challenges of strengthening the Russia-ASEAN relationship. She points out that Russia is not even among ASEAN's top ten biggest trading partners. In contrast to the large shares of ASEAN's trade with China (11.7 per cent), the EU (11.4 per cent), Japan (9.8 per cent) and the US (8.3 per cent), Russia's share of ASEAN trade is only 0.6 per cent. From 2006 to 2011, FDI flows from Russia to ASEAN declined.

Even the symbolic relations have been inconsistent. In 2005, President Putin participated in the first East Asia Summit as an observer. He expressed a desire to join the group, but his application was politely denied at the time. Yet, after Russia was admitted as a member of EAS in 2010, President Putin failed to turn up for the 2012 EAS meeting, even though President Obama attended.

Martynova suggests that this lack of a strong relationship between Russia and ASEAN reflects a deeper problem. She says, "Both the president and the prime minister on several occasions have pointed to the need to turn to Asia. However, Russia has yet to develop a long-term and comprehensive Asian strategy." In short, the Russia-ASEAN relationship can begin to blossom only after Russia works out a comprehensive Asian strategy. This may well happen in a decade or two, but it will also depend on global geopolitical developments. Right now, ASEAN is not a major preoccupation in Moscow.

---

2. Elena S. Martynova, "Strengthening of Cooperation between Russia and ASEAN: Rhetoric or Reality?" *Asian Politics & Policy* 6, 3 (2014): 397–412.

Similarly, this chapter will not discuss ASEAN-Australia relations, even though Australia is a key dialogue partner of ASEAN. Australia is not a great power, by any definition. It makes it to the list of "middle powers" by virtue of the size of its GNP. This is why it is a member of the G20.

Yet, as Kishore points out in an essay titled "Australia's Destiny in the Asian Century: Pain or No Pain?" Australia has made some serious geopolitical mistakes in its management of ASEAN. This is what he says:

> Australia has been blessed with an unexpected but valuable geopolitical buffer: ASEAN. For all its flaws and defects, ASEAN has enhanced Australian security by keeping Southeast Asia at peace (with no refugee spillover onto an empty continent), keeping Asian powers (like China and India) at arms' length and increasing multilateral webs of cooperation which have created greater geopolitical stability. One of the biggest geopolitical mistakes Australia made in recent decades was to take ASEAN's geopolitical success for granted. Even worse, Australia has, from time to time, tried to undermine or bypass ASEAN in its diplomatic initiatives.[3]

In its efforts to undermine or bypass ASEAN, Australia has demonstrated geopolitical folly of the highest order. It has been poking holes into a geopolitical umbrella that ASEAN has created over Australia. This is why Australians, perhaps more than any other people in the Asia-Pacific region, need to develop a deep understanding of ASEAN, and the Australian government needs to work out a consistent long-term strategy towards ASEAN that will survive the frequent changes of governments and prime ministers in Australia. If ASEAN were to fall apart, one of the biggest losers will be Australia. If ASEAN were to do well, Australians would be among the biggest beneficiaries. All this is patently obvious. This is why this book needs to be read and understood by all Australian policy makers, present and future.

The most valuable contribution Australia can make to ASEAN today is to use its special relationship with America to educate America on the long-term values and strategic significance of ASEAN. As the

---

3. Kishore Mahbubani, "Australia's Destiny in the Asian Century: Pain or No Pain?" *Australian National University*, 31 July 2012, https://asiapacific.anu.edu.au/researchschool/emerging_asia/papers/Mahbubani_final.pdf/, accessed 12 Oct. 2016.

following section on ASEAN and America makes clear, American policy towards ASEAN has been driven by short-term considerations. Indeed, if America persists in using ASEAN as a short-term instrument to embarrass China on the South China Sea, America could end up breaking apart ASEAN. And if ASEAN breaks up, Australia loses big time. It is a sad reflection of the quality of Australian strategic thinking that this obvious danger does not seem to have dawned on Australians. And Australia has done virtually nothing to educate America (or other great powers) on the long-term strategic value of ASEAN.

To reverse this self-destructive policy of apathy and neglect of ASEAN-American relations, Australians should study the lessons of this chapter carefully and ask themselves how they can serve their own long-term interests by being a more intelligent and shrewd strategic long-term partner of ASEAN.

The overview of ASEAN relations with each great power will proceed in alphabetical order, with America, China, the EU, India and Japan reviewed in this order.

ASEAN and America

ASEAN was born pro-American. Indeed, for most of its existence it has had, broadly speaking, a pro-American orientation. Unfortunately, inconsistent American policies towards ASEAN have led to ups and downs in ASEAN's relationship with America.

There have been three phases in this relationship. In phase 1, during the Cold War, a clear strategic alignment of interests led to a very close relationship. Phase 2 began with the end of the Cold War. In the 1990s America, for various reasons, lost interest in its erstwhile allies, such as ASEAN. ASEAN felt abandoned by America. Phase 3 began with America rediscovering the strategic value of ASEAN following the tragic 9/11 attacks in 2001. This section will describe these three phases.

Yet, through all these ups and downs, ASEAN never lost its essential pro-American character. ASEAN speaks in one language, English, because of American—not British—influence. When ASEAN drifted closer to America politically in the Cold War, it also drifted closer to America in economic and cultural terms. This is why many Americans feel comfortable with the texture of civic life in ASEAN societies. All ASEAN societies have adopted free market economics and welcome American investment. Chambers of commerce and Rotary Clubs in ASEAN capitals reflect American influence. The children of ASEAN elites have studied primarily in American universities. As children, both of us were overawed by the arrival of the American fast food chain A&W in Singapore. To us, living in a poor Third World society then, it seemed like the dawn of a new civilization. That is how alluring American culture looked to us during the Cold War—an allure that was reinforced by the prevalence of Hollywood and American TV dramas. In short, while the political relationship went through ups and downs, America maintained a steady course of accumulating reservoirs of goodwill in ASEAN societies. American soft power, which Joe Nye speaks eloquently about, has been woven into the hearts of many Southeast Asians. Sadly, few Americans, barring Barack Obama, seem to be aware of these reservoirs of goodwill. America needs to be more consistent towards ASEAN, acknowledging the goodwill that has built up over the years. Unfortunately, the election of Donald Trump will lead to a greater distance between America and ASEAN as Trump is woefully ignorant about ASEAN.

Phase 1

Phase 1, the very close relationship, lasted through the Cold War. ASEAN was born in August 1967 with the primary goal of warding off Communist expansion in Southeast Asia. America shared this goal. This is why China was perfectly justified in condemning ASEAN as an American creation.

From 1967 to 1989, when the Cold War ended, the United States worked closely with ASEAN. America's catastrophic defeat in Vietnam in 1975 led to a brief traumatic interruption when America lost its nerve; but fortunately, its policy towards ASEAN was led by a gifted American diplomat, Richard Holbrooke, who fought to retain a strong American presence in Southeast Asia. When Holbrooke retired, he proudly displayed in his office a letter from Lee Kuan Yew praising his ability to maintain a consistent policy towards Southeast Asia.

As will be explained in the ASEAN-China section, when Vietnam invaded Cambodia in December 1978, ASEAN, America and China worked together to pressure Vietnamese forces to withdraw. This period of closeness and shared interests was symbolized by Washington's decision to invite Singapore Prime Minister Lee Kuan Yew to address a joint session of Congress on 9 October 1985. Kishore accompanied Lee Kuan Yew on this visit to Washington, DC, and saw at first hand the close relations between the Reagan administration and Southeast Asia. During this period, US Secretary of State George

Shultz regularly attended the annual ASEAN meetings and extolled the benefits of closer US-ASEAN relations. Somewhat remarkably, President Ronald Reagan attended an ASEAN ministerial meeting in May 1986 and said the following:

> The United States sees ASEAN's unity and decisiveness as an example to other free people. The ASEAN collective voice of responsible international behavior has been amplified throughout the world, and I am here to listen to you. Support for and cooperation with ASEAN is a linchpin of American Pacific policy. Nowhere has your leadership been more inspiring than in molding the world's response to the Vietnamese invasion and occupation of Cambodia.[4]

Singapore was not alone in developing close ties with the US in the 1980s. The United States' relations with Thailand, based on the 1962 Rusk-Thanat Agreement and the 1964 Manila Pact, were very close, and the two countries engaged in annual joint military exercises. In 1985 Thailand purchased 12 F-16 fighter-bombers from General Dynamics in the United States, perhaps as a response to Vietnam's acquisition of Soviet-piloted MiG-23s the same year. The US and Thailand signed an accord in October 1985 setting up a war reserve weapons stockpile in Thailand, making it the first country without a US military base to have such an arrangement. Political relations between the countries also strengthened.[5]

The United States also viewed President Suharto as a vital ally in its struggle against the Soviet Union. Indonesia's strategic location in the Indian Ocean and its control of the Melaka and Sunda Straits made the country exceptionally important for US strategic and security interests in the region. The US provided Indonesia with large amounts of military aid, and even today it remains the largest supplier of arms to Indonesia's armed forces. Indonesia has also benefited from US security arrangements with its neighbours Australia and the Philippines.[6]

---

4. "Address to the Ministerial Meeting of the Association of South East Asian Nations in Bali, Indonesia", Ronald Reagan Presidential Library & Museum, 1 May 1986, https://reaganlibrary.gov/34-archives/speeches/1986/5513-50186c/, accessed 12 Oct. 2016.
5. For this and following accounts of US relations with individual countries in this section, see *Country Studies/Area Handbook Series*, Federal Research Division of the Library of Congress, http://countrystudies.us/.
6. *Country Studies/Area Handbook Series*, Indonesia.

After Marcos was eased out of power with some help from the Reagan administration in 1986, Corazon Aquino became president of the Philippines. Aquino, who did part of her schooling and earned her undergraduate degree in the US, was well liked there. When she visited in 1986, she addressed a joint session of the United States Congress and received a pledge of strong support for her government. US development assistance to the Philippines in 1990 amounted to nearly US$500 million, while private investment exceeded US$1 billion. The Philippines also received debt relief and new credit arrangements through a multilateral aid initiative that counted the US and Japan as its major donors. Linkages between the two countries were further strengthened by politically active Filipino-American communities in the US.[7]

The geopolitical links between the US and ASEAN also led to close ties being developed in other spheres. Trade between the US and ASEAN more than doubled between 1980 and 1990, rising from US$22.6 billion in 1980 to US$47.57 billion in 1990.[8] During the same period, American investment in the ASEAN countries surged. Between 1980 and 1992, the total stock of US FDI in the ASEAN-5 increased from US$3.15 billion to US$14.67 billion.[9]

American foreign investment produced more than economic benefits. American MNCs, unlike those in Japan, made a conscious effort to train local talent, and American investment created a whole new managerial and entrepreneurial class in Southeast Asia. Koh Boon Hwee, who served as chairman of several Singapore corporations, including Singapore Airlines, DBS Bank and Singtel, said that his years with Hewlett-Packard in the 1980s transformed him and paved the way for his successful career. Similarly, many successful bankers in Southeast Asia, especially in Singapore, were trained and developed by Citibank.[10]

Close ties between ASEAN and America also grew out of the experiences of young ASEAN citizens who studied in North American

7. *Country Studies/Area Handbook Series*, Philippines.
8. "Direction of Trade Statistics", International Monetary Fund, https://www. imf.org/external/pubs/cat/longres.aspx?sk=19305.0/, accessed 12 Oct. 2016.
9. Chia Siow Yue, "Foreign and Intra-regional Direct Investments in ASEAN and Emerging ASEAN Multinationals", in *Asia & Europe: Beyond Competing Regionalism*, ed. Kiichiro Fukasaku, Fukunari Kimura and Shujiro Urata (Eastbourne: Sussex Academic Press, 1998), p. 56.
10. Personal communication from Peter Seah, chairman of DBS, to Kishore Mahbubani.

universities. Many personal networks in East Asia took shape as a result of students forging lifelong bonds while attending leading American universities. When many of these students went on to become successful leaders, the ties they developed with their East Asian peers became instrumental to the peaceful development of the region. This is probably one reason why America has a greater reservoir of "soft power" in East Asia, including Southeast Asia, than in any other region.

Phase 2

But a new, second phase began with the end of the Cold War. With the collapse of the Soviet Union, America lost its obsessive fear of Communist expansionism. As a result, ASEAN was no longer seen in Washington as a valuable geopolitical asset. And an ally that was not a positive asset soon began to seem more like a political liability that America had to carry on its shoulders. No American statesman or historian will admit on the record that ASEAN was used by America during the Cold War and dropped like a hot potato after the end of the Cold War. In Kishore's book *Beyond the Age of Innocence*, he shows how America was completely instrumental in its relations with many of its Cold War allies. Once their practical use diminished, America began to discover "human rights" defects in many of them and began to turn away.[11]

As a result of this policy shift, America lost a golden opportunity to lift its relations with ASEAN to a much higher level of cooperation. Because there has been very little honest American accounting of this change in US-ASEAN relations after the Cold War, it is useful to discuss it in some detail. The blossoming of ties between ASEAN countries and the US in the 1980s should have led to a close partnership in the 1990s between the two sides. Instead, the opposite happened. If one could describe the first phase of relations between ASEAN and America during the Cold War as the "honeymoon" era, phase 2 was "rejection". This is a harsh word to use, but we feel it is justified. American policy makers need to wake up to the harsh reality in America's history of relations with Southeast Asia. By refusing to acknowledge the rejection phase in US-ASEAN relations, American policy makers will fail to understand the mistakes they have made

---

11. Kishore Mahbubani, *Beyond the Age of Innocence: Rebuilding Trust between America and the World* (New York: Public Affairs, 2005), pp. 181–2.

towards ASEAN. A refusal to acknowledge the mistakes made will lead to another great failure to learn lessons from the mistakes. This means that the mistakes could be repeated. To avoid this, we must deal squarely with harsh realities.

To be fair, ASEAN was not the only victim in this rejection phase. Many other countries in the Third World were rejected at the same time. And why were they rejected? The simple truth is that during the Cold War, since the United States was engaged in what it believed was a life-and-death struggle with the Soviet Union, it was prepared to work with anyone, including unsavoury dictators and brutal killers. Few Americans, for example, are aware that Osama bin Laden and his ilk were key allies of America in the Cold War. So, too, were unsavoury dictators like Mobutu of Zaire and Muhammad Zia-ul-Haq of Pakistan.

With the Cold War at an end, there was widespread joy and relief that America had prevailed against the Soviet Union. During a private conversation with Kishore, one American captured this spirit well when he remarked that it was a relief to wake up in the morning without fearing that a nuclear war could break out at any moment. However, America also began to see its many Cold War allies in a new light, questioning their usefulness and seeing their flaws in sharper relief. Since it would have been seen as unethical (not to mention ungrateful) to use and then abandon allies, America needed an ethical justification. Under Jimmy Carter in the 1980s, America started bringing human rights into foreign policy conversations. By the 1990s, human rights were used as a tool to create distance from inconvenient or former allies.

On the surface, things appeared to carry on as normal. American secretaries of state continued to attend the annual ASEAN ministerial meetings (AMM), but the tone of the relationship changed significantly. Long after James Baker (of the George H.W. Bush administration) stepped down from office, he told the Senate Foreign Relations Committee, "We have ... the widest array of strategic alliances, from NATO to ASEAN."[12] Technically, ASEAN does not have a "strategic alliance" with America, but Baker's positive attitude towards ASEAN shines through in his statement. By contrast, the next two secretaries of state, Warren Christopher and Madeleine Albright, showed less

---

12. "Opening Remarks, James A. Baker, III, Senate Foreign Relations Committee", United States Senate Committee on Foreign Relations, 12 May 2016, http://www.foreign.senate.gov/imo/media/doc/051216_Baker_Testimony.pdf/, accessed 12 Oct. 2016.

enthusiasm for attending AMMs. They either skipped them altogether or left early. During the Cold War the apparently dubious human rights record of several countries had not been an obstacle, but post-Cold War it became an issue. In 1997 Albright threatened not to attend an ASEAN meeting, prompting the Thai journalist Kavi Chongkittavorn to write:

> What is at stake is insurmountable: Asean will put at risk its relations with the United States if the grouping goes ahead with its decision to admit Burma tomorrow. Washington had made it clear to Asean senior officials at last week's meeting of the Asean Regional Forum (ARF) on Langkawi Island that the new US Secretary of State Madeleine Albright would have to reconsider the US' participation in the ARF and post ministerial conference this July in Kuala Lumpur.[13]

In this way, ASEAN went from asset to liability, although America did not publicly acknowledge this strategic shift. The Clinton administration's lack of enthusiasm for ASEAN was not surprising. America under Clinton enjoyed a unique "unipolar" moment, and allies were not needed. Later, in his second term, President Clinton became preoccupied with domestic matters and was distracted by the Lewinsky affair.

As ASEAN declined in strategic importance for America, negative episodes began to dominate US relations with ASEAN countries. Singapore had been one of America's most trusted friends in the Cold War, and Singaporean leaders enjoyed regular access to the White House. However, the US froze ties with Singapore after Singapore caned an American teenager in May 1994. During the Cold War, such a minor episode would not have disrupted relations. Indeed, in the 1980s, Singapore had had bigger bilateral disputes with America, for example over the gazetting of the *Wall Street Journal* (in February 1987) and the expulsion of an American diplomat (Hank Hendrikson, in May 1988). The Cold War trumped all other considerations in the 1980s, but when the Cold War ended, allies like Singapore became dispensable and small issues became big problems.

In some instances, the United States went further and bullied former allies. An ASEAN Regional Forum Meeting took place in Singapore in April 2000, not long after the bombing of the Chinese Embassy in Belgrade by US Air Force planes (on 7 May 1999). Since this was an

---

13. Kavi Chongkittavorn, "Asean to Push back New Admission to December", *The Nation* (Bangkok), 30 May 1997.

event of some significance, the Singaporean hosts of the ARF added a reference to it in the chairman's statement at the end of the meeting. The wording was negotiated between the US diplomats Kurt Campbell and Stan Roth and their Singaporean counterpart, Bilahari Kausikan, and the matter appeared to have been settled.

However, when Albright arrived at the meeting, she strongly opposed any reference to the bombing. Singapore Foreign Minister S. Jayakumar wrote in his book *Diplomacy*, "Albright adopted a hectoring and bullying approach and insisted on having her own way."[14] When the argument became heated, Albright asked for a suspension. An observer who was present in the room reported that with a wave of her arm, she summoned her allies to join her, and most of them scurried to her side. The South Korean delegate, apparently feeling insulted to be so publicly summoned, walked as slowly as possible, but even he could not resist a summons by a US secretary of state. American power was invincible and irresistible.

Malaysia incurred the wrath of the United States in 1999 when then Prime Minister Dr Mahathir Mohamad decided to arrest and charge his former deputy prime minister, Anwar Ibrahim. DPM Anwar was beaten when he was arrested, something that was clearly unacceptable, but American Vice President Al Gore broke all rules of diplomatic courtesy by publicly chastising PM Mahathir while he was a guest of Malaysia. America was claiming the moral high ground in its foreign policy in the 1990s and saw no costs in alienating Malaysia.

The traumas suffered by Singapore and Malaysia pale in comparison with the travails suffered by Thailand and Indonesia in the 1990s. The Asian Financial Crisis broke out in Thailand in May 1997 and quickly spread to other countries. Indonesia became another major victim by July 1997. Between 1997 and 1999, Thailand's economy shrank from US$143 billion to US$138 billion.[15] Many major corporations went bankrupt, and unemployment rose from 0.9 per cent to 3 per cent. Indonesia suffered even more. Its GDP fell from US$262 billion to US$230 billion,[16] and unemployment increased from 4.7 per cent to 6.3 per cent.

---

14. S. Jayakumar, *Diplomacy: A Singapore Experience* (Singapore: Straits Times Press, 2011), p. 121.
15. Constant US dollars. "National Accounts Main Aggregates Database", United Nations Statistics Division, http://unstats.un.org/unsd/snaama/dnllist.asp/, accessed 7 Sept. 2016.
16. Ibid.

A treaty ally of the United States since 1954, Thailand was an exceptionally good friend. During the Vietnam War, for example, it allowed air bases in the country to be used by American bombers. When the Asian Financial Crisis broke out in July 1997, there was therefore a general expectation in Bangkok that if the situation got really bad, Washington would come to the rescue, as it had done for Mexico in 1995. Had the situation arisen during the Cold War, there is little doubt that Thailand would have quickly received assistance. However, by 1997 memories of Thailand's strong support for America during the Cold War had long faded in Washington. Thailand was left twisting in the wind. It would be an understatement to say that the Thai establishment felt deeply betrayed. The sense of betrayal become more acute when Washington rushed to rescue South Korea in December 1997. The contrast between the American inaction in Thailand and the rapid American response to South Korea's financial problems could not have been more striking, and it clearly indicated that Thailand had become dispensable. By contrast, China tried to help out Thailand and the other ASEAN countries by refusing to devalue the Chinese RMB, at some cost to the Chinese economy. Accordingly, there is a belief today in Bangkok that China is a more reliable friend than America.

Indonesia, by contrast, was formally non-aligned but also a close friend of the US during the Cold War, and the sense of betrayal was equally strong. Washington did intervene to help Indonesia during the crisis, but it prescribed ideologically doctrinaire solutions that were socially and economically painful. For example, Washington insisted that all of Indonesia's struggling banks should be shut down. Barely a decade later, when America suffered a similar problem with its banks, it bailed them out. The double standard could not have been clearer. As Mari Pangestu, a former trade minister of Indonesia, explained:

> During the 1997 Asian Financial Crisis IMF conditionalities required for closure of banks and no bail outs, budget cuts and austerity measures, and tight monetary policy. In contrast in the 2009 financial crisis, the US government response was to bail out banks, providing support to some sectors, and a program of fiscal stimulus and easy monetary policy. The IMF under European influence, provided assistance in multiple amounts of the quota to troubled European economies and with soft conditions compared with what the IMF did during the East Asian Financial crisis. It should be noted that some of the key players that provided advice and implemented the programs in

the 1997 crisis in East Asia, were also the same key actors in the 2008 crisis.[17]

Phase 3

The second phase, or negative trend in the ASEAN-America relationship, could have persisted into the 21st century. However, a major geopolitical event intervened. After the terrorist attack on 11 September 2001, America realized that it once again needed global allies in the fight against international terrorism, and ASEAN's perceived value to Washington changed.

The moderate Muslim countries in Southeast Asia, which had seemed unimportant in the 1990s, became valuable strategic assets in the first decade of the 21st century, and the discussions of human rights issues that had hounded US-ASEAN relations vanished. To the absolute shock of the ASEAN countries, the Americans began to practice as routine the same human rights violations (such as torture and detention without trial) that they had accused the ASEAN countries of carrying out. America went seamlessly from being a defender to a violator of human rights when its national interests changed.

The ASEAN countries could have reacted churlishly when America came knocking on their doors for support after 9/11. Instead, ASEAN chose to respond positively to American suggestions of closer cooperation. Intelligence collaboration between America and several ASEAN countries increased, and in August 2002 ASEAN and the US signed a Joint Declaration on Cooperation to Combat International Terrorism. The crisis of 9/11 led Washington to rediscover the value of ASEAN and eventually come to ASEAN with several proposals to strengthen relations. The concrete steps forward in US-ASEAN relations included the following milestones:

- 2005: A Joint Vision Statement on the ASEAN-US Enhanced Partnership

- 2006: A Trade and Investment Framework Agreement (TIFA) that strengthened ASEAN-US economic ties

---

17. From the authors' e-mail correspondence with Dr Pangestu.

- 2009: Adoption of a declaration of the first ASEAN-US Leaders' Meeting on Enhanced Partnership for Enduring Peace and Prosperity

- 2010: Establishment of a US Permanent Mission to ASEAN

- 2013: The first ASEAN-US Summit—an institutionalization of the annual meeting between the leaders of ASEAN and the US. Leaders committed to further strengthening ASEAN-US cooperation in many areas such as non-proliferation, cyber security, counterterrorism, trafficking in persons, trade and investment, science and technology, and education.

In February 2016, Obama became the first American president to host all ASEAN leaders, as well as the secretary-general of ASEAN, on American soil. The Sunnylands summit is widely regarded as an important milestone in ASEAN-US relations. At its conclusion, the participants released a joint declaration outlining principles for increased economic and security cooperation as well as the launching of US-ASEAN Connect, which would coordinate American economic engagement in Southeast Asia and enable firms to take advantage of increased connectivity between the US and ASEAN. The final joint statement spoke about the following:

> Shared commitment to maintain peace, security and stability in the region, ensuring maritime security and safety, including the rights of freedom of navigation and overflight and other lawful uses of the seas, and unimpeded lawful maritime commerce as described in the 1982 UN Convention on the Law of the Sea (UNCLOS) as well as non-militarisation and self-restraint in the conduct of activities; Shared commitment to promote cooperation to address common challenges in the maritime domain; Strong resolve to lead on global issues such as terrorism and violent extremism, trafficking in persons, drug trafficking, and illegal, unreported, and unregulated fishing, as well as illicit trafficking of wildlife and timber.[18]

ASEAN-US relations improved also in matters of security. An ASEAN-US security dialogue was added to the dialogue partnership.

---

18. "Joint Statement of the ASEAN-U.S. Special Leaders' Summit: Sunnylands Declaration", Permanent Mission of the Republic of Singapore, ASEAN, Jakarta, 17 Feb. 2016, http://www.mfa.gov.sg/content/mfa/overseasmission/asean/latest_news_in_asean/2016/2016-02/Latest_News_In_ASEAN_2016-02-17.html/, accessed 12 Oct. 2016.

Cooperation intensified in the area of transnational crime, and ASEAN senior officials dealing with transnational crime meet periodically with their US counterparts (SOMTC+US). An ASEAN-U.S. cybercrime workshop took place in May 2014, and the US proposed enhancing collaboration and cooperation with ASEAN in addressing human trafficking. The US has also begun participating more actively in various regional meetings, including the ASEAN Regional Forum, ASEAN Defence Ministers Meeting Plus, East Asia Summit and Post-Ministerial Conferences.

The purpose of highlighting America's inconsistent track record vis-à-vis ASEAN here is not to score political points, but to emphasize that ASEAN's great potential as a strategic asset for America will go to waste unless Washington works out a clear and consistent long-term policy towards ASEAN. Policies change in Washington when administrations change, but in some delicate areas of American foreign policy (the status of Israel and Saudi Arabia, for example) there is a "deep consensus" that shields these relationships from short-term changes in administration. Washington might usefully develop a deep consensus on its policy towards ASEAN built on three key principles: consistency, delicacy and education. Call them the C, D and E principles.

Consistency is key. A modicum of consistency is needed to keep a relationship stable, and a stable foundation allows relationships to grow closer. The best way to demonstrate the importance of consistency is to look at ASEAN's relationship with the Obama administration (2009–16). Relations between ASEAN and America might have been expected to prosper under President Obama, the only American president to have spent a significant amount of time in the region. He described his personal commitment to Southeast Asia during a Myanmar town hall meeting on 14 November 2014, when he said:

> As President of the United States, I've made it a priority to deepen America's ties with Southeast Asia—in particular, with the young people of Southeast Asia. And I do this for reasons that go beyond the fact that I spent some of my childhood in Southeast Asia, in Indonesia. And that gives me a special attachment, a special feeling for Southeast Asia and this region. But I do it mainly because the 10 nations of ASEAN are home to about one in ten of the world's citizens. About two-thirds of Southeast Asia's population is under 35 years old. So this region—a region of growing economies and emerging democracies, and a vibrant diversity that includes oceans and

islands, and jungles and cities, and peoples of different races and religions and beliefs—this region will shape the 21st century.[19]

Obama's words demonstrate a deep understanding of Southeast Asia and its unique value to America, and it would have been natural to expect American policy towards ASEAN to reflect this. Unfortunately, it did not. Obama had to cancel several trans-Pacific trips: in March 2010 (Indonesia and Australia, due to the healthcare bill); June 2010 (again Indonesia and Australia, due to the Gulf oil spill); and October 2013 (Bali, Brunei, the Philippines and Malaysia, due to the US government shutdown). While he had no way of escaping the vagaries of politics in the US capital, he could have done more to take advantage of the opportunities that presented themselves, including more use of his personal charisma. Obama spent part of his childhood in Indonesia, travelled around Southeast Asia while young, and even spoke Bahasa Indonesia. If he had made a major visit to Indonesia soon after being elected, he would have been greeted with large cheering throngs. The image of an American president being received like a rock star in the world's largest Islamic country would have done much to repair the damage done by the Bush administration in alienating the 1.6 billion Muslims in the world after the disastrous invasion of Iraq. No such opportunity will present itself to Donald Trump, who has spoken so disparagingly of Muslims. This makes Obama's failure to capitalize on his special relationship with Indonesia even more sad.

Another opportunity arose when Obama decided to deliver two major speeches on America and Islam: one in West Asia, in Istanbul on 6 April 2009; and the other in Middle Eastern Africa, in Cairo on 4 June 2009. The speeches were brilliant, but the choice of venues was flawed. Istanbul, which represents the crossroads of East and West, was a good choice for the first speech. However, Obama would have done well to deliver the second speech in the eastern part of the Islamic world, which is less troubled by dysfunctional societies than the western part. Southeast Asia alone is home to almost as many Muslims as the Arab world. Indonesia, where Obama would have received a hero's welcome, might have been a good choice.

When the White House papers are eventually declassified 25 years from now, it will be interesting to discover whether any of his foreign

---

19. "Remarks by President Obama at Young Southeast Asian Leaders Initiative Town Hall, 11/14/14", White House, 14 Nov. 2014, https://www.whitehouse.gov/the-press-office/2014/11/14/remarks-president-obama-young-southeast-asian-leaders-initiative-town-ha/, accessed 12 Oct. 2016.

policy advisers recommended that he speak in Southeast Asia instead of in the Middle East. If none did (and we believe no one did), it would confirm that senior American advisers are woefully unaware of the strategic assets and opportunities they have in Southeast Asia. This is why it is important for the American establishment to rediscover ASEAN and internalize the history of America's relations with it. A strong consensus in Washington to give greater strategic priority to ASEAN would yield great dividends to America.

The second principle of an improved American diplomacy would be delicacy, a crucial element in dealing with Southeast Asia. As Sino-American geopolitical competition rises in the coming decades, as it inevitably will, there will be a strong temptation for both sides to attempt to use ASEAN as a geopolitical instrument against the other. If Sino-American geopolitical competition ends up destroying ASEAN, it will be a great historical irony as it was Sino-American geopolitical collaboration, especially in the 1980s, that led to the strengthening of ASEAN. A key strategic decision point for Washington is to understand whether American national interests are better served by an ASEAN that is strong and united or by one that is weak and divided. If it is to be the former, Washington must refrain from using ASEAN as a weapon against China.

For example, Americans will be tempted to embarrass China over its assertive actions in the South China Sea. Several American leaders have already spoken out on the issue, including President Obama, who said, "Regional aggression that goes unchecked—whether it's southern Ukraine, or the South China Sea, or anywhere else in the world—will ultimately impact our allies, and could draw in our military."[20] When she was secretary of state, Hillary Clinton said, "We oppose the threat or use of force by any claimant in the South China Sea to advance its claims or interfere with legitimate economic activity."[21] Charles Hagel, the former US secretary of defence, spoke at greater length at the Shangri-La Dialogue in Singapore in 2014:

---

20. "Remarks by the President at the United States Military Academy Commencement Ceremony", White House, 28 May 2014, https://www. whitehouse.gov/the-press-office/2014/05/28/remarks-president-united-states-military-academy-commencement-ceremony/, accessed 12 Oct. 2016.
21. "The South China Sea, Press Statement, Hillary Rodham Clinton, Secretary of State, Washington, DC", U.S. Department of State, 22 July 2011, http://www. state.gov/secretary/20092013clinton/rm/2011/07/168989.htm/, accessed 12 Oct. 2016.

China has called the South China Sea "a sea of peace, friendship and cooperation." And that's what it should be. But in recent months, China has undertaken destabilizing, unilateral actions asserting its claims in the South China Sea. It has restricted access to Scarborough Reef, put pressure on the longstanding Philippine presence at the Second Thomas Shoal, begun land reclamation activities at multiple locations, and moved an oil rig into disputed waters near the Paracel Islands.[22]

American officials may be tempted to enlist all or part of ASEAN in their campaign to embarrass China. Such a step would be a huge strategic mistake. It will do nothing to deter China, but ASEAN could be seriously damaged. This is why it is important that in the growing Sino-American geopolitical competition, both sides should treat ASEAN as a delicate Ming vase that could easily be destroyed. As American and Chinese interests will both suffer if ASEAN is damaged or destroyed, delicacy in dealing with ASEAN is critical for both sides.

The final principle to guide ASEAN-America relations, education, may seem surprising. If asked to name America's biggest asset in the region, most American leaders would undoubtedly point to its military or economic presence, both of which are significant. However, over time the relative American share in both these spheres will diminish. For example, US investment flows to ASEAN declined from US$9.13 billion in 2011 to US$3.757 billion in 2013, and the US share of FDI in the ASEAN region decreased from 9 per cent to 3 per cent over the same period.[23]

However, one American asset is growing: its "mind-share" of the elites of Southeast Asia, which arises from the fact that even more young Southeast Asians are studying in American universities now than in the 1980s. In 2014–15, there were 50,865 students from Southeast Asia enrolled in American universities, a 47 per cent increase from 34,590 ten years earlier. Moreover, many leading Southeast Asian universities derive their curriculums from American educational institutions.

---

22. "The United States' Contribution to Regional Stability: Chuck Hagel", International Institute for Strategic Studies, IISS Shangri-La Dialogue: The Asia Security Summit, 31 May 2014, https://www.iiss.org/en/events/shangri%20la%20dialogue/archive/2014-c20c/plenary-1-d1ba/chuck-hagel-a9cb/, accessed 12 Oct. 2016.

23. "ASEAN Investment Report 2013–2014: FDI Development and Regional Value Chains", ASEAN Secretariat and United Nations Conference on Trade and Development, 2014, http://www.asean.org/storage/images/pdf/2014_upload/AIR%202013-2014%20FINAL.pdf/, accessed 12 Oct. 2016.

As yet, no American administration has developed a long-term strategy to take advantage of this long-term and growing asset. More educational exchanges between Southeast Asian and American institutions along the lines of Yale-NUS College and Duke-NUS Medical School would help. They have benefited both the American institutions and their Singapore counterpart and contributed to strengthening the ASEAN-American relationship.

Educational exchange also has other benefits. In an essay titled "The Fusion of Civilizations", which Kishore wrote with Larry Summers, the authors put it this way:

> There is every reason to be confident that the condition of the world will continue to improve as pragmatism and the use of reason become universal. Western universities have been a crucial driver of this trend. It is not just that their curricula have been copied around the world; the entire ecosystem of a modern research university is being replicated, and it is the graduates of these Western-style universities who have in turn introduced modern methods into education, public health, economic management, and public policy more generally.[24]

In sum, through educational exchanges America can further cultivate a political and economic ecosystem sympathetic to American perspectives in Southeast Asia.

ASEAN and China

The history of the ASEAN-China relationship can also be divided into three phases: an initial phase of hostility, a second of "falling in love", and a third (and current) phase of uncertainty. Each phase has been influenced by larger geopolitical currents, suggesting that the ASEAN-China relationship is driven by global trends as well as bilateral considerations. This is a key point that both sides should bear in mind as they reflect on the future.

The first phase can be easily described. When ASEAN was born in August 1967, China reacted with hostility. The following extract from a *Peking Review* article of 18 August 1967 captures the spirit of China's response to the creation of ASEAN very well:

---

24. Kishore Mahbubani and Lawrence H. Summers, "The Fusion of Civilizations", *Foreign Affairs*, May–June 2016.

In its Joint Declaration issued on August 8, this alliance of US stooges openly supported the existence of the US military bases in Southeast Asia, not even bothering to make any excuses for them. All this proves that this reactionary association formed in the name of "economic cooperation" is a military alliance directed specifically against China.[25]

Why did China respond in this way? The simple answer is global geopolitics. At that time, China was aligned with the Soviet Union in the Cold War against America. Since the five founding members of ASEAN tended to be more pro-American than pro-Soviet, and since they were banding together in fear of Communist expansion in Southeast Asia, it was only to be expected that China would denounce ASEAN's creation. The Soviet Union also warned that ASEAN would be subjected to American pressures. The *Diplomatic Dictionary*, edited by Andrei Gromyko, suggested that ASEAN was "under undisguised pressure from the US and other countries, which hope to impart on the association an anti-socialist orientation".[26]

At that point China did not have diplomatic relations with any of the five founding ASEAN states. Moreover, it supported radio broadcasts by various Southeast Asian Communist parties that originated in Chinese territory[27] and strongly criticized all five governments. These broadcasts included vitriolic criticism of ASEAN.

Fortunately for ASEAN, this hostile phase did not last long. China had a major falling out with the Soviet Union, and there were military skirmishes in 1969 on the Ussuri River. Chinese historians call this the Zhenbao Island Incident. The United States tried to exploit the Sino-Soviet division by pulling China into its orbit against the Soviet Union, and an entente took shape starting with Henry Kissinger's famous visit to China in July 1971.

This entente between China and America inaugurated phase 2 of the ASEAN-China relationship: the "falling in love" phase. China began courting ASEAN slowly and steadily, and Malaysia established

25. "Puny Counter-Revolutionary Alliance", *Peking Review* 10, 3 (18 Aug. 1967): 40, https://www.marxists.org/subject/china/peking-review/1967/PR1967-34.pdf/, accessed 12 Oct. 2016.

26. Cited in Jim Nichol, *Soviet Views of the Association of Southeast Asian Nations: An Examination of Unclassified Soviet Sources* (Washington, DC: Federal Research Division for the Library of Congress, 1985).

27. Jing Sun, *Japan and China as Charm Rivals: Soft Power in Regional Diplomacy* (Ann Arbor: University of Michigan Press, 2012), pp. 64–5.

diplomatic relations with China in May 1974, followed by Thailand in July 1975.

One major event triggered a period of extraordinary closeness between ASEAN and China: the Vietnamese invasion of Cambodia in December 1978. China and ASEAN both opposed the invasion, as did the Americans, and opposition to the Soviet-supported Vietnamese invasion of Cambodia led to a decade of close collaboration in the 1980s between ASEAN, China and America. Kishore served as Singapore's ambassador to the UN from 1984 to 1989 and experienced at first hand this close collaboration. He also witnessed an extraordinary episode in the UN at the International Conference on Kampuchea in July 1981. When ASEAN opposed a Chinese effort to return Pol Pot to power, America supported China against ASEAN, effectively supporting the restoration of the genocidal Pol Pot regime. This episode taught the ASEAN countries a valuable lesson: even when relations are good, great power interests trump ethical and human rights principles.

For most of the 1980s, there was close collaboration between ASEAN and China. This could have ended when the Cold War ended with the collapse of the Berlin Wall in November 1989, but the habits of cooperation continued. China appreciated, in particular, ASEAN's continued hand of friendship after several Western countries, including America, tried to isolate it after the June 1989 Tiananmen incident. The West believed then that it could afford to isolate China, since China had become dispensable after the end of the Cold War.

ASEAN did not join in the Western ostracism of China, and by remaining friendly with China it reaped some extraordinary rewards. When several ASEAN countries, especially Indonesia, Malaysia and Thailand, suffered enormously from the Asian Financial Crisis of 1998–99, China helped out by refusing to devalue the RMB. This act of friendship was deeply appreciated. In addition, Zhu Rongji, then premier of China, made an extraordinary proposal for a free trade agreement (FTA) between ASEAN and China at the ASEAN-China Summit in Singapore in November 2000. The formal proposal from Zhu Rongji came a year later in Brunei in 2001.

This proposal for an ASEAN-China FTA was truly extraordinary because the hitherto pro-Western ASEAN countries had enjoyed close relations with Western-oriented free market economies, including Japan, South Korea and Australia. Yet, none of these countries had proposed an FTA with ASEAN. Instead, the Communist government of China was the first to do so. What was even more remarkable was that China did not just propose an FTA, it offered unilateral concessions to the ASEAN countries and an "early harvest" as part of the agreement. The ASEAN-China FTA was negotiated in record time. A framework agreement signed in November 2002 provided the legal basis for ASEAN and China to negotiate the ACFTA. An Agreement on Trade in Goods was signed in November 2004, an Agreement on Trade in Services on 14 January 2007, and an Investment Agreement in August 2009. The ACFTA officially came into effect on 1 January 2010. The ceremony for the establishment of the China-ASEAN Free Trade Area was held on 7 January 2010 in Nanning, China. The first decade of the 21st century was clearly positive for the ASEAN-China relationship.

By contrast, the second decade of ASEAN-China relations proved to be far more challenging. The lowest point was seen in July 2012, when the ASEAN foreign ministers held their annual ministerial meeting (AMM) in Phnom Penh. For 45 years, without exception, the ministers had agreed to issue a joint communiqué, but in Phnom Penh they failed to do so. Why? The general perception was that the Cambodian government, which chaired the meeting, had come under pressure from China not to allow any references to the South China Sea in the joint communiqué. Since the other nine countries felt, as a matter of principle, that such a reference should be included, political gridlock developed. ASEAN unity was shattered in Phnom Penh as a result of perceptions of Chinese pressure.

This event symbolized the fact that the long phase 2 (falling in love) had given way at some point to phase 3, a new period of uncertainty. It is impossible to establish a specific point in time when phase 3 began, but the 2012 Phnom Penh meeting indicated that the South China Sea issue was beginning to affect the ASEAN-China relationship.

Key Factors in ASEAN-China Relations

Given the major uncertainties surrounding the ASEAN relationship, it would be wise for both sides to engage in deep reflection on the future of this relationship. There are some big questions: Is China better off with an ASEAN that is strong and united, or one that is weak and divided? Does China get greater global benefits from a positive ASEAN-China relationship? What adjustments do the ASEAN countries need to make as China emerges as the number one power in the world? China needs to ponder the first two questions; ASEAN needs to reflect on the third.

Given China's recent difficulties with certain ASEAN member states, especially the Philippines, it would be natural for some of the strategic planners in Beijing to believe that China may be better off with a broken rather than a united ASEAN. Traditionally, great powers have engaged in the practice of divide-and-rule, and one might argue that China's interests could be better served with a divided and broken ASEAN. The temptation to divide ASEAN might attract some in Beijing.

However, any Chinese strategic planners so tempted should ponder carefully the short-term benefits vis-à-vis long-term losses. One of the modern miracles of our time has been the peaceful re-emergence of China as a great power. A lot of this has been due to the wisdom displayed by Chinese leaders, especially Deng Xiaoping and Zhu Rongji. However, China's peaceful re-emergence was due also to ancillary factors. One such factor was ASEAN.

Normally, shifts among great powers generate a great deal of friction. It would be perfectly normal to see, for example, increased friction between China and Japan or China and India. Yet, there has been relatively little friction in either case. One reason for this, to use an engineering analogy, is that ASEAN played a kind of "lubricating" role by "softening" the interactions among the great powers in the Asia-Pacific region. ASEAN's role in providing a neutral geopolitical platform for great-power engagement is particularly valuable in the current context of major great-power shifts. The reason only ASEAN can do this is that it is the only party trusted by all the powers in the region. As Kishore said in *The New Asian Hemisphere*, "new patterns of cooperation are emerging. ASEAN has played a key role, being single-handedly responsible for spawning a new alphabet soup of cooperation ventures: ARF, APEC, ASEAN+3, ASEM and EAS."[28]

Another scholar, Amitav Acharya, has also documented ASEAN's critical role in providing a key geopolitical platform for the emerging Asian powers to engage with each other. In his words, "[ASEAN] acts as the hub, if not the leader, of regional multilateral forums for East Asia. ... Despite ASEAN's limitations, no other organization can challenge its role as the hub of regional multilateral diplomacy."[29]

---

28. Kishore Mahbubani, *The New Asian Hemisphere: The Irresistible Shift of Global Power to the East* (New York: Public Affairs, 2008), p. 84.
29. Amitav Acharya, "ASEAN at 40: Mid-Life Rejuvenation?" *Foreign Affairs*, 15 Aug. 2007, https://www.foreignaffairs.com/articles/asia/2007-08-15/asean-40-mid-life-rejuvenation/, accessed 12 Oct. 2016.

If ASEAN did not exist it would have been perfectly conceivable for Chinese strategic planners to look for alternative ways and means of smoothening China's rise. But it would not have been easy to find such alternatives. Organizations such as ASEAN cannot be created overnight. It takes years of effort and astute leadership to create a viable and functioning regional organization. In short, the very existence of ASEAN is a geopolitical gift to China. ASEAN is clearly an imperfect organization (as are all regional organizations, including the European Union). Yet even such an imperfect organization could not be created overnight to serve China's interests. China's strategic planners should consider ASEAN as one of their biggest strategic assets and work towards strengthening instead of undermining it. It is too early to tell whether Donald Trump's election will lead to new storms emerging in the US-China relationship. Yet a rough ride in US-China relations is plausible, if not likely. In this scenario, close relations between ASEAN and China would be a valuable strategic asset to the latter.

Strategic planners should also be aware that ASEAN's continued existence and success could bring other and larger global benefits to China. One obvious example can be cited here. It is no secret that many Western countries, especially the Anglo-Saxon countries, are troubled by China's rise. This is why there has been a steady outpouring of negative articles on China in the Anglo-Saxon media. To put it simply, bad relations between ASEAN and China will be exploited by the Anglo-Saxon media to portray China negatively. Good relations between ASEAN and China will deprive them of this weapon.

Were the Chinese to analyze the impact of their recent activities in the South China Sea on global perceptions of the country, they would surely conclude that these actions have done damage to China's efforts to present its rise as a world power as peaceful.

One small micro-indicator will tell a lot. Chinese analysts should study the weekly cartoons produced by *The Economist*, which is a globally influential journal. It regularly portrays "Uncle Sam" (the United States) as a hapless old and well-intentioned gentleman, and China as an angry dragon with many sharp teeth. This portrayal is the exact opposite of the truth when one looks objectively at the global military roles of the United States and China in recent years. Yet, the exact opposite of the truth has become the conventional perception of China today. This shows the power of the Anglo-Saxon media. In the example here, a peace-loving US confronts China's militant dragon. Yet, in the Asia-Pacific waters, the American military presence is stronger than the Chinese.

Source: Courtesy Kevin Kallaugher, first appeared in *The Economist*, 11 June 2016.

Kishore warned a group of Chinese foreign policy analysts during a think tank discussion in Beijing in the middle of 2014 that the Anglo-Saxon media were using China's assertive actions in the South China Sea to portray China as aggressive and belligerent. Indeed, Kishore used stronger words. He said that the Anglo-Saxon media had been trying to unleash a "tiger of anti-China sentiment" globally. China's actions in the South China Sea had finally enabled them to do so.

It needs to be emphasized here that good relations between ASEAN and China will bolster the claim that China is committed to a peaceful rise. China's leaders have spoken eloquently about their goal of emerging peacefully. Zheng Bijian was one of the first Chinese senior officials to refer to his country's emergence as a "peaceful rise". He said, "Some emerging powers in modern history have plundered other countries' resources through invasion, colonization, expansion or even large-scale wars of aggression. China's emergence thus far has been driven by capital, technology and resources acquired through peaceful means."[30]

---

30. Zheng Bijian, "China's 'Peaceful Rise' to Great-Power Status", *The Foreign Affairs*, Sept./Oct. 2005, https://www.foreignaffairs.com/articles/asia/2005-09-01/chinas-peaceful-rise-great-power-status/, accessed 12 Oct. 2016.

Xi Jinping reinforced this message with equally strong comments. He said, "There's no gene for invasion in Chinese people's blood, and Chinese people won't follow the logic that 'might is right.'"[31] He also said, "Today, the lion has woken up. But it is peaceful, pleasant and civilized." The first leader to implement the policies of "peaceful rise" was, of course, the great Chinese leader Deng Xiaoping, who said firmly, "We are opposed to the establishment of hegemony and spheres of influence by any country in any part of the world in violation of these principles."[32] He added something even more shocking:

> If one day China should change her colour and turn into a superpower, if she too should play the tyrant in the world, and everywhere subject others to her bullying, aggression and exploitation, the people of the world should identify her as social-imperialism, expose it, oppose it and work together with the Chinese people to overthrow it.[33]

China can continue to make eloquent speeches about its commitment to a peaceful rise, and it should do so. However, as is often the case in human affairs, deeds speak louder than words. China needs to demonstrate that its emergence is peaceful, and abide by Deng's categorical assertion that it is "opposed to the establishment of hegemony and spheres of influence". The best such laboratory is the ASEAN region. Why? The simple answer is that ASEAN serves China in the same way as Latin America has served the United States: as a geopolitical backyard. The United States demonstrated the nature of its great-power behaviour through its deeds in Latin America. Similarly, China can demonstrate it through its deeds in the ASEAN region. This is why if China wants to prove that—unlike the United States—it will emerge as a peaceful power, the best place to show the contrast is with ASEAN.

Fortunately, China will not have to work hard to prove that it will treat its geopolitical backyard better than the United States did in Latin America. In Kishore's book *Beyond the Age of Innocence*, he documents

---

31. Jin Kai, "Building 'A Bridge between China and Europe'", *The Diplomat*, 23 Apr. 2014, http://thediplomat.com/2014/04/building-a-bridge-between-china-and-europe/, accessed 12 Oct. 2016.
32. "Speech by Chairman of the Delegation of the People's Republic of China, Teng Hsiao-Ping, at the Special Session of the U.N. General Assembly" (Beijing: Foreign Languages Press, 10 Apr. 1974), https://www.marxists.org/reference/archive/deng-xiaoping/1974/04/10.htm, accessed 12 Oct. 2016.
33. Ibid.

in great detail the role that the United States has played as a great power. He begins by asserting an incontestable truth: "America has done more good for the rest of the world than any other country."[34] Yet, it is also true that America has harmed the world in several ways. The one region that has suffered the most from American power is Latin America.

Few Americans know or understand the bitterness they have generated in their own backyard. To make Americans aware of this, Kishore quoted the famous Latin American writer Gabriel Garcia Marquez, in a message he delivered to a meeting in New York held in November 2003 to celebrate his writing. Instead of thanking the Americans for honouring him, he said in a video message to a somewhat shocked American audience:

> How does it feel now that horror is erupting in your own yard and not in your neighbor's living room? ... Do you know that between 1824 and 1994 your country carried out 73 invasions in countries of Latin America? ... For almost a century, your country has been at war with the entire world. ... How does it feel, Yank, knowing that on September 11th the long war finally reached your home?[35]

Marquez describes eloquently the troubled relationship between America and its backyard, Latin America. By contrast, China has had, overall, a good relationship with its backyard, Southeast Asia. China's leaders, especially President Xi Jinping, have declared their commitment to building stronger ASEAN-China relations. In his address to the Indonesian Parliament on 2 October 2013, President Xi put forward many concrete proposals to further strengthen the China-ASEAN relationship:

> China is ready to open itself wider to ASEAN countries on the basis of equality and mutual benefit, to enable ASEAN countries to benefit more from China's development. China is prepared to upgrade the China-ASEAN Free Trade Area and strive to expand two-way trade to $1 trillion by 2020. China is committed to greater connectivity with ASEAN countries. ... China will propose the establishment of an Asian infrastructure investment bank that would give priority to ASEAN countries' needs [emphasis added]. Southeast Asia has since ancient times been an important hub along the ancient Maritime Silk Road. China

---

34. Mahbubani, *Beyond the Age of Innocence: Rebuilding*, p. 1.
35. Ibid., p. 144.

will strengthen maritime cooperation with ASEAN countries to make good use of the China-ASEAN Maritime Cooperation Fund set up by the Chinese government, and vigorously develop maritime partnerships in a joint effort to build the Maritime Silk Road of the 21st century.[36]

He added, "Last year saw 15 million people traveling between China and ASEAN countries, with over 1,000 flights between the two sides each week. Increased interactions have nurtured deeper bonds between us and enabled our people to feel ever closer to each other."

As a result of the initiatives undertaken by Chinese leaders from Deng Xiaoping to Xi Jinping, China-ASEAN relations have grown from strength to strength. Trade has grown exponentially, from US$2.4 billion in 1980 to US$350 billion in 2013, an increase of over 100 times in 30 years. Two-way investment has also grown. ASEAN investment in China grew to US$8.35 billion in 2013. China's investment in ASEAN grew from US$4.4 billion in 1991 to US$8.6 billion in 2013. China and ASEAN have provided mutual support and partnered with each other in confronting a series of severe natural disasters and epidemics, such as the 2004 Indian Ocean tsunami, the Myanmar cyclone, the Wenchuan earthquake, SARS and avian flu.

President Xi called for "a new type of great-power relations". It was very wise of him to do so. History teaches us when one great power (in this case China) is about to surpass another great power (in this case the United States) as the world's greatest power, conflicts can arise. Xi has referred to this problem as the "Thucydides trap", saying, "We all need to work together to avoid the Thucydides trap—destructive tensions between an emerging power and established powers, or between established powers themselves."[37]

It would be equally wise for President Xi to also call for a new model of relations between great powers and small/medium powers. Contrary to the conventional Western wisdom that China will inevitably emerge as a belligerent and aggressive power, China can demonstrate that, unlike the United States, it can treat small and medium powers with respect. The best place for China to start demonstrating this is with ASEAN.

---

36. "Speech by Chinese President Xi Jinping to Indonesian Parliament", ASEAN-China Centre, 2 Oct. 2013, http://www.asean-china-center.org/english/2013-10/03/c_133062675.htm, accessed 12 Oct. 2016.
37. Nicolas Berggruen and Nathan Gardels, "How the World's Most Powerful Leader Thinks", *Huffington Post*, 30 Sept. 2015.

Were China to establish a new model of relations between great powers and small states/medium powers, the Anglo-Saxon media would find it harder to portray China as a belligerent and aggressive power. Many in the Anglo-Saxon media (as well as Anglo-Saxon governments) believe that they have found the perfect ammunition in the Nine-Dash Line that China has drawn in the South China Sea. Since this line is difficult to justify under any contemporary international law or any contemporary international consensus on maritime claims, it provides the Anglo-Saxon media with an opportunity to project a negative portrayal of China.

In this geopolitical context, China-ASEAN relations become even more important. If China succeeds in developing a new model of great power-middle/small power relations to govern relations with ASEAN, it would significantly blunt the efforts of the Anglo-Saxon media to portray China as an aggressive actor on the global scene. A comprehensive review of China-ASEAN relations would show Beijing how that relationship can help serve China's larger foreign policy interests.

The big message that this section is trying to convey is that China should not underestimate the many collateral benefits of a good relationship with ASEAN. As the second-most successful regional organization in the world, after the EU, ASEAN can raise its standing and prestige in the world if it continues to present a united stand and increases levels of inter-regional cooperation by undertaking projects such as the AEC and working to meet its targets. China can be part of that global success story if it develops a good relationship with ASEAN. We hope therefore that as a result of a significant and comprehensive policy review, China will come to the conclusion that it is in its interests to strengthen, not weaken, ASEAN.

As in any bilateral relationship, clapping requires two hands. Just as China should engage in deep reflection on the ASEAN-China relationship, ASEAN needs to do the same. It is more difficult for ASEAN to do this as there are ten national actors involved, and their national interests vis-à-vis China are each different. ASEAN member states will factor in their own bilateral interests as they consider what ASEAN's policy towards China might be. Their assessment of their bilateral interests will of course be conditioned by geography and history, and also by the nature and personality of the leaders in power, because policies often change when leaders change. It would not be surprising if different ASEAN countries reached different conclusions on the ASEAN-China relationship. Indeed, as of 2016, this has already happened.

The two ASEAN countries that will always be the most wary of China are Vietnam and Myanmar. Why? The simple answer is history. Both have fought wars against invading Chinese armies. The Qianlong Emperor invaded Myanmar four times between 1765 and 1769, conflicts that led to the creation of the present-day border with China.[38] The Myanmar border was also the scene of skirmishes resulting from the civil war between Chinese nationalists and Communists. The war between China and Vietnam in 1979 left more than 50,000 Vietnamese dead,[39] although the conflict lasted only three weeks and six days. Vietnam is particularly suspicious about Chinese interests and intentions because it was occupied by China for more than 1,000 years, from 111 BC to AD 938. Nayan Chanda, a well-known journalist, has written that less than a decade after Hanoi was bombed by American war planes during the Vietnam War, visitors to the Hanoi Museum were given historical accounts of "Vietnam's thousand-year fight for independence against China".[40] A Vietnamese journalist, Dien Luong, wrote in an article for *The Diplomat*:

> In 1970, during a short hiatus in the U.S. bombing of North Vietnam, Noam Chomsky, the leading American political activist and one of the most vociferous critics of America's foreign policies, was invited to visit the capital Hanoi and lecture at the Polytechnique University there. Chomsky recalled that the first morning he arrived, he was taken to the war museum to listen to long lectures with dioramas about Vietnamese wars with China many centuries ago. "The lesson was clear," he said in an interview, "you happen to be destroying us now, but you'll leave. China will always be here."[41]

38. Charles Patterson Giersch, *Asian Borderlands: The Transformation of Qing China's Yunnan Frontier* (Cambridge, MA, and London: Harvard University Press, 2006).
39. Michael Sullivan, "Ask the Vietnamese about War, and They Think China, Not the U.S.", *NPR*, 1 May 2015, http://www.npr.org/sections/parallels/2015/05/01/402572349/ask-the-vietnamese-about-war-and-they-think-china-not-the-u-s/, accessed 12 Oct. 2016.
40. Nayan Chanda, *Brother Enemy: The War after the War* (New York: Harcourt, 1986), p. 93.
41. Dien Luong, "Why Vietnam Loves the Trans-Pacific Partnership", *The Diplomat*, 16 Mar. 2016.

The fate of Vietnam and China will always be joined because of geography. Bilahari Kausikan, a senior Singapore diplomat, addressing a forum in the lead-up to the G7 Summit in Japan in 2016, told the audience:

> Some years ago, I asked a senior Vietnamese official what leadership changes meant for Vietnam's relations with China. Every Vietnamese leader, he replied, must be able to stand up to China and get along with China and if anyone thinks this cannot be done at the same time, he does not deserve to be a leader.[42]

Curiously, while the national interests of China and Vietnam are the most divergent (especially over the South China Sea disputes), the two countries have one contemporary interest in common: to preserve the legitimacy of the ruling Communist parties in Beijing and Hanoi. This helps to soften the differences between Vietnam and China.

Thailand does not share a border with China, nor has it ever fought Chinese forces. Thai courts traditionally sent tributes to Chinese emperors, and modern Thailand has assimilated residents of Chinese descent very comfortably. Thailand remains an American ally, but it has received a great deal of Chinese aid and is emerging as a country sympathetic to China's interests. Ian Storey describes this shift well:

> ... for the past four decades Thailand has always been able to rely on China's support during crisis periods: e.g. during the 1973 energy crisis when China sold oil to Thailand at "friendship prices"; China was Thailand's primary strategic ally during the decade-long Cambodian Crisis; Beijing provided financial support when the Thai economy buckled during the 1997–98 Asian Financial Crisis; and after the 2006 coup, China recognized the new government immediately and bilateral relations continued as normal. In Thailand, these events, among others, have created a very positive image of China as a country that always has the Kingdom's national interests at heart, irrespective of who holds power in Bangkok.[43]

---

42. Bilahari Kausikan, "Standing up to and Getting Along with China", *Today*, 18 May 2016,
    http://www.todayonline.com/chinaindia/standing-and-getting-along-china/, accessed 12 Oct. 2016.
43. Ian Storey, "Thailand's Post-Coup Relations with China and America: More Beijing, Less Washington", *Trends in Southeast Asia* 20 (Singapore: ISEAS–Yusof Ishak Institute, 2015), p. 14.

In recent years, American criticism—and indeed ostracism—of military-dominated governments has pushed Thailand closer to China. Just as Western isolation of Myanmar in the 1980s and 1990s drove Myanmar into the hands of the Chinese, Western criticism of Thailand's military governments could mean that country's geopolitical gift to China. As Storey put it:

> Thailand's domestic political situation has largely determined the country's tilt towards Beijing. The junta has expressed appreciation for China's understanding that after nearly a decade of political turmoil, the Kingdom requires a period of stability that only the army can provide. The Thai government contrasts this with Washington's repeated calls for the immediate restoration of democracy, and has rejected as unfair and hypocritical U.S. allegations that Thailand's human rights and people trafficking situation has deteriorated since the coup … Chinese and U.S. responses to the coup have strengthened the Thai narrative that since the late 1970s, the Kingdom has always been able to rely on China's support in times of crisis, while America behaves as a fair weather friend.[44]

China has also been exceptionally generous to Cambodia and Laos, and they have emerged as the two most pro-China governments within the ASEAN constellation.

In maritime Southeast Asia, there is greater political as well as physical distance from China and, from time to time, greater wariness of China. However, the policies of individual countries have been inconsistent. The Philippines under President Benigno Aquino III (2010–16) was very critical of China and took China to court in the Permanent Court of Arbitration in The Hague. However, barely two decades earlier, in 1991, the Philippines had expelled American carriers from Subic Bay and Clark Airbase. The Philippines has tended to be inconsistent and erratic in its foreign policy behaviour, partially for cultural reasons. With the election of Rodrigo Duterte as president in May 2016, China-Philippines tensions have subsided as President Duterte has said that he will try to work together with China to resolve issues in the South China Sea bilaterally. Duterte followed up by visiting China in October 2016 with a delegation that included 400 businessmen. US$24 billion worth of trade deals were signed. Soon after he returned home, China once again allowed Filipino fishermen to fish near Scarborough Shoal.

---

44. Ibid., pp. 1–2.

Malaysia, like Thailand, has a long history of good relations with China. Malaysia was the first ASEAN country to establish diplomatic relations with China (in 1974); and successive Malaysian prime ministers, including Dr Mahathir and the current incumbent Najib Razak, have maintained close relations with Beijing. Najib is always treated royally in Beijing since it was his father, PM Tun Razak, who established diplomatic relations with China. In November 2016, Najib visited Beijing and received many sweet deals. China agreed to build a new port in Melaka for US$1.9 billion and a new railway line between Kuala Lumpur and Kelantan for US$13.1 billion. However, despite the bonhomie among the leaders, structural factors complicate China-Malaysia relations. The two countries have competing claims in the South China Sea, and Malaysia's ruling elite views the country's ethnic Chinese community with suspicion. These and other issues have the potential to complicate China-Malaysia relations.

Indonesia's relations with China are complicated by several factors. With its aspirations towards becoming a middle power, Indonesia is not naturally deferential to China. Indonesia was one of the last ASEAN countries to establish diplomatic relations with China because President Suharto believed that the Chinese Communist Party had supported the PKI's attempted coup in 1965. Suharto only allowed diplomatic relations to be established in 1990. Suharto is gone, but the wariness of China remains. The Nine-Dash Line China has drawn in the South China Sea intrudes on Indonesia's own Exclusive Economic Zone. China has given various private assurances to Indonesian leaders that it does not claim those Exclusive Economic Zone waters but will not say this publicly. There have also been incidents between Indonesian and Chinese government vessels in the South China Sea.

This brief survey of bilateral relations between China and some ASEAN states shows how complicated each bilateral relationship is. However, it would be a mistake for any of the ASEAN countries to allow bilateral interests to determine the future of the ASEAN-China relationship. Instead, that should be based on an enlightened calculation of ASEAN's long-term interests as a group vis-à-vis China.

Any such calculation of ASEAN's long-term interests will show that either of the two extreme options—being supplicant to China or being confrontational against China—is potentially disastrous for the ten ASEAN countries. The ASEAN group needs to agree, by traditional ASEAN consensus, to walk a middle path between being supplicant and hostile to China. This group should make it clear to China that an independent ASEAN would be best for China's long-term interests as it would provide an independent and neutral presence that could help lubricate and soften China's relations with other major powers, especially Asian powers such as India and Japan.

ASEAN has demonstrated in its first 50 years, and especially in the last 30, that it can benefit China's long-term interests by helping to bridge the gap between China and other major powers. To understand the value of ASEAN, China should understand the depth of suspicion it faces in Northeast Asia and compare that to the relative lack of suspicion in Southeast Asia. The difference in political chemistry between Northeast Asia and Southeast Asia can be credited to ASEAN. If China wants to have a positive dynamic around its borders, it should see that a stronger rather than a weaker ASEAN offers the most satisfactory way forward.

Leaders in ASEAN and China need to engage in subtle and sophisticated long-term calculations to ensure that ASEAN-China relations remain on a steady and positive course despite the few hiccups that have affected these relations in recent years. This approach requires a deep understanding on the part of all parties of the critical interests of each side. One goal of the present book is to help each great power develop a better understanding of its long-term interests vis-à-vis ASEAN.

ASEAN and the EU

The European Union is the world's most successful regional organization, and ASEAN is the second-most successful one. Their strengths are complementary, and an alliance between them would unleash many synergies that would benefit both enormously.

The EU is a group of developed countries. ASEAN (barring Singapore) is a group of developing countries. Their economic strengths complement each other. The groups could also complement each other culturally. The EU is a mono-civilizational club of Christian countries. ASEAN is a multi-civilizational club of many different religions and cultures. As a group of developed countries dispensing aid and development advice, the EU could help the ASEAN countries grow economically. ASEAN could reciprocate by helping the EU in the geopolitical dimension. ASEAN has been singularly successful in helping to create a relatively stable geopolitical environment through regional arrangements centred on ASEAN processes. This last point will come as a surprise to some readers.

To understand it, one has to understand the geopolitical deficiencies of the European Union. The EU is a short-sighted geopolitical animal. Its decision-making processes unfortunately focus on the short-term interests of individual member states rather than the larger and longer-term interests of the EU as a whole. Quite often, the short-term electoral interests of politicians in office also trump regional interests.

In 2015, the Syrian refugee crisis overwhelmed the EU. When more than a million refugees arrived, the EU response was characteristically chaotic. Although politicians feigned surprise, this could have been seen coming. Kishore wrote in *Europe's World* on 26 November 2015:

> Europe's current migration crisis, like the Mexican migration problem, could have been anticipated. The EU should have signed a North African Free Trade Area (NAFTA) to match the American NAFTA. Yet none was proposed or even considered. Why not? The simple answer is that the U.S. has intelligence and security agencies that focus on long-term challenges, and they anticipated the Mexican challenge. The EU has had none, and failed to identify the looming migratory pressures. To make matters worse, the EU allowed the U.S. to set the agenda for the EU's relations with its Islamic neighbours. When the Arab spring began in Tunisia in December 2010, the EU allowed the U.S. to take the driver's seat in dealing with the uprisings in Tunisia, Egypt and Libya. The U.S. was able to take ideological positions because, separated by the Atlantic Ocean, it could walk away from these problems. The EU can never walk away from North Africa's problems, and should have been careful and pragmatic in dealing with them instead of allowing the ideological interests of the U.S. to trump its own pragmatic interests.[45]

The EU's failure to see such an obvious point is a result of a deep structural flaw in its decision-making arrangements. EU leaders spend most of their time negotiating internal arrangements, but the challenges facing the EU are now largely external. Anyone who doubts this should look at the EU's failure to deal with the demographic explosion in Africa (which will inevitably lead to more migrants to Europe), the turbulence in North Africa and the Middle East (which has opened the tap for more migrant flows to Europe), and the disaster in Ukraine.

---

45. Kishore Mahbubani, "Here's How the EU Should Start to Think Long-term", *Europe's World*, 26 Nov. 2015, http://europesworld.org/2015/11/26/heres-how-the-eu-should-start-to-think-long-term/, accessed 12 Oct. 2016.

So, what lessons can the EU learn from ASEAN in geopolitics? The EU would do well to consider two countries that have faced similar challenges: Myanmar and Syria. Both had military regimes and were countries divided by deep ethnic and religious fault lines. Both quashed efforts at democratic reforms. The EU response in both cases was the same: it imposed sanctions on both regimes. The ASEAN reaction was the opposite: it engaged with Myanmar.

ASEAN-EU differences over Myanmar peaked during the 1990s. The timing was unfortunate. The outcome of the Cold War made the EU insufferably arrogant. During an ASEAN-EU meeting in the early 1990s, Belgian Foreign Minister Willy Claes led the European delegation because Belgium held the presidency of the EU at the time. He proudly proclaimed that with the end of the Cold War, there were only two superpowers left in the world: the United States and the European Union. He exuded arrogance. (Curiously, Belgium, despite its domestic difficulties, has a tradition of producing arrogant ministers. Two decades later, European Commissioner for Trade Karel De Gucht showed much the same arrogance when dealing with his ASEAN counterparts.)

The EU suspended some ties with ASEAN when Myanmar was admitted as a member in 1997, and ASEAN was forced to call off an ASEAN-EU meeting because the EU refused to give a visa to the Myanmar representative. S. Jayakumar, the then foreign minister of Singapore, wrote:

> The EU and ASEAN had biennial dialogues with the venue alternating between ASEAN countries (and chaired by ASEAN) and Europe (in the country holding the EU presidency). When held in ASEAN, the EU delegation had no problem sitting together with the foreign ministers from all ASEAN countries, including Myanmar. However, when it was their turn to host, they refused to give a visa to the Myanmar Foreign Minister due to their strong stand on Myanmar's human rights record. Naturally, we could not agree to the divide-and-rule approach, and we refused to attend without the presence of Myanmar's Foreign Minister. As a result, the ASEAN-EU dialogue got stalled. The breakthrough came in January 2003 when they devised a face-saving approach of having the dialogue in Brussels, the seat of the EU. The Myanmar Deputy Foreign Minister attended.[46]

---

46. Jayakumar, *Be at the Table or Be on the Menu*, pp. 77–8.

Jayakumar later explained that "The EU's single issue was Myanmar and human rights. Myanmar was a convenient whipping boy."[47] According to Tommy Koh:

> When Jayakumar visited Sweden, he was asked by F[oreign] M[inister] Lindh to explain why he took such a hard line on Myanmar. He said that it was not a hard line and pointed out the inconsistency in the fact that the EU would speak to North Korea yet refused to speak to Myanmar. Lindh agreed that he was right.[48]

It has been 20 years since ASEAN admitted Myanmar. Myanmar has made a peaceful evolution towards a more democratic regime. By contrast, Syria is in flames, and Syrian refugees are pouring into Europe. Clearly the ASEAN policy of engaging the military regime in Myanmar succeeded, while the EU policy of isolating Syria failed. Perhaps the EU should offer ASEAN an apology for criticizing and maligning its engagement with Myanmar.

Such an apology would help with the full realization of the potential harmonization of ASEAN and EU relations, which need to be completely reset. In order to scrub out the dysfunctional aspects of the relationship, the EU needs to admit openly that its policies on Myanmar were dead wrong. It also needs to dispense with the arrogance and condescension it has displayed towards ASEAN.

ASEAN, for its part, needs to be more self-confident in dealing with the EU. Since many ASEAN countries receive aid from the European Commission and from individual EU member states, they are accustomed to behaving as supplicants. This has to stop. ASEAN can learn from India, which also receives aid from the EU. The EU gave India US$78 million in aid during 2014, while ASEAN countries received US$304 million.[49] When the EU tried to impose conditions on India by demanding that certain standards of democracy and human rights be met, India, which is the world's largest democracy, told the EU to go fly a kite. In 2011 Shashi Tharoor, the then minister of state for foreign affairs, explained India's position:

> Sometimes Europe has a tendency to give too much advice on things that are domestic affairs, which is something we do not

---

47. Authors' interview with Professor S. Jayakumar, 19 Aug. 2016.

48. Authors' interview with Ambassador Tommy Koh, 23 Dec. 2015.

49. *Development Co-operation Directorate (DCD-DAC)*, http://www.oecd.org/dac/, accessed 12 Oct. 2016.

always appreciate. I believe that if we treat each other with the respect that is necessary for sovereign countries, we will have no problem in developing a real strategic partnership. But we will start with trade, because that is the easiest starting point.

He continued:

For example, human rights. We are very proud to say that violations of human rights are mostly exposed, even in Kashmir, by either civil society, the media or public administration. India is a country that likes to solve its own problems. Because of our colonial past, we don't like it when someone from outside India comes to gives us lessons. I am convinced that if Europe were to insist on imposing conditionality of such a sort on the FTA, then India would refuse to cooperate. You can't forget history, you can't forget that for 200 years others have led India's business and politics, and it is much more important for us to insist on our own rights than to strike an FTA. As simple as that.[50]

The big question that the EU needs to ask itself is whether it has taken this piece of advice to heart.

If the EU and ASEAN could engage in a dialogue of equals, each side could learn from the other. Although this idea is probably inconceivable in many European minds, there are many lessons that the EU might learn from ASEAN. And the lessons that ASEAN could learn from the EU are equally important. Let me suggest three examples each way.

First, Europe has an existential problem dealing with the Islamic world. This was clearly demonstrated by the Charlie Hebdo affair and by the tragic killings in Paris on 13 November 2015. In this area, geography is destiny. Europe will always live with Islamic neighbours, and at the moment its neighbours are not particularly successful or well off. By contrast, three of the most successful Islamic countries in the world are ASEAN members: Brunei, Malaysia and Indonesia. Europe's future would look a lot more secure in the long term if countries like Libya, Tunisia and Algeria could emulate the successful examples of Brunei, Malaysia and Indonesia.

Were the EU to sponsor a massive programme of scholarships to send young North African students to study in ASEAN countries, those students would see at first hand that Islam is compatible with both

50. "Indian MP Tharoor: Europe Must Stop Lecturing India", *EurActiv*, 19 Apr. 2011, http://www.euractiv.com/section/global-europe/interview/indian-mp-tharoor-europe-must-stop-lecturing-india/, accessed 12 Oct. 2016.

democracy and development. Some of them might study governance at the Lee Kuan Yew School of Public Policy (where Kishore serves as dean). In short, ASEAN could do the EU a substantial favour by instilling hopes for development and democracy in North Africa. Should this sense of hope grow, fewer migrants would feel a need to cross the Mediterranean to Europe. This is an obvious area where the EU can gain by collaborating more closely with ASEAN. Why hasn't a single senior EU policy maker thought of the obvious? The tragic and honest answer to this question is that European arrogance created this appalling blindness.

Second, the EU can learn from ASEAN the policy approaches of engagement instead of isolation. The examples of Myanmar and Syria mentioned earlier have demonstrated this. The EU should also emulate ASEAN's policies of engagement in dealing with Russia. Why? Sanctions do not work! Kofi Annan and Kishore published an article together in December 2015 arguing that sanctions rarely change policies, saying:

> After all, public policy should be guided by evidence, not intuition and emotion. And the evidence indicates that, in order to achieve success and avoid unintended consequences, carefully calibrated sanctions must be pursued in tandem with political engagement. Imposing sanctions may feel good. But if they are actually to do good, we must refine how they are used.[51]

A major country like Russia cannot be humiliated into submission. ASEAN has displayed a special genius in engaging previous adversaries. When the association was formed in 1967, both China and Vietnam denounced its creation as an imperialist plot. Yet, 30 years later, Vietnam joined ASEAN and China became the first country to sign a free trade agreement with ASEAN.

EU member states are richer and more powerful than ASEAN member states. Yet, they have allowed key aspects of their foreign policy to be hijacked and run by the United States, their major ally. Geopolitics is always about geography. The United States will never be a neighbour of Russia, except in Alaska. The EU will always be a neighbour of Russia. Given these circumstances, why does the EU allow the ideological priorities of the US to override its pragmatic

---

51. Kofi A. Annan and Kishore Mahbubani, "Rethinking Sanctions", *Project Syndicate*, 11 Jan. 2016, https://www.project-syndicate.org/onpoint/rethinking-economic-sanctions-by-kofi-a-annan-and-kishore-mahbubani-2016-01, accessed 12 Oct. 2016.

priorities in dealing with Russia? Why allow the US to expand NATO right up to Russia's doorstep? Why threaten Russia by offering to bring Ukraine into NATO?

In contrast to the lack of geopolitical wisdom shown by the EU, ASEAN has often demonstrated its wisdom in this area. Here, again, the case of Myanmar is instructive. In the mid-1990s, both the US and EU applied enormous pressure on ASEAN to isolate and ostracize Myanmar. ASEAN wisely ignored these pressures and continued engaging with Myanmar. The then Indonesian Foreign Minister Ali Alatas explained that ostracism would drive Myanmar into the arms of China and India, which would make it a centre of geopolitical struggle. Similarly, by isolating Russia, the EU is forcing it to cooperate and collaborate more with China.

Many Europeans may argue over the specific rights and wrongs of this case, but the key issue is how to change Russia's behaviour. The traditional EU answer has been sanctions. The traditional ASEAN answer has been engagement. Looking at their experiences over the past 25 years since the end of the Cold War, ASEAN's policies have worked better than the EU's. This is why the EU should learn lessons from ASEAN on geopolitics.

The third area where the EU can learn from ASEAN is administrative pragmatism. The EU has 28 member states. ASEAN has ten. Yet, ASEAN is far more diverse culturally and linguistically than the EU. The EU has 24 official languages because every EU member state feels that its language is equally important. This creates a massive amount of work, just to translate and interpret across many languages. By contrast, ASEAN uses English, which is not native to any ASEAN country. If the EU could learn to emulate ASEAN, it could save €1 billion. The EU website says, "According to certain very rough estimates, the cost of all language services in all EU institutions amounts to less than 1% of the annual general budget of the EU. Divided by the population of the EU, this comes to around €2 per person per year."[52] As the combined population of the EU is 500 million, the total cost of all the translations comes to €1 billion. Adopting a common language would also foster greater understanding among EU leaders and officials. As Lee Kuan Yew wrote in his memoirs:

---

52. "Frequently Asked Questions about DG Translation", European Commission, last updated 21 Sept. 2016, http://ec.europa.eu/dgs/translation/faq/index_en.htm/, accessed 14 Oct. 2016.

One serious obstacle to European cohesion and unity is the absence of a common language. Schmidt spoke to Giscard in English and told me they could establish a close rapport. Mitterrand and Chirac communicated with Kohl through an interpreter. I have always found it difficult to feel the texture of another person's mind when an interpreter stood in between.[53]

The fourth area where the EU can learn lessons from ASEAN is to consider adopting the ASEAN-X principle. The ASEAN countries have long recognized that it would be a mistake to get all ten ASEAN members to sign on to a project if some are not ready to join in. Hence, when it came to trade liberalization under AFTA, ASEAN had a two-tier system to give the newer members of ASEAN, especially Myanmar, Cambodia, Laos and Vietnam, more time before joining AFTA. If the EU had taken a similar approach, it could have avoided the Grexit problem.

The Grexit episode clearly demonstrated that a certain rigidity had developed in the EU cooperation process. In the years 2012–14, the world watched with bated breath as the EU went through a wrenching struggle to see whether Greece would remain in the Eurozone. The prospect of a "Grexit" was real, and it caused nervousness in world markets. Greece did not leave the EU, but the country might have been better off outside the Eurozone with a flexible currency that could be devalued to make Greek exports competitive again. Also, when accounts of Greece's application to join the Eurozone emerged, it became clear that massive deception had taken place. Greece lied and provided false statistics to indicate that it qualified for Eurozone entry, and the EU officials processing the application knew that Greece was lying but pretended that the statistics Greece submitted were correct. Angela Merkel said in 2013:

> Greece shouldn't have been allowed into the euro. Chancellor Schroeder accepted Greece in [in 2001] and weakened the Stability Pact, and both decisions were fundamentally wrong, and one of the starting points for our current troubles. That [a unified euro area] is such a treasure, such a boon, that we can't place it in doubt. That's why the euro is more than a currency. For this reason we've shown solidarity, but solidarity always

---

53. Lee, *From Third World to First*, p. 487.

linked to responsibility for reforms in those countries that experience our solidarity.[54]

In essence, Merkel admitted publicly that the admission of Greece was a mistake. Since the EU has preached the virtues of zero corruption and transparency, it is shocking that senior EU leaders participated in such massive self-deception. This is one reason why the bloom is off the rose of the EU as a model of regional cooperation.

When prospects of a Grexit loomed large, it became clear that the Eurozone had a major design flaw. It had worked out a strict set of criteria and rules for entry into the Eurozone, but it had absolutely no criteria or procedures to cover an exit. The implicit and hugely arrogant assumption underlying this situation was that when an EU country entered the Eurozone, it would automatically succeed. The EU had locked itself into an ideological straitjacket that the EU could only move forward. It could not take a step backwards. The world will also be watching carefully how the EU handles Brexit.

Brexit was a major shock to the EU. Indeed, it was a major shock to the whole world. Only when the dust of history has settled will we learn the fundamental structural reasons why the British voted to leave. Yet, to use a simple military analogy, the EU experiment may have tried to capture a bridge too far. It tried to bring about regional integration in areas where the people were not ready.

The principal reason that many British voters gave for their choice was that too many foreigners, especially from the EU, had moved to live in the UK. This increased migration followed an EU decision that regional economic cooperation would work better if free trade could be accompanied by free movement of people. The decision was correct on economic grounds, but in the UK a large influx of Polish and Romanian workers created discomfort about strangers in residents' familiar neighbourhoods.

Here, too, the ASEAN practice of moving ahead slowly and pragmatically may hold some lessons for the EU. Indeed, the ASEAN countries have occasionally backtracked from their commitments to ASEAN integration. In theory, this is wrong. In practice, this flexibility in the ASEAN method of cooperation and collaboration may be the most viable way of moving forward. While it may be difficult for

54. Andrew Trotman, "Angela Merkel: Greece Should Never Have Been Allowed in the Euro", *The Telegraph*, 27 Aug. 2013, http://www.telegraph.co.uk/finance/financialcrisis/10269893/Angela-Merkel-Greece-should-never-have-been-allowed-in-the-euro.html, accessed 12 Oct. 2016.

the legalistic European mind to accept the idea of backtracking from explicit legal commitments, the ASEAN culture of pragmatically handling such situations may be worth studying by the EU.

In short, if the EU and ASEAN made a strong, conscious effort to work together more closely, each side could learn implicit lessons from the other. ASEAN has always accepted the idea that it can learn lessons from the EU experiment. The big question, then, is whether EU policy makers are willing to accept the idea that they can learn from ASEAN.

ASEAN and India

In December 1995 the leaders of the ASEAN countries attended a summit meeting in Bangkok, Thailand. A key question on the agenda was whether India would be admitted as a full dialogue partner of ASEAN, joining Japan (1973), Australia (1974), New Zealand (1975), the US (1977), Canada (1977) and South Korea (1991). (China and Russia would both join later, in 1996.) As permanent secretary of the Singapore Foreign Ministry, Kishore served as the ASEAN Senior Officials Meeting (SOM) leader from Singapore.

Singapore had tried previously at the SOM level to get India admitted but without success. Out of a sense of Islamic solidarity, Indonesia and Malaysia felt that Pakistan should also be admitted as a full dialogue partner. The other ASEAN countries baulked at the idea of admitting India and Pakistan at the same time, fearing that their deep rivalry would be carried into ASEAN meetings and disrupt them.

In Bangkok, the ASEAN leaders retreated into a small room with no advisers present to deliberate a number of sensitive matters in private, including the question of India's admission. Before the meeting, Kishore warned Singapore Prime Minister Goh Chok Tong that Indonesia's President Suharto and Malaysia's PM Dr Mahathir were unlikely to agree to India's admission without Pakistan. PM Goh entered the room knowing that his chances of success were slim. When this meeting ended and the leaders came streaming out, PM Goh spotted Kishore in the crowd and gave him the thumbs up, indicating that India had got in alone. That scene remains one of the more memorable moments of Kishore's life.

India's gratitude towards Singapore for engineering its participation in ASEAN meetings was enormous, and more than two decades later that gratitude has not diminished. However, while India and Singapore have an unusually close friendship, Singapore has candidly told India that the gap between the potential of the ASEAN-India relationship and concrete outcomes is very large. Why is this so?

In theory, the dialogue partnership between ASEAN and India should be particularly productive because India has a long-standing and deeply rooted relationship with Southeast Asia. Of the ten ASEAN countries, only Vietnam and the Philippines do not have cultural roots in Indian civilization.

In practice, the ASEAN-India relationship is less productive than it might be. As a trading partner of ASEAN, India ranks seventh, below China, the EU, Japan, the United States, South Korea and Australia (see Table 1). India ranks seventh in investments in the ASEAN region as well, behind the EU, Japan, the United States, China, Australia and South Korea (see Table 2).

Table 1. Trade figures between ASEAN and dialogue partners (2013) (descending order of total)

Partner country/ region	Value (in billions of US$)		
	Exports	Imports	Total trade
China	152.5	198.0	350.5
EU 28	124.4	121.8	246.2
Japan	122.9	117.9	240.8
United States	114.5	92.3	206.9
Republic of Korea	52.8	82.1	135.0
Australia	45.5	22.5	68.1
India	41.9	25.9	67.9
Russia	5.2	14.7	19.9
Canada	7.2	6.2	13.5
New Zealand	5.7	4.1	9.8

Source: http://asean.org/resource/statistics/asean-statistics/, accessed 27 July 2015.

Table 2. FDI inflows from dialogue partners to ASEAN
(descending order of 2012–14 total)

Partner country/ region	Value (in billions of US$)			
	2012	2013	2014	2012–14
European Union	6.5	22.3	29.3	58.1
Japan	21.2	21.8	13.4	56.4
United States	14.4	4.9	13.0	32.4
China	5.7	6.8	8.9	21.4
Australia	3.2	3.5	5.7	12.4
Republic of Korea	1.6	3.7	4.5	9.7
India	4.3	1.3	0.8	6.4
Canada	1.0	1.0	1.3	3.3
Russian Federation	0.2	0.5	-0.02	0.7
New Zealand	-0.1	0.3	0.3	0.6

Source: http://asean.org/resource/statistics/asean-statistics/, accessed 27 July 2015.

India is a relative latecomer in developing close relations with Southeast Asian countries. Even though it became politically decolonized in 1947, it remained mentally colonized for several decades and continued to look west towards Europe and America for inspiration. In his book *The Intimate Enemy*, the Indian sociologist Ashis Nandy describes this mindset as "colonialism which survives the demise of empire".[55]

India drifted towards the Soviet Camp during the Cold War, while the ASEAN countries were clearly pro-American. These differing political orientations occasionally led to sharp diplomatic clashes between ASEAN and India in the UN, especially over the Vietnamese invasion of Cambodia. When the Cold War ended, India could have made a sharp U-turn, as China did, and prioritized strategic engagement with ASEAN. Instead, it allowed events rather than strategy to shape the ASEAN-India relationship. It is a very strong

---

55. Ashis Nandy, *The Intimate Enemy: Loss and Recovery of Self under Colonialism* (New Delhi: Oxford University Press, 1988), p. xi.

statement to suggest that India has no long-term strategy towards ASEAN, but it is probably fair. It would also be fair to add that it is harder to get consistent long-term strategic plans from a democracy like India than from a single-party system like China.

The election of Prime Minister Modi created a unique window of opportunity to shift the ASEAN-India relationship. In PM Modi India has a strong leader who is willing to make risky long-term strategic decisions. On 20 December 2012, the leaders of ASEAN and India adopted the ASEAN-India Vision Statement and declared that their relationship should be elevated to a strategic partnership at the ASEAN-India Commemorative Summit held in New Delhi.

As ASEAN comes under renewed stress from the growing geopolitical rivalry between the US and China, India could provide a strategic balance. India has an opportunity to develop a 20-year plan to enhance its relationship with ASEAN. In working out the details, it will come to realize that its relations with ASEAN rest on three pillars: cultural, economic and geopolitical. A tripod is stable when all three legs are equally strong, but the tripod supporting the ASEAN-India relationship still needs a great deal of work.

Most of the statements and declarations issued at ASEAN-India meetings have focussed on the economic aspects of the relationship. An ASEAN-India Eminent Persons group (EPG) was established in 2010 to take stock of ASEAN-India relations over the past 20 years, explore ways to widen and deepen existing cooperation between ASEAN and India, as well as recommend measures to further strengthen relations in the future. Its report concentrated on economic recommendations, and even the non-economic recommendations had economic ramifications. For example, the first item under socio-cultural cooperation concerned using corporate social responsibility to promote socioeconomic development in ASEAN and India. Other key recommendations of the EPG are listed below:[56]

- Conclude agreements in the areas of services and investment as early as possible, bearing in mind the fact that such Agreements would supplement the Free Trade Agreement in Goods, cement existing ties and take economic relations to a higher plane.

---

56. "ASEAN-India Eminent Persons' Report to the Leaders", ASEAN, Oct. 2012, http://www.asean.org/storage/images/2012/documents/Asean-India%20 AIEPG%20(29%2010%2012)-final.pdf, accessed 12 Oct. 2016.

- Declare a target of US$200 billion for bilateral ASEAN-India trade by the year 2022 under the ASEAN-India Free Trade Area. [Note: In 2015–16, ASEAN-India trade stood at US$65 billion.[57]]

- Facilitate a mutually beneficial business visa regime, including the granting of long-term, multiple entry business visas and stay permits for professionals and their families.

- Set up an ASEAN-India panel of experts to draw up a Food Security Plan for the region.

- Conclude as soon as possible an Open Skies agreement between ASEAN and India.

While the economic relationship is important, India needs to strengthen the cultural relationship. No other partner, not the US, not Europe and not even China, can match India's long historical association with Southeast Asia.

In Jakarta, large statues depicting scenes from the Hindu epics, the *Ramayana* and *Mahabharata*, stand at major traffic intersections. The most famous of these statues—the Arjuna Wijaya Statue in Central Jakarta—was installed in 1987, under Suharto, but all the statues are well cared for today. Similarly, the famous Javanese shadow play, *wayang kulit*, features characters from the *Ramayana* and the *Mahabharata*. Further examples from Thailand and Java demonstrate that Indian cultural influences remain alive and vibrant today, even though they have been overlaid by other more recent cultural waves (as documented in Chapter 1). Clearly a carefully articulated campaign by India reminds Southeast Asians of the cultural heritage they share with India. Many ordinary Southeast Asians are well acquainted with figures from, say, the *Ramayana* and *Mahabharata*. Yet, they would be surprised to learn that these figures, which they consider to be part of their heritage, come from India.

India's soft power turns up also in contemporary art and pop culture. Bollywood productions have enjoyed extraordinary success in many Southeast Asian countries. The Indian TV show *Mahabharata*, dubbed into Indonesian and broadcast in March 2014, became very popular in Indonesia and led to a reality show called *Panah Asmara*

---

57. *India ASEAN Trade and Investment Relations: Opportunities and Challenges* (Delhi: Associated Chambers of Commerce and Industry of India, July 2016), http://www.assocham.org/upload/docs/ASEAN-STUDY.pdf/, accessed 29 Sept. 2016.

Arjuna (Arjuna's Arrow of Love) hosted by the Indian actor who played the character of Arjuna in the Indian TV show. The ability of contemporary Bollywood films to strike a cultural chord with young Southeast Asian populations with no historical knowledge of ancient India-Southeast Asia links demonstrates that the cultural connectivity between India and Southeast Asia is still alive. India can expect a warm welcome if it launches a major push to build new cultural bridges with Southeast Asia.

Singapore, where 75 per cent of the population is Chinese, provides an interesting case study in this regard. Only 8 per cent of the population has Indian roots, but Singapore invested US$18 million to build and develop an Indian Heritage Centre that houses more than 440 artefacts. These include jewellery, stone sculptures, costumes and woodcarvings, along with items such as vintage suitcases that were used by Indian immigrants. The collection includes a 3.4m-tall wooden Chettinad doorway from the late 19th century with 5,000 minute carvings that reflects the architectural style of South India's Chettiar community, which acquired much of its wealth from moneylending businesses in Southeast Asia. Singapore's sixth president, the late S.R. Nathan, donated a series of wartime publications from the 1940s that illustrate the involvement of the region's Indian community with the wartime Indian National Army in its fight for Indian independence from Britain. The museum also pays tribute to Indian pioneers.[58] If India and Southeast Asia do re-establish and strengthen ancient cultural links, it will provide added meaning to the well-known phrase "culture is destiny".

Culture, though, cannot trump economics. Mexico is a case in point. Its culture is deeply rooted in the Spanish-speaking world, but its economic future will be shaped by twists and turns in American domestic politics. Similarly, as Southeast Asia's economic links with China grow stronger, and they inevitably will, India will find it increasingly difficult to counterbalance China's influence in Southeast Asia. This is why India should heed the recommendations of the ASEAN-India EPG. It is a good sign that India has implemented the recommendation to establish a separate diplomatic mission by

---

58. Melody Zaccheus, "Five Things to Know about the New Indian Heritage Centre", *Straits Times*, 8 May 2015, http://www.straitstimes.com/singapore/five-things-to-know-about-the-new-indian-heritage-centre/, accessed 12 Oct. 2016.

appointing an ambassador accredited to ASEAN. It should now work on implementing the following EPG recommendations:[59]

- Provide further support for the establishment of an ASEAN Promotional Chapter of Tourism (APCT) in Mumbai to further strengthen the tourism cooperation between ASEAN and India.

- Establish an ASEAN-India Centre in India to promote trade, investment, tourism, and cultural exchanges.

- Support ASEAN Community Building, the implementation of Master Plan on ASEAN Connectivity, and the attainment of ASEAN Community, avoiding redundancy with the existing Plan of Action.

Beyond the cultural and economic dimensions, India has a great opportunity on the geopolitical front. As indicated earlier, the worst-case scenario for ASEAN would be a schism resulting from member countries being forced to choose sides between China and the United States. If this rivalry intensifies, the only power that can provide ASEAN with a geopolitical buffer is India. If India were to strengthen its political presence and play a stronger role in Southeast Asia in the coming decades, it would receive a positive response from ASEAN countries.

ASEAN and Japan

Since the Meiji Restoration in the 1860s, the Japanese have viewed the rest of Asia with cultural condescension. The Meiji reformer Yukichi Fukuzawa captured this spirit when he said, "Our immediate policy, therefore, should be to lose no time in waiting for the enlightenment of our neighbouring countries in order to join them in developing Asia, but rather to depart from their ranks and cast our lot with the civilized countries of the West."[60] At the time, Fukuzawa was right: Asia was in decline, and the West was in the ascendant.

---

59. *ASEAN-India Eminent Persons' Report to the Leaders* (Jakarta: ASEAN, Oct. 2012), http://www.asean.org/storage/images/2012/documents/Asean-India%20AIEPG%20(29%2010%2012)-final.pdf, accessed 12 Oct. 2016.

60. Fukuzawa Yukichi, "Datsu-A Ron", *Jiji-Shimpo*, 12 Mar. 1885, trans. Sinh Vinh, in *Fukuzawa Yukichi nenkan*, Vol. 11 (Tokyo: Fukuzawa Yukichi kyokai, 1984), cited in "Fukuzawa Yukichi (1835–1901)", Nishikawa Shunsaku, *Prospects: The Quarterly Review of Comparative Education* 23, 3/4 (1993): 493–506.

The era of Western domination is clearly over, and we are seeing a powerful resurgence of Asian societies. The Japanese need to decide whether they have shed their long-established attitude of condescension towards their Asian neighbours and adjust to the realities of the Asian century. Thus far, the Japanese are providing mixed signals. In their rhetoric, Japanese leaders do acknowledge the return of Asia, although they rarely celebrate the Asian century. However, in their deeds, Japanese leaders and opinion-makers continue to prioritize their membership in "dying" Western clubs, such as the G7 and the OECD. This is natural. People take time to change their deep-seated cultural attitudes.

If Japan does not adjust quickly, it risks being left out as the rest of Asia forms economic and cultural communities that exclude it. Japan also faces an extraordinary geopolitical challenge after the election of Donald Trump, who threatened to make Japan pay more before agreeing to defend Japan. The Japanese could feel unusually isolated if they became estranged from both America and Asia at the same time. In this context, ASEAN becomes strategically important for Japan. Japan cannot re-engage with Asia through China or South Korea because the cultural and political divide between Japan and its nearest neighbours remains deep. By contrast, the ten ASEAN countries are willing to engage Japan. The residue of suspicion left behind since World War II is mostly gone. Moreover, as earlier chapters of this book have shown, ASEAN offers a valuable geopolitical platform for the great powers to re-engage in East Asia. It is telling that even though the Association of Southeast Asian Nations was created some 50 years ago, the Northeast Asian nations have yet to create an equivalent regional grouping. When relations between Japan and its neighbours have become difficult, Japanese leaders have at times used ASEAN meetings to re-engage with their immediate neighbours. Furthermore, as ASEAN grows and develops economically, it will provide growing markets for Japanese products. As Prime Minister Lee Hsien Loong of Singapore said in 2013, "The growing middle class in ASEAN countries will be important for Japanese exporters, whether you are talking about Toyota cars, Fujitsu laptops, Shiseido cosmetics and many other Japanese products."[61]

61. "Speech by Prime Minister Lee Hsien Loong at the 19th Nikkei International Conference on the Future of Asia", Prime Minister's Office Singapore, 26 May 2013, http://www.pmo.gov.sg/mediacentre/speech-prime-minister-lee-hsien-loong-19th-nikkei-international-conference-future-asia/, accessed 12 Oct. 2016.

On the economic front, there is a strong positive legacy in ASEAN-Japan relations. Former Singapore Minister George Yeo stated, "The Japanese were the most important integrator of ASEAN, I think in the '80s, because they were manufacturing in different countries. Member countries had to modify their rules to make that possible." He continued:

> They were producing and distributing in different ASEAN countries under different local conditions, all part of a global manufacturing process directed from Japan. Naturally, they were the ones who developed close links with governments who lobbied. And because their investments were important, governments accommodated them. This is my sense of that period. It preceded my time in MTI. Japan played the most important role. After the Plaza Accord in 1985, Japan's economy went into the doldrums for 20 years. Japanese influence receded.[62]

If Japan is to succeed in engaging ASEAN deeply, it must first understand why several decades of ASEAN-Japan engagement have failed to produce a close relationship. Simply put, there is no heart-to-heart engagement. Japanese leaders should ask themselves why China has succeeded in engaging ASEAN more deeply than Japan. This should not have happened. When ASEAN was formed as a perceived pro-Western club, Japan supported the new organization while China condemned it. Under the Fukuda Doctrine, Japan engaged ASEAN deeply as early as 1977. China's rapprochement with ASEAN began much later. Indonesia and Singapore established formal diplomatic relations with China as late as 1990. Yet, despite this late start, China pulled ahead of Japan and established a China-ASEAN Free Trade Area in 2005 while Japan only caught up in 2008.

Where and how did Japan go wrong with ASEAN? This is a complex question with a simple answer: Japan has never treated ASEAN with great respect. S. Jayakumar has described how slowly Japan moved when approached by ASEAN to sign the Treaty of Amity and Cooperation:

> We wanted Japan to sign in the same year as China did. China said, "No problem." But the Japanese bureaucracy insisted on checking the treaty line by line. I pulled the Japanese FM, Yoriko Kawaguchi, aside and said, "This is really a symbolic move.

---

62. Authors' interview with George Yeo, 5 Feb. 2016.

We want you to be a major player in the region. It is better if both China and Japan sign it together." But Japan took another year to sign it, and as a result, China signed first and got all the publicity. When Japan signed a year later, they did not get much publicity.[63]

Japan's failure to engage with ASEAN has deep roots. In 1977, in the course of a visit to the five ASEAN countries and Burma, Prime Minister Takeo Fukuda delivered a major speech[64] that launched what is often called the Fukuda Doctrine. Fukuda made many excellent points in his superbly drafted speech. Three stand out. First, he said, "A true friend is one who offers his hand in understanding and cooperation, not only in fair weather, but in adverse circumstances as well. I know Japan will be such a friend to ASEAN." Second, he called for "'heart-to-heart' understanding among the peoples of Japan and Southeast Asia" and "expressed Japan's readiness to extend our full cooperation in this regard in response to the concrete formulation by ASEAN of a workable scheme for such enhanced intraregional exchanges". Third, he announced that Japan would be "more than doubling its official development assistance within the next five years". The American scholar William Haddad wrote:

> The showpiece of the Fukuda Doctrine was no doubt the promise to loan the ASEAN members yen totalling US$1 billion for the five major industrial projects, one in each of the members' countries. They are two urea plants, one each in Indonesia and Malaysia; a superphosphate factory in the Philippines; a soda ash plant in Thailand; and a diesel engine factory for Singapore. The promise of credits was, however, conditional. The timing of the US$1 billion loan, for example, was unclear.[65]

The promise of US$1 billion for these five industrial projects generated great excitement in the ASEAN countries. The ASEAN countries viewed this as a strong signal of support from Japan for the economic development of ASEAN, and if the projects had been successful, it would have significantly boosted Japan's standing in ASEAN.

---

63. Authors' interview with Professor S. Jayakumar, 19 Aug. 2016.
64. "Speech by Takeo Fukuda", *Contemporary Southeast Asia* 2, 1 (1980): 69–73.
65. William Haddad, "Japan, the Fukuda Doctrine, and ASEAN", *Contemporary Southeast Asia* 2, 1 (1980): 18.

In the event, only two projects were carried out,[66] and Japan's poor track record honouring explicit commitments seriously damaged its standing with ASEAN. Japan's reluctance to implement these five projects was signalled soon after Fukuda returned to Japan. As Haddad reports:

> One paper demanded to know what exactly the Prime Minister intended to do about the five ASEAN industrial projects. It quoted the Prime Minister as having said in Kuala Lumpur that he had made a "concrete promise" of US$1 billion in aid but when he returned to Japan he said that he had "only promised to look into the problem" (*Asahi*, 25 Aug. 1977).[67]

While it may have been difficult for Japan to deploy US$1 billion for the five industrial projects, it even found it difficult to deliver on a pledge of ¥5 billion (approximately US$18.7 million) promised for the ASEAN Cultural Fund. Haddad notes, "Though the Foreign Ministry supported the project, Finance Minister Hideo Boo walked out of a governmental meeting when the subject turned to cultural cooperation" (Ibid.).

In short, PM Fukuda failed to deliver on two of the three commitments in his famous Manila speech, and exactly two decades later Japan also failed to deliver on the third: that Japan would be a true friend "not only in fair weather but in adverse circumstances as well". When adverse circumstances came in the form of the 1997–98 Asian Financial Crisis, Japan did little to help the ASEAN countries.

To be fair, some Japanese policy makers wanted to provide a lot more help. The famous "Mr. Yen", Japanese Vice Minister of Finance for International Affairs Eisuke Sakakibara, proposed setting up an Asian Monetary Fund to help ASEAN countries. Emilio de Miguel, a Spanish diplomat, described this Japanese initiative:

> Then, in August [1997] Japan came with a revolutionary idea: the creation of an Asian Monetary Fund. The AMF would be a 100 billion $ fund. Its members would be: Australia, China, Hong Kong, Indonesia, Japan, Malaysia, Philippines, Singapore, South Korea and Thailand. As a show of the new assertiveness of Japan, US was neither invited nor consulted previously and

---

66. Fertilizer plants in Indonesia were completed in 1983 and in Malaysia in 1986. Takeshi Imagawa, "ASEAN-Japan Relations", *Keizaigaku-Ronsan* 30, 3 (May 1989): 121–42, http://civilisations.revues.org/1664?file=1/, accessed 12 Oct. 2016.
67. Haddad, "Japan, the Fukuda Doctrine, and ASEAN": 24.

it was stated that the AMF would not necessarily coordinate its activity with the IMF.[68]

This proposal was scuttled by the United States, which vehemently opposed any measure that would diminish American influence in the region. As de Miguel says, the effects of this failure were profound:

> The Asian financial crisis showed the shortcomings of Japan's leadership. The episode of the AMF was reminiscent of the shyness deployed by Japan in the late 70s in Indochina. Japan's prestige in the region never recover[ed] fully from the failure to create the AMF because of the US opposition. In contrast China managed to use the Asian financial crisis as an opportunity to introduce herself as a meaningful player in the region. Japan was neither able nor willing to stop this development. The creation of ASEAN + 3 meant that Japan could not invoke for itself the role of main Asian interlocutor of the region anymore.[69]

Japan's position reflected a long-standing tendency to bow meekly to demands from the US government. Effectively, Japan sacrificed its interests in ASEAN in favour of maintaining close ties with the US government.

All this does not mean that the Japanese government has done nothing for the ASEAN countries. Following the announcement of the Fukuda Doctrine, Japan provided more than US$50 billion in ODA to the Southeast Asian nations. Despite this generosity, Japan found out in 2005 that it had few friends in ASEAN. That year Japan—in the face of firm opposition from China—made a strong effort to secure support from UN member states for its bid for a permanent seat on the UN Security Council. Japan was surprised to discover that of the ten ASEAN member states, only Singapore publicly supported its campaign. Vietnam supported it privately, but the other eight ASEAN member states remained silent or neutral.

In reflecting on its relations with the ten ASEAN states, Japan might want to ponder why so few ASEAN states were prepared to support it, publicly or privately, despite its friendship with ASEAN and despite having provided much more aid to the ASEAN countries than China did. One obvious answer that some Japanese could provide is that the relatively weak ASEAN states have become frightened of a rising

---

68. Emilio de Miguel, "Japan and Southeast Asia: From the Fukuda Doctrine to Abe's Five Principles", UNISCI Discussion Paper 32, May 2013, https://revistas. ucm.es/index.php/UNIS/article/viewFile/44792/42219/, accessed 12 Oct. 2016.
69. Ibid.

and powerful China, and there would be an element of truth in this response. However, the absence of ASEAN support for Japan grew also out of Japan's failure to honour Fukuda's promise of developing a "heart-to-heart" relationship with the ASEAN countries. This is why this section on ASEAN-Japan relations began with a harsh assessment of Japan's attitude towards its fellow ASEAN societies. Many people in ASEAN feel that the Japanese in their hearts do not respect the rest of Asia but continue to feel that theirs is a culturally superior society. The writer and human rights activist Debito Arudou describes this feeling of cultural superiority in an article in the *Japan Times*:

> ... the "Japanese only" signs and rules that refuse entry and service to "foreigners" on sight (also excluding Japanese citizens who don't "look Japanese"); the employers and landlords who refuse employment and apartments—necessities of life—to people they see as "foreign"; the legislators, administrators, police forces and other authorities and prominent figures that portray "foreigners" as a national security threat and call for their monitoring, segregation or expulsion. But this exclusionism goes beyond a few isolated bigots in positions of power, who can be found in every society. It is so embedded that it becomes an indictment of the entire system. In fact, embedded racism is key to how the system "works." ... Japanese are constantly fed a mantra about their country's uniqueness and, therefore, by definition, how Japanese are different from non-Japanese. It's one thing to be made to feel special (national narratives have precisely that role), but it's another to constantly infer that foreigners are merely temporary guest workers (if not criminals, terrorists, etc.) and can never really belong in Japanese society.[70]

It is an open question whether a change in government policies can alter Japanese cultural attitudes towards the ASEAN countries and make Japan treat them with genuine respect. One symbolic move would be easy to accomplish. Japan has routinely sent senior-ranked ambassadors to EU capitals and more junior ambassadors to ASEAN capitals. Since the EU today represents the past and Asia, including ASEAN, represents the future, Japan could reverse this policy and assign senior diplomats to ASEAN capitals.

Japan could also step up the implementation of its commitments in the ASEAN countries. For example, China has offered to build a

---

70. Debito Arudou, "Tackle Embedded Racism before It Chokes Japan", *Japan Times*, 1 Nov. 2015, http://www.japantimes.co.jp/community/2015/11/01/issues/tackle-embedded-racism-chokes-japan/, accessed 12 Oct. 2016.

Kunming–Singapore railway. The *Bangkok Post* reported in January 2016 that Japan had agreed in principle to build an East-West line from Cambodia to Myanmar "linking a border village in Kanchanaburi with Cambodia".[71] The ASEAN region will be watching to see whether China or Japan will build a better train system, and whether Japan will share advanced transportation technology with ASEAN countries.

Another way Japan might demonstrate support for ASEAN would be a "big-bang" project in a field such as energy, where it is clearly a world leader. Japan uses one-tenth as much energy as China for every unit added to GNP. In part this is because Japan has moved many heavy-duty manufacturing plants overseas, including some to China. But the Japanese have also devised ingenious ways to reduce energy consumption. The economically and culturally diverse ASEAN countries could provide Japan an opportunity to test their energy-efficient technology in a variety of contexts, benefiting not only the rest of Asia but also the entire planet.

In short, 38 years after launching the Fukuda Doctrine, Japan needs to re-engage with ASEAN. The year 2017 marks the 50th anniversary of the birth of ASEAN and would be an ideal time to relaunch the Fukuda Doctrine by preparing a new plan of engagement with ASEAN for the next 50 years. Such a plan could embrace exciting new projects, such as building new high-speed train networks and helping ASEAN countries manage and reduce their energy consumption. However, economic cooperation alone is not sufficient to change the chemistry of ASEAN-Japan relations.

That would require a major effort to fulfil one of the key pillars of the Fukuda Doctrine: the development of what Fukuda called "heart-to-heart" understanding. Fukuda emphasized that a heart-to heart relationship could not be a "one-way street serving only to introduce Japan's culture to our neighbours", and that "We are also introducing the ancient and glorious cultures of Southeast Asia to the Japanese people".[72] It would be instructive for the Japanese Ministry of Education, Culture, Sports, Science and Technology (Monbushō) to examine whether Japanese awareness and understanding of Southeast Asian cultures has increased during the last 40 years. Anecdotal

---

71. Chatrudee Theparat, "Tokyo to Help with East-West Rail Link", *Bangkok Post*, 28 Jan. 2015, http://www.bangkokpost.com/news/general/460975/tokyo-to-help-with-east-west-rail-link/, accessed 12 Oct. 2016.
72. "Speech by Takeo Fukuda": 69–73.

evidence suggests that there is little awareness of Southeast Asia among the Japanese public.

Many Japanese would be surprised to learn about the extraordinary cultural diversity of Southeast Asia. The success of ASEAN in managing cultural diversity is a key reason why the Japanese should make a deep effort to understand the heart and soul of ASEAN regional cooperation. In addition to offering valuable lessons in the management of diversity, ASEAN also provides an ideal platform for Japan to launch a process of deeper re-engagement with the rest of Asia. Every major culture and civilization of Asia is represented within ASEAN. By developing warm relations with the diverse ASEAN cultures, the Japanese people will also develop a cultural sensitivity to the diversity of the Asian population as well as a deeper cultural understanding of Theravada Buddhists and Christians, Confucianists and Hindus, Muslims and Taoists, all of whom can be found within Southeast Asian societies.

Southeast Asian nations have distinctive national costumes made from locally produced fabrics, and these fashions could also provide one way to help the Japanese understand the region's diversity. In 2006, several Japanese ministers (including Yuriko Koike, who was then minister of environment) were supporting a "Cool Biz" campaign that encouraged the wearing of lighter clothing in hot weather to reduce the need for air conditioning. Kishore was invited along with other policy makers and diplomats from other Asian countries to become fashion models and walk down a catwalk wearing clothing that was in line with that concept. The ability to cross cultures comfortably is a Southeast Asian strength. Kishore was raised as a Hindu in Singapore, which opened the door to a wide range of clothing. However, for this Cool Biz event he chose to wear a silk batik shirt from Indonesia, the world's largest Islamic society. Japan's Cool Biz campaign is an annual affair, and Japan might consider introducing this ASEAN style to the Japanese public, encouraging the use of clothing from Southeast Asia that is specially designed for hot tropical weather. Japanese perceptions of Southeast Asia would change if the people of Tokyo were confronted by a dazzling array of Southeast Asian clothes when they boarded their commuter trains to go to work. These could include the *sue phraratchatan* (Thailand), *teluk beskap* (a combination of the Javanese jacket and sarong), *longyi* (Myanmar), *áo dài* (Vietnam — although Vietnamese men wear it now only for special occasions), *kebaya* (a women's garment worn in several countries), and *barong Tagalog* (Philippines). Japanese would experience the diversity of

Southeast Asia at first hand, and it would be a real eye-opener and a pleasure for them.

Other measures are needed to develop a deeper knowledge of the diversity of Southeast Asia. One small step would be to insert a chapter on Southeast Asian history into school textbooks. If every Japanese child knew the names of the ten ASEAN countries, it would be a substantial step forward. Today, we would guess that the average Japanese citizen knows the names of more European than ASEAN countries.

If the Japanese population can, over time, develop a deeper knowledge and understanding of Southeast Asian cultures and societies, Japan will have taken a first critical step towards engaging the Asian century. If this leads to a deeper respect for Southeast Asia, even though its societies are much poorer than Japan's, it will help Japan learn to engage with the rest of Asia in a more heart-to-heart fashion. Japan would do well to make a deeper understanding of and deeper engagement with the ASEAN countries a strategic priority.

Chapter

4

Pen Sketches

This book emphasizes the remarkable diversity of Southeast Asia. This chapter's pen sketches of each of the ten ASEAN countries have an ambitious goal: to draw out the "soul" of each country. These sketches also share the main achievements of each country and the significant challenges they face (which are often, fortunately, problems that flow from success). Each country has something to contribute to ASEAN, and each can benefit from ASEAN in different ways.

When children in the 28 EU member states study their history, their textbooks inevitably emphasize their shared Greco-Roman heritage. If they visit the Roman Parthenon or the Greek Acropolis, they can identify these ancient monuments as part of their own heritage. By contrast, Southeast Asia's amazing historical monuments do not signify a common heritage. Cambodians identify with Angkor Wat, and Myanmar people identify with Pagan. Each ASEAN country emphasizes its own distinct cultural identity, drawing on different civilizations, not a single one.

The diversity is demonstrated also in the writing scripts that ASEAN countries use. Europeans write in many languages: English and French, Spanish and German. But they use the same Latin script and alphabet (aside from the older Greek alphabet, of course). By contrast, the ten ASEAN countries write in at least six scripts (Latin, Thai, Lao, Burmese, Khmer and Jawi[1]), and that is only counting official languages. This linguistic diversity is almost unique to Southeast Asia,

---

1. The Jawi script is used in daily life in more conservative Malay-populated areas in Malaysia, in signboards and religious schools in Brunei, and in government signs in some provinces of Indonesia.

as members of other regional organizations, such as the Arab League and Mercosur, share a common script.

In the European Union, there is only one form of government. All EU members are democracies. Indeed, it is a condition of EU membership that an EU member state must be a democracy. Spain and Portugal could only join the EU in 1986, after they abandoned the Franco and Salazar dictatorships. By contrast, there is a great diversity of governments in the ten ASEAN countries: from democracies to military rule, from an absolute monarchy to Communist Party rule. This diversity of governance systems could make meaningful regional cooperation difficult, but the pragmatic working culture of ASEAN has overcome the differences.

The real diversity of the ten ASEAN countries comes out in the religions they practise. There are Christians, Muslims, Buddhists, Hindus, Confucianists and Taoists in Southeast Asia, and within each of these traditions there is even more diversity. Malaysia and Brunei have adopted Islam as their official religion. Indonesia has many more Muslims, but it advocates the Pancasila philosophy, which is based on five key principles, one of which is respect for different religions. Myanmar, Thailand, Laos, Cambodia and Vietnam have Buddhist populations. But the predominant Mahayana form of Buddhism practised in Vietnam is very different from the Theravada Buddhism practised in the other four countries. This remarkable religious diversity of Southeast Asia stands in sharp contrast to the common Christian heritage of the EU member states, the common Islamic heritage of the Arab League, and the common Christian heritage of the Organization of American States, even accounting for religious minorities (Christian Arabs, European Jews, Bosnian Muslims). Of course, religious conflicts can break out within a great religious faith— for instance, between Catholics and Protestants, or between Shias and Sunnis. That makes it all the more striking that Southeast Asia seems to have both the deepest diversity and the greatest levels of tolerance.

The long-standing diversity of Southeast Asia is enhanced by the different colonial experiences of the different ASEAN countries. Brunei, Malaysia, Myanmar and Singapore experienced British colonialism. Cambodia, Laos and Myanmar were colonized by the French, Indonesia by the Dutch, and the Philippines by the Spanish and Americans. Thailand is the only Southeast Asian country not to have been colonized by any European power.

These different colonial experiences mattered a great deal, especially in the early years of ASEAN. Even though Southeast Asian countries had been neighbours for millennia and had organic links over the ages, many of these traditional links had been abruptly cut off by the different colonial masters. Growing up in Singapore, for example, we learned a lot about British history. We had almost zero exposure to the history of our neighbours, such as Indonesia or Thailand, the Philippines or Vietnam.

The situation has improved somewhat in recent years, but there is still much to be done to build an understanding of the unique character of each ASEAN country. In a 1,000-word pen sketch it will, of course, be difficult to draw out the complex character of each ASEAN country. At best, each pen sketch can provide an appetizer that we hope will stimulate a desire to understand each ASEAN country better. These pen sketches will follow alphabetical order, beginning with Brunei and ending with Vietnam.

Brunei

With a population of less than half a million, Brunei is the smallest member state of ASEAN by population. Yet, it is the second wealthiest in per capita terms, after Singapore. A small, wealthy state is in a vulnerable position, but few in Brunei feel vulnerable as the ASEAN ecosystem of peace has created a congenial environment for the country.

The Sultanate of Brunei ruled a territory that encompassed the island of Borneo and even parts of the Philippines from the 15th to 17th centuries, but it later faced the real possibility of extinction as an independent political entity. As Brunei weakened, it ceded territory, river valley by river valley, to James Brooke, who became the White Rajah of Sarawak in 1841. Brunei became a British protected state in 1888, but the British stood by when Sarawak annexed the Limbang District in 1890, dividing Brunei into two parts. Nevertheless, the British did preserve Brunei from total extinction. Brunei came close again to losing its independent existence in 1963, when Lee Kuan Yew of Singapore encouraged the ruler of Brunei, Sultan Omar Ali Saifuddien III, to join Singapore, Sarawak and Sabah in the Federation of Malaysia. The Sultan demurred. Two years later, when Singapore left Malaysia, his decision not to join Singapore in Malaysia was vindicated.

Even though contemporary Brunei represents a tiny fraction of the Bruneian empire at its zenith, the people of Brunei are lucky that they were left with a tiny fraction of land that has proven to be immensely wealthy in oil and gas reserves. Prudent management of these oil and gas resources and a policy of sharing wealth with its citizens has led to Brunei having the second-highest Human Development Index among the ASEAN countries, second only to Singapore.

As two relatively small and wealthy states in Southeast Asia, Brunei and Singapore have developed close relations. Singapore helped Brunei to develop its civil service and foreign service. When Kishore served as Singapore's ambassador to the UN in the 1980s, he hosted several young Brunei diplomats who came to the Singapore Mission for diplomatic training. The two countries have an interchangeable currency, and Brunei has generously allowed the Singapore military to train in its territory.

Having been independent for more than 30 years, Brunei has matured into a self-confident small state. It successfully held the chairmanship of ASEAN in 2001 and again in 2013, and hosted an East Asia Summit in October 2013. (Sadly, President Obama had to cancel his participation in the East Asia Summit that year because of the threatened US government shutdown. That meant Brunei lost a rare opportunity to host an American president.)

As a result of its deft diplomacy, Brunei faces few external threats, but it does need to deal with internal challenges. Brunei has an absolute monarchy. Sultan Hassanal Bolkiah has proven to be a deft and capable leader since his accession to the throne in 1967, and Brunei has prospered under his rule. However, the aspirations of the country's growing middle class may require the ruling family to adjust its style of governance over time. While Brunei is not likely to become a democracy in the near future, like Indonesia, Malaysia and Singapore, it could enhance its consultative mechanisms to provide an opportunity for its middle-class population to express their political views. The global trend towards greater democratization is not a trend that Brunei can ignore.

Lee Kuan Yew, who was a close friend of both Sultan Hassanal Bolkiah and his father, once suggested to Brunei that it should consider looking at the successful monarchies in the Persian Gulf region as models for the modernization of Brunei. Gulf kingdoms have succeeded in retaining their conservative values, yet they have also successfully opened up to the world. Brunei cannot rely forever on its oil and gas revenues. Indeed, the BP World Energy Outlook projects that if no new sources are found, Brunei may run out of oil reserves in 22 years. It would be wise for Brunei to begin diversifying its economy before then. Tourism will be an easy revenue earner and job creator. To get the tourism industry growing, Brunei should emulate the Gulf kingdoms and allow liquor sales to tourists in five star hotels. If the UAE and Qatar can allow this, Brunei can do so too.

Overall, the future for Brunei looks bright. Having shrewdly preserved its independence and progressively developed its human resources, the country has many assets in place to ensure continual peace and prosperity. It also enjoys close relations with all of its neighbours. A territorial dispute with Malaysia has been contained, and Malaysia and Brunei cooperate closely, especially in the management of oil and gas resources off the coast.

Like Malaysia, the Philippines and Vietnam, Brunei has claims to some islands and rocks in the South China Sea. Like them, it will also have to deal with the competing claims made by China and Taiwan. The only way for Brunei to retain some bargaining leverage in this "great game" is to ensure that ASEAN remains strong and united. Clearly when Brunei defines its strategic priorities for the 21st century, ASEAN will have to be number one on its list. Fortunately, Brunei has the material resources to implement its strategic priorities. It can make no better use of these resources than to invest more in ASEAN.

Cambodia

Is Cambodia a lucky or an unlucky country? One can easily make the case for both sides. In some respects, modern Cambodia is the unluckiest country in Southeast Asia since it is the only country in the region to have experienced genocide. In less than four years, from 1975 to 1979, an estimated 1.7 million Cambodians—one-fifth of the population—died during Pol Pot's brief but brutal rule.[2] This genocide was preceded by five years of civil war after King Sihanouk was deposed in March 1970. And after Cambodia was "liberated" from Pol Pot's rule by Vietnamese forces in 1979, it endured and resisted foreign occupation.

Yet, Cambodia can also be described as a lucky country. Many peoples and nations have disappeared in the past few centuries, and Cambodia could easily have been extinguished as a nation. Angkor

---

2. "Cambodian Genocide Program", Yale University Genocide Studies Program, http://gsp.yale.edu/case-studies/cambodian-genocide-program, accessed 13 Oct. 2016.

was the largest pre-industrial city in the world at its peak in the 12th century, but after its glorious period as the seat of the Khmer empire from the 9th to the 15th centuries, Cambodia weakened and lost territory to two powerful neighbouring states, Thailand and Vietnam. Cambodia could easily have been absorbed by its neighbours, but as it was on the verge of extinction, the Europeans stepped in. In 1863 King Norodom I of Cambodia, who had been installed as the ruler by the Thais, sought the protection of France from Siamese rule. In 1867, the King of Siam gave up his claim over Cambodia to the French, receiving in return control over two large provinces, Battambang and Siem Reap. Both were returned to Cambodia as part of a new border treaty between France and Thailand in 1907. There can be no doubt that the French saved the Cambodian nation from extinction.

Modern Cambodia is associated with two key names: Norodom Sihanouk and Hun Sen. Sihanouk was installed by the French as the King of Cambodia in 1941, in the belief that this young ruler (who was then 18 years old) would be pliable. The French were wrong. Sihanouk wrested independence from the French on 9 November 1953 and soon emerged as one of the leaders of the Third World, hobnobbing with Mao Zedong, Zhou Enlai, Jawaharlal Nehru, Gamal Abdel Nasser and Josip Broz Tito. Sihanouk alternated between being King and prime minister. In either position, he retained absolute power. His rule was mercurial. Unfortunately for him, as a neighbour of Vietnam, Cambodia was sucked into the Vietnam War. The North Vietnamese used Cambodian territory to ferry supplies to South Vietnam. The Americans retaliated by bombing Cambodia. In this maelstrom, Sihanouk was deposed on 18 March 1970 by Lon Nol. Many people believe that the CIA instigated the coup.

The story of Sihanouk's life mirrors the tragedies Cambodia was experiencing. He fought against the Lon Nol regime, became a prisoner of the Khmer Rouge, and struggled against the Vietnamese occupation. In the 1990s, he returned home to become a titular ruler while Hun Sen dominated the political scene. Kishore had become a friend of his in the 1980s. He remained politically active until he died in October 2012.

Hun Sen's life also encompasses the travails of recent Cambodian history. He started off as a Khmer Rouge cadre working for Pol Pot. In 1977 he defected to the Vietnamese and effectively served as the quisling ruler of Cambodia from 1985 to 1989. When the Vietnamese were forced to leave Cambodia in 1989, Hun Sen's political career should have ended. Instead, with great shrewdness, he reinvented himself politically and even managed to win subsequent elections (although he brutally removed a political competitor, Norodom Ranariddh, in 1997).

Hun Sen switched his allegiance to China after the Vietnamese forces left, to increase Cambodia's geopolitical space vis-à-vis its traditional rivals of Thailand and Vietnam. His strong authoritarian rule has been strongly criticized by the Western media. Still, the two decades of Hun Sen's rule — from 1995 to 2015 — were the most peaceful and productive Cambodia had experienced in a long time. Under his rule, small miracles were achieved. Cambodia's GNP increased from US$900 million in 1990 to US$11.3 billion in 2010. Phnom Penh's water authority under Ek Son Chan outperformed all the British water authorities privatized to great acclaim by Margaret Thatcher, and won the Stockholm Water Prize in 2010.

In recent years, Cambodia's closeness to China has created challenges for ASEAN. In 2012, Cambodia single-handedly blocked an ASEAN joint communiqué because it contained a reference to the South China Sea. In 2015, Cambodia did the same at the ASEAN-China meeting in Kunming. By being helpful to China, Cambodia has received generous assistance from China. As Veasnar Var notes, "Between 1994 and 2013, Chinese investment in Cambodia was about US$10 billion, focused mainly on agriculture, mining, infrastructure projects, hydro-power dams and garment production. Since 1992, China has also provided around US$3 billion in concessional loans and grants to Cambodia."[3]

Yet, Cambodia also faces a paradox here. It can be most useful to China by remaining a member of ASEAN. If its membership were to be cancelled or suspended, its usefulness to China would diminish significantly. It is not in Cambodia's interest to alienate its fellow ASEAN members too much. China should also understand this and demonstrate its good judgement by allowing Cambodia more political space to take independent positions. In short, Cambodia will have to learn to dance more nimbly in the geopolitical game to retain its usefulness and relevance.

---

3. Veasna Var, "Cambodia Should Be Cautious When It Comes to Chinese Aid", *East Asia Forum*, 9 July 2016, http://www.eastasiaforum.org/2016/07/09/cambodia-should-be-cautious-when-it-comes-to-chinese-aid/, accessed 13 Oct. 2016.

Indonesia

One key word should always be used to describe Indonesia: resilient.

As the world's largest archipelagic state, with islands stretching nearly one-eighth of the world's circumference from east to west and more than 1,000 miles from north to south and with enormous ethnic, religious and linguistic diversity, Indonesia could have come apart (like Yugoslavia) at several points in its history. Instead, through several major crises, Indonesia has hung together and remained relatively peaceful, while steadily growing its economy.

Indonesia's relative success is not easy to explain. It is a large and complex country. But one reason why it eventually succeeded may be that it had the right leader for each epoch of its history. Three in particular stand out: Sukarno, Suharto and Susilo Bambang Yudhoyono (SBY). Sukarno delivered unity, Suharto delivered prosperity, and SBY consolidated Indonesia's democracy.

Sukarno ruled Indonesia from 1945 to 1967. He was a fiery nationalist leader who declared Indonesia's independence, then led the violent struggle that eventually achieved it. His economic policies were disastrous (with the Indonesian economy growing at only 2 per cent per year during his term). However, he may have delivered something more important in the early years of Indonesia: a sense of nationhood.

This sense of belonging to one country was a remarkable achievement as the current configuration of Indonesia as a single unit did not exist until the Dutch, over a period of nearly 400 years, created a single colony. The great empires of Srivijaya (7th to 13th centuries CE) and Majapahit (13th and 14th centuries CE) could command obedience from ports and chiefs across much of Indonesia (and parts of contemporary Malaysia) but not all of it. The Bataks of Sumatra and the Papuans of West Papua could not be more different culturally.

Yet, Sukarno was able to take the enormously diverse cultural fabric of Indonesia and weave together a single nation. He was a brilliant orator. With his great speeches, he spun a dream of a common destiny. Years later, in the 1990s, when Indonesian national TV ran a series of programmes on the different ethnic groups of Indonesia, many Indonesians were surprised to discover the extent of their own ethnic diversity. Sukarno engendered national unity with the principles of Pancasila and by getting the Indonesians to adopt a common language, Bahasa Indonesia, based on Malay, and not Javanese, the first language of the largest single ethnic group in Indonesia.

General Suharto came to power on the back of a violent transition in 1965. Millions died. Under a military strongman, Indonesia could have suffered the same fate as Burma, Pakistan, Iraq and Syria. Instead, Suharto modernized his country by gradually opening up its economy and providing much needed political stability. During his reign, Indonesia's economy grew from US$8.42 billion in 1967 to US$135.08 billion in 1998. More important, he eradicated poverty and significantly improved living standards. This is why the UN's Food and Agriculture Organization conferred a gold medal on Suharto in November 1985 for Indonesia's achieving self-sufficiency in growing rice.

After Suharto stood down during the Asian Financial Crisis in 1998, the popular Western verdict was that his downfall was due to crony capitalism. Undoubtedly, there was corruption involving his family. Yet it is also true that Suharto laid the foundations for a strong Indonesian economy. As Adam Schwarz said at the time:

> Economically speaking, the Suharto regime has done many things right. It has used the country's oil wealth relatively wisely, investing in rural infrastructure, schools, and health clinics. By developing a manufacturing base before its reserves were depleted, Indonesia, unlike almost all other OPEC members, has avoided a crippling dependency on petroleum ... Lower tariffs beginning in the mid-1980s and a plentiful supply of cheap labour have combined to make the country a major exporter of light manufactures.[4]

Without the strong economic foundations laid by Suharto, Indonesia may not have emerged as a stable democracy in the 21st century.

After Suharto fell in 1998, he was succeeded by relatively weak presidents who did not stay long in office. Fortunately, SBY was elected president in 2004 and ruled Indonesia for ten years. A former general, President SBY was an astute military strategist[5] as well as a scholar who read widely and worked hard to strengthen Indonesia's democratic institutions. Even though he was not able to replicate the rapid economic growth of the Suharto years, the development of democracy in his time made any return to military rule impossible. This democratic spirit enabled the election as his successor of the

---

4. Schwarz, "Indonesia after Suharto".
5. Endy M. Bayuni, "SBY, the Military Strategist Besieged by War on Two Fronts", *Jakarta Post*, 25 Nov. 2009, http://www.thejakartapost.com/news/2009/11/25/sby-military-strategist-besieged-war-two-fronts.html, accessed 10 Oct. 2016.

improbable Jokowi, a former city mayor who comes from a remarkably humble background.

We can be optimistic about Indonesia's future. McKinsey has predicted that by 2030, Indonesia will have the seventh-largest economy in the world. It bases its optimism on the large consuming class, rapid urbanization, abundance of skilled workers, and market opportunities in consumer services, agriculture, fisheries, resources and education.[6]

Despite these many favourable trends, Indonesia continues to face real challenges that Jokowi will have to deal with. On the economic front, Indonesia could be held back by a strain of economic nationalism that has been around since Sukarno's days. Many Indonesian tycoons understandably want to keep the large Indonesian market for themselves. They resist opening the economy to competitors, including businesses from ASEAN. If Jokowi cannot outmanoeuvre the economic nationalists, he could end up making the same tragic mistake that another middle power, Brazil, made: relying on its domestic market to promote economic growth. Indonesia should follow the example of China instead. If Indonesia is unwilling to open up and compete with fellow ASEAN countries in what, in global terms, would be described as a "baby pool" of competition, it is only crippling its ability to develop an economy that can compete with the world.

The other challenge that Indonesia faces is from jihadists. Indonesia's track record of promoting tolerance and understanding among different religious communities is excellent. Yet it is also true that Jakarta is the only ASEAN capital to have experienced a car bombing of a hotel, on 5 August 2003. The ability of ISIS to recruit 514 fighters[7] (as of March 2015) from Indonesia to fight in Iraq and Syria is also troubling, though it is a much lower number in per capita terms than in many European countries. Any Indonesian leader, even one as popular as Jokowi, will find it difficult to come down hard on extremists while preserving Indonesia's culture of openness and

---

6. Raoul Oberman *et al.*, "The Archipelago Economy: Unleashing Indonesia's Potential", McKinsey & Company, http://www.mckinsey.com/insights/asia-pacific/the_archipelago_economy, accessed 13 Oct. 2016.

7. Catriona Croft-Cusworth, "Beware ISIS' Threat to Indonesia", *National Interest*, 24 Mar. 2015, http://nationalinterest.org/blog/the-buzz/beware-isis-threat-indonesia-12472, accessed 13 Oct. 2016.

tolerance. One key goal of many of these extremists is to promote polarization. Such polarization could well test Indonesia's resilience.

One important reason why ASEAN has succeeded is because of Indonesian wisdom. As the largest ASEAN member (with over 40 per cent of ASEAN's population) Indonesia could have stifled ASEAN's growth by trying to dominate it. Instead, Suharto wisely decided to take a step back and allowed smaller ASEAN states, such as Malaysia and Singapore, to take the lead. He was always supportive of ASEAN.

So too was President SBY. President Jokowi is still warming up to ASEAN. Unfortunately, President Jokowi attended his first ASEAN meeting on 12 November 2014 soon after taking office on 20 October 2014. He was not psychologically prepared for it. After listening to a series of mechanical speeches from various leaders of the meetings with ASEAN's dialogue partners, President Jokowi complained to Singapore PM Lee Hsien Loong about the long, boring speeches, which he saw as a waste of time.[8]

President Jokowi's impatience was understandable. He wanted to focus on economic development, not listen to speeches. Yet, Indonesia's success also depends on a stable geopolitical environment enveloping Indonesia. Boredom in geopolitics is a good thing. It signifies that peace and harmony is dominating the region. By contrast, excitement in ASEAN Plus One meetings would signify geopolitical turbulence. Given the significant weight that Indonesia has in ASEAN affairs, President Jokowi should show more forbearance towards ASEAN processes. Strong Indonesian support for ASEAN is critical for ASEAN's success. Fortunately, the latest signals from Jakarta indicate that President Jokowi is getting more enthusiastic about ASEAN.

President Barack Obama, who spent four years of his childhood in Indonesia—from 1967 to 1971—described the extraordinary optimism Indonesia radiates. In a speech in November 2010, he said: "While my Indonesian friends and I used to run in fields with water buffalo and goats—a new generation of Indonesians is among the most wired in the world—connected through cell phones and social networks."[9] More important, he praised the spirit of tolerance that radiates through Indonesia. In his words: "Bhinneka Tunggal Ika—unity in diversity.

---

8. This was told to Kishore by an Indonesian diplomat.
9. "Remarks by the President at the University of Indonesia in Jakarta, Indonesia", White House, 10 Nov. 2010, https://www.whitehouse.gov/the-press-office/2010/11/10/remarks-president-university-indonesia-jakarta-indonesia, accessed 12 Oct. 2016.

This is the foundation of Indonesia's example to the world, and this is why Indonesia will play such an important part in the 21st century."

Laos

There was no guarantee that Laos would emerge as an independent country in the 20th century. Like Cambodia, Laos' identity was protected by French colonial rule. What is now the People's Democratic Republic traces its roots to the 14th-century Lan Sang kingdom, which held sway on both sides of the Mekong River, in what is now Laos and Thailand's northeast. By the 17th century an independent Lao cultural identity was well established, but Lan Sang had split into a series of small principalities under the sway of Siam. For centuries upland Laos has been affected by the rise and fall of the powers to the south, as well as its neighbours over the mountains, Burma, Vietnam and China to the north. Vietnam took the lead in the 20th century, with the Communist takeover of Indochina in 1975. Now Vietnamese influence is being replaced by Chinese influence. In short, landlocked, mountainous Laos is one of the most vulnerable states of Southeast Asia.

Laotian language and culture stem from the same roots as Thailand's. Indeed, the Isan people of Northeast Thailand feel a greater cultural affinity with the people of Laos than with Bangkok. Laos' links with Siam were always strong, and the Laotian principalities were Siamese provinces for most of the 19th century. It was the French who liberated Laos from Siamese rule in 1893 and sealed Laotian independence by treaties with Thailand in 1904 and 1907. If not for this French intervention, Laos would have probably remained part of the Siamese kingdom in the 20th century.

The Vietnam War had devastating consequences for Laos. As the United States believed that North Vietnamese forces were using Laotian territory to transport men and weapon to South Vietnam, Laos was bombed mercilessly by American aircraft. More than two million tons of bombs were dropped on Laos (2.5 million tons compared to 2.7 million and 4.6 million tons of bombs dropped on Cambodia and Vietnam respectively). President Obama, the first American president to visit Laos, admitted that America had over-bombed Laos. He said, "Over the course of roughly a decade, the United States dropped more bombs on Laos than Germany and Japan during World War II. Some 270 million cluster bomblets were dropped on this country ... By some estimates, more bombs per capita were dropped on Laos than any other country in the world."[10]

Despite this, Laos was not wracked by a major civil war, unlike Cambodia and Vietnam. A coalition government composed of right-wing, left-wing and neutral factions continued to function in Laos during much of the Vietnam War. After the fall of Saigon, the Communists also took over Laos, but it was a relatively peaceful affair. This may at least partially explain why the Laotian Communist rulers were far less brutal than their Cambodian and Vietnamese counterparts. The benign influence of the neutralist leader, Prince Souvanna Phouma, who remained an adviser to the Communist Laotian regime until his death in 1984, may have been another reason.

Laos remained under Vietnamese domination from 1975 to 1990. When the Soviet Union collapsed and Vietnam was forced to change, to give up its occupation of Cambodia, and to open its economy to the world, Laos followed suit. Vietnam joined ASEAN in 1995. Laos followed in 1997.

The foundations for Laos' economic progress were laid in the 1990s, as the country progressively engaged America's allies, especially Japan. The building of two bridges across the Mekong to Thailand in 1994 and 2006 further reinforced Laotian engagement with Thailand and other free market economies. Laos has also been exporting energy, especially hydropower, to Thailand. Its energy exports to Thailand have grown. In 1993 Laos and Thailand signed their first MOU, by which Laos supplied 1,500MW of power to Thailand. According to the most recent power purchase scheme, this figure has gone up to 7,000MW.[11] Given its close cultural affiliations with Thailand, Laos will always have to worry about excessive economic dependence on Thailand as that could increase Thailand's ability to dominate Laos. This is why it would be wise for Laos to hedge its bets and develop close economic ties with its other neighbours, including Vietnam and China.

In the 1990s, China emerged as a major foreign aid donor to Laos. Its annual aid went up from US$10 million in 1990 to US$85 million

---

10. "Remarks by President Obama at the Cooperative Orthotic and Prosthetic Enterprise (COPE) Centre", White House, 7 Sept. 2016, https://www.whitehouse.gov/the-press-office/2016/09/07/remarks-president-obama-cooperative-orthotic-and-prosthetic-enterprise, accessed 12 Oct. 2016.
11. "Country Profile: Laos", International Hydropower Association, http://www.hydropower.org/country-profiles/laos, accessed 13 Oct. 2016.

in 2012. Laotian foreign policy in turn became more pro-Chinese and noticeably less pro-Vietnamese. As a small and relatively vulnerable state bordering China, Laos has wisely trimmed its sails and moved with the prevailing geopolitical winds. Yet Laos has also worked hard to strengthen ASEAN. It recognizes that ASEAN provides a valuable strategic umbrella for the smaller Southeast Asian states.

Over the long term, there are few guarantees of independence and self-determination for a country like Laos. The presumption that small states have the right to be independent and sovereign is a gift from the UN Charter of 1945. As long as the norms of the UN Charter and also the ASEAN Charter remain in force, Laos need not worry about losing its political independence. But for most of its history, there was no such guarantee.

What is certain is that Laos will continue to be subject to contending geopolitical forces. In the 21st century, Laos must deal with greater geopolitical rivalry between the US and China. Its neighbours will face a similar challenge. The wisest thing that Laos can do to protect its independence and freedom of manoeuvre is to become one of the leading champions of ASEAN.

When Laos assumed the chair of ASEAN in January 2016, several questions were asked about its ability to lead the group. Would Laos emulate Cambodia and block references to the South China Sea in ASEAN communiqués? Could it comfortably host leaders of both America and China on its soil? In the end, Laos passed the test of ASEAN chairmanship with flying colours. It secured agreement on a joint communiqué with reference to the South China Sea at the AMM in July. In September 2016, President Obama's visit to Laos for the ASEAN Summit meetings attracted global attention. At the same summit, Chinese Premier Li Keqiang cut a cake to mark the 25th anniversary of ASEAN-China dialogue relations. For a small and relatively poor country with a population of only 6.8 million, Laos showed its fellow ASEAN neighbours what deft diplomacy could accomplish.

Malaysia

Malaysia is truly a paradoxical country. When viewed through a microscope, it appears to be full of problems. Yet a helicopter view makes clear that Malaysia is one of the most successful Third World countries.

Its economic track record is hard to beat. Since Malaysia gained independence from the British in 1957, its GNP has grown from US$7 billion to US$208 billion. Its per capita income has also grown significantly. This was already clear in the early 1990s. Greg Lopez of the Australian National University notes:

> In 1993, the World Bank in its publication *The East Asian Miracle: Economic Growth and Public Policy* identified eight miracle East Asian economies—including Malaysia—that had real GDP growth of around or above four per cent from 1960 to 1990, which was far better than the rates achieved since the Industrial Revolution. More importantly, this economic growth benefited the poorest in society. Malaysia was also one of thirteen countries identified by the Growth Report to have recorded average growth rates of more than 7 per cent per year for twenty five years or more. Malaysia achieved this spectacular performance from 1967 to 1997.[12]

A visitor arriving in Malaysia today will be impressed by the modern airport, the tallest buildings in Southeast Asia (the Petronas Towers), beautiful highways, thriving plantations and industries, and world-class resorts. Indeed, Malaysia's track record is envied by most Third World countries. Its economic development record in Southeast Asia is second only to Singapore's in the last 50 years.

Yet, from the micro perspective, it seems to be a country riddled with problems. Ethnic tensions between the majority Malay population and the minority Chinese population continue to fester, although there has been no repetition of the bloody ethnic riots of 1969.

The ruling party, the United Malays National Organisation, has proven resilient despite decades of internal political turmoil. The much-loved first prime minister of Malaysia, Tunku Abdul Rahman, was deposed by his deputy, Tun Abdul Razak, in 1970, in the wake of the 1969 riots. Razak also made enormous contributions to Malaysia's economic development. When he died relatively young, at the age of 54, in 1976, his brother-in-law Tun Hussein Onn held office briefly before handing over power to Malaysia's strongest ruler, Dr Mahathir, who served as PM for over two decades from 1981 to 2003.

---

12. Greg Lopez, "Malaysia: A Simple Institutional Analysis", *Malaysia Today*, 22 Aug. 2011, http://www.malaysia-today.net/malaysia-a-simple-institutional-analysis/, accessed 13 Oct. 2016.

Dr Mahathir deserves much of the credit for the success of modern Malaysia. He was a determined and hands-on PM who insisted on seeing results, not papers. His Vision 2020 captured the imagination of Malaysians. Under his rule, the capital city was transformed. He made Malaysia a car-owning society, promoting a national car and massive highway projects, with the total road length in Malaysia more than doubling from 31,568km in 1981 to 79,667km in 2003.

He also launched Malaysia on the global stage with his rhetoric. At the tenth session of the Islamic Summit Conference in Putrajaya, on 16 and 17 October 2003, he shook his fellow Islamic leaders by asking why the Islamic world had fallen so far behind the rest of the world. He received a standing ovation for his remarkably courageous speech in which he said the unsayable, including the following paragraphs:

> Over the centuries the *ummah* and the Muslim civilisation became so weak that at one time there was not a single Muslim country which was not colonised or hegemonised by the Europeans. But regaining independence did not help to strengthen the Muslims. Their states were weak and badly administered, constantly in a state of turmoil. The Europeans could do what they liked with Muslim territories …

> We are now 1.3 billion strong. We have the biggest oil reserve in the world. We have great wealth. We are not as ignorant as the Jahilliah who embraced Islam. We are familiar with the workings of the world's economy and finances. We control 57 out of the 180 countries in the world. Our votes can make or break international organisations. Yet we seem more helpless than the small number of Jahilliah converts who accepted the Prophet as their leader. Why?[13]

Sadly, Dr Mahathir's final years in office were marked by controversies, both at home and abroad. The West disowned him after he fell out with Anwar Ibrahim. Then American Vice President Al Gore unwisely and discourteously attacked Dr Mahathir while attending the 1998 APEC Business Summit in Kuala Lumpur, ignoring a key Asian custom of always showing respect to one's host.

---

13. "Dr Mahathir Bin Mohamad at the Opening of the Tenth Session of the Islamic Summit Conference at Putrajaya Convention Centre on October 16", *Sydney Morning Herald*, 22 Oct. 2003, http://www.smh.com.au/articles/2003/10/20/1066502121884.html, accessed 13 Oct. 2016.

How resilient is Malaysia? Certainly, the case for a strong Malaysia can be made. Despite having endured several political crises from 1969 to 2015, the Malaysian economy kept chugging along. The lives of ordinary Malaysians have improved by leaps and bounds. Education has become almost universal. Even more remarkably, Malaysia has practically moved to virtually universal health care. Dr Ravi P. Rannan-Eliya has documented how Malaysia has made astonishing progress in health care. Its mixed public and private system has resulted in high levels of access to medical care, cost savings, and good health outcomes.[14]

Globally, Malaysia has become a highly respected country. When Ian Bremmer, a renowned public intellectual, was asked to name seven countries he would bet on for the future, he included Malaysia in the list.[15] In a *Fortune* article on 22 January 2015, he argued that India, Indonesia, Mexico, Columbia, Poland, Kenya and Malaysia were good places for companies to make strategic investments because they were stable and resilient. "These are markets where it would seem good governance and sustainable growth are likely to go hand in hand," he wrote. "In Malaysia, an incumbent government is offering credible pledges for smarter economic management."

Yet, it is also clear that Malaysia as a society faces many structural challenges, especially in the political sphere. A new social contract of harmonious coexistence needs to be worked out between the Malays and Chinese. Sadly, PM Najib Razak's bold initiative of 1Malaysia failed to gain traction. The growing voice of Islamic fundamentalists in Malaysia is undermining the relatively secular social culture that the two founding PMs of Malaysia, Tunku Abdul Rahman and Tun Abdul Razak, left as their legacy.

This is why in December 2014, 25 prominent Malaysians (including former director-generals of government ministries and former ambassadors) signed an open letter calling for a rational dialogue on Islam in Malaysia. They cited concerns with

---

14. Ravi P. Rannan-Eliya, "Achieving UHC with Limited Fiscal Resources: Lessons for Emerging Economies", Speech, Ministerial Meeting on Universal Health Coverage (UHC): The Post-2015 Challenge, Singapore, 2015, https://www.moh.gov.sg/content/dam/moh_web/PressRoom/Highlights/2015/Universal Health Coverage/Session 2 Slides 3 Rannan-Eliya.pdf, accessed 14 Oct. 2016.

15. Ian Bremmer, "The New World of Business", *Fortune International*, 22 Jan. 2015, http://fortune.com/2015/01/22/the-new-world-of-business/, accessed 12 Oct. 2016.

the current situation where religious bodies seem to be asserting authority beyond their jurisdiction; where issuance of various *fatwa* violate the Federal Constitution and breach the democratic and consultative process of *shura*; where the rise of supremacist NGOs accusing dissenting voices of being anti-Islam, anti-monarchy and anti-Malay has made attempts at rational discussion and conflict resolution difficult; and most importantly, where the use of the Sedition Act hangs as a constant threat to silence anyone with a contrary opinion.[16]

As a result, they argued, "It is urgent that all Malaysians are invested in finding solutions to these long-standing areas of conflict that have led to the deterioration of race relations, eroded citizens' sense of safety and protection under the rule of law, and undermined stability."

There are other problems. Malaysia's steady economic growth has sucked in about two million illegal foreign workers, and this seems to have made Malaysia much less safe than it used to be. The number of violent crimes per 100,000 people increased from 84 in 2004 to 98 in 2013, a 16.7 per cent increase.[17] And sadly, Malaysia's universities are underperforming. The highest-ranked Malaysian university, Universiti Malaya, is ranked number 133 in the world in the QS World University Rankings 2016–17. Dr Ong Kian Ming, the MP of Serdang, said, "even our local universities would admit that they have much progress to make in terms of teaching quality, infrastructure and funding for research, before they can reach the standards of universities in the UK and Australia."[18] This is partially a result of moving away from meritocracy to a *bumiputera* (indigenous Malay) dominated university environment.

A perception of being disadvantaged has created dissatisfaction amongst many non-*bumiputera* Malaysians. A 2011 World Bank report stated, "Brain drain—the migration of talent across borders—touches the core of Malaysia's aspiration to become a high-income nation …

16. "Group of Prominent Malays Calls for Rational Dialogue on Position of Islam in Malaysia", *The Star*, 7 Dec. 2014, http://www.thestar.com.my/news/nation/2014/12/07/group-prominent-malays-calls-for-moderation/, accessed 9 Nov. 2016.

17. Muhammad Amin B. *et al.*, "A Trend Analysis of Violent Crimes in Malaysia", *Health and the Environment Journal* 5, 2 (2014).

18. Haikal Jalil, "Malaysia's Tertiary Education Not up to Par, Says Nurul Izzah", *Sun Daily*, 22 Feb. 2015, http://www.thesundaily.my/news/1335663, accessed 1 Dec. 2016.

Malaysia needs talent, but talent seems to be leaving."[19] Ethnic Chinese make up a disproportionately large proportion of the Malaysian diaspora.

In short, despite its remarkably successful development record, Malaysia cannot afford to rest on its laurels. Fortunately, PM Najib realizes that Malaysia can do better by further opening up its economy. His decision to join the Trans-Pacific Partnership was a bold one. In the short run, it will create economic disruptions. In the long run, it will make Malaysia more economically competitive.

Malaysia is also a strong supporter of ASEAN. Geopolitically, Malaysia is the biggest beneficiary of ASEAN's ecosystem of peace as it has more common borders with fellow ASEAN countries than any other ASEAN country. Its geopolitical location puts it in the heart of ASEAN. Hence, Malaysia is also one of the biggest, if not the biggest, beneficiary of ASEAN economic liberalization. This is one reason why Malaysia under PM Najib was able to launch the ASEAN Economic Community (AEC) on schedule under its chairmanship of ASEAN in 2015. Despite his domestic political travails that year, PM Najib did not lose his focus on ASEAN economic liberalization. If the AEC takes off and boosts ASEAN GDP growth, the Malaysian economy will get a significant boost. Several dynamic Malaysian trade ministers, including Rafidah Aziz (1987–2008) and Mustapa Mohamed (2009–present) have provided sound leadership on ASEAN economic liberalization. If Malaysia continues with this track record of solid commitment towards ASEAN, we will have less to worry about with regard to ASEAN's future.

Myanmar

One of the modern miracles of our time has been the peaceful transition of Myanmar away from decades of military rule. This miracle demonstrates the power of the "ASEAN Way". When the West intervened militarily to remove long-standing military dictators like Saddam Hussein and Gaddafi, it left behind disasters in Iraq and Libya. Western sanctions also failed to remove Assad in Syria. By

---

19. "Malaysia Economic Monitor 2011", World Bank, 2011, http://siteresources. worldbank.org/INTMALAYSIA/Resources/324392-1303882224029/malaysia_ ec_monitor_apr2011_execsumm.pdf, accessed 14 Oct. 2016.

contrast, ASEAN's policy of engaging, not isolating, Myanmar has led to a peaceful transition.

So why did Myanmar finally decide to end decades of self-imposed isolation in the 1990s? Many factors must have contributed. Myanmar leaders travelling to other Southeast Asian countries would have seen how far behind the Myanmar economy had fallen. An equally important factor was geopolitical. When the legendary Indonesian Foreign Minister Ali Alatas was asked why ASEAN had decided to admit Myanmar, he replied that with Myanmar inside ASEAN, it would be protected from Indian and Chinese efforts to pull Myanmar into their respective spheres of influence. And Alatas was dead right.

The Indian belief that Myanmar fell within its sphere of influence was clearly expressed at the Non-Aligned Movement Summit meeting in Colombo, Sri Lanka, in August 1976. Kishore attended a meeting of the Asian group to discuss how seats should be allocated between South Asia and Southeast Asia. The Indian delegation proclaimed that Myanmar belonged to South Asia. When the then Myanmar foreign minister meekly said that Myanmar belonged to Southeast Asia, then Indian Minister of External Affairs Yashwantrao Chavan bellowed, "You don't know! You don't know! Myanmar belongs to South Asia."

Chavan demonstrated a poor understanding of Myanmar's history. For most of its history, its destiny was more closely intertwined with its Southeast Asian neighbours than with South Asia. Indeed, at the height of Burmese power in the 16th century, it created the largest empire ever seen in mainland Southeast Asia. It covered an area including modern Myanmar, Thailand and Laos. Myanmar was ruled from India only when the British arrived and conquered both India and Myanmar.

Traditionally, Myanmar has had a greater fear of China than India. It has fought more wars with China. During the brief period 1765–69, Myanmar repelled four Chinese invasions. This was a key reason why Myanmar decided to end decades of isolation in the 1990s. The leaders of Myanmar could see that self-imposed isolation was only pulling them into the Chinese sphere of economic influence. The decision by the Myanmar government to unilaterally cancel a deal with China to build a major dam in 2011 demonstrated this great desire to balance Chinese influence.

While Myanmar's decision to join ASEAN in 1997 and, as a consequence, to also open up its economy, was a wise one, the country has still not resolved its internal political challenges. The military rulers, led from 2011 by Thein Sein, wisely decided to share political power. However, they have refused to change a constitutional clause preventing Nobel Peace Prize winner Daw Aung San Suu Kyi from assuming the presidency of Myanmar despite her party's famous victory in 2015. She is disqualified as her children are British citizens.

Aung San Suu Kyi has achieved global iconic status. She is almost as widely respected and admired as Nelson Mandela, as she suffered decades of house confinement during various periods of military rule: July 1989 to October 1995, September 2000 to May 2002, and September 2003 to November 2010. The military government could not suppress her completely since she was the daughter of the legendary military figure Aung San, who was sadly assassinated in July 1947. Her global stature means that she can be a real asset for Myanmar.

The challenge that Myanmar faces now is to find a political compromise that is acceptable to both Aung San Suu Kyi and the military leaders. In theory, a full return to democracy and the return of the military to the barracks would solve the problem. However, the military leaders believe that they should have a say in the running of the country. Their experience has taught them that Myanmar's territorial integrity is vulnerable to challenges, mostly from ethnic minorities in the highland areas at Myanmar's borders. Even during the decades of harshest military rule, Myanmar struggled to keep peace with rebel Karen and Shan forces. The civil war with these groups has been going on since 1948. A coalition of six Kachin groups is still fighting the government.

As a member of the majority Burmese ethnic group, Aung San Suu Kyi shares the concerns of the Burmese to preserve national unity. Given her global iconic status as a human rights fighter, many in the West were puzzled and disappointed that she did not speak up against the poor treatment of the Muslim Rohingya population in Arakan province. Kenneth Roth, the executive director of Human Rights Watch, said:

> Aung San Suu Kyi has been disappointing as well. Aware that the army will determine her ability to run for president, she has refrained from criticizing its abuses. And because the vulnerable and stateless Rohingya are so unpopular in Burma, she has refused to come to their verbal defense as they have been violently attacked.[20]

---

20. Kenneth Roth, "Rights Struggles of 2013", Human Rights Watch, 2014, https://www.hrw.org/world-report/2014/essays/rights-struggles-of-2013, accessed 13 Oct. 2016.

Such criticism of both Aung San Suu Kyi and Myanmar's military may not be totally fair. Myanmar is undergoing a messy and complicated political transition. It is never easy for a country to walk out of decades of isolation, even if the isolation was self-imposed. It will take time to rebuild the many public institutions, especially in the public service sector, that were ossified during the decades of isolation. At the same time, Myanmar is a highly multi-ethnic country, with many of the different ethnic groups having a history of controlling their own territories, especially in the highlands. Keeping peace in such a country is always a challenge. The best that the outside world can do is to be patient and allow the people of Myanmar to find the right political compromises. Aung San Suu Kyi may have to make painful political compromises to keep the country together.

The significant economic progress Myanmar has made since joining ASEAN in 1997 demonstrates the country's current potential. Its Human Development Index rose from 0.347 in 1990 to 0.524 in 2013.[21] Its GDP per capita also rose, from US$190.70 in 1990 to US$1,308.70 in 2015 (in constant 2010 prices).[22] Its GDP grew from US$8 billion in 1990 to US$60.8 billion in 2013 and $70.5 billion in 2015 (using the same constant 2010 prices).[23] Myanmar's economic success, though impressive, is just beginning. After Vietnam joined ASEAN in 1995, its GNP went up from US$20.74 billion in 1995 to US$193.6 billion in 2015,[24] an increase of nine times. Myanmar has the same potential for rapid growth as Vietnam.

Even though Myanmar joined ASEAN in 1997, it could only begin to open up its economy after the political transition to Aung San Suu Kyi in 2015. Myanmar can learn economic lessons from its fellow ASEAN countries. It can also take full advantage of the Integration for ASEAN Initiative, which was set up to help Cambodia, Laos, Myanmar and Vietnam integrate into ASEAN. The record of ASEAN

---

21. Expansión, "Myanmar: Human Development Index", Country Economy, http://countryeconomy.com/hdi/burma, accessed 12 Oct. 2016.
22. "GDP Per Capita of Myanmar (Constant 2010 US$)", World Bank, http://data.worldbank.org/indicator/NY.GDP.PCAP.KD?locations=MM, accessed 10 Oct. 2016.
23. "GDP at Market Prices (Constant 2010 US$)", World Bank, http://data.worldbank.org/indicator/NY.GDP.MKTP.KD?locations=MM, accessed 10 Oct. 2016.
24. "GDP of Vietnam (Current US$)", World Bank, http://data.worldbank.org/indicator/NY.GDP.MKTP.CD?locations=VN, accessed 10 Oct. 2016.

development shows that the faster Myanmar opens up its economy, the better it will do in social and economic development.

Myanmar has another advantage. It is emerging as a geopolitical darling of the major powers. It is being actively courted by China and India, the US and Japan. Hence, Myanmar is likely to receive more aid than most other ASEAN countries. China has helped Myanmar significantly with its massive gas pipeline project from the Bay of Bengal to Kunming in China. The pipeline alone contributes US$1.8 billion to the Myanmar treasury per year.[25] India is building the Kaladan Multi-Modal Transit Transport Project, which links its northeastern state of Mizoram with Sittwe Port in Myanmar. In January 2015, Japan agreed to participate in the Dawei Port Project along with Thailand; this aims to develop Dawei in Myanmar into Southeast Asia's largest industrial and trade zone.

At the same time, Myanmar should show its appreciation to ASEAN for having helped with its peaceful political transition by becoming a louder champion of ASEAN. Until recently, Aung San Suu Kyi was somewhat ambivalent about ASEAN personally as she had witnessed the close ties between the previous military rulers and ASEAN. Yet she should accept that these close ties also persuaded the military rulers that they should make political compromises. These compromises paved the way for Aung San Suu Kyi to assume power. An enthusiastic endorsement of ASEAN by Aung San Suu Kyi would be a win-win proposition. It would win her significant regional dividends and also help to boost ASEAN's standing. Indeed, as a Nobel Peace Prize winner herself, she should be the one to nominate ASEAN for the prize.

The Philippines

Within the ASEAN community, the Philippines faces a unique cultural problem. While the other nine ASEAN states have no doubt that they are Asian states, Filipinos are culturally torn between their Asian and Western identities. History explains why. The Philippines endured the longest period of Western colonial rule. From 1565 to 1898, for over 330

---

25. Hong Zhao, "China–Myanmar Energy Cooperation and Its Regional Implications", *Journal of Current Southeast Asian Affairs* 30, 4 (2011): 89–109, http://journals.sub.uni-hamburg.de/giga/jsaa/article/view/502, accessed 14 Oct. 2016.

years, the Philippines was run by the Spanish. This was followed by almost 50 years of American colonial rule, from 1898 to 1946.

The political colonization of the Philippines ended in 1946. However, the mental colonization continued. For several decades after independence, some prominent Filipinos indicated a preference for giving up their independence to become the 51st state of the United States of America. No other population in Southeast Asia would have tolerated such a movement. Rufino D. Antonio, a former congressman, launched a campaign for Philippine statehood—for the Philippines to become the 51st state of the United States. In a letter to the *Manila Times* in May 1972, he said: "I cannot see any treachery in the hearts and souls of six million members of the organization who are fed up with the present corrupt and abusive system and merely want to aspire for a better way of life."[26]

Fifteen years later, in a famous article in the *Atlantic Monthly*, James Fallows pointed out this continuing Filipino dependence on American culture. He said:

> In deeper and more pernicious ways Filipinos seem to have absorbed the idea that America is the center and they are the periphery. Much local advertising plays to the idea that if it's American, it's better. "It's got that stateside caste [*sic*]!" one grinning blonde model says in a whiskey ad. An ad for Ban deodorant warns, "Hold It! Is your deodorant making your skin dark?" The most glamorous figures on TV shows are generally light-skinned and sound as if they grew up in Los Angeles ... "This is a country where the national ambition is to change your nationality," an American who volunteers at Smoky Mountain told me.[27]

When combined with economic uncertainty, this uncertain cultural identity may also explain a certain lack of confidence. Of all the ASEAN countries, the Philippines has the highest degree of emigration. About 100 million Filipinos live in the Philippines. An additional 12 million live overseas. This desire to emigrate reflects a lack of confidence that success can come at home. By contrast, Indonesia, which in per capita terms is poorer than the Philippines,

---

26. Rufino Antonio, "We, the People" (Letters to the Editor), *Manila Times*, 11 May 1972.
27. James Fallows, "A Damaged Culture: A New Philippines?" *The Atlantic*, 1 Nov. 1987, http://www.theatlantic.com/technology/archive/1987/11/a-damaged-culture-a-new-philippines/7414/, accessed 13 Oct. 2016.

has only 5.3 million Indonesians living overseas, or 2 per cent of its population (in contrast to 12 per cent of the Philippines).

This huge Filipino diaspora could now prove to be one of the Philippines' biggest assets. Just as the Indian diaspora, especially in Silicon Valley, has helped to spark India's economic development, the Philippines' diaspora can do the same. The Philippines government should mount a new national strategy to take greater advantage of the country's diaspora.

Yet, these cultural challenges must also be part of the explanation for the troubled history that the Philippines has had since independence. In the 1950s, several major economists predicted that the Philippines would shine as one of the best-performing economies. The United States had left behind a decent public administration. The country enjoyed special access to the large American market. In the 1950s, pundits predicted that South Korea would fail and the Philippines would succeed. Instead, the opposite happened.

Other structural factors no doubt played their part. The many years of Spanish rule had entrenched a feudal system akin to the worst Latin American societies. At the end of World War II, the Philippines failed to carry out any significant land reform. Hence, the Philippines has one of the most concentrated landowning classes amongst the ASEAN countries. As Bonifacio S. Macaranas, assistant professor at the University of the Philippines School of Labor and Industrial Relations, writes, "Poverty in the Philippines has its historical roots in its colonial past, particularly in the feudal work practices and influences that characterized the mode of governance by the Spanish colonial administration for more than 300 years, and sustained as well in other forms by American rule for almost 50 years." [28]

This Latin American–style feudal system may have also contributed to the Philippines suffering probably the worst dictatorial rule in Southeast Asia. Both Thailand and Indonesia also had military dictators. The families of Suharto and Ferdinand Marcos both benefited from their respective reigns. Yet while Suharto also focussed on improving Indonesian livelihoods, Marcos mainly enriched his family. Remarkably, even after the dramatic People Power Revolution that overthrew Marcos in 1986, the Philippines was once again

---

28. Bonifacio S. Macaranas, "Feudal Work Systems and Poverty: The Philippine Experience", International Labour and Employment Relations Association, 2009, http://www.ilera-directory.org/15thworldcongress/files/papers/Track_4/Poster/CS2T_2_MACARANAS.pdf, accessed 13 Oct. 2016.

perceived as having suffered from corrupt presidential rule under Gloria Macapagal-Arroyo from 2001 to 2010, even though she was cleared by the courts.

Despite these challenges, the Philippines has emerged as one of the most promising economies in ASEAN, if not Asia. A few honest and hard-working presidents, including Corazon Aquino, Fidel Ramos and Benigno Aquino, have provided bouts of good governance that have begun to stabilize prospects for the Philippines. Increasingly, several sectors of the Philippines economy have begun to shine. India pioneered the global outsourcing business, especially call centres. Now the Philippines has outstripped India. The Philippines' Contact Center Association estimates that 350,000 call handlers are employed in the Philippines, compared with approximately 330,000 in India.[29]

Like India, the Philippines is becoming a centre of software development. According to the Philippine Software Industry Association their business is among the fastest growing of all the outsourcing sectors in the Philippines, growing by 37 per cent in 2011, with total revenue of US$993 million, and adding nearly 50,000 additional full-time employees.[30] The development of this software industry only confirms that the Philippines has a young, energetic and talented population that can be put to good use. All that the Philippines really needs is good governance. With a modicum of good governance, the Philippines can do well, as demonstrated by the rule of Benigno Aquino from 2010 to 2016. During his years of rule, the Philippines' GDP growth went up from the previous decade's average rate of 4.45 per cent per annum to more than 6 per cent per annum.

So even though the Philippines failed to live up to its promise 50 years ago, it now has the prospect of doing so. Its main challenges used to be internal. They are now being resolved, as there is a strong national consensus that the Philippines should open up its economy and integrate with the world. It is too early to tell what impact the mercurial rule of Duterte will have, but the good news is that he is

---

29. Gregory Walton, "Sarcasm Gives Call Centres in Manila the Edge", *The Telegraph*, 9 Mar. 2015, http://www.telegraph.co.uk/news/newstopics/howaboutthat/11460424/Sarcasm-gives-call-centres-in-Manila-the-edge.html, accessed 13 Oct. 2016.

30. "PHL Emerging as a Strong Software Development Hub", Team Asia, 26 Nov. 2012, http://www.teamasia.com/newsroom/read-client-news.aspx?id=407:phl-emerging-as-a-strong-software-development-hub, accessed 14 Oct. 2016.

likely to be as honest as Ramos and the Aquinos. The Philippines' main challenges are geopolitical, especially because of its dispute with China on the South China Sea. Three other ASEAN member states have similar disputes with China. However, while Brunei, Malaysia and even Vietnam tried to resolve these disputes quietly and pragmatically, the Philippines chose to publicly confront China by taking it to compulsory arbitration at the Permanent Court of Arbitration in the Hague. The Philippines won the judgement, but the Duterte administration recognizes that it cannot be enforced on China. Hence, it is likely to become as pragmatic as its ASEAN neighbours and try bilateral negotiations. Duterte initiated this process of bilateral negotiations by visiting China in October 2016. If these differences can be managed and contained, there is nothing to hold back the Philippines emerging as one of the "tiger" economies of the 21st century.

However, even if the Philippines continues its economic resurgence, its relationship with its fellow ASEAN member states may remain awkward for a while. As the Philippines remains torn between its Asian and Western identities, it risks remaining a cultural misfit within the ASEAN family. These cultural differences surfaced early in the history of ASEAN. President Nathan of Singapore, who attended the inaugural ASEAN meeting in August 1967, told us that the drafting of the final ASEAN declaration was held up by the insistence of the Filipino representative to focus on style rather than substance. He insisted on using American spelling rather than the more commonly used British spelling.

Fortunately, the Philippines has had many brilliant foreign ministers, starting with Carlos Romulo, one of the signatories of the UN Charter. These foreign ministers, including Carlos Romulo's son Bobby and the late Domingo Siazon, developed over time a deep understanding of how the ASEAN family worked. So too did Rod Severino, the successful Filipino secretary-general of ASEAN. This knowledge of ASEAN needs to be more deeply institutionalized in Manila to overcome the cultural distance between the Philippines and the other ASEAN members.

Under Philippines chairmanship, the negotiation on the ASEAN Charter made slow progress, as the Philippines took a Westernized legalistic approach to the drafting. However, when Singapore Ambassador Tommy Koh took over the chairmanship, the negotiation proceeded smoothly. He injected Asian, or, more accurately, ASEAN pragmatism into the drafting process. That episode confirmed that the cultural gap between the Philippines and the rest of ASEAN remains real. It needs to be narrowed.

Changing the Western mindset of the Filipinos and the Filipino elites will not be easy. In a survey of 36 countries worldwide by Gallup Poll in 2014, Filipinos emerged as the most pro-American, followed by Israel. In fact, the survey revealed that Filipinos are more pro-American than Americans themselves.

This is about to change under President Duterte's leadership. In less than four months of his presidency, he travelled to Laos, Indonesia, Brunei, Vietnam, China and Japan. He has said that he wants to prioritize his relations with ASEAN, China and Japan, but his officials have added that he does not want to abandon the United States. In fact, the first country he wanted to visit as president was Brunei—a symbolic and powerful gesture.

President Duterte can become one of ASEAN's most effective leaders. This is important at a time when ASEAN needs strong leadership. Our Filipino friends have several suggestions for President Duterte.

First, he can reaffirm the importance of ASEAN to the Philippines' foreign and trade policy. Of the Philippines' trade, 60 per cent is now with ASEAN and Asia, compared to 60 per cent with the US and EU in previous years. The Philippines benefited greatly from the help of Brunei, Indonesia and Malaysia in settling the Muslim insurgency in Mindanao. The Philippines depends on Vietnam and Thailand for its rice supply. It is in the interest of the Philippines, therefore, to change course and put ASEAN front and centre of its foreign policy.

Second, as chair of ASEAN's 50th anniversary celebrations in 2017, Duterte can use that occasion to bring ASEAN and China together to sign a binding code of conduct on the South China Sea. He can also use this occasion to promote more economic integration between ASEAN and China through the Maritime Silk Road as well as more economic and social integration within ASEAN.

Third and finally, President Duterte can demonstrate his leadership of ASEAN by personally inviting Donald Trump to come and attend the ASEAN Summit, along with President Xi and President Putin. If Duterte can successfully invite these key leaders to attend the 50th Anniversary Summit, it would be a major diplomatic feather in his cap. It would also symbolically demonstrate that the gap between the Philippines and its fellow ASEAN members has narrowed.

Singapore

Singapore was not born. It was aborted. It was expelled from Malaysia on 9 August 1965, when the leaders of Malaysia and Singapore developed irreconcilable differences in their visions for the future direction of Malaysia. And when Singapore was expelled, the only thing that the Malaysian and Singaporean leaders could agree on was that Singapore was likely to fail, as a city cut off from its hinterland could not possibly survive.

For a nation that was destined to fail, Singapore has done extraordinarily well. Sometimes, to liven up a conversation, Kishore likes to make the following claim: not since human history began has any society improved the living standards of its people as quickly and as comprehensively as Singapore. So far, no one has been able to disprove this statement. Singapore's remarkable success deserves note in the Guinness World Records.

What explains this extraordinary success? The simple answer is extraordinary leadership. Like the United States, Singapore was blessed with great founding fathers. The whole world has heard of Lee Kuan Yew. Indeed, the remarkable turnout of global leaders and the magnificent tributes he received at his funeral in March 2015 demonstrated his global standing.

Without Lee Kuan Yew, Singapore would not have had its extraordinary success. Yet, what is less well known is that Lee Kuan Yew worked with a remarkable team of men, especially two other outstanding leaders, Dr Goh Keng Swee and S. Rajaratnam.

The strong camaraderie of this extraordinary bunch was forged by the life-and-death struggle they fought against stronger Communist forces in pre-independence Singapore. Dr Goh Keng Swee colourfully said, "We were like innocent virgins roaming a brothel area. Misfortune could hardly be avoided."[31] Lee Kuan Yew had the courage of a lion in fighting the Communists. Both Dr Goh Keng Swee and S. Rajaratnam were also lions.

They were also great intellectuals. They read voraciously and understood the world well. Dr Goh Keng Swee succeeded as the architect of the Singapore miracle because he studied the Meiji

---

31. Goh Keng Swee, "A Holy Order to Scale New Heights: Dr. Goh Keng Swee's Last Major Speech before Retiring from Politics, 25 September 1984", in *Goh Keng Swee: A Legacy of Public Service*, ed. Emrys Chew and Chong Guan Kwa (Singapore: World Scientific, 2012), p. 311.

Restoration intensively. He was the ultimate pragmatist. Rajaratnam delivered brilliant speeches and rallied the international community to support Singapore. In short, Singapore's success was also a result of brilliant teamwork.

This exceptional team implemented three exceptional policies: Meritocracy, Pragmatism and Honesty (MPH). Indeed, Kishore at the Lee Kuan Yew School shares this MPH formula with every foreign student, assuring them that their country will succeed as well as Singapore if they can implement the formula. Meritocracy means a country picks its best citizens, not relatives of the ruling class, to run the country. Pragmatism means that a country does not try to reinvent the wheel. As Dr Goh Keng Swee would say: "No matter what problem Singapore encounters, somebody, somewhere, has solved it. Let us copy the solution and adapt it to Singapore."[32] Copying best practices is something any country can do. However, implementing honesty is the hardest of the three policies. Corruption is the single biggest reason why most Third World countries have failed. The greatest strength of Singapore's founding fathers was that they were ruthlessly honest. It helped that they were also exceptionally shrewd and cunning.

Yet, it is also true that Singapore has had its fair share of critics. The Western media has been merciless in its criticism. Indeed, many ostensibly well-informed people in the West grew to believe that Singapore was no different from North Korea, run by a dictator called Lee Kuan Yew. One prominent critic was William Safire of the *New York Times*. He wrote, "The determinedly irreplaceable Lee Kuan Yew is the world's most intelligent, and to some most likable, despot."[33] He also described Goh Chok Tong as "the puppet who is keeping the Prime Minister's seat warm for one of Dictator Lee Kuan Yew's sons".[34] In the 1980s and 1990s, Singapore's leaders won multiple legal suits against leading Western newspapers and journals, including the *New York Times*, the *International Herald Tribune*, the *Wall Street Journal*,

---

32. Kishore Mahbubani, "Why Singapore Is the World's Most Successful Society", *Huffington Post*, 4 Aug. 2015, http://www.huffingtonpost.com/kishore-mahbubani/singapore-world-successful-society_b_7934988.html, accessed 12 Oct. 2016.

33. William Safire, "Essay; The Dictator Speaks", *New York Times*, 15 Feb. 1999, http://www.nytimes.com/1999/02/15/opinion/essay-the-dictator-speaks.html, accessed 14 Oct. 2016.

34. William Safire, "Essay; Singapore's Fear", *New York Times*, 20 July 1995, http://www.nytimes.com/1995/07/20/opinion/essay-singapore-s-fear.html, accessed 14 Oct. 2016.

The Economist and the *Far Eastern Economic Review*. They paid the fines, but it led to a history of bad blood between Singapore and the Western media, which damaged Singapore's reputation, especially in the West.

Domestically, too, the Singapore government has had its share of critics. The well-known Singapore novelist Catherine Lim said in June 2014, "We are in the midst of a crisis where the people no longer trust their government, and the government no longer cares about regaining their trust."[35] She cited the use by Singapore's leaders of defamation suits against their opponents as a key factor in engendering such mistrust, saying, "Singaporeans have long got used to a certain belief that colours all their perceptions, namely, that here, there is no level playing field but one massively tilted in favour of an all-powerful, vindictive government that will have no qualms about reducing its opponents to bankruptcy." While the mainstream print media is supportive of the government, social media can be vociferous in its criticism. For this and other reasons, a new political environment is developing in Singapore.

Singapore is fortunate that the two prime ministers who succeeded Lee Kuan Yew have been popular and effective. Goh Chok Tong served as PM from 1990 to 2004 and is widely credited with liberalizing Singapore's political environment. Lee Hsien Loong, the son of Lee Kuan Yew, has also been a great leader of Singapore. His commitment and dedication to Singapore are total. Like his parents, he has an extraordinary intellect. Singapore is blessed to have had three good prime ministers in a row.

What is new in Singapore is that for the first time in almost three decades, Singaporeans do not know the name of their next PM. Several possibilities have surfaced. However, there is not yet a clear consensus on any one. Since Lee Hsien Loong has announced that he plans to step down when he turns 70 in 2022, Singapore may face political uncertainty within a few years.

Political succession is only one of the many challenges that Singapore will face in the coming decades. In his book *Can Singapore Survive* (2015), Kishore has spelled out at least three possible dangers that could dramatically affect Singapore: the danger of a populist party taking off; the danger of US-China geopolitical rivalry tearing Singapore apart; and the danger of black swan events such as the

---

35. Catherine Lim, "An Open Letter to the Prime Minister", 7 June 2014, http:// catherinelim.sg/2014/06/07/an-open-letter-to-the-prime-minster/, accessed 14 Oct. 2016.

emergence of an Arctic maritime route that diminishes the importance of Singapore's port.

One open secret about Singapore is that it has for many years played a quiet but significant leadership role within ASEAN. The idea of an ASEAN Free Trade Area (AFTA) was germinated in Singapore. So too was the idea of an ASEAN Regional Forum (ARF). Similarly, it was PM Goh Chok Tong who first proposed the idea for an Asia-Europe Meeting (ASEM). Yet Singapore also wisely decided that it was not a good idea to take too much credit for these initiatives. It would generate envy and resentment. Hence, it was happy to see other ASEAN states launch these initiatives. As a Thai journalist once commented pithily, whenever Singapore gets a new idea, Thailand becomes pregnant. It was Thailand that launched both AFTA and ASEM.

Singapore plays a valuable role for ASEAN by serving as an intellectual hub. Given its relative political stability and strong political leadership, it can suggest and promote far-sighted ideas. This is why Singapore's short-sighted policies on the ASEAN Secretariat are truly puzzling. As indicated in the concluding chapter, Singapore's insistence on equal payments by ten unequal states to the budget of the ASEAN Secretariat is crippling the growth of the secretariat. To put it bluntly, Singapore is undermining its own national interests by advocating this policy. This policy prevents ASEAN from growing naturally. As one of the biggest beneficiaries of the ASEAN ecosystem of peace, Singapore is shooting itself in the foot with this short-sighted policy.

Singapore needs to continue strengthening ASEAN because, despite its own extraordinary success, it remains vulnerable—as all small states do. The existential challenge Singapore faces is a simple one. To survive, it has to remain paranoid and keep worrying about new challenges. Yet, it also has to retain strong faith in its future to prevent massive migration out of Singapore. Being paranoid and confident at the same time requires an exceptional mental ability.

Thailand

Thailand stands out in at least three respects. First, it is the only Southeast Asian country not to have been colonized by Europeans—a striking fact, but perhaps only a sort of accident. The British (after colonizing Burma and Malaya) and the French (after colonizing

Indochina) may have decided that it was wiser for both of them to maintain a buffer state between their respective spheres of influence. Or one might see Thailand's success in retaining its independence as reflecting the deep tradition of wise Thai diplomacy. For centuries, Thai royal families have learnt geopolitical lessons from the Chinese classic novel the *Romance of the Three Kingdoms*.[36]

Second, Thailand has a rich culture. Japanese scholars have observed privately to Kishore that Japan is drawn to work closely with Thailand because it has a "sweet smell of culture". Other observers of Thailand have made similar comments. Nattavud Pimpa said, "Thai culture is unique and renowned for its complexities."[37]

Third, with China and India re-emerging as great powers hovering over Southeast Asia, Thailand may be uniquely placed to understand both, as its culture draws on both traditions. The Thai monarchy can trace its roots to the 13th century. Thai court traditions are heavily influenced by Indian culture. Even today, many Thai court rituals are carried out by Brahmin priests, in a striking continuity with the first few centuries of our era. Sanskrit is widely used in Thai royal ceremonies. Yet, while the Thai royal court is deeply influenced by Indian traditions, Thailand, more than any other Southeast Asian country (with the obvious exception of Singapore), has absorbed its overseas Chinese community almost completely.

The founder of the Chakri dynasty, King Rama I, was of Chinese descent. He ruled Thailand from 1782 until his death in 1809. King Mongkut, who ruled from 1851 to 1868, was also very proud to proclaim his Chinese lineage. Unlike in, say, Malaysia or Indonesia, Brunei or Vietnam, the overseas Chinese community in Thailand is not seen as foreign. It has been fully integrated and absorbed. Most Chinese have adopted Thai names. They speak Thai fluently and in their souls probably feel more Thai than Chinese. As the scholars Christopher Baker and Pasuk Phongpaichit explain, "The Chinese learnt the Thai language, adopted new forms of behaviour, and identified themselves as citizens of the Thai nation. But at the same

---

36. Malinee Dilokwanich, "A Study of Samkok: The First Thai Translation of a Chinese Novel", *Journal of the Siam Society* 73 (1985): 77–112.
37. Nattavud Pimpa, "Amazing Thailand: Organizational Culture in the Thai Public Sector", *International Business Research* 5, 11 (16 Oct. 2012), http://www. ccsenet.org/journal/index.php/ibr/article/view/21408/13905, accessed 12 Oct. 2016.

time they helped to mould an urban culture that included speech, taste, and aesthetics from their own heritage."[38]

Despite its rich history and culture, and the benefits of not being colonized, Thailand has had remarkable difficulty emerging as a successful modern Asian society. The first Southeast Asian country to have emulated the Japanese or South Korean societies in thoroughly modernizing both its political and economic systems should have been Thailand. Instead, it was Singapore.

Certainly, its economic modernization has succeeded. Thailand's GNP grew from US$14.58 billion in 1965 to US$232.01 billion in 2015, an increase of almost 16 times (Singapore's GNP increased 35.6 times during the same period).[39] The IMF predicts that Thailand's GDP in PPP terms will be US$1,378 billion in 2020. Thailand has a happy economic story to tell overall. Yet, even in the economic realm, it may be missing opportunities. As Dr Chitriya Pinthong told us, "Thailand should at least have participated in the TPP discussion even if it might finally decide not to join. But we were much preoccupied with domestic issues at the time and did not have spare resources to do so."

The political story is much less cheerful. The Thai military continues to play a determining role in politics, with the country put under martial law in 2014. During the Cold War, as Thailand felt threatened by Communist expansion in Indochina, America was happy to support military regimes in Thailand as they were reliable allies for American interests. When the Cold War ended, Thailand was among the first Southeast Asian countries to move towards a more open and liberal democracy. Thai politicians in the 1990s even began preaching the virtues of democracy to their fellow ASEAN countries. Thai newspapers published commentaries criticizing other Southeast Asian governments as undemocratic.

Given this Thai period of democratic preachiness, it is ironic that Thailand has reverted to military rule. All this was the result of Thaksin Shinawatra's party winning several elections in a row—in 2001, 2005 and 2006. Thaksin succeeded because he was able to win the votes of the large and relatively poor population in the northeastern areas of Thailand. He won by delivering goodies to them, such as massively

---

38. Christopher John Baker and Pasuk Phongpaichit, *A History of Thailand* (New York: Cambridge University Press, 2005), p. 207.

39. "GDP of Thailand (Constant 2010 US$)", World Bank, http://databank. worldbank.org/data/reports.aspx?source=wdi-database-archives-(beta), accessed 10 Oct. 2016.

subsidized healthcare services, a three-year debt freeze, grants to villages for creating small businesses, and agricultural subsidies.

Thaksin's success resulted in a shift of power away from the traditional Bangkok establishment that had long dominated political power in Thailand. This powerful Bangkok establishment counter-attacked by starting a Yellow Shirts movement to oppose Thaksin's Red Shirts. Unfortunately, as the Yellow Shirts were a relative minority in numbers, they had to resort to undemocratic means to try to regain power. Some of their measures were quite extreme. They stormed and captured the Bangkok airports, stormed Government House, and blockaded Parliament in 2008.

The Thai people inevitably became tired of this persistent civil strife, more or less continuous since 2006. As a consequence, they passively accepted the return of military rule in 2014. The military coup was led by General Prayuth Chan-o-cha. General Prayuth has declared that this period of military rule will be temporary and Thailand will return to democracy. He said, "We want to see an election that will take place under the new constitution ... that will be free and fair, so that it can become a solid foundation for a complete Thai democracy."[40] He added, "Today, if we go ahead and hold a general election, it will lead to a situation that creates conflict and the country will return to the old cycle of conflict, violence, corruption by influential groups in politics, terrorism and the use of war weapons." In August 2016 a new military-sponsored constitution (Thailand's 17th since 1932) was approved in a national referendum.

The metaphor of Pandora's box may be the most appropriate. As Thaksin has successfully awoken Thai rural voters to the power they can exercise through the ballot box, this empowered rural population cannot be put back to sleep again. They will exercise their power again whenever elections return to Thailand. Thailand faces an uncertain political future as at the time of writing. This political uncertainty could become more acute now that King Bhumibol Adulyadej has passed away, on 13 October 2016.

How resilient is Thailand? In some ways, it has already demonstrated its resilience. Despite the political uncertainties that have gripped Thailand since 2006, the Thai economy has continued to grow slowly and steadily. Thailand also continues to sail dexterously through recent troubled diplomatic waters. It has maintained close

---

40. "Thai Army Promises Elections in October 2015", *BBC News*, 28 June 2014, http://www.bbc.com/news/world-asia-28069578, accessed 1 Dec. 2016.

ties with all the great powers contending for influence in Southeast Asia, from America to China, from India to Japan. It has not lost its diplomatic skills.

However, there is no doubt that Thailand's domestic political preoccupations have weakened ASEAN. ASEAN was born in Thailand. As Professor Suchit Bunbongkarn recalls:

> In 1967 when their meetings to draft the ASEAN Declaration were going nowhere, the ASEAN leaders returned to Bangsaen beach, where they managed to draft the final ASEAN Declaration in a peaceful and restful atmosphere. It was drafted by Sompong, who was private secretary to Thanat Khoman at the time.[41]

Ever since the founding of ASEAN in Bangkok in August 1967, Thailand has served as a valuable anchor for the association. Many ASEAN initiatives took off because they were launched by Thailand, including AFTA and ASEM. One of Thailand's advantages is that it is trusted by its fellow ASEAN founding members, Singapore and Malaysia, Indonesia and the Philippines. This is why the ASEAN countries have a stake in the early resolution of Thailand's domestic difficulties.

Yet, it would be unwise for the ASEAN states to intervene in Thailand's domestic affairs. One of the lowest points in ASEAN's history occurred when the leaders of ASEAN had to be suddenly evacuated when demonstrators broke through Thai police ranks and invaded the hotel where an ASEAN Summit meeting was held in April 2009. The world was subjected to the unsavoury sight of leaders being helicoptered away. Despite this embarrassing episode, the ASEAN leaders wisely decided not to comment or intervene in Thailand's internal affairs. There is wisdom in patience. Thailand will eventually come out of its current political travails. It is a proud and ancient country, and it will find its feet again.

Vietnam

Each Southeast Asian country is unique. Yet Vietnam may be more unique than most. Why? It is the only Southeast Asian country with Chinese culture deep in its roots. Vietnam's identity was formed in a

---

41. Authors' interview with Professor Suchit Bunbongkarn, 23 Apr. 2015.

2,000-year struggle with China; and so, paradoxically, Vietnam both shares deep common cultural roots with China and is the ASEAN state that is most wary of China.

For over a thousand years, from 111 BC to AD 938, Vietnam was occupied by China. It then spent the next thousand years trying to preserve its hard-fought independence. Vietnamese folklore is full of names of heroes who fought against China. The Trung sisters fought against the first Chinese occupation of Vietnam. They liberated Nanyue and ruled over the country for three years before being defeated again by the Chinese in AD 43. The most famous hero in Vietnamese history is Lê Lợi. He fought against the Ming empire and won Vietnam's independence from them in 1427 after a decade-long war. He was then crowned emperor of the country.

At the risk of being politically incorrect, we would describe Vietnam as the "hardest" country in Southeast Asia. This is a perception shared by both of us, a matter of intuition. Most Southeast Asian cultures are soft and supple; Vietnam's is hard and unyielding. Thailand has preserved its independence by bending with the winds, like a strong and supple bamboo. This is how Thailand escaped colonial rule. By contrast, Vietnam is like a hard rock. It stands firm and strong, even in the most violent storms. Hence, when the United States, as the world's greatest military power, attacked Vietnam with all its military might, Vietnam did not flinch. Indeed, Vietnam defeated America, and American diplomats had to flee ignominiously as Vietnamese tanks entered Saigon.

In yet another paradox, having defeated America, with help from China, Vietnam is now hoping that America will help it deal with the growing pressures from a rising China. This is not the only amazing reversal Vietnam has made in recent times. After vociferously condemning the ASEAN countries as being "lackeys of US imperialism",[42] Vietnam joined ASEAN with great alacrity after the end of the Cold War. After the collapse of the Soviet Union in 1991, Vietnam rushed to join ASEAN in 1995. Significantly, even though Vietnam was not an original founding member, it has emerged as one of the strongest supporters of ASEAN.

As it joined ASEAN, Vietnam also joined the ASEAN mainstream in opening up its economy to trade with the rest of the world. Even

---

42. Stephen Vines, "Vietnam Joins ASEAN Grouping", *The Independent*, 29 July 1995, http://www.independent.co.uk/news/world/vietnam-joins-asean-grouping-1593712.html, accessed 14 Oct. 2016.

though for several decades Vietnam had a Soviet-style centrally planned economy, it was able to implement economic reforms quickly; as a result, Vietnam's economy has been among the fastest growing in the world since 2000. Vietnam's total trade stood at around 164 per cent of its GDP in 2013,[43] more than three times the ratio for both China and India. Quite remarkably, even though Vietnam started its reforms much later, its percentage of people living in extreme poverty is less than those of China and India, Indonesia and the Philippines.[44] President Kim of the World Bank has heaped enormous praise on Vietnam, saying, "In just three decades, Vietnam has been transformed from one of the world's poorest nations to one of the world's greatest development success stories."[45]

Despite its significant economic successes, Vietnam faces serious problems. Ironically, again, its problems are the largely the same as China's. Like China, it has succeeded because a strong and competent Communist Party has provided a stable government. Also, like China, Party rule is weakened by perceptions of corruption in the ranks and also at the top (a deputy minister of transport was arrested in 2006).

Vietnam will be helped by various geopolitical forces. While it will have to delicately handle a fast-rising China, it can rely on the fact that other countries will be working to balance China. In recent years, both America and Japan have drawn much closer to Vietnam.

In theory, it should be difficult for America and Vietnam to cooperate. America lost a bitter war in Vietnam. It has been critical of human rights violations and one-party rule in Vietnam. Yet, as usual, geopolitical calculations trump ethical principles. America enthusiastically welcomed Vietnam into the negotiations for the Trans-Pacific Partnership (TPP). Vietnam signed the final agreement on 4 February 2016. Equally strikingly, American military vessels have begun calling at Cam Ranh Bay. Even more significantly, on 23 May 2016 Obama announced that the United States would lift the ban on the sale of military equipment to Vietnam that had been in place

43. "Trade (% of GDP)", World Bank, http://data.worldbank.org/indicator/ NE.TRD.GNFS.ZS, accessed 14 Oct. 2016.
44. "Millennium Development Goals Database", UNDATA, http://data.un.org/ Data.aspx?d=MDG&f=seriesRowID%3A580, accessed 14 Oct. 2016. Extreme poverty is defined as a household living on an income of less than US$1.25 per day.
45. Jim Yong Kim, "Lessons from Vietnam in a Slowing Global Economy", *Straits Times*, 24 Feb. 2016, http://www.straitstimes.com/opinion/lessons-from-vietnam-in-a-slowing-global-economy, accessed 14 Oct. 2016.

for close to 50 years. Kishore saw this close relationship between the US and Vietnam coming over 30 years ago, predicting in a speech at the Council on Foreign Relations in New York in 1985 that the US naval base in Subic Bay would eventually relocate to Cam Ranh Bay. It did not take a genius to predict this. Geopolitical calculations can sometimes be as precise and predictable as mathematical calculations.

A leading indicator of Vietnam's economic prospects is provided by annual flows of foreign direct investment (FDI). They grew from US$1.7 billion[46] in 1995 to US$15.58 billion in 2015,[47] an increase of nine times in 20 years. The leading investors in Vietnam come from Singapore, South Korea and Japan (as of 2014).[48] It is not surprising that Japan has emerged as a leading investor. This is again a result of political calculations. Japan, like America, is looking for a balance against China. Hence, Vietnam is seen as a natural country to support.

The ultimate political challenge for Vietnam's leaders is a simple one: how to take geopolitical advantage of rising concerns about China without alienating and antagonizing China. However, this is not a new challenge for Vietnam. It has been dealing with it for over 2,000 years. Hence, it must have accumulated, over the centuries, political wisdom about dealing with China.

Given Vietnam's profound geopolitical concerns about a rising China, it clearly has the most to lose if ASEAN is weakened. ASEAN provides Vietnam with a valuable geopolitical buffer. So it is clearly in Vietnam's national interest to make a deep commitment to strengthen ASEAN. In theory, this should be easy to do. In practice, it may be difficult as Vietnam, a "hard" country, may find it difficult to dance with its "soft" fellow ASEAN countries. A small practical example will illustrate this challenge. When China sent an oil rig to explore for oil in waters disputed with Vietnam on May 2014, there was widespread political anger in Vietnam. Demonstrations erupted against China. At that point of time, the ASEAN secretary-general was a Vietnamese named Le Luong Minh. He decided to publicly criticize

46. "Foreign Direct Investment, Net Inflows (BoP, Current US$)", UNDATA, http://data.un.org/Data.aspx?d=WDI&f=Indicator_Code%3ABX.KLT.DINV. CD.WD, accessed 14 Oct. 2016.
47. "Vietnam's FDI Pledges Dip, but Actual Inflows Jump in 2015", *Reuters*, 29 Dec. 2015, http://www.reuters.com/article/vietnam-economy-fdi-idUSL3N14J1I120151230, accessed 14 Oct. 2016.
48. "Vietnam", US Department of State, http://www.state.gov/documents/organization/229305.pdf, accessed 14 Oct. 2016.

China. This was unwise. He should not have used his ASEAN position to criticize China, since this was not a dispute between China and ASEAN. In short, Vietnam will have to learn to become more subtle and sophisticated in using ASEAN to balance China. It should not use ASEAN as a battering ram against China. Instead, it should try to gradually enhance ASEAN's soft power. This will help to restrain China over the long term.

Overall, it is not difficult to be optimistic for Vietnam. In all likelihood, it will emerge as a significant economic power, like South Korea today. The remarkable progress it has made since it opened up its economy demonstrates its real potential to become the economic superpower within the ASEAN family.

5 ASEAN: Strengths and Weaknesses

This book is being written in 2016. There is no doubt that ASEAN will be around on 8 August 2017 to celebrate its 50th anniversary, and built-in momentum alone will keep ASEAN going for a decade or more after that. However, one cannot be so certain that ASEAN will be around to celebrate its 100th anniversary on 8 August 2067.

Like any living organism, ASEAN faces the threat of mortality. Curiously, even though regional organizations have been proliferating and have been around for decades, we are not aware of any recent efforts to classify the different types of regional organizations and their unique strengths and weaknesses.[1] American political scientists are unlikely to do this today, because in an effort to make politics a science, they prefer to study quantitative indicators. Yet, what makes up the unique character of each regional organization and differentiates one from the other is a unique combination of geography and history, economics and politics, culture and national psychologies. In short, each regional organization is a unique beast.

Curiously, among these beasts, ASEAN is, in relative terms, strong and healthy. It suffers from fewer dysfunctions than other regional organizations. A brief comparison with the other major regional organizations will illustrate this. The list of major regional organizations

---

1. Before he invented the term "soft power", in 1971 political scientist Joseph Nye published *Peace in Parts: Integration and Conflict in Regional Organization* (Boston: Little, Brown, 1971). There he did discuss different regional organizations and the ways they could contribute to peace. ASEAN was too new to be mentioned in his book, but the association has proved a textbook example of the process he was promoting.

would include the following (in alphabetical order): African Union, ASEAN, EU, Gulf Cooperation Council (GCC), Mercosur, Organization of American States (OAS), Shanghai Cooperation Organisation (SCO), and South Asian Association of Regional Cooperation (SAARC).

In this short list, the strongest beast is, of course, the EU. Its combined GDP of US$16 trillion[2] dwarfs those of the other organizations. Yet, its nature is not easy to discern. In theory, it is an economic beast designed to promote economic integration. In practice, it was set up primarily to block another major war in Europe. Even though it is organizationally strong, it has faced unique challenges, with the threat of Grexit in 2012 and the surprise development of Brexit in 2016. The strongest beast in the family of regional organizations is also vulnerable.

A quick survey of the other regional organizations will show that each has a particular dysfunctionality that cripples its development. The OAS is dysfunctional because it is dominated by the United States. This means that, unlike ASEAN, it cannot be inclusive and incorporate a Communist-Party-run state like Cuba. SCO is dysfunctional because it is dominated by China, which sets the agenda. Undoubtedly, China is generous to its fellow SCO members, but the other SCO members do not feel the sense of ownership of their organization that ASEAN and EU members do.

SAARC, founded in 1985, is dysfunctional because the bitter India-Pakistan rivalry prevents any real cooperation. The GCC is dysfunctional because the level of trust among its members is low, despite the organization's having been around since 1981. In principle, the level of trust and confidence should have been high within the GCC since the member states share a common language (Arabic), religion (Islam), social structure (traditional ruling families), geopolitical interests (fear of Iran), and so on. Yet, having interacted frequently with policy makers from the GCC, and also with those from SAARC and ASEAN, Kishore can say with confidence that the level of trust is highest within ASEAN.

Each regional organization is unique, and ASEAN is clearly more functional than many of the others. The goal of this chapter is to draw out the unique characteristics of ASEAN using the methodology of SWOT (strengths, weaknesses, opportunities and threats) analysis. We will swop the Opportunities and Threats sections to conclude on a high note.

---

2. "European Union", World Bank, http://data.worldbank.org/region/european-union, accessed 1 Dec. 2016. Data from 2015 in current USD.

Strengths

ASEAN has many strengths, and this book has already highlighted some of them. The first and most important is a sense of community among the ten nations of Southeast Asia despite their remarkable diversity. The sense of identity that the people of ASEAN have developed is not the same as the sense of identity that the people of Europe have clearly developed. As Singapore's late President S.R. Nathan reminded us: "The people-to-people relationship in ASEAN has not been established, even now. No school in ASEAN teaches about ASEAN as a subject."[3]

Still, the governments and leaders of ASEAN feel a sense of responsibility to maintain and strengthen the sense of ASEAN community. No two ASEAN member states have gone to war against each other since ASEAN was formed in 1967, although member states have occasionally been involved in tense military standoffs: Cambodia and Thailand almost came to blows over the Preah Vihear temple in 2008, while Indonesia and Malaysia both carried out aggressive naval patrols around the disputed islands of Sipadan and Ligitian in 2005.

The absence of war may seem a low baseline for a sense of community. This is why it is important to emphasize that an invisible but real psychological sense of community has developed among the elites and policy makers of ASEAN. Chapter 2, "Ecosystem of Peace", documented how ASEAN began and developed during and after the Cold War period. Since this time, thousands of formal meetings and less formal games of golf have developed invisible networks of trust and cooperation amongst thousands of key Asian officials. The reference to golf may puzzle some readers. Explaining why the ASEAN Eminent Persons Group (EPG) agreed to a draft report he prepared, S. Jayakumar, former Singapore foreign minister, wrote in his book: "It helped that Ramos, Ali Alatas, Musa, Jock Seng and I had also been long-time golf buddies!"[4] Golf has been critical to ASEAN's success from the beginning. S. Dhanabalan, the former foreign minister of Singapore, also mentioned the importance of golf when he spoke to us, adding:

---

3. Authors' interview with the late President Nathan, 27 June 2015.
4. The group included Ali Alatas, former minister for foreign affairs of Indonesia; Tan Sri Musa Hitam, former deputy prime minister of Malaysia; Fidel V. Ramos, former president of the Philippines; Kasemsamosorn Kasemsri, former deputy prime minister of Vietnam; and Pehin Dato Lim Jock Seng, minister of foreign affairs and trade of Brunei Darussalam. Jayakumar, *Diplomacy*.

The frequent meetings of senior officials, ministers and so forth are actually a great strength, even if they don't result in anything concrete. They are seen as a waste of time. But they develop a sense of identity, of coming together as a group; they develop the idea that we are an entity. If not for the frequent meetings at all levels, we would not have that sense of identity and unity.[5]

Mutual trust and confidence among the leadership corps of member states, although often invisible to the international community, is one of ASEAN's greatest strengths. It explains why key Indonesian policy makers, including President Susilo Bambang Yudhoyono and his foreign minister, Marty Natalegawa, rushed to repair the wounds when the ASEAN foreign ministers failed to reach an agreement over a joint communiqué in July 2012 in Phnom Penh. This impulse to protect and heal ASEAN showed that a real sense of commitment to the ASEAN community had developed among ASEAN elites.

The second major strength is that ASEAN is developing institutions to reinforce the invisible sense of community. The process of ASEAN's institutionalization took a significant leap forward with the adoption of the ASEAN Charter in 2007. It was remarkable that the first stages of this complex process of transforming the institutional character of ASEAN went relatively smoothly. It began with the establishment of the Eminent Persons Group (EPG) in 2005 to propose the outlines of an ASEAN Charter, whose members included some of ASEAN's most respected statesmen, among them Fidel Ramos, Musa Hitam, Ali Alatas and S. Jayakumar. As a result, their report had a high level of credibility. A High Level Task Force (HLTF) set up to implement the EPG report agreed to most of its recommendations. Indeed, it is a political miracle that the HLTF was able to complete the drafting of the ASEAN Charter in less than a year in 2007.

Termsak Chalermpalanupap, a keen observer of ASEAN, looks at the different roles of the two groups in the process. He points out that the EPG members "neither represented their respective governments nor countries. They were given full liberty to think outside of the box". Termsak adds:

[T]he EPG members were not concerned about how to implement what they recommended; they would rather leave this operational question to bureaucrats. The [HLTF] drafters, on the other hand, were fully aware of the need to ensure implementation of and compliance with every provision in the

---

5.   Authors' interview with S. Dhanabalan, 30 July 2015.

Charter. They would be held responsible if they put in something that turned out to be too idealistic and impracticable.[6]

Clearly, the drafting of the ASEAN Charter was a complex process. The EPG members tried to be bold and visionary in their recommendations. The HLTF members had to be careful and practical in choosing which recommendations to include. They also had to consider inputs from various other sources in drafting the charter, including consultations with ASEAN leaders and ministers, and with the High Level Task Force on Economic Integration, senior officials from ASEAN sectoral bodies and other stakeholders. They also took existing ASEAN commitments into consideration. As a result of these consultations, some EPG ideas had to be abandoned, including the following:

- No mentioning of ASEAN Union as the ultimate goal;

- No provisions for suspension, expulsion and withdrawal from ASEAN membership;

- No voting (actually the EPG recommended voting only in non-sensitive areas if consensus could not be achieved);

- No ASEAN Institute; and

- No special fund for narrowing the development gap.

Yet, while it is true that the final charter did not include some recommendations from the EPG, the EPG and the HLTF carried ASEAN over a significant threshold. Until then, while the ASEAN countries had engaged in political and economic and other forms of cooperation, there had been an aversion to building strong institutions.

This is why the EPG report was pathbreaking. The EPG report forged a new consensus within ASEAN, enshrined in the ASEAN Charter, in favour of strengthening its common institutional framework. The success of the EPG can also be an example of something Dr Chitriya Pinthong mentioned in her interview with us: "ASEAN has succeeded because it adapted to find its relevance."[7]

The efforts of the EPG and HLTF have caused several institutions and processes to be strengthened. Two good books have been published

---

6. Termsak Chalermpalanupap, "In Defence of the ASEAN Charter", in *The Making of the ASEAN Charter*, ed. T. Koh, R.G. Manalo and W.C. Woon (Singapore: World Scientific, 2009), pp. 117–36.
7. 23 Apr. 2015.

on the ASEAN Charter: *The ASEAN Charter: A Commentary* by Walter Woon (2015); and *The Making of the ASEAN Charter*, edited by Tommy Koh, Rosario Gonzalez Manalo and Walter Woon (2009). These books draw out in some detail the significant improvements made by the agreement on the charter. The ASEAN statement on the institutional changes introduced by the charter highlighted the following points:

- ASEAN leaders had to meet at least twice a year;

- A Committee of Permanent Representatives to ASEAN was set up, with a permanent representative from each member state residing in Jakarta;

- Non-member states and international organizations were allowed to appoint ambassadors to ASEAN;

- Three ASEAN Community Councils were set up, with one for each ASEAN Community Pillar;

- A single ASEAN chairmanship was implemented, such that the ASEAN chair chaired all the key ASEAN bodies;

- An ASEAN human rights body was set up;

- The ASEAN secretary-general had an expanded role and mandate; and

- The ASEAN Foundation was to report directly to the ASEAN secretary-general instead of to the board of trustees.

The advantage of visible ASEAN institutions and institutional processes over the invisible ASEAN sense of community documented earlier lies precisely in the institutions' visibility. The fact that the citizens of ASEAN countries can see these institutions at work may help them to develop a greater sense of ownership of ASEAN. Moreover, by their nature institutions can keep ASEAN going even if the invisible sense of community that binds the association occasionally falters. Once a bridge is built, it will continue to connect. The larger and more complex ASEAN institutional frameworks that emerged after the EPG and HLTF reports serve as bridges to hold together the detached ASEAN nations. These institutions also develop a dynamic of their own, and, as the EU institutions have done, create new avenues of ASEAN cooperation.

The third strength of ASEAN is that many great powers have a vested interest in keeping ASEAN going. Chapter 3 has documented how some key great powers, including the United States, China,

Japan and India, have a common interest in ASEAN's survival and success despite divergences in their interests vis-à-vis the ASEAN region. ASEAN has become indispensable in the Asia-Pacific region, and no other organization can replace it. Only ASEAN is trusted by all the great powers to be a neutral and effective platform through which they can engage with one another. After several decades, the foreign ministers of the United States, China, Japan, India and even Russia and the EU have come to see the value of attending the annual ASEAN meetings. Similarly, with ASEAN+3 and ASEAN+6 meetings raised to summit level, the presidents and prime ministers of these countries also find value in attending ASEAN meetings. According to Ambassador Tommy Koh:

> The EU is driven by its two biggest economies, but here, the US, China and India are not able to take the role of driving the region because they have no common agenda. ASEAN is able to drive precisely because the three great powers cannot agree. And we can continue to do so as long as the major powers find us neutral and independent.[8]

In the past, ASEAN foreign ministers invited their non-ASEAN counterparts to perform skits at dinners during the annual ASEAN ministerial meetings, a practice that regrettably has ceased. There were some memorable performances by distinguished personalities, including Madeline Albright and Gareth Evans, who would sing, dance or act at these events. These distinguished, and often stiff, leaders would let their hair down at ASEAN dinners, and in the process of demonstrating that they were human they enhanced the camaraderie among participants.

One of the miracles of the Asia-Pacific region is that we have prevented significant great-power conflict even though there have been enormous shifts of power among the great nations in the region. The reasons for this lack of conflict are, of course, complex. One reason could be that ASEAN's neutrality helps it retain its centrality in the region. As George Yeo explained earlier in this volume:

> In the end, everybody came to the conclusion that however ungainly, however inefficient, however elliptical ASEAN's ways are, it's still better than not having an ASEAN. That is the genius of ASEAN foreign policy. In the end, almost with a sneer, they accepted that ASEAN should be in the driving seat.

---

8.   Authors' interview with Ambassador Tommy Koh, 23 Dec. 2015.

Yes, ASEAN's leadership is the most preferred because no other
driver would be trusted by the others.

There can be no doubt that the ASEAN gatherings have altered the
chemistry of relations among the great powers and, as a result, helped
to diminish rivalry and enhance cooperation among them. If this
was ASEAN's sole achievement after 50 years, it would be sufficient
to prove that ASEAN was a truly valuable regional organization and
fully deserving of the Nobel Peace Prize.

Weaknesses

ASEAN has some serious weaknesses. The first is that it has no
natural custodian. The EU has remained strong and resilient because
France and Germany accepted a common responsibility to keep the
organization going. Hence, strong leaders such as Charles De Gaulle,
Konrad Adenauer, François Mitterrand and Helmut Kohl believed
that they had a great responsibility to maintain and strengthen the
EU. The EU never faced any danger of being neglected.

The absence of a natural custodian poses a challenge for ASEAN.
Who owns ASEAN? Who will nurture it, protect it and develop it for
the long run? As Chapter 2 has shown, an unusual combination of
factors, among them fear, luck and wise leadership, lay behind the birth
and early development of ASEAN. Many of the factors that boosted
ASEAN development are gone. Those who believe in and care for
ASEAN should now ask themselves: Who can provide custodianship
for ASEAN? Interested parties such as America, Europe, China and
India cannot perform this role; the custodian must be internal.

Indonesia, which is home to about 40 per cent of ASEAN's
population, would be a logical choice. A large and geographically
dispersed nation, Indonesia is the largest beneficiary of the effective
ecosystem of peace that ASEAN has created. President Suharto
understood this point very well, having experienced considerable
turmoil in his younger days and seen how the occupation of even a
small state like East Timor stressed Indonesia. He fully understood
the virtues of peace and worked hard to nurture and develop ASEAN,
even though he was ambivalent about opening up the Indonesian
economy to competition from other ASEAN economies. In this matter,
as Chapter 2 has shown, President Suharto was pulled between two
opposing strains in Indonesian economic thinking: the liberal free

marketers led by the Berkeley Mafia and the nationalists led by Widjojo Nitisastro.

This ambivalence remains a constant feature of the Indonesian political landscape. President Susilo Bambang Yudhoyono, who ruled Indonesia from 2004 to 2014, tried to push Indonesia towards the liberal and open end of the economic spectrum. President Jokowi was initially inclined to listen to the voices of the Indonesian nationalists, but in his second and third years in office he began to support more liberal approaches in trade. Indonesian Trade Minister Thomas "Tom" Lembong told Rappler's Maria Ressa that in recent years APEC economies had been adopting protectionist policies that hampered economic growth: "Let's be honest. We all talk about free and even fair trade but what we do in practice, the truth is, since the global financial crisis in 2008, more countries including Indonesia have been quietly rolling out protectionist measures."[9] Quite remarkably, President Jokowi has started to buck this trend, even suggesting that Indonesia might join the Trans-Pacific Partnership. During a meeting with the US president at the White House, he risked angering economic nationalists at home by declaring, "Indonesia intends to join the TPP. Indonesia is an open economy and with a population of 250 million, we are the largest economy in south-east Asia."[10] Lembong had said in October 2015 that investment in Indonesia would continue "If the government can give that, in 2–3 years we would have TPP and the European (agreement)".[11]

It remains to be seen whether Jokowi can continue in this direction. When the largest member state of ASEAN turns inward, it is natural for ASEAN to appear to be drifting. The Indonesian establishment needs to have an open and robust debate on the value of ASEAN to Indonesia, and fortunately one of Indonesia's strengths is its capacity to have such open debates.

9. Maria Ressa, "Indonesia's Tom Lembong: 'Let's Move Away from Playing Games'", Rappler, 20 Nov. 2015, http://www.rappler.com/thought-leaders/113434-indonesia-minister-tom-lembong-trade-politics, accessed 10 Oct. 2016.

10. Agence France-Presse, "Indonesia Will Join Trans-Pacific Partnership, Jokowi Tells Obama", *The Guardian*, 27 Oct. 2015, https://www.theguardian.com/world/2015/oct/27/indonesia-will-join-trans-pacific-partnership-jokowi-tells-obama, accessed 13 Oct. 2016.

11. Bernadette Christina, "Indonesia's Trade Minister Calls for TPP Membership in Two Years", *Reuters*, 9 Oct. 2015, http://www.reuters.com/article/us-trade-tpp-indonesia-idUSKCN0S312R20151009, accessed 13 Oct. 2016.

Jusuf Wanandi is one of Indonesia's leading public intellectuals. As head of the Centre for Strategic and International Studies in Jakarta, he has participated in meetings of ASEAN-ISIS (Institute of Strategic and International Studies), the group of ASEAN think tanks that provides a "Track Two" (NGO) route for ASEAN cooperation. Kishore knows Jusuf well, and also knows that Jusuf appreciates the importance of the ASEAN community. But as an Indonesian nationalist, Jusuf has also been critical of ASEAN's shortcomings.

The future of ASEAN will depend a great deal on the consensus that develops within the Indonesian establishment. If the strong nationalist voices win out, they could persuade the Indonesian population that Indonesia is losing out economically by sharing its large market with its fellow ASEAN citizens, and politically because ASEAN constrains it from emerging as a strong and independent power in its own right. Indonesian nationalists might argue that as the fourth-largest country by population in the world (after China, India and the US), Indonesia should not need to belong to or support a regional organization like ASEAN. Without question this uncertainty in Indonesia is the strongest internal threat that ASEAN faces. If the nationalists win out and, in the worst-case scenario, pull Indonesia out of ASEAN, ASEAN will not be around to celebrate its 100th anniversary in August 2067. Indonesia is likely to remain a member of ASEAN, but it could become a relatively unenthusiastic member. In this case, ASEAN would not be able to rely on Indonesian leadership to keep it going.

If Indonesian leadership is not forthcoming, the three other natural candidates as custodians of ASEAN are Malaysia, Singapore and Thailand. To understand why, look at the map of ASEAN. Unlike Myanmar, Vietnam or the Philippines, Malaysia, Singapore and Thailand are, in geographic terms, the core countries of the ASEAN community. Hence, a combination of geography and politics — geopolitics — should drive Malaysia, Singapore and Thailand to provide leadership and become the next set of primary custodians of ASEAN. But it is unlikely that such leadership will be forthcoming from them any time soon.

In the years since PM Thaksin was forced to leave Thailand in 2006, the country has been wracked by political turmoil. Although the turmoil subsided after General Prayut Chan-o-cha's interim military government was established on 30 August 2014, Thailand remains in a zone of political uncertainty. The demise of the beloved Thai

King Bhumibol Adulyadej on 13 October 2016 has aggravated this uncertainty.

This is unfortunate, as Thai leadership has often given ASEAN development a significant boost. ASEAN was born under the tutelage of Thai Foreign Minister Thanat Khoman in 1967. The ASEAN Free Trade Area (AFTA) concept was launched by another Thai PM and elder statesman, Anand Panyarachun. Thai leadership has influenced ASEAN's development positively, but given the current domestic challenges, Thailand is unlikely to provide leadership for ASEAN in the medium term. The absence of Thai leadership could negatively impact ASEAN.

Malaysia is also unlikely to provide leadership to ASEAN in the short term. Prime Minister Najib is a strong and dedicated supporter of ASEAN, and he has a sentimental attachment to the organization because his father was a signatory of the Bangkok Declaration in 1967. He was the chairman of ASEAN in November 2015, when ASEAN's economic, political-security and sociocultural communities were launched. But for much of 2015 and 2016, Prime Minister Najib's government was, like the Thai government, wracked with political turmoil. Any ambitious move to push ASEAN cooperation to a much higher level had to be forgone to deal with domestic political crises; and the goals set for ASEAN cooperation within these communities were less ambitious than they might have been. As Wong Kan Seng, Singapore's minister for foreign affairs from 1988 to 1994, pointed out: "When leaders are strong domestically, they are not so concerned that vested interests might attack them on their foreign policy decisions."[12]

Singapore has not experienced such political turmoil. The passing of Lee Kuan Yew in 2015 led to deep national mourning, but there was no political uncertainty and nothing like a political vacuum. Prime Minister Lee Hsien Loong is clearly one of the most capable leaders within ASEAN, if not in the world; but given Singapore's small size, no leader of Singapore can compensate for the lack of political leadership for ASEAN from Indonesia, Malaysia and Thailand. Indeed, in the past, there has been resentment when Singapore pushed hard for greater ASEAN cooperation.

Leadership for ASEAN cannot be provided by the other three small countries (Brunei, Cambodia and Laos) or by the three large but geographically fringe countries (Myanmar, the Philippines and

---

12. Authors' interview with Wong Kan Seng, 24 July 2015.

Vietnam), at least not for many years. Even though it joined ASEAN late—in 1995—Vietnam has become one of its most enthusiastic supporters because membership provides Vietnam with a small but valuable geopolitical buffer from the strong and rising China at its border. However, for cultural and historical reasons, Vietnam can never serve as the leader of the ASEAN community.

The absence of a natural custodian is the first key weakness of ASEAN. This weakness is aggravated by a second one: the absence of strong institutions. Having said earlier in the chapter that one of ASEAN's strengths is its institutions, the reader may be surprised by this observation, but the paradox is easily explained. ASEAN developed more complex institutional frameworks after the launch of the ASEAN Charter in 2008, built organically on the solidarity established over previous decades. These institutions help hold ASEAN together, but they are not strong enough to provide leadership for ASEAN, as the EU Commission often does. Neither are they strong enough to discourage ASEAN national leaders from putting their national interests ahead of ASEAN's interests.

According to S. Jayakumar, the EPG interviewed several former ASEAN secretary-generals while working on its report. The EPG asked each of them separately: "If there's one thing you wish ASEAN could do, what would it be?" All of them said: implementing of decisions. The biggest issue with ASEAN was that there was no enforcement of decisions, no monitoring of compliance, and no sanctions. The secretary-generals might make proposals and even get the member states to agree to them, but there is no way to ensure there is a follow through.

There are structural reasons for the absence of strong ASEAN institutions. One of these is the insistence of some of the member states, including Malaysia, Singapore and Thailand, that each ASEAN member state should pay an equal share of the annual cost of funding the ASEAN Secretariat. Hence, in the year 2015, each ASEAN country paid an equal annual contribution of US$1.9 million to the ASEAN Secretariat, for a total budget of US$19 million. By comparison, the EU set a total of commitment appropriations for 2015 of €145.3 billion (US$159 billion). Even though the EU's population is smaller than ASEAN's, its secretarial budget is 8,000 times larger.

The size of the GDPs of ASEAN countries varies enormously. They include the large GDPs of Indonesia (US$888.7 billion), Thailand (US$373.8 billion) and Malaysia (US$326.9 billion) (2014 figures). By contrast, the three smallest GDPs are those of Cambodia (US$16.6

billion), Brunei (US$15.1 billion) and Laos (US$11.7 billion). Given these enormous disparities in the size of the ten ASEAN GDPs, it would appear to be both inequitable and unwise to insist on equal payments by all ten nations. Fortunately, there is a simple and easily acceptable solution to this problem. All ten ASEAN member states have accepted the concept of "capacity to pay" when they pay their annual contributions to major international organizations, especially those in the UN family. Hence, ASEAN should be able to adapt the principle of capacity to pay and apply it also to the annual expenses of the ASEAN Secretariat. A simple step like that could help to alleviate the second critical weakness of ASEAN.

The third critical weakness ASEAN faces is that even the limited ownership of this organization is felt primarily by the governments of the region. The great strength of the EU is that most of its citizens feel a deep sense of ownership and often identify themselves as Europeans. The great weakness of ASEAN is that its citizens do not feel a deep sense of ownership of ASEAN. There is no doubt that if ASEAN is to survive until 2067, its primary ownership must gradually shift from the governments to the people. If there is no popular support for the organization, politicians will have little incentive to keep it going. Sourav Roy, a Singapore-based media analyst, has written about this in the *Huffington Post*:

> The story remains same [*sic*] in almost every ASEAN country. I have plenty of anecdotes to weave an encyclopedia of what ordinary Southeast Asians thought ASEAN to be. A few hawker-centre stall owners in Singapore thought it to be a British football club, mistaking it for Arsenal, while others thought it to be arsenic, the poisonous chemical. The stories and the innocent ignorance don't end. The bottom-line being, ASEAN might be one lofty political and economic bloc from Asia, preparing itself for the shift of power from the West to East, yet its own people remain the most ignorant about it. Is ASEAN ready for a unified common market, which it is heading to, and in turn, play a greater global role?[13]

Some small symbolic steps have been taken to help promote a sense of ownership. For example, when ASEAN citizens travel overseas, they

---

13. Sourav Roy, "ASEAN: What's That and Who Cares? Certainly Not the Common Man in Asia", *Huffington Post*, 9 Oct. 2013, http://www.huffingtonpost.com/sourav-roy/asean-whats-that-and-who-cares_b_3894984.html, accessed 13 Oct. 2016.

are intrigued to find that their overseas embassies fly two flags: the national flag and the ASEAN flag. ASEAN got this idea from the EU. And it was a good one, because for many "man on the street" citizens of ASEAN, seeing the flags together may be their first encounter with their ASEAN status.

This is one of the key goals of this book: to persuade the ASEAN man on the street that he should feel a greater sense of ownership of the living and breathing political miracle that ASEAN has become. Towards this end, it would be helpful if primary school children in all ten ASEAN countries were given a common textbook on ASEAN. All the children in ASEAN should be aware of the basic facts of their ASEAN neighbours, especially their history and geography, culture and identity. A survey on attitudes and awareness towards ASEAN was commissioned by the ASEAN Foundation in 2007. It surveyed 2,170 undergraduates in the ten member states. Of the respondents, 39 per cent said that they were only a little familiar or not at all familiar with ASEAN. On average, respondents could list only nine of the ten ASEAN countries and could identify only about seven on a map; 26 per cent could not correctly identify the ASEAN flag; and more than 50 per cent did not know when ASEAN was founded.

If this ASEAN Foundation survey is accurate, it shows an alarming weakness in ASEAN. If the populations of ASEAN are barely aware of the key facts about ASEAN as a community, how can they feel any sense of ownership? The conclusion of this book contains some concrete recommendations on how to strengthen the ownership of ASEAN among its people.

Threats

Geopolitical rivalries are the most obvious threat that ASEAN faces. In coming years the Asia-Pacific region will see significant shifts of power, especially with the US giving up its position as the number one economy in the world to China by 2030, or even earlier. History shows that when the world's number one power (today, the US) is about to be surpassed by an emerging power (today, China), rivalry between these powers intensifies. Donald Trump's mercurial nature could make things worse and increase the level of unpredictability in US-China relations. ASEAN will face great stress in the coming decades because of the heightened US-China rivalry. ASEAN will also be buffeted by increased Sino-Japanese and Sino-Indian rivalry. The geopolitical storms are coming, and if ASEAN fails to prepare for them it could be torn apart.

One early warning sign came at the Phnom Penh ASEAN ministerial meeting in July 2012. Cambodia, under pressure from China, objected to a paragraph on the South China Sea. The Philippines and Vietnam, with American support, insisted on including a reference to the South China Sea. This book is not the place to discuss the merits of China's South China Sea claim, although China would plainly find it difficult to justify its Nine-Dash Line under international law. Clearly the US will find it in its national interest to embarrass China over its South China Sea claims. In the ASEAN Regional Forum in Hanoi in July 2010, US Secretary of State Hillary Clinton made a statement on the South China Sea. Yang Jiechi, the Chinese foreign minister, responded with a fierce denial that the South China Sea issue was a cause for international concern, saying, "Nobody believes there's anything that is threatening the region's peace and stability." In a statement on the Chinese Foreign Ministry website, he said, "The seemingly impartial remarks were in effect an attack on China and were designed to give the international community a wrong impression that the situation in the South China Sea is a cause for grave concern."[14]

The failure to agree to the joint communiqué might in the end have turned out to be fortuitous. The events in Phnom Penh in 2012 and Hanoi in 2010 provide sufficiently clear warning to ASEAN that it will be affected by US-China rivalry. Another indication of things to come was provided in October 2014, when China launched its initiative to set up an Asian Infrastructure Investment Bank (AIIB). The US opposed this step, and several Asian capitals, including those of ASEAN, received calls from the US Treasury lobbying them against joining the AIIB. Tokyo, Seoul and Canberra stayed out, but the ASEAN countries wisely decided to join, as they were intended to be the prime beneficiaries.

On other issues the ASEAN countries adopt a different stance. With regard to the South China Sea, most ASEAN countries are seen as being more pro-American. On the AIIB issue, the ASEAN countries are seen as more pro-Chinese.

---

14. "Chinese FM Refutes Fallacies on the South China Sea Issue", *China Daily*, 25 July 2010, http://www.chinadaily.com.cn/china/2010-07/25/content_11046054. htm, accessed 10 Oct. 2016.

Many other challenging issues will surface between the US and China in the coming decades. In the worst-case scenario, which cannot be ruled out, ASEAN's integrity as a unified organization could be threatened. A strongly pro-China government in Cambodia, for example, could clash with a strongly pro-American government in the Philippines. When that happens, ASEAN could well break apart. It would therefore be truly unwise for ASEAN as a community not to prepare for such worst-case scenarios.

It is worth reiterating the key message of Chapter 3. The leaders of the US, China, Japan and India, in particular, should reflect carefully on whether it is in their long-term interest for ASEAN to remain united as a single community providing stability to Southeast Asia, or to break apart. Chapter 3 explains in detail why each of the four powers should see that it is in its interest for ASEAN to "hang together" (to quote the memorable words of S. Rajaratnam). Fortunately, key policy makers in Washington, Beijing, Tokyo and New Delhi share a fairly strong conviction that it is in their respective national interests to see ASEAN holding together as a cohesive regional organization.

That is the good news. The bad news is that great powers do not always make wise decisions. More often than not, they are driven by events or short-term political interests. In retrospect, it was unwise for China to block the ASEAN joint communiqué in Phnom Penh in July 2012. It was equally unwise for the US to try to block the ASEAN countries from joining China's AIIB initiative. Such zero-sum initiatives by either Beijing or Washington will surely surface again. ASEAN needs to develop the resilience to deal with such geopolitical stresses and strains.

One way of achieving resilience is to develop deep relations with other great powers, declining or emerging. Both Japan and India have declared a long-term commitment to help protect and strengthen ASEAN, and ASEAN should make it a priority to work with New Delhi and Tokyo. Similarly, while the EU and Russia have been relatively weak in their courtship of ASEAN, ASEAN should work hard to develop close and extensive relations with both the EU and Russia.

Another geopolitical buffer that ASEAN could develop is a closer partnership with Australia and New Zealand. When Goh Chok Tong and Paul Keating were the prime ministers of Singapore and Australia respectively, there were discussions of creating a new "community of twelve" consisting of the ten ASEAN countries plus Australia and New Zealand. Any reasonable assessment of this proposal would show that the benefits outweigh the costs. If this had been done in 2015, the combined GDP of ASEAN (US$2,328 billion), Australia (US$1,252 billion) and New Zealand (US$191 billion) would have amounted to US$3,772 billion, making the "community of twelve" the fourth-largest economy in the world.

To understand the importance of developing such additional geopolitical buffers, the ASEAN countries need to better understand the history of ASEAN. ASEAN did exceptionally well in the 1970s and 1980s because it benefited from the strategic alignment of interests between the US and China. Favourable geopolitical conditions also contributed to the development of an ecosystem of peace in Southeast Asia. When favourable geopolitical winds are replaced by unfavourable geopolitical storms, the ASEAN countries need deeper sources of resilience.

The second threat that ASEAN faces is that its political leaders are focussed on domestic challenges rather than regional concerns. Looking back now, it is clear that one reason for ASEAN's golden era in the 1980s and 1990s is that it had strong leaders such as Lee Kuan Yew, Mahathir Mohamad and Suharto at the helm. Because they were strong domestically, they could find the time and political resources to work on regional cooperation.

As ASEAN approaches its 50th anniversary, most ASEAN leaders—including President Jokowi, Prime Minister Najib and Prime Minister General Prayut Chan-o-cha—are preoccupied by domestic challenges. Prime Minister Lee Hsien Loong has commented on the dangers associated with a domestic focus:

> Domestic agendas have to be attended to but if that becomes all-consuming and you don't have space for ASEAN cooperation or you're unable to make the case for ASEAN cooperation—for example in investment guarantees, trade, technical cooperation or human resources—then we'll have the form of it, but not have fully fulfilled the substance.[15]

As noted above, this issue is aggravated by the growing but still relatively weak institutions of ASEAN, which cannot provide leadership for the organization. Some EU officials have expressed frustration with regard to ASEAN-EU Programme for Regional

---

15. "Dialogue with Prime Minister Lee Hsien Loong at the Singapore Summit on 19 September 2015", Singapore Summit, https://www.singaporesummit.sg/downloads//Dialogue%20with%20PM%20Lee%20Hsien%20Loong_SS2015.pdf, accessed 12 Oct. 2016.

Integration Support initiatives, saying of the ASEAN Secretariat, "There is a lack of personnel and resources, the mandate is weak, it doesn't have executive powers and members are travelling all the time."[16]

In theory, the absence of top-down leadership of ASEAN could be compensated for by bottom-up leadership, and some Track Two (non-governmental) processes within ASEAN have functioned in this way. For example, a group of ASEAN think tanks meet regularly under the ASEAN-ISIS (ASEAN Institute of Strategic and International Studies) framework. As a result of their regular meetings, they have come up with some interesting suggestions for enhancing ASEAN cooperation. According to Kripa Sridharan and T.C.A. Srinivasa-Raghavan, "ASEAN-ISIS confabulations, particularly the annual Asia-Pacific Roundtable hosted by them, have been instrumental in creating a climate of trust and confidence within the region."[17]

Given that ASEAN is facing a particularly challenging environment of heightened geopolitical challenges and domestically distracted leaders, the time may have come for it to call for the establishment of Version 2.0 of the Eminent Persons Group. ASEAN is fortunate to have a group of recently retired ASEAN leaders who dedicated themselves to strengthening ASEAN while in office. Each of these individuals is highly respected in their country and in the region. The list includes President Susilo Bambang Yudhoyono of Indonesia, PM Goh Chok Tong of Singapore, PM Anand Panyarachun of Thailand, and President Ramos of the Philippines. These leaders know each other well, and they were less domestically distracted and more focussed on ASEAN than their successors.

When ASEAN celebrates its 50th anniversary in August 2017, it would do well to convene a second Eminent Persons Group (EPG) and call on this group of leaders to look at ASEAN's key challenges over the coming 50 years. Their mandate could be simply to ask what ASEAN needs to do to ensure that it remains a vibrant organization in 2067. In short, the second ASEAN EPG should be mandated to produce a Project 2067 report for ASEAN.

---

16. Laura Allison, *The EU, ASEAN and Interregionalism: Regionalism Support and Norm Diffusion between the EU and ASEAN* (Houndmills: Palgrave, 2015), p. 108.
17. Kripa Sridharan and T.C.A. Srinivasa-Raghavan, *Regional Cooperation in South Asia and Southeast Asia* (Singapore: ISEAS, 2007).

The third threat that ASEAN could face grows out of failing to deal with the first two threats. If ASEAN is hit by geopolitical conflicts and its leaders are distracted by domestic affairs, the organization could well be seriously weakened or torn apart. Were that to happen, Southeast Asia's underlying fault lines could emerge.

The British historian Charles Fisher was right to point out that the underlying cultural fabric of Southeast Asia could make it the Balkans of Asia; sectarian strife could break out in many corners of the region. One indication of this is provided by the tensions between the Muslim Rohingya population and the dominant Buddhist majority population of Myanmar. The tensions became so acute in May 2015 that there was a surge of boat people from the Rohingya population fleeing to other parts of Southeast Asia. Initially, Thailand, Malaysia and Indonesia turned away the boats. When these actions generated international criticism, the ASEAN countries were put under some pressure to respond. Fortunately, ASEAN formulated a regional response that helped alleviate the problem. The measures included establishing a joint task force to assist the Rohingya, and setting up a humanitarian fund to which Singapore committed an initial sum of US$200,000.

ASEAN was able to respond in this way because it remains a functioning organization. However, if ASEAN were to become dysfunctional, with weak leadership, it is not clear that there would be an alternative organization or enough of a remaining regional sense of community to manage any new outbursts of sectarian strife, especially across borders.

ASEAN scholars need to make an intensive effort to study and document the fault lines in Southeast Asia's cultural landscape. For example, there has been a long-standing low-level insurgency in Southern Thailand led by some Thai Muslims who are fighting for greater autonomy. In their statement of first requests in the peace negotiations with the Royal Thai Government in 2013, the Barisan Revolusi Nasional Melayu Patani wrote, "The Thai Royal Government must acknowledge the rights of the Melayu Patani nation for the Patani land."[18] When Bangkok handles Southern Thailand well, the insurgency goes down in intensity. But when Bangkok makes unwise

---

18. N. Hayipiyawong, "The Failure of Peace Negotiation Process between Government of Thailand and Revolution National Front (BRN) in Southern Thailand Conflict (Patani)", BA thesis, Universitas Muhammadiyah Yogyakarta, 2014, http://thesis.umy.ac.id/datapublik/t39343.pdf, accessed 12 Oct. 2016.

moves, the insurgency heats up. According to Zachary Abuza's conservative count, the violence peaked in mid-2007, when Thailand was under junta rule. It declined in 2008, when the People Power Party was in power, led by Prime Minister Samak Sundaravej. The number of casualties stabilized at about 86 per month between 2009 and 2014. After the May 2014 coup, the number of casualties fell to just 27 in February. Insurgents interviewed by Abuza cited fierce flooding, arrests, and fear of the security forces as reasons for this initial decline. However, the number of casualties rose again to 80 in May 2015, perhaps because the military withdrew half of its army battalions from the deep south and replaced them with soldiers from the Ministry of Interior, rangers, village security teams and local defence volunteers—personnel who, Abuza says, were ill equipped to handle the insurgency.[19]

ASEAN also needs an independent study of recent developments in the Middle East. The sectarian divisions in Iraq, Syria, Lebanon, Yemen and Bahrain are not new, but while there were simmering tensions, they did not erupt into open fighting until the American invasion of Iraq. In short, an external geopolitical shock triggered long-dormant sectarian conflict.

Since Southeast Asia could well be subject to some significant external geopolitical shocks in the coming decades, ASEAN needs to ponder whether such shocks would have a similar outcome. For example, if Thailand were to emerge as a pro-China country while Malaysia took a pro-American stance, the geopolitical tensions between the two could heighten the sectarian strife in Southern Thailand. The majority of Thai Muslims are ethnically Malay and might readily support the foreign policy stances of Malaysia. Geopolitical shocks often have unintended consequences. ASEAN should psychologically prepare itself for some surprising, perhaps even shocking, resurfacing of long-buried fault lines.

---

19. Zachary Abuza, "The Smoldering Thai Insurgency", *CTC Sentinel*, 29 June 2015, https://www.ctc.usma.edu/posts/the-smoldering-thai-insurgency, accessed 10 Oct. 2016.

Opportunities

While ASEAN faces many threats, it also has a sea of opportunities before it. To extend this maritime analogy a little further, ASEAN can take advantage of at least three rising tides.

The first is multilateralism. This simple statement may shock many readers, especially in America, where it is fashionable, even among academics, to pour scorn on multilateral institutions such as the United Nations. In the American popular imagination, multilateral institutions are seen as fat, bloated, inefficient and unnecessary. The overwhelming power of America allows it to act unilaterally, and it has often done so. Hence, most Americans are unaware that the rest of the world is creating more and more multilateral institutions.

Brexit is another event that may give the impression that multilateralism is dying. Clearly, Britain's decision to leave the EU was a big shock, but we should wait and watch carefully how the British negotiate their exit. It seems the British will try to remain attached to as many of the EU's institutions and processes as possible. Withdrawal from them will have painful costs. When the folly of Brexit sinks in, the world will see why more and more countries are joining multilateral institutions.

In *The Great Convergence* (2013), Kishore describes how Bill Clinton explained the value of multilateral institutions and processes. Clinton said:

> If you believe that maintaining power and control and absolute freedom of movement and sovereignty is important to your country's future, there's nothing inconsistent in that [the US continuing to behaving unilaterally]. [The US is] the biggest, most powerful country in the world now. We've got the juice and we're going to use it. ... But if you believe that we should be trying to create a world with rules and partnerships and habits of behavior that we would like to live in when we're no longer the military political economic superpower in the world, then you wouldn't do that. It just depends on what you believe.[20]

---

20. William J. Clinton, "Transcript of 'Global Challenges': A Public Address Given by Former US President William J. Clinton at Yale University on October 31, 2003", *YaleGlobal*, 31 Oct. 2003, http://yaleglobal.yale.edu/content/transcript-global-challenges, accessed 13 Oct. 2016.

Clinton was wisely anticipating a global trend of accelerating multilateralism. Many Americans view with suspicion the international behaviour of China and Russia, two countries that are involved with various new multilateral institutions. For example, China launched the Shanghai Cooperation Organisation in 2001 and Russia the Eurasian Economic Union in 2014.

Multilateralism is promoted not only by governments but also by the people of our world. A 2013 paper noted, "Over the twentieth century, more than 38,000 IGOs [intergovernmental organizations] and INGOs [international non-governmental organizations] were founded—a rate of more than one per day."[21] Figure 1 from the same paper indicates how steep the increase is, especially in international non-governmental organizations. This chart demonstrates clearly that multilateralism is a sunshine industry.

Figure 1: Number of IGOs and INGOs, 1909-2009

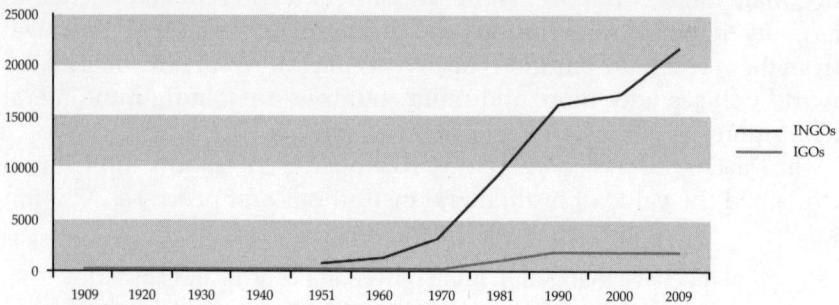

Source: Weiss 2013.

The new organizations exhibit a natural desire to identify role models that demonstrate the gold standard of multilateral cooperation. Until recently, the institution that clearly embodied this gold standard was the EU. It is the most densely packed regional organization, with thousands of agreements that bind the member states together. As noted earlier, the EU is ahead of ASEAN because while there have been no wars between any two ASEAN states, there is zero prospect of war between any two EU member states. Still, ASEAN is number two in the world. Tan Sri Mohamed Jawhar Hassan, the chairman of Malaysia's Institute of Strategic and International Studies (ISIS),

---

21. Thomas G. Weiss *et al.*, "The Rise of Non-State Actors in Global Governance: Opportunities and Limitations", One Earth Future Foundation, 2013, http://acuns.org/wp-content/uploads/2013/11/gg-weiss.pdf, accessed 13 Oct. 2016.

commented, "Just compare ASEAN with other regional ventures. Besides the EU, nothing else comes close."[22]

Take the example of economic cooperation. After the EU, the second-most successful regional organization is ASEAN. The ASEAN Economic Community (AEC), formally established in 2015, "envisions ASEAN as a single market and production base characterized by free flow of goods, services, and investments, as well as freer flow of capital and skills".[23] In the run-up to the AEC, ASEAN had been virtually tariff-free since 2010. FDI into ASEAN increased from about US$76 billion in 2010[24] to US$120 billion in 2015.[25] ASEAN connectivity has been greatly enhanced—for example, intra-ASEAN air travel increased at a compounded growth rate of 10 per cent between 2009 and 2014, and between 2000 and 2014 Internet penetration grew from 8 per cent to 44 per cent.[26]

Even though the EU is ahead in market integration, it has tended towards rigidity in its methods and procedures while ASEAN has tended towards flexibility and pragmatism. Unlike the EU, which works out detailed agreements to bind countries in various areas of cooperation, ASEAN is based on simple and general agreements that allow for flexibility.

The most notable example of the lack of pragmatism in the EU and the abundance of it in the ASEAN is in the area of language policy. Europeans rightly believe that each national language should be treated with respect; but given the multitude of EU languages, it would have been wiser to confine use of all the official languages to symbolic occasions. Working documents for use at the bureaucratic level are a different matter. Sadly, such basic pragmatism is out of the grasp of EU

22. Authors' interview with Tan Sri Mohamed Jawhar Hassan, 17 June 2016.
23. "ASEAN Economic Community: How Viable Is Investing?" Invest in ASEAN, http://investasean.asean.org/index.php/page/view/asean-economic-community/view/670/newsid/758/single-market-and-production-base.html, accessed 13 Oct. 2016.
24. "Foreign Direct Investment into Asean in 2010", ASEAN, http://www.asean.org/storage/images/resources/Statistics/2014/StatisticalPublications/fdi_statistics_in_focus_2010_final.pdf, accessed 13 Oct. 2016.
25. "Foreign Direct Investment Net Inflows, Intra and Extra ASEAN", ASEAN, http://asean.org/storage/2015/09/Table-252.pdf, accessed 11 Oct. 2016.
26. "The ASEAN Economic Community (AEC) 2015: A Guide to the Practical Benefits", Ministry of Trade and Industry Singapore, https://www.mti.gov.sg/MTIInsights/MTIImages/MTI%20AEC%202015%20Handbook.PDF, accessed 11 Oct. 2016.

officials, who work in 24 official languages. At an everyday level they function in two languages, but tons of EU documents (and this is no exaggeration) must be translated into 22 languages.

The ASEAN countries function in a single language, English, that is not native to any ASEAN country. ASEAN leaders, of course, need translation when they meet at the summit level. For the most part, officials and ministers meet and do business in English, and documents are produced in the same language.

As multilateralism grows globally, especially at the regional level, the world should continue to study the EU as a model of regional cooperation, but we should also understand the sources of its weaknesses. Moreover, world leaders should start to look at ASEAN as an alternative model. Since most countries are part of the developing world, ASEAN may work better as a model for them. For example, African countries may have made a mistake in choosing the EU as a model for the African Union. The very inclusion of the word "Union" implies that Africans are going to march down the European road of regional cooperation. By choosing the wrong model, the African Union may have set itself on a course towards failure. Had they followed ASEAN, where the A stands for "Association", the Africans would have been better off aspiring for a lower and more pragmatic model of regional cooperation.

Fortunately, more and more regional organizations in the developing world are developing ties with ASEAN, including the Gulf Cooperation Council in 2000, the Shanghai Cooperation Organisation in 2005, and Mercosur in 2008. In addition, ASEAN has been informally fostering ties with the South Asian Association for Regional Cooperation, the Organization of American States, the African Union, the Economic Cooperation Organization, the Arab League, the Eurasian Economic Union and the Southern African Development Community. Inevitably, as these regional organizations get to know ASEAN better, they will begin to emulate some of ASEAN's best practices.

If ASEAN becomes a model for regional cooperation, it will add value not only to the 630 million people who live within the ASEAN region but also to the lives of the almost 5.5 billion who live in the rest of the developing world. In fact, the EU might also benefit from studying the ASEAN model of cooperation. In the past it was inconceivable that the EU had anything to learn from other regional organizations, but the inconceivable is becoming conceivable.

The second tide that could lift ASEAN's standing in the world is the growing geopolitical competition in the Asia-Pacific region. This book has explained how and why geopolitical competition is likely to increase in the region, and the danger geopolitical competition poses to ASEAN's very survival. However, if ASEAN can retain a certain degree of cohesion, it could also take advantage of geopolitical competition. For example, while China was first off the block to offer free trade agreements to ASEAN, South Korea and Australia, the US has tried to get back into the game by bringing several Asian countries, including four members of ASEAN (Brunei, Malaysia, Singapore and Vietnam), into a Trans-Pacific Partnership (TPP).

While geopolitics is often a zero-sum game, this is not true of geoeconomics. Linda Lim, a Singaporean professor in the University of Michigan at Ann Arbor, has argued that win-win outcomes are possible:

> From an economic perspective, both the TPP and AIIB are not "zero-sum games". Despite the internal operational challenges that each faces, both have the potential to benefit China and the US, neither of which is precluded from joining either. Rather, it is the current domestic political context in each country that has transformed both institutional innovations into an apparent struggle for international dominance.[27]

She also called upon both the US and China to tone down their statements:

> Politicians and pundits on both sides of the Pacific should ratchet down their rhetoric that privileges domestic political myth over international economic reality. If not, a rising risk of conflict over the other's hegemonic aspirations that each rails against, might make the rest of us both poorer, and less secure.

Lim suggests that journalists' and politicians' rhetoric about rising US-China rivalry is overly simplistic when it comes to economic arrangements but may be self-fulfilling. Such rhetoric presents the TPP as an attempt by the United States to prevent China from setting the rules of the game for Pacific trade, rouses fears that the AIIB will have lax practices, and engenders conspiracy theories that China is a currency manipulator and that the US will go to any lengths to

---

27. Linda Lim, "The Myth of US-China Economic Competition", *Straits Times*, 16 Dec. 2015, http://www.straitstimes.com/opinion/the-myth-of-us-china-economic-competition, accessed 13 Oct. 2016.

defend the dollar. Lim points out that the evidence for these claims is shaky, and that continuing to use such rhetoric is dangerous as the climate of fear it creates can produce real tensions between the US and China. ASEAN should join Lim in calling upon the US and China to emphasize the positives, instead of the negatives, of geoeconomic competition.

If the US and China, followed by Japan and India and possibly the EU, continue to shower ASEAN with geoeconomic goodies, the ASEAN countries could end up as the biggest winners from the rising geopolitical competition in the Asia-Pacific region. Several ASEAN countries have already benefited from the growing competition between Japan and China. When Indonesia announced that it would build a high-speed rail line between Jakarta and Bandung, two of the biggest cities in Java, both Japan and China competed ferociously for this project. Initially it appeared that Japan would get the contract, but to the surprise of many, including the Japanese, it went to the Chinese. There is no doubt that as a result of this intense competition, Indonesia obtained very sweet terms for the long-term financing of this railway.

Japan and China have also competed to help ASEAN by bidding to build railways and roads in Thailand, Laos, Cambodia and Vietnam. Such competition clearly benefits ASEAN. A report published by the S. Rajaratnam School of International Studies describes this competition well:

> Japan has been the key partner in supporting the Initiative for ASEAN Integration (IAI), which aims to reduce the development gap among ASEAN member states. Tokyo was the largest contributor of the first phase of the IAI (2002–2008), focusing mainly on human resource development. China also contributed to the IAI, but focused more on the inland waterway improvement in CLMV countries. The Mekong region, which includes all the CLMV countries plus Thailand and some provinces of China, presents a good example of the competition between the two economic powerhouses. Tokyo opted for the multilateral Green Mekong Initiative (GMI) which promotes shared values, rule of law and sustainable development. This differentiates Japan's strategy from China's ... For Beijing,

collaboration with CLMV also brings benefits for domestic economy. The CLMV countries are located adjacent to Yunnan, hence a prosperous Mekong sub-region would directly benefit China's south-western region. Aid provision is also a fulfilment of China's "Good Neighbourliness" and "Going Global" policies, all aimed at building a benign image and denying the "China threat" perception. The development assistance in CLMV complements the Western Development Strategy (WDS).[28]

Myanmar has benefited from competition between China and India. Myanmar's outgoing military-controlled government awarded Citic Group, China's largest state conglomerate, contracts to develop Kyaukphyu Special Economic Zone and a nearby deep-sea port in Rakhine state, close to Myanmar's border with India.[29] On 13 February 2001 India and Burma inaugurated the 250km Tamu-Kalewa-Kalemyo highway, popularly called the Indo-Myanmar Friendship Road, built mainly by the Indian Army's Border Roads Organisation and designed to provide a major strategic and commercial transport route connecting Northeast India and South Asia, as a whole, to Southeast Asia.[30] India and Myanmar have agreed to a four-lane, 3,200km highway connecting India, Myanmar and Thailand, which is expected to be completed by 2020. The route runs from India's northeastern states into Myanmar, where over 1,600km of roads will be built or improved.[31] The Kaladan Multi-modal Transit Transport Project will connect the eastern Indian seaport of Kolkata with Sittwe seaport in Myanmar by sea; it will link

28. "Impact of the Sino-Japanese Competitive Relationship on ASEAN as a Region and Institution", Report, S. Rajaratnam School of International Studies (RSIS), Nanyang Technological University, 24 Dec. 2014, https://www.rsis.edu.sg/wp-content/uploads/2014/12/PR141224_Impact_of_Sino-Japanese.pdf, accessed 10 Oct. 2016.

29. Thurein Hla Htway, "Military Party Awards Major Projects to China", *Nikkei Asian Review*, 13 Jan. 2016, http://asia.nikkei.com/Business/Companies/Military-party-awards-major-projects-to-China, accessed 10 Oct. 2016.

30. Tony Allison, "Myanmar Shows India the Road to Southeast Asia", *Asia Times*, 21 Feb. 2001, http://www.atimes.com/reports/CB21Ai01.html#top5, accessed 13 Oct. 2016.

31. Dean Nelson, "India to Open Super Highway to Burma and Thailand", *The Telegraph*, 29 May 2012, http://www.telegraph.co.uk/news/worldnews/asia/india/9297354/India-to-open-super-highway-to-Burma-and-Thailand.html, accessed 13 Oct. 2016.

Sittwe seaport to Lashio in Myanmar via the Kaladan river boat route and then Lashio on to Mizoram in India by road.[32]

The third rising tide that can benefit ASEAN is the general rise of Asia in world affairs, what Kishore often refers to as the coming Asian century. The idea of the Asian century was first triggered by the emergence of Japan and the great success of the "four tigers" of Hong Kong, South Korea, Singapore and Taiwan. However, the rise of China and India has given real weight to the sense of the inevitability of the Asian century, as their large populations serve as the basis of massive economies. This is a return to normalcy, as China and India had the world's largest economies through most of human history.

ASEAN stands to benefit enormously from this situation. A simple look at the world map will explain why. Geography is destiny, and Southeast Asia is geographically close to both China and India. Central Asia may also enjoy the same physical closeness, but it is far from China's economic growth centres, and the natural barrier of the Himalayan mountains stands between Central Asia and India. By contrast, major trading routes have linked Southeast Asia with China and India for over 2,000 years.

The former PM of Singapore Goh Chok Tong used a vivid and memorable analogy to explain ASEAN's prospects:

> I like to think of new Asia as a mega jumbo jet that is being constructed. Northeast Asia, comprising China, Japan and South Korea, forms one wing with a powerful engine. India, the second wing, will also have a powerful engine. The Southeast Asian countries form the fuselage. Even if we lack a powerful engine for growth among the 10 countries, we will be lifted by the two wings.[33]

Hence, as China and India take off, the ASEAN region will naturally take off economically with them. In many respects, this is already happening, as demonstrated by the growing trade and investment links between ASEAN and both countries.

---

32. Government of India, Ministry of Development of Northeastern Region, *Kaladan Multi-Modal Transit Transport Project*, 2014, http://www.mdoner.gov.in/content/introduction-1, accessed 12 Oct. 2016.

33. "Singapore Is the Global City of Opportunity", Ministry of Communications and Information Singapore, 2005, http://www.mci.gov.sg/web/corp/press-room/categories/speeches/content/singapore-is-the-global-city-of-opportunity, accessed 12 Oct. 2016.

While geographical proximity will allow ASEAN to profit from the growth of China and India, cultural compatibility and comfort are equally important. Having interacted for thousands of years, it is only natural to anticipate a reconnection between Southeast Asia and China and India as the grip of European colonization fades into the past.

With each decade, the governments of China and India have moved closer to Southeast Asia. Their current leaders, President Xi Jinping and Prime Minister Narendra Modi, are dynamic reformists who have spoken about bringing their countries closer to Southeast Asia. At the 37th Singapore Lecture on 23 November 2015, PM Modi said:

> ASEAN is the anchor of our Act East Policy. We are linked by geography and history, united against many common challenges and bound by many shared aspirations. With each ASEAN member, we have deepening political, security, defence and economic ties. And, as ASEAN Community leads the way to regional integration, we look forward to a more dynamic partnership between India and ASEAN that holds rich potential for our 1.9 billion people.[34]

President Xi stated in a speech to the Indonesian Parliament in October 2013:

> China and ASEAN countries are linked by common mountains and rivers and share a historical bond. This year marks the tenth anniversary of the China-ASEAN strategic partnership. Our relationship now stands at a new historical starting point. China places great importance on Indonesia's status and influence in ASEAN. China wishes to work with Indonesia and other ASEAN countries to ensure that China and ASEAN are good neighbors, good friends and good partners who would share prosperity and security and stick together through thick and thin. By making joint efforts, we will build a more closely-knit China-ASEAN community of common destiny so as to bring more benefits to both China and ASEAN and to the people in the region.[35]

---

34. "Text of 37th Singapore Lecture 'India's Singapore Story' by Prime Minister Narendra Modi during His Visit to Singapore", 23 Nov. 2013, https://www.iseas.edu.sg/images/event_highlights/37thsingaporelecture/ Textof37thSingaporeLecture.pdf, accessed 10 Oct. 2016.
35. "Speech by Chinese President Xi Jinping to Indonesian Parliament", ASEAN-China Centre, 2 Oct. 2013, http://www.asean-china-center.org/english/2013-10/03/c_133062675.htm, accessed 10 Oct. 2016.

Chinese Premier Li Keqiang told the China-ASEAN Summit in November 2015 in Kuala Lumpur:

> China and ASEAN countries are good neighbors enjoying geographical proximity and cultural affinity ... In recent years, we have accelerated the building of the 21st-Century Maritime Silk Road, implemented the 2+7 cooperation framework, and forged a sound momentum of China-ASEAN relations featuring shared future, integrated interests and close emotional bond. Our relations have gone far beyond the bilateral scope to become a major cornerstone underpinning peace, stability and development in East Asia.[36]

Conclusion

The strengths and weaknesses, as well as threats and opportunities, that ASEAN faces are easily identified, and clearly the region faces serious challenges. However, the strengths are far more substantial than the weaknesses, and the opportunities outweigh the threats. If ASEAN can find the right leaders to drive it forward in the 21st century, the strengths it has developed can propel it forward at an even faster pace. The purpose of this book is to make more ASEAN policy makers and the populations of ASEAN countries aware that they have inherited a precious resource that they should not neglect or take for granted (as some Asian leaders have been wont to do in recent years). ASEAN is a gift from outstanding founding fathers to the current generation of leaders. It would be a great tragedy if this gift were to be lost through neglect or poor leadership.

---

36. "Remarks by H.E. Li Keqiang Premier of the State Council of the People's Republic of China at the 18th China-ASEAN Summit", Ministry of Foreign Affairs of the People's Republic of China, 22 Nov. 2015, http://www.fmprc.gov.cn/mfa_eng/zxxx_662805/t1317372.shtml, accessed 10 Oct. 2016.

Chapter

6 ASEAN's Peace Prize

The primary purpose of this book is to celebrate the many benefits ASEAN has provided for Southeast Asia and for the world. ASEAN has achieved a miraculous peace dividend. Its extraordinary achievements are deserving of the Nobel Peace Prize. But the prize is unlikely to be awarded to ASEAN anytime soon. There is a widespread lack of knowledge about ASEAN, and a baffling tendency to belittle its many accomplishments. It must also be said that ASEAN is not always its own best advocate.

Even your authors, who have lived in Southeast Asia all our lives, have missed some important ASEAN developments. For example, neither of us knew that in 2008 the ASEAN countries had adopted an anthem. The text of the anthem, which is titled "The ASEAN Way", reads as follows:

> Raise our flag high, sky high
> Embrace the pride in our heart
> ASEAN we are bonded as one
> Look-in out to the world.
> For peace, our goal from the very start
> And prosperity to last.
>
> We dare to dream, we care to share.
> Together for ASEAN
> We dare to dream,
> We care to share, for it's the way of ASEAN.

The fact that people deeply involved with ASEAN have never heard the official ASEAN anthem illustrates perfectly the challenges ASEAN faces in building knowledge about itself as an organization.

This concluding chapter will reiterate the three massive achievements of ASEAN, and highlight some ongoing positive processes within ASEAN that need to be nurtured and strengthened. It will conclude with three bold recommendations for lifting regional cooperation within ASEAN to a much higher level. None of these recommendations can or will be implemented soon, but ASEAN can and should be ambitious about its future goals.

First a word about how far we must go to persuade the world of ASEAN's achievements. As we mentioned in the Introduction, *The Economist*, one of the most influential news magazines in the world, regularly demonstrates ignorance about ASEAN and seems to have a blind spot about its achievements. On 17 May 2014 *The Economist* published an article about "the ASEAN Way". It pointed out all of ASEAN's deficiencies. It noted that a dangerous standoff was taking place between China and Vietnam over a Chinese oil rig drilling off the coast of Vietnam. In discussing ASEAN's goal of creating an ASEAN Economic Community (AEC) in 2015, it started with a typically condescending Anglo-Saxon observation: "*The Economist*'s own style book is leery of the word 'community'", which, it sniffily suggests, often "purports to convey a sense of togetherness that may well not exist". The writer then quotes a study by the Asian Development Bank and the Institute of Southeast Asian Studies which argues that ASEAN "has no prospect of coming close to … [a] single market by the AEC's 2015 deadline—or even 2020 or 2025." The *Economist* piece concludes: "The ASEAN way frustrates the ASEAN project."[1]

It may be unfair to judge *The Economist* on the basis of one column, but as regular readers of the magazine, we have noticed that this condescending dismissal of ASEAN and its achievements is par for the course. When *The Economist* (and other Western publications) report on ASEAN, they fail to note that ASEAN has consistently disappointed its sceptics. That "dangerous" confrontation between China and Vietnam over the oil rig was peacefully and pragmatically resolved. Similarly, contrary to most expectations, the proposed AEC was launched on schedule in November 2015. The ASEAN Way may be imperfect, but ASEAN will make progress with the AEC.

There is nothing imperfect about ASEAN's three major achievements. The first is to deliver 50 years of peace to ASEAN

---

1.   "Getting in the Way", *The Economist*, 17 May 2014, http://www.economist. com/news/asia/21602265-south-east-asia-finds-decorum-its-regional-club-rather-rudely-shattered-getting-way, accessed 12 Oct. 2016.

member states. To drive home the importance of this achievement, think of a world in which war is inconceivable between Israel and Palestine, Iran and Saudi Arabia, India and Pakistan, China and Japan, North and South Korea. Southeast Asia was rife with painful bilateral disputes in the 1950s and 1960s, and maintaining the peace in one of the most troubled regions in the world—the Balkans of Asia—is without question a magnificent achievement. For this alone, ASEAN should have won a Nobel Peace Prize years ago. The fact that it has never been seriously considered for this honour illustrates the global ignorance about ASEAN. Apart from the EU, no other regional organization comes close to matching ASEAN's record in delivering five decades without any major conflicts. In many ways, the ASEAN project is synonymous with peace. Yet, even though the EU was awarded a Nobel Peace Prize in 2012, ASEAN has not even been considered for one.

The second big achievement of ASEAN has been to improve the livelihoods of the more than 600 million people living in Southeast Asia. Here, too, the best way to illustrate the region's progress is to compare the record of its members with their counterparts in other regions. In 1965, Singapore's per capita income was the same as Ghana's. Today, the difference is amazing; the figure for Singapore is US$38,088, while that for Ghana is US$763. While Singapore may be an outlier, the record of ASEAN's most populous country, Indonesia, compares favourably with the most populous countries in Africa (Nigeria) and Latin America (Brazil). In 1967, when ASEAN was founded, their respective per capita incomes were US$1,902 for Brazil, US$484 for Nigeria, and US$274 for Indonesia. Some 50 years later, in 2014, the figures were US$5,881 for Brazil (a 300 per cent increase), US$1,098 for Nigeria (220 per cent), and US$1,853 for Indonesia (670 per cent).[2] It is not surprising that Indonesia outperformed Nigeria since conditions in Africa are much more difficult, but Indonesia's ability to outperform Brazil in percentage terms is an exceptional achievement. Brazil was a far more developed country than Indonesia when ASEAN was founded. National leadership drives economic development, but ASEAN provides the hidden X-factor.

Vietnam is the one country in the region that experienced major conflict over the past half-century. It achieved real peace only in 1992,

2. "Adjusted Net National Income Per Capita (Constant 2005 US$)", IndexMundi, http://www.indexmundi.com/facts/indicators/NY.ADJ.NNTY.PC.KD, accessed 12 Oct. 2016.

when the Cambodian peace settlement was signed. Vietnam joined ASEAN, its erstwhile enemy, in 1995. Vietnam's per capita income rose from US$409 in 1995 to US$1,077 in 2014, and its GDP increased from US$29.5 billion to US$97.7 billion. Jim Yong Kim, president of the World Bank, said on 23 February 2016:

> Vietnam's development achievements over the last 25 years are remarkable. Over this period, the lives of the Vietnamese people have changed dramatically. We have seen economic growth averaging nearly 7 percent, which enabled Vietnam, one of the world's poorest countries in the 1980s, to leapfrog to middle-income status in a single generation. In an especially remarkable achievement, Vietnam has reduced extreme poverty from 50 percent about 25 years ago to just 3 percent today.[3]

Just 45 per cent of the population had access to sanitation facilities in 1995, compared to 78 per cent in 2015. Vietnam's under-five mortality rate fell from 41 per 1,000 in 1995 to 22 in 2015, and its gross enrolment ratio for tertiary education (the proportion of the total population of the five-year age group following on from secondary school leaving) rose from 3 per cent in 1995 to 25 per cent in 2013.

It is hard to find any other country that experienced more than 50 years of continuous conflict (in the case of Vietnam, from 1942 to 1992) and which then turned around to achieve so much economically. Vietnam's achievements demonstrate that ASEAN has been able to deliver economic and social development to its members.

ASEAN's third big achievement has been to "civilize" the big powers that have been dealing with the region. Over the past few decades, each of the major powers involved with Southeast Asia (the United States, China, Japan, India, the EU and Russia) has come to ASEAN bearing gifts. No other regional organization has been as assiduously courted as ASEAN has been by the great powers. As one example, when President Obama invited all the ASEAN leaders to attend the first-ever US-ASEAN Summit meeting on US soil in February 2015, he told the opening session:

---

3. "World Bank Group President Jim Yong Kim Opening Remarks at the Vietnam 2035 Report Launching", World Bank, 23 Feb. 2016, http://www.worldbank.org/en/news/speech/2016/02/23/world-bank-group-president-jim-yong-kim-opening-remarks-at-the-vietnam-2035-report-launching, accessed 12 Oct. 2016.

> It is my privilege to welcome you to this landmark gathering—
> the first U.S.-ASEAN Summit hosted by the United States. This
> reflects my personal commitment and the national commitment
> of the United States, to a strong and enduring partnership
> with your 10 nations individually and to Southeast Asia as one
> region, as one community—ASEAN.[4]

Obama's track record with ASEAN was imperfect—he cancelled
at least three proposed trips to the region—but he recognized the
long-term importance of cultivating ASEAN. A *Straits Times* article
documenting the results of that summit shows that his assessment was
correct:

> The move could be seen as the Obama administration walking
> the talk since it said in 2011 that the US needs to make a "strategic
> pivot" in its foreign policy, with greater attention to the South-
> east Asian region. In nearly eight years of the Obama presidency,
> this is the third attempt to economically connect the US to
> South-east Asia, earlier ones being the US-ASEAN Expanded
> Economic Engagement in 2012 and the Trans-Pacific Partnership
> (TPP) last year … for the US, a strong and developed ASEAN
> can buffer the economic rise of China, especially in regional
> organisations such as the ASEAN+3 and the East Asia Summit.[5]

The value of ASEAN to most of the great powers is likely to increase
in the coming decades, and so, accordingly, will their courtship of
ASEAN. Great-power courtship of ASEAN has already brought
massive social and economic benefits. ASEAN has signed nearly
as many free trade agreements as the EU, seven versus ten, even
though ASEAN is much younger and less developed. Trade between
ASEAN and China grew from US$20 billion in 1995[6] to US$480 billion

---

4. "Remarks by President Obama at Opening Session of the U.S.-ASEAN
   Summit", White House, 2016, https://www.whitehouse.gov/the-press-
   office/2016/02/15/remarks-president-obama-opening-session-us-asean-
   summit, accessed 12 Oct. 2016.
5. Sanchita B. Das, "What US-Asean Connect Means for the Region", *Straits
   Times*, 17 Mar. 2016, http://www.straitstimes.com/opinion/what-us-asean-
   connect-means-for-the-region, accessed 12 Oct. 2016.
6. Yu Sheng *et al.*, "The Impact of ACFTA on People's Republic of China-ASEAN
   Trade: Estimates Based on an Extended Gravity Model for Component
   Trade", Asian Development Bank, July 2012, https://www.adb.org/contact/
   tang-hsiao-chink, accessed 12 Oct. 2016.

in 2014,[7] an increase of 24 times. Japanese trade and investment in ASEAN has also grown rapidly. In 2014 Japan was ASEAN's third-largest trading partner, with two-way trade of US$220.4 billion, nearly double the figure of US$126.3 billion in 1995.[8] Japan is also ASEAN's second-largest source of FDI flows (US$20.4 billion in 2014, up from US$5.2 billion in 1997).[9] Amazingly, even though the US has slipped behind China, Japan and the EU in trade with ASEAN, it remains the second-largest investor in ASEAN after the EU.

In addition to these three major achievements, three ongoing processes within ASEAN have brought significant benefits to the ASEAN countries and their neighbours. The first of these is a strong camaraderie among the leaders, ministers and senior officials in ASEAN. Scholarship in the West often overlooks the personal dimension in international relations. One man who has spoken to us eloquently about the strength and power of the camaraderie among ASEAN officials is George Yeo, who has spent more than two decades interacting at senior levels of the ASEAN system, working on two very different tracks of ASEAN cooperation: political and economic.[10]

Having only worked on the Foreign Ministry track of ASEAN cooperation, Kishore had always assumed that ASEAN foreign ministers, who practised diplomacy, would develop closer relations than ASEAN trade ministers, who were busy trying to protect their economies from excessive competition. It came as a surprise to learn from Yeo that ASEAN trade ministers were actually closer, an

---

7. "ASEAN-China Economic and Trade Cooperation Situation in 2014", Asian-China Centre, 16 Mar. 2015, http://www.asean-china-center.org/english/2015-03/16/c_134071066.htm, accessed 12 Oct. 2016.

8. Calculated from data available at http://www.customs.go.jp/toukei/info/index_e.htm and in the IMF database.

9. Japan External Trade Organization, "East Asia Economic Integration and the Roles of JETRO", Ministry of Foreign Affairs of Japan, http://www.mofa.go.jp/region/asia-paci/cambodia/workshop0609/attach5.pdf, accessed 12 Oct. 2016; Japan External Trade Organization, "JETRO Global Trade and Investment Report 2015: New Efforts Aimed at Developing Global Business", http://www.jetro.go.jp/en/news/2015/ea96c87efd06f226.html, accessed 12 Oct. 2016.

10. From 1988 to 1991 George Yeo served as a senior official in the Ministry of Foreign Affairs (as minister of state for foreign affairs; from 1990 to 1991, as senior minister of state for foreign affairs; from 1991 to 1994, as second minister for foreign affairs; and from 2004 to 2011, as minister of foreign affairs). From 1997 to 1999 he also served as second minister for trade and industry, and from 1999 to 2004 as minister for trade and industry. In each role he had frequent meetings with his ASEAN counterparts.

observation that goes a long way towards explaining why ASEAN trade and economic cooperation has progressed steadily even though some ASEAN countries tend to be protectionist at times. The cordial relations among trade ministers and officials has created peer pressure, which has led to the progressive opening up of ASEAN economies. Yeo emphasized that unlike the EU, which moved towards economic cooperation within a rigid and legalistic framework, the ASEAN countries did so in a loose and pragmatic fashion. Rather than big-bang change in ASEAN trade liberalization, there has been a slow but steady lifting of both tariff and non-tariff barriers.

Ambassador Tommy Koh, a veteran Singaporean diplomat, has worked with ASEAN for many years, but even he was surprised to learn from a doctor he met that regular meetings took place among ASEAN paediatric surgeons, resulting in improved paediatric care in ASEAN countries. In short, the thousands of meetings that take place among the ASEAN countries each year have created hundreds of networks that substantially increase cooperation among the countries.

It is fashionable among conservative American scholars to be cynical about the value of multilateral processes. Were sceptics to attend and study ASEAN meetings, they would be surprised by the high levels of cooperation among ASEAN officials in many areas. From health to environment, and from education to defence, there has been a steady rise in multilateral cooperation among ASEAN countries, all facilitated by the personal relations that have developed among ASEAN leaders and officials.

Yeo also notes that ASEAN camaraderie has defused many potential crises. Three powerful examples occurred during his time in government. In 2007, the world was shocked when monks in Yangon were shot during street protests after the unexpected removal of fuel subsidies on 15 August 2007 led to a drastic overnight rise in commodity prices. Since ASEAN had admitted Myanmar as a member in 1997, there was a lot of pressure on the ASEAN countries to issue a statement criticizing these shootings. As an ASEAN member state, Myanmar had two options. It could have vetoed an ASEAN joint statement or disassociated itself from such a statement. Then there would have been a statement by the remaining nine countries criticizing Myanmar. Many people, including the nine other ASEAN foreign ministers, expected this to be the outcome.

At the time of the shootings, which began on 26 September 2007, the ten ASEAN foreign ministers held meetings in New York, where they had gone to participate in sessions of the UN General Assembly. Singapore was then chairman of ASEAN, so Yeo chaired these

meetings. When the group drafted a strong statement criticizing the
shootings, Yeo suggested that the ASEAN statement be of the nine
less Myanmar. It was widely expected that the Myanmar foreign
minister, Nyan Win, would disassociate himself and his delegation
from the statement. To the surprise of Yeo and the other ASEAN
foreign ministers, Nyan Win agreed that all ten countries, including
Myanmar, should endorse the statement. This was truly remarkable as
the statement said that the ASEAN foreign ministers

> were appalled to receive reports of automatic weapons being
> used and demanded that the Myanmar government immediately
> desist from the use of violence against demonstrators. They
> expressed their revulsion to Myanmar Foreign Minister Nyan
> Win over reports that the demonstrations in Myanmar are being
> suppressed by violent force and that there has been a number
> of fatalities.[11]

In short, Myanmar Foreign Minister Nyan Win endorsed a statement
criticizing his own government. Even at the press conference that
followed the meeting, Myanmar was represented by a senior official.
In assessing this surprising development, Yeo said:

> To Myanmar, ASEAN was everything they had. They would
> attend all ASEAN meetings. They would have set pieces,
> prepared statements. They would be thick-skinned in receiving
> criticism, but they stuck it out, because we were their only hope.
> They didn't want to be too close to China, even though they
> depended on China. India supported Aung San Suu Kyi initially
> and took an intermediate position, but was never close to them.
> The Western powers were pretty hostile.

In short, even when there were sharp disagreements between
Myanmar and its fellow ASEAN countries, Myanmar decided
that sticking with ASEAN was preferable to opting out. ASEAN
camaraderie helped to create this deep sense of solidarity, which
would prove to be useful in crises.

A crisis arose in May 2008 when Cyclone Nargis killed thousands
of people in Myanmar and left hundreds of thousands homeless,
without food and medicine. According to a report by Crisis Group

---

11. "Statement by ASEAN Chair, Singapore's Minister for Foreign Affairs George
    Yeo in New York, 27 September 2007", Embassy of the Republic of Singapore,
    Washington, DC, http://www.mfa.gov.sg/content/mfa/overseasmission/
    washington/newsroom/press_statements/2007/200709/press_200709_03.html,
    accessed 12 Oct. 2016.

Asia, "Critical infrastructure, including electricity, communication and transportation networks, health facilities and schools across an area half the size of Switzerland, sustained massive damage. The scale of destruction is comparable to the 2004 Indian Ocean tsunami."[12] The international community expected to be called upon by the government of Myanmar to provide assistance, but the ruling military government was suspicious of foreign intervention, and especially of Western intervention, and it turned down all offers of help.

The international community was horrified. Sarah Ireland, Oxfam's regional director for East Asia, said: "With the likelihood of 100,000 or more killed in the cyclone there are all the factors for a public health catastrophe which could multiply that death toll by up to 15 times in the coming period."[13] As usual, many Western leaders claimed the moral high ground and vehemently condemned the Myanmar government. A British paper published this account of PM Gordon Brown's reaction:

> In the UK's strongest criticism of Burma's military rulers so far, the prime minister said the junta was turning a natural disaster into a manmade catastrophe. "This is inhuman. We have an intolerable situation, created by a natural disaster," Brown told the BBC World Service. "It is being made into a manmade catastrophe by the negligence, the neglect and the inhuman treatment of the Burmese people by a regime that is failing to act and to allow the international community to do what it wants to do. The responsibility lies with the Burmese regime and they must be held accountable."[14]

French Foreign Minister Bernard Kouchner made a particularly damaging statement. Referring to the decision by the UN General Assembly at the 2005 UN World Summit to endorse the concept of "Responsibility to Protect", he said that if the government of Myanmar refused international assistance to help the victims of the cyclone, the

12. "Burma/Myanmar after Nargis: Time to Normalise Aid Relations", International Crisis Group, 2008, https://www.files.ethz.ch/isn/93248/161_burma_myanmar_after_nargis.pdf, accessed 12 Oct. 2016.
13. "Oxfam Warns up to 1.5 Million in Danger if Aid Effort Cannot Reach Cyclone Victims", Oxfam America, 11 May 2008, https://www.oxfamamerica.org/press/oxfam-warns-up-to-15-million-in-danger-if-aid-effort-cannot-reach-cyclone-victims/, accessed 12 Oct. 2016.
14. Ian MacKinnon and Mark Tran, "Brown Condemns 'Inhuman' Burma Leaders over Aid", *The Guardian*, 17 May 2008, https://www.theguardian.com/world/2008/may/17/cyclonenargis.burma2, accessed 12 Oct. 2016.

international community had a responsibility to protect the victims and should therefore intervene militarily and provide assistance against the wishes of the Myanmar government.

This was a particularly unwise and infelicitous statement, one that reinforced the paranoia of Myanmar's military government. This government was accustomed to rebuffing and ignoring Western criticisms of Myanmar and was ready to ride out another wave of criticism. Its response to Kouchner's threat to intervene militarily was to send troops to a base in Irrawaddy to ward off any Western military incursion. Rather than helping cyclone victims, the military was deployed to fight off foreign forces. The standoff lasted a few weeks. Had it continued, hundreds of thousands of cyclone victims would have experienced even more suffering. Fortunately, ASEAN came to the rescue.

At a meeting of ASEAN foreign ministers convened on 19 May 2008 in Singapore, the Myanmar delegation persisted in refusing all foreign assistance. When the discussions became tense, Indonesian Foreign Minister Hassan Wirajuda looked Myanmar Foreign Minister Nyan Win in the eye and said, "What do you mean to us, and what do we mean to you?" It was a powerful statement. George Yeo jumped in, telling Nyan Win, "Why don't you check back with Naypyidaw?" Nyan Win said, "Okay, I'll do it." Yeo said, "Take your time." Nyan Win came back after lunch and said, "I got the go-ahead."

After the Myanmar government said yes, ASEAN encountered practical difficulties in delivering aid. In their book *Myanmar: Life after Nargis*, Pavin Chachavalpongpun and Moe Thuzar explain the challenges ASEAN faced:

> Following the pledging conference, the ASEAN Secretariat … found itself pressed for time and space to establish its presence in Yangon. Up to that point, the Secretariat officers had been operating out of office space and with equipment provided by the UN. For the first time in the Secretariat's operational history, its officers were now faced with the challenge of opening a field office, with limited resources. Dr Surin [Pitsuwan] himself scouted for possible office space, and used his personal networks to negotiate favourable terms and obtain sufficient funds to tide over the initial operations of the ASEAN field office in Yangon.[15]

---

15. Pavin Chachavalpongpun and Moe Thuzar, *Myanmar: Life after Nargis* (Singapore: ISEAS, 2009), p. 56.

This was a revealing episode. It showed that the level of trust and friendship among ASEAN ministers had reached a high level. Myanmar, especially its courageous foreign minister, Nyan Win, felt real pressure to accommodate the interests of fellow ASEAN members. This is turn saved hundreds of thousands of lives in Myanmar, after the Myanmar government finally announced that it would allow in foreign aid workers on 23 May 2008. The episode forcefully demonstrates why ASEAN should continue to nurture and strengthen regional networking.

The third example provided by Yeo concerned the dispute between Cambodia and Thailand over the Preah Vihear temple. The two countries came close to open military conflict over this territorial dispute. Tension started brewing in January 2008, when Cambodia registered the temple as a UNESCO World Heritage Site without seeking agreement from Thailand. The Thais eventually agreed on the UNESCO registration, and Preah Vihear was named a UNESCO World Heritage Site on 8 July. However, the decision gave rise to protests in Thailand, and on 15 July three Thais were arrested by the Cambodians as they tried to plant a flag near the temple. Both countries moved more troops and heavy artillery into the area over the next few days, and on 3 October 2008 the troops exchanged fire. Several clashes took place during the next few years, and the situation again escalated in February 2011. Towards the end of the month, though, the two countries agreed to allow Indonesian observers on the scene. In July, the International Court of Justice ordered both countries to withdraw their troops. The situation de-escalated, but there were two more clashes later in the year. The International Court of Justice ruled in November 2013 that the promontory belonged to Cambodia.

In theory, this was a bilateral dispute between two countries over a border issue. In practice, the dispute was a result of a political crisis in Thailand. The government in Thailand, which was sympathetic to former Thai Prime Minister Thaksin Shinawatra, had built up a good relationship with the Cambodian government and did not take a hard line on the Preah Vihear dispute. The political forces supporting the pro-Thaksin government were known as the Red Shirts and their opponents the Yellow Shirts. In an effort to embarrass the Red Shirt movement, the Yellow Shirts accused the foreign minister of being a traitor for giving away Thai national territory to Cambodia. An acute political crisis ensued, and the Thai government was forced to adopt a hard-line position. The two countries came close to military conflict in June and July 2008.

Once again, ASEAN intervened to defuse the situation. An ASEAN foreign ministers meeting was convened on 22 July 2008. Yeo described what happened at this meeting:

> Then, they were close to blows. We were in the chair and Thailand had no foreign minister at that time. They sent one of the deputy prime ministers, who, by his own admission, only came because all the other deputy prime ministers knew that it was going to be very difficult, and found reasons not to come. So he was volunteered and represented Thailand. And we said we were going to discuss Preah Vihear. He said, "I got no mandate to discuss Preah Vihear." I said to him, "You represent Thailand!" He said, "Yeah—but I cannot, because everything has to be referred back to Parliament; otherwise I will be accused of treason." I said, "If that is the case, we will meet without you." He said, "No, you can't do that. You know—ASEAN meeting— Thailand must be there." I said, "You decide. You want to be there, then be there when we discuss Preah Vihear. If you cannot discuss Preah Vihear, then we'll meet without you." So he went back and consulted Bangkok. After doing so, he came back and said, "I will attend the meeting." So he attended the meeting, and in fact, I have a picture of that meeting in my book. It was held in the Botanic Gardens, in one of the bungalows there. Very intense meeting. We offered the offices of ASEAN [to mediate]. Thailand refused; Cambodia said, "Why not?" After the chair passed to Indonesia, Marty, the Indonesian foreign minister, on his own initiative visited both countries and helped to broker something. It worked out in the end. Through patience and persistence, we overcame a crisis.[16]

These positive results within ASEAN were possible because of the deep sense of camaraderie and community that has developed among senior ASEAN leaders and officials over the course of thousands of ASEAN meetings. Even if they do nothing else, the ASEAN countries need to carry on with these meetings because they have clear payoffs.

The second ongoing process is the development of stronger cooperation among the intellectual communities of different ASEAN countries. The SWOT analysis of ASEAN in the previous chapter showed that one of its key weaknesses is the absence of a sense of ownership by the people of ASEAN. One stepping stone towards developing a sense of ownership is to strengthen further cooperation among intellectual elites, especially those working in foreign policy.

---

16. Authors' interview with George Yeo, 5 Feb. 2016.

In academic parlance such cooperation is called Track Two cooperation. It refers to cooperation among non-governmental organizations, as opposed to Track One cooperation, which is cooperation among governments. ASEAN cooperation has proceeded primarily on Track One, but Track Two cooperation is becoming significant. The primary venue for Track Two cooperation has been ASEAN-ISIS meetings. (ISIS here refers to Institute of Strategic and International Studies, not the terrorist group in Syria.) Each ASEAN country has designated one strategic issues think tank to represent it in the ASEAN-ISIS network.[17]

The spiritual father of this network is the renowned Indonesian intellectual Jusuf Wanandi, whose Centre for Strategic and International Studies in Jakarta is one of the most effective think tanks in Southeast Asia. Jusuf took the lead in assembling a group of ASEAN intellectuals he knew well, including Noordin Sopiee (Malaysia), Simon Tay (Singapore) and Carolina Hernandez (Philippines). Formed in 1988, the network's founding members include the Centre for Strategic and International Studies, ISIS of Malaysia, the Institute of Strategic and Development Studies (ISDS) of the Philippines, the Singapore Institute of International Affairs, and the Institute of Security and International Studies (ISIS) of Thailand.

Kishore was the ASEAN-SOM leader from Singapore from 1994 to 1998 and participated in several meetings between ASEAN senior officials and ASEAN-ISIS representatives. Meetings between government and non-government representatives in other countries often turn negative and confrontational because the parties represent different constituencies. Fortunately, these ASEAN meetings never turned negative. There was always a friendly spirit of openness in the room as both sides listened to each other. During each session, the ASEAN-ISIS representative would present proposals for enhanced ASEAN cooperation. Evaluating this approach, Maria Ortuoste of California State University has written:

> This assertion of the exportability of the ASEAN model was aided by the ASEAN-ISIS and supported (if not acquiesced to) by other countries. By this time, ASEAN-ISIS had developed an extensive network of linkages in Southeast Asia and in the Asia-Pacific (particularly with Japan, Canada and Australia) which allowed for the preliminary exchange of ideas on a regional security dialogue. This culminated in the ASEAN decision

---

17. For more information, see http://www.siiaonline.org/page/isis/.

to tackle political and security issues in its Post-Ministerial Conference (PMC) with its dialogue partners and later with the establishment of the ARF.[18]

A paper presented by the chairman of ASEAN-ISIS, Malayvieng Sakonhnihom, at the ARF Inter-Sessional Support Group in 2007 states:

> During almost two decades [since its launch in 1988], ASEAN-ISIS has established itself as a very important Track 2 network recognized by the governments of ASEAN countries ... Acting as "Track 2", ASEAN-ISIS provides policy inputs to their respective Track 1 by organizing regional workshops, meetings, conferences, seminars, etc. ... It is significant to recognize that among these important venues, some have become the "flagship activities" of ASEAN-ISIS namely the Asia Pacific Roundtable (APR) for Confidence Building and Conflict Resolution, the ASEAN-ISIS Colloquium on Human Rights (AICOHR), and the ASEAN People's Assembly (APA).[19]

The third ongoing process that ASEAN needs to strengthen further is multilateral meetings involving all great powers in the Asia-Pacific region. As this book has documented, ASEAN has done a good job of "civilizing" the great powers. However, the real challenges for ASEAN are just beginning. Huge shifts of power will take place in the Asia-Pacific region, and it is reasonable to predict growing tension involving the US, China, Japan and India as the relative weights of these powers vis-à-vis each other shift significantly in the coming decades. Painful readjustments will have to be made.

ASEAN can help ease the pain of these adjustments by continuing its practice of inviting leaders and ministers of the great powers to regularly attend ASEAN meetings. Their informal encounters on these occasions can lubricate and reduce the inevitable friction among these great powers.

For this to happen, the parties concerned need to understand the value of these gatherings. From time to time, as new leaders emerge,

18. Maria Consuelo C. Ortuoste, "Internal and External Institutional Dynamics in Member-States and ASEAN: Tracing Creation, Change and Reciprocal Influences", PhD dissertation, Arizona State University, 2008, http://gradworks.umi.com/33/27/3327250.html, accessed 10 Oct. 2016.
19. Malayvieng Sakonhninhom, "Flagships and Activities of ASEAN-ISIS", ASEAN Regional Forum, Mar. 2007, http://aseanregionalforum.asean.org/files/Archive/14th/ARF_Inter-sessional_Support_Group/Annex(34).pdf, accessed 10 Oct. 2016.

they will question the value of having meetings simply for the sake of having meetings. President Jokowi of Indonesia, for example, was appalled by the ASEAN and ASEAN-plus meetings that he attended after he was elected president of Indonesia in July 2014. After his first meeting with his fellow ASEAN leaders, he reportedly turned to ask PM Lee Hsien Loong of Singapore whether it was necessary for ASEAN leaders to make such routine statements at each ASEAN meeting. He preferred to avoid these rituals and work on solving real problems at home.

But rituals matter. When leaders assemble together in ritualistic fashion each year, they get to know each other as human beings and not as officials representing different countries. Hence, we would call on leaders like President Jokowi to be patient and allow the positive effects of these encounters to unveil themselves after attending a few ASEAN and ASEAN-plus meetings. Moreover, President Jokowi's continued participation in ASEAN meetings will encourage other leaders to attend. American leaders and officials such as President Obama and former Secretary of State Condoleezza Rice have shown a tendency to skip ASEAN meetings. If this becomes a habit for future American officials, ASEAN will be less able to lubricate relations among great powers. ASEAN must use all its persuasive powers to persuade the great powers to attend ASEAN-plus meetings without fail, and they will not come if the president of the largest ASEAN country, Indonesia, does not turn up himself. Just being present is important. If we can ensure that the leaders of America, China, India and Japan come regularly to ASEAN-plus meetings, we will have laid a foundation for smooth relations among the great powers in the Asia-Pacific region.

Three Bold Recommendations

We will conclude this book by making three bold recommendations to lift ASEAN cooperation to a higher level and ensure that ASEAN remains a strong, dynamic and vibrant regional organization half a century from now. Each of these suggestions will meet some resistance, and there may be difficulties when it comes to implementation, but if ASEAN leaders fail to set ambitious goals for the next 50 years, they will not fulfil their responsibility to build on the good work done by their predecessors.

The first recommendation is the most obvious one. If ASEAN is going to survive and succeed over the long term, ownership of the organization must shift from the governments to the people.

Governments come and go. People do not. The relative enthusiasm of the member countries for ASEAN changes when governments change. President Suharto was a staunch defender of ASEAN during his long reign, but his immediate successor, President Habibie, was initially less enthusiastic. As Amitav Acharya has noted, this approach changed: "Despite an initial sign of an unwitting neglect of ASEAN on the part of the Habibie and Wahid government in Jakarta, Jakarta signalled a more activist attitude towards ASEAN."[20] Similarly, President SBY was a more enthusiastic supporter of ASEAN processes than his successor, President Jokowi, but President Jokowi has become more supportive of ASEAN with each passing year. The trade minister he appointed in 2015, Tom Lembong, was more enthusiastic about implementing the AEC than his immediate predecessor, Rachmat Gobel.

To protect ASEAN from the vicissitudes of changes in government, the people of ASEAN need to feel a greater sense of ownership. If the people of ASEAN applied pressure on their respective governments to pay more attention to the organization, that would be the ultimate insurance policy to ensure that no ASEAN member state withdraws or otherwise jeopardizes its future. The sense that the "people" own ASEAN has grown over the years as a result of some unusual ASEAN initiatives. It was a brilliant idea, for example, for each ASEAN country to follow the EU practice of having two flags, the ASEAN flag and the national flag, flying over each ASEAN embassy. Since most citizens feel a surge of national pride when they visit their embassies, they will associate this pride with both their own country and ASEAN.

The best way to generate a deep sense of ownership of ASEAN by its people is to embed ASEAN into the curricula of national education systems. Each primary school child should be able to name the ten ASEAN countries and know at least a little bit about the history and culture of each one. In the British colony of Singapore, our primary education included information about the history and culture of Great Britain. There was a lot about the Queen of England but almost nothing about the King of Thailand. Textbooks do matter. Each ASEAN country should be encouraged to incorporate ASEAN in the textbooks used in its schools. Without doubt the result would then be ten very different versions of ASEAN, and so the ASEAN countries might exchange textbooks to help understand the diversity that lies at the heart of the organization.

---

20. Acharya, *Constructing a Security Community in Southeast Asia*, p. 221.

ASEAN has already taken steps to widen and deepen a sense of public ownership. Visa-free travel and an explosion of budget carrier flights among ASEAN countries have significantly increased face-to-face contact among the different ASEAN populations and thereby promoted intra-ASEAN understanding. According to the ASEAN Travel website:

> Some 105 million travellers are recorded in the 10 ASEAN member countries while the market share of ASEAN travellers represent on average a little less than half of these arrivals—46% to 48% according to official data. But they could grow to 152 million by 2025 while intra ASEAN arrivals could overpass the 90-million traveller's mark. GDP contribution of ASEAN tourism could potentially increase from 12% today to 15% in 2025 while tourism could represent 7% of all employments in a decade time compared to 3.7% today.[21]

BBC reported in 2012 that one-third of Southeast Asia's airline capacity was fulfilled by low-cost carriers.[22] A May 2014 article in *The Economist* states:

> In just ten years, according to the Centre for Asia Pacific Aviation (CAPA), a research firm in Sydney, low-cost carriers' share of the region's aviation market has soared from almost nothing to 58% ... Now South-East Asia's skies are looking crowded ... Of the world's 15 busiest low-cost international routes, nine are in South-East Asia.[23]

Another unintended positive benefit of the explosion of intra-ASEAN budget carrier flights is that poets and artists of ASEAN countries can visit each other more easily. Inevitably, this led to more references to fellow ASEAN countries in the art and literature of the region. Matthew Isaac Cohen observed in an article published in the *Asian Theatre Journal*:

---

21. Luc Citrinot, "ASEAN for ASEAN: Focus Will Be Given to Strengthening Intra-ASEAN Tourism", ASEAN Travel, 2016, http://asean.travel/2016/01/24/asean-for-asean-focus-will-be-given-to-strengthening-intra-asean-tourism/, accessed 12 Oct. 2016.
22. Nick Easen, "In Asia, a Boom in Low-cost Flights", BBC, 2 Apr. 2012, http://www.bbc.com/travel/story/20120402-low-cost-flights-in-asia-booms, accessed 12 Oct. 2016.
23. "Too Much of a Good Thing", *The Economist*, 15 May 2014, http://www.economist.com/news/business/21602241-after-binge-aircraft-buying-and-airline-founding-it-time-sober-up-too-much-good, accessed 12 Oct. 2016.

Long considered an isolated backwater of global cultural flows, a proud possessor of artistic traditions seemingly immune to international fashions, Southeast Asia is now coming into its own as a cultural powerhouse, refashioning old traditions and taking on new forms and ideas, with connections being rapidly formed between ASEAN member states ... The current generation of collaborators is more cosmopolitan and curious, experienced and agile in cross-art collaborations, hungry for enriching their practices and generating new expressive possibilities and linkages. A Thai contemporary dancer confesses that his peers are located in Indonesia and Cambodia, not Bangkok. A young puppeteer from Kuala Lumpur makes it clear he gained far more understanding of shadow puppetry from a brief trip he took to Java to talk to experimental puppeteers than in his sponsored studies with the conservative puppet masters of the northern Malaysian state of Kelantan. Indonesian playwrights and directors are reading, translating, and performing plays by Singaporean playwrights.[24]

While these initiatives have had a positive incremental effect in building awareness and ownership of ASEAN among its population, ASEAN would benefit from some big-bang initiatives, and two have already been proposed. At their retreat in January 2011, the ASEAN foreign ministers discussed the possibility of jointly hosting the World Cup, and after the International Olympic Committee voted in December 2014 to allow countries to co-host the Olympics, an ASEAN Olympics also became a possibility. News agencies quoted Olympic Committee members from various ASEAN countries supporting this idea. Since Brazil hosted the World Cup in 2014 and the Olympics in 2016, there is no reason why ASEAN collectively cannot host either or both of these events. Hosting one of the world's most important athletic competitions would have an electrifying effect on ASEAN by building awareness of ASEAN in the region and throughout the world.

Either initiative would give rise to intense haggling—for example, over which capital should host the World Cup Final, the most-watched game in the competition—but ASEAN is accustomed to haggling. When Japan proposed setting up an institute to promote economic research in the ASEAN countries, Malaysia and Indonesia fought hard to host it. Both countries had strong and dynamic trade ministers: Mari Pangestu in Indonesia and Rafidah Aziz in Malaysia. In the end, after

---

24. Matthew Isaac Cohen, "Introduction: Global Encounters in Southeast Asian Performing Arts", *Asian Theatre Journal* 31, 2 (2014): 353–68.

intense lobbying, Indonesia won. The Economic Research Institute for ASEAN and East Asia was set up in Jakarta in 2008 and has produced valuable economic studies on ASEAN. In short, even though hosting an event like the World Cup or the Olympics would give rise to intense competition among ASEAN countries, ASEAN is well equipped to resolve such disagreements and arrive at a consensus.

ASEAN could also take a leaf from Europe's book and create cultural events similar to the Edinburgh Fringe Festival or the Eurovision contest to showcase the rich artistic and cultural heritage of the Southeast Asian region. Any such mega-event would have a cascading effect of developing the consciousness of an ASEAN identity among the region's populations.

The second bold recommendation is equally obvious: to change the current stunted and severely limited secretariat into a vibrant institution that will serve ASEAN well. As organizations (and companies) grow and succeed, their administrative capabilities must grow and keep pace. It is true that ASEAN must not replicate the huge expenditures of the European Commission. ASEAN, unlike the EU, is an intergovernmental organization, not a supranational body like the European Commission. Singapore Ambassador Bilahari Kausikan was right in pointing out the differences between the EU and ASEAN when he said:

> The EU is meant to be a post-nationalist construct. Paradoxically, it was inspired by very nationalist fears of a superior nationalism … ASEAN did not deny the reality of nationalism or try to supplant it with some delusional higher purpose. In a region whose geopolitical location at the intersection of major power interests puts sovereignty at continual risk, ASEAN harnessed the nationalisms of its members to a mechanism that could enhance our capacity to retain autonomy and sovereignty by channelling our nationalisms to this end which, whatever our other differences, we all shared.[25]

However, the secretariat should not remain stunted while ASEAN grows. Why has it failed to expand? The simple answer is a design flaw that has not been remedied. When the ASEAN Secretariat was established in 1976, ASEAN had only five members, each with similar national capabilities, and they agreed on the simple principle that each member should pay the same amount to the ASEAN Secretariat to avoid squabbling over who should pay more and who should pay

---

25. Bilahari Kausikan, "Hard Truths and Wishful Hopes about the AEC", *Straits Times*, 2 Jan. 2016.

less. At that time, it was a generous gesture on the part of Singapore as it had agreed that despite its small population of 2.2 million people, it would pay the same as Indonesia, which then had a population of 132.4 million, 60 times larger.

By 2014 ASEAN had ten member states, and the disparities among them had also grown enormously. Laos and Cambodia, for example, had GDPs of US$11.8 billion and US$16.7 billion in 2014, while Indonesia's GDP stood at US$890 billion, 75 times more than the smallest ASEAN GDP.[26] This structural problem that has stunted the growth of the ASEAN Secretariat grows directly out of the policy of equal payments because annual payments for the secretariat cannot exceed the capacity to pay of the poorest ASEAN member state.

An ADB report has strongly recommended that ASEAN reconsider its principle of equal funding from all ten members:

> Anchoring funding on equal shares not only hampers budget growth: it also makes the group intrinsically dependent on external funding from international donors. In practice, while funds are typically available, donor and ASEAN priorities do not always match. Thus, ASEAN is unable to independently accomplish its plans and realize its strategies as decisions are distorted by accommodating requests from the many external stakeholders contributing to the association's budget. If ASEAN is to become a mature and thriving institution, member countries should realize that the principle used in funding the budget is obsolete.[27]

As a dynamic regional organization, ASEAN needs a correspondingly strong and dynamic secretariat. Why are we crippling the capacity of the secretariat to grow with the principle that its funding should be determined by the capacity to pay of the poorest member state? All ten ASEAN member states are also members of the UN, where their annual dues are determined by a complex formula that allocates to each country a certain proportion to pay for the annual UN budget based on each member state's "capacity to pay".

26. "World Economic Outlook Database", International Monetary Fund, https://www.imf.org/external/data.htm, accessed 12 Dec. 2016.
27. "ASEAN 2030: Toward a Borderless Economic Community", Asian Development Bank Institute, 2014, http://www.adb.org/sites/default/files/publication/159312/adbi-asean-2030-borderless-economic-community.pdf, accessed 10 Oct. 2016.

Since the ten ASEAN members have accepted this principle of "capacity to pay" for the UN, which is far less important for their national interests than ASEAN, why not agree on the same principle for the ASEAN Secretariat? The ASEAN countries could determine how much each should pay to the ASEAN Secretariat based on the percentages they pay to the UN Secretariat. In 2014 these percentages were: Brunei 0.026 per cent, Cambodia 0.004 per cent, Indonesia 0.346 per cent, Laos 0.002 per cent, Malaysia 0.281 per cent, Myanmar 0.010 per cent, Singapore 0.384 per cent, Thailand 0.239 per cent, the Philippines 0.154 per cent, and Vietnam 0.042 per cent.[28] Using this simple scheme, the contributions of each ASEAN country (based on the 2014 figures) to the ASEAN Secretariat budget would be as follows:

Brunei	1.75%
Cambodia	0.27%
Indonesia	23.25%
Laos	0.13%
Malaysia	18.88%
Myanmar	0.67%
Singapore	25.81%
Thailand	16.06%
Philippines	10.35%
Vietnam	2.82%

Asking the larger ASEAN states (like Indonesia) and the more prosperous ones (like Singapore) to pay a larger percentage of the ASEAN Secretariat budget would only be fair and just. Equally important, it would release the secretariat from the principle that has limited its capacity, and would allow it to grow organically in tandem with the rising GDPs of each ASEAN country. An ADB study has recommended a ten-fold increase to the budget for the ASEAN Secretariat:

> As its mandate has been expanding, it is clear resources must increase exponentially to meet ASEAN's needs. Based on an

---

28. "Assessment of Member States' Advances to the Working Capital Fund for the Biennium 2014–2015 and Contributions to the United Nations Regular Budget for 2014", United Nations Secretariat, 27 Dec. 2013, http://www.un.org/ga/search/view_doc.asp?symbol=ST/ADM/SER.B/889, accessed 12 Dec. 2016.

exercise prepared for this study, by 2030 the ASEAN Secretariat
will need an estimated yearly budget of $220 million and more
than 1,600 employees if it is to fulfil its expanded mandate.[29]

To those who would object to such a large increase, including many
in Singapore, we would emphasize that the absolute amount that
each country would have to pay would be peanuts. For Singapore,
for example, the new annual sum would be US$56.78 million if we
adopted the ADB recommendation of a budget of US$220 million.
By contrast, the annual budgets for Singapore's Defence and Foreign
Ministries were US$9.8 billion and US$353 million respectively in
2014. Given ASEAN's contribution to enhancing the long-term security
and prosperity of Singapore, it would be both churlish and unwise
for Singapore not to agree to this increased payment. Moreover, a
formula based on the UN principle of capacity to pay will work in
Singapore's long-term interests as Singapore is one of the smallest
states in ASEAN. Over time, the GNPs of the other ASEAN states will
grow much larger, and Singapore's share of the ASEAN budget will
shrink accordingly.

This criticism of Singapore's policy of equal payments, by two
Singaporean former diplomats, reflects our desire to set an example. If
other ASEAN governments protest against an increase of their annual
dues for the ASEAN Secretariat, other ASEAN citizens should be
equally critical of their own countries. Each ASEAN country, without
exception, has benefited from the ecosystem of peace and prosperity
that ASEAN has created. Instead of complaining against an increase in
their annual dues, ASEAN citizens should petition their governments
to contribute more to the ASEAN Secretariat.

Singapore can also try to influence the working culture of the
ASEAN Secretariat by sharing the excellent working culture of
its institutions with ASEAN institutions. How might this transfer
happen? There are several simple steps that can be taken. First,
Singapore has an unusual supply of senior civil servants, including
permanent secretaries, who have retired relatively early, in their
early 60s. They still remain active and dynamic, and the Singapore
government could compensate them well and offer their services on
a voluntary basis to the ASEAN Secretariat. This is not a new idea.
Other organizations have done this. For example, in 1964 retired
American businessmen set up SCORE (the Service Corps of Retired

---

29. Ibid.

Executives), a body that has counselled more than 8.5 million clients. A study by SBA Entrepreneurship Education says that SCORE's work helps create an estimated 25,000 new jobs annually in America. Similar informal counselling could improve the performance of the ASEAN Secretariat.

Second, Singapore can offer free training courses to ASEAN Secretariat officials in Singapore organizations. Singapore has world-class training institutions, including the Civil Service College, Lee Kuan Yew School of Public Policy, NUS and SMU business schools, and INSEAD, to name a few. It is in Singapore's national interest to use Singapore Cooperative Programme funds to provide training courses in Singapore for ASEAN civil servants. The benefits will not be felt overnight, but over time the working culture and efficiency of the ASEAN Secretariat will improve.

Deepak Nair has documented the periods when the ASEAN Secretariat was able to recruit talented staff and the periods when it could not.[30] Clearly, the times when it could not attract talented staff were the times when it had relatively few resources. With the new formula, the ASEAN Secretariat would have the resources to recruit talented and dynamic staff.

Might the ASEAN Secretariat waste a lot of money if it were suddenly flooded with new resources? Admittedly there is a risk, but there are many ways of averting this danger. For example, the major consulting firms working in Southeast Asia, including McKinsey, Bain, BCG and Oliver Wyman, have a good practice of doing pro bono work for worthwhile non-profit organizations. In 2003, at the request of the ASEAN trade ministers, McKinsey & Company did a study on the benefits of an ASEAN Free Trade Area. Some ASEAN countries had been anxious that AFTA could be a zero-sum game and that not all members would benefit from integration. However, the study found that integration would allow complementarities to emerge between member economies while also incentivising each economy to improve its competitiveness. Furthermore, McKinsey concluded that an integrated ASEAN would have more leverage in negotiating future trade pacts and would also be a more attractive destination for FDI.

ASEAN has the financial and intellectual means to develop a strong and dynamic secretariat that could provide a valuable host to many

---

30. Deepak Nair, "A Strong Secretariat, a Strong ASEAN? A Re-evaluation", *ISEAS Perspective*, 2016, https://www.iseas.edu.sg/images/pdf/ISEAS_Perspective_2016_8.pdf, accessed 10 Oct. 2016.

recently launched ASEAN cooperative programmes. The secretariat could become an active and dynamic agency spawning new ideas in addition to implementing agreed-upon decisions. Under the right leadership, the ASEAN Secretariat has the clear ability to lift ASEAN cooperation to even greater heights.

The third recommendation is a truly bold initiative: to promote ASEAN as a new beacon for humanity. Traditionally, it has been America's role to provide a beacon of hope for humanity. In many ways, despite the troubling election of Donald Trump, America will continue to do so. But the American model of handling cultural differences is to create a melting pot in which all differences disappear and a single American identity emerges. Our world will never become a melting pot. Indeed, with the ongoing resurgence of different Asian civilizations, the need is to handle a world of greater, not less, diversity.

This is why ASEAN, the only truly multi-civilizational regional organization in the world, can serve as an alternative beacon of hope. As the world moves away from two centuries of dominance by Western civilizations and towards a multi-civilizational world, ASEAN provides a valuable model for how very different civilizations can live and work together in close proximity. No other region can act as a living laboratory of cultural diversity, so the whole world has a stake in the success of ASEAN. Every day and every year ASEAN succeeds provides a valuable beacon of hope.

The importance of demonstrating that different civilizations can work together has become more pressing as there is growing global pessimism, especially prevalent in the West, that different civilizations cannot cooperate with one another. The pessimism became all the more acute after the killings by jihadist terrorists in Paris on 13 November 2015, in California on 2 December 2015, and in Brussels on 22 March 2016. A number of sophisticated Western pundits began to suggest publicly that the Harvard scholar Samuel Huntington may have been right when he predicted a "clash of civilizations".

Responding to this growing pessimism in the West, in the May/ June 2016 issue of *Foreign Affairs*, Kishore co-authored an essay with Larry Summers—the former US Treasury secretary and former president of Harvard University—titled "The Fusion of Civilizations". In this essay, the authors use "fusion of civilizations" to refer to the areas of commonality between the great world civilizations, driven by the spread of a modern outlook originating in the West that relies on science and rationality to solve problems.

The facts make it clear that the world is experiencing a fusion rather than a clash of civilizations, and the essay explains ways in which the world is becoming a far better place as a result of this process. Steven Pinker has documented a dramatic long-term decline in conflict and violence.[31] The world's infant mortality rate decreased from an estimated 63 deaths per 1,000 live births in 1990 to 32 in 2015. This translates into more than four million fewer infant deaths each year. Globally, middle-class populations are growing by leaps and bounds.

Empirical evidence alone is not enough to convince the world that the dominant global dynamic is a fusion of civilizations. The world also needs to see that the process is actually happening, and ASEAN can provide this evidence because it demonstrates on a daily basis that different civilizations can coexist and cooperate on the basis of what they have in common, while working around their differences. Given the deep pessimism in the West and the growing distrust of Islam, the success of Malaysia and Indonesia provides hope that the Islamic world can continue to modernize. Their success also demonstrates that Islam is compatible with many modern Western values. For example, Malaysia has created one of the best universal health coverage schemes in the developing world, and women outnumber men 65 per cent to 35 per cent in Malaysian universities.[32]

Indonesia is the world's most populous Islamic country, with a population of 250 million. It is also the most successful Islamic democracy. Its two most recent presidents, Susilo Bambang Yudhoyono and Joko Widodo, have been committed to integrating Indonesia into the modern world. Nahdlatul Ulama, Indonesia's largest Muslim organization (with 50 million members), is taking up the challenge to promote moderate Islam to the world. If the 250 million people in Indonesia continue along this trajectory—and they are likely to do so—they will demonstrate that the positive impact of the fusion of civilizations is also working well in the Islamic world.[33]

With its hugely diverse population of 625 million people, ASEAN serves as a microcosm of the diverse global population, where seven

---

31. Steven Pinker, *The Better Angels of Our Nature: Why Violence Has Declined* (New York: Viking, 2011).
32. Latifah Ismail, "Factors Influencing Gender Gap in Higher Education of Malaysia: A University of Malaya Sample", Faculty of Education, University of Malaya, 2014, https://umexpert.um.edu.my/file/publication/00000380_116971.pdf, accessed 10 Oct. 2016.
33. Mahbubani and Summers, "Fusion of Civilizations".

billion people are being squeezed daily into what is literally becoming a global village. Many in the West question whether we can live together in peace in this tiny global village. The ability of Christians and Muslims, Hindus and Confucianists, Taoists and Communists to live and work together within the ASEAN family provides daily proof to a sceptical West that this is possible. This may well turn out to be one of ASEAN's biggest contributions to world history in the 21st century.

Yet, it is vital to emphasize that ASEAN will succeed imperfectly. As suggested earlier, ASEAN's movements are often erratic and never proceed forward in a straight line. However, these imperfections only reinforce the message of hope that ASEAN provides. If such an imperfect corner of the world can deliver both peace and prosperity to its 625 million citizens, the rest of the world can surely replicate ASEAN's imperfect record. This is the ultimate paradox of the ASEAN story: its strength lies in its imperfection.

This is another reason why ASEAN should be awarded the Nobel Peace Prize, perhaps in 2017 on the occasion of its 50th anniversary. The prize would draw global attention to another beacon of hope emerging on the world stage and would send a positive message to the West that Islamic and non-Islamic civilizations can live together in peace. It would also inspire the billion other Muslims who live outside Southeast Asia to study the ASEAN model carefully, since three of the most successful Islamic societies can be found in the ASEAN family. Fifty years of hard work by ASEAN should not go to waste. The association's success should be used to inspire other societies and cultures to emulate the ASEAN spirit.

Bibliography

"Address to the Ministerial Meeting of the Association of South East Asian Nations in Bali, Indonesia", Ronald Reagan Presidential Library & Museum, 1 May 1986. https://reaganlibrary.gov/34-archives/speeches/1986/5513-50186c/, accessed 12 Oct. 2016.

"Adjusted Net National Income Per Capita (Constant 2005 US$)", IndexMundi. http://www.indexmundi.com/facts/indicators/NY. ADJ.NNTY.PC.KD, accessed 12 Oct. 2016.

"ASEAN 2030: Toward a Borderless Economic Community", Asian Development Bank Institute, 2014. http://www.adb.org/sites/default/files/publication/159312/adbi-asean-2030-borderless-economic-community.pdf, accessed 10 Oct. 2016.

"ASEAN Economic Community: How Viable Is Investing?" Invest in ASEAN. http://investasean.asean.org/index.php/page/view/asean-economic-community/view/670/newsid/758/single-market-and-production-base.html, accessed 13 Oct. 2016.

"ASEAN-China Economic and Trade Cooperation Situation in 2014", Asian-China Centre, 16 Mar. 2015. http://www.asean-china-center.org/english/2015-03/16/c_134071066.htm, accessed 12 Oct. 2016.

"ASEAN-India Eminent Persons' Report to the Leaders", ASEAN, Oct. 2012. http://www.asean.org/storage/images/2012/documents/Asean-India%20AIEPG%20(29%2010%2012)-final.pdf/, accessed 12 Oct. 2016.

"ASEAN Investment Report 2013–2014: FDI Development and Regional Value Chains", ASEAN Secretariat and United Nations Conference on Trade and Development, 2014. http://www.asean.org/storage/images/pdf/2014_upload/AIR%202013-2014%20FINAL.pdf/, accessed 12 Oct. 2016.

"Assessment of Member States' Advances to the Working Capital Fund for the Biennium 2014–2015 and Contributions to the United Nations Regular Budget for 2014", United Nations Secretariat, 27 Dec. 2013. http://www.un.org/ga/search/view_doc.asp?symbol=ST/ADM/SER.B/889, accessed 12 Dec. 2016.

"Burma/Myanmar after Nargis: Time to Normalise Aid Relations", International Crisis Group, 2008. https://www.files.ethz.ch/isn/93248/161_burma_myanmar_after_nargis.pdf, accessed 12 Oct. 2016.

"Cambodian Genocide Program", Yale University Genocide Studies Program. http://gsp.yale.edu/case-studies/cambodian-genocide-program, accessed 13 Oct. 2016.

"Chinese FM Refutes Fallacies on the South China Sea Issue", *China Daily*, 25 July 2010. http://www.chinadaily.com.cn/china/2010-07/ 25/ content_11046054.htm, accessed 10 Oct. 2016.

"Country Profile: Laos", International Hydropower Association. http://www. hydropower.org/country-profiles/laos, accessed 13 Oct. 2016.

"Dialogue with Prime Minister Lee Hsien Loong at the Singapore Summit on 19 September 2015", Singapore Summit. https://www.singaporesummit. sg/downloads//Dialogue%20with%20PM%20Lee%20Hsien%20Loong_ SS2015.pdf, accessed 12 Oct. 2016.

"Direction of Trade Statistics", International Monetary Fund. https://www. imf.org/external/pubs/cat/longres.aspx?sk=19305.0/, accessed 12 Oct. 2016.

"Donald J. Trump Statement on Preventing Muslim Immigration", Donald J. Trump for President, 7 Dec. 2015. https://www.donaldjtrump.com/press-releases/donald-j.-trump-statement-on-preventing-muslim-immigration/, accessed 12 Oct. 2016.

"Dr Mahathir Bin Mohamad at the Opening of the Tenth Session of the Islamic Summit Conference at Putrajaya Convention Centre on October 16", *Sydney Morning Herald*, 22 Oct. 2003. http://www.smh.com.au/ articles/2003/10/20/1066502121884.html, accessed 13 Oct. 2016.

"Establishment of the Group of 77", G77. http://www.g77.org/paris/history/ establishment-of-g77.html/, accessed 12 Oct. 2016.

"European Union", World Bank. http://data.worldbank.org/region/european-union, accessed 1 Dec. 2016.

"Foreign Direct Investment into Asean in 2010", ASEAN, http://www.asean. org/storage/images/resources/Statistics/2014/StatisticalPublications/fdi_ statistics_in_focus_2010_final.pdf, accessed 13 Oct. 2016.

"Foreign Direct Investment, Net Inflows (BoP, Current US$)", UNDATA. http://data.un.org/Data.aspx?d=WDI&f=Indicator_Code%   3ABX.KLT. DINV.CD.WD, accessed 14 Oct. 2016.

"Foreign Direct Investment Net Inflows, Intra and Extra ASEAN", ASEAN. http://asean.org/storage/2015/09/Table-252.pdf, accessed 11 Oct. 2016.

"Foreign Relations 1964–1968, Volume XXVI, Indonesia; Malaysia-Singapore; Philippines", U.S. Department of State Archive, 10 Dec. 1966. http://2001-2009.state.gov/r/pa/ho/frus/johnsonlb/xxvi/4432.htm, accessed 12 Oct. 2016.

"Frequently Asked Questions about DG Translation", European Commission, last updated 21 Sept. 2016. http://ec.europa.eu/dgs/translation/faq/index_ en.htm/, accessed 14 Oct. 2016.

"GDP at Market Prices (Constant 2010 US$)", http://data.worldbank.org/ indicator/NY.GDP.MKTP.KD?locations=MM, accessed 10 Oct. 2016.

"GDP of Thailand (Constant 2010 US$)", World Bank. http://databank. worldbank.org/data/reports.aspx?source=wdi-database-archives-(beta), accessed 10 Oct. 2016.

"GDP of Vietnam (Current US$)", World Bank. http://data.worldbank.org/ indicator/NY.GDP.MKTP.CD?locations=VN, accessed 10 Oct. 2016.

"GDP Per Capita of Myanmar (Constant 2010 US$)", World Bank. http://data. worldbank.org/indicator/NY.GDP.PCAP.KD?locations=MM, accessed 10 Oct. 2016.

"Getting in the Way", *The Economist*, 17 May 2014. http://www.economist. com/news/asia/21602265-south-east-asia-finds-decorum-its-regional-club-rather-rudely-shattered-getting-way, accessed 12 Oct. 2016.

"Group of Prominent Malays Calls for Rational Dialogue on Position of Islam in Malaysia", *The Star*, 7 Dec. 2014. http://www.thestar.com.my/ news/nation/2014/12/07/group-prominent-malays-calls-for-moderation/, accessed 9 Nov. 2016.

"Impact of the Sino-Japanese Competitive Relationship on ASEAN as a Region and Institution", Report, S. Rajaratnam School of International Studies (RSIS), Nanyang Technological University, 24 Dec. 2014. https://www.rsis. edu.sg/wp-content/uploads/2014/12/PR141224_Impact_of_Sino-Japanese. pdf, accessed 10 Oct. 2016.

"Indian MP Tharoor: Europe Must Stop Lecturing India", *EurActiv*, 19 Apr. 2011. http://www.euractiv.com/section/global-europe/interview/indian-mp-tharoor-europe-must-stop-lecturing-india/, accessed 12 Oct. 2016.

"Indonesia Will Join Trans-Pacific Partnership, Jokowi Tells Obama", *The Guardian*, 27 Oct. 2015. https://www.theguardian.com/world/2015/ oct/27/indonesia-will-join-trans-pacific-partnership-jokowi-tells-obama, accessed 13 Oct. 2016.

"Joint Statement of the ASEAN-U.S. Special Leaders' Summit: Sunnylands Declaration", Permanent Mission of the Republic of Singapore, ASEAN, Jakarta, 17 Feb. 2016. http://www.mfa.gov.sg/content/mfa/ overseasmission/asean/latest_news_in_asean/2016/2016-02/Latest_News_ In_ASEAN_2016-02-17.html/, accessed 12 Oct. 2016.

"Malaysia Economic Monitor 2011", World Bank, 2011. http://siteresources. worldbank.org/INTMALAYSIA/Resources/324392 -1303882224029/ malaysia_ec_monitor_apr2011_execsumm.pdf, accessed 14 Oct. 2016.

"Memorandum of Conversation, Washington, May 8, 1975, noon–1 p.m.", *Foreign Relations of the United States, 1969–1976, Volume E–12, Documents on East and Southeast Asia, 1973–1976*, 8 May 1975. https://history.state.gov/ historicaldocuments/frus1969-76ve12/d297/, accessed 12 Oct. 2016.

"Millennium Development Goals Database", UNDATA. http://data.un.org/ Data.aspx?d=MDG&f=seriesRowID%3A580, accessed 14 Oct. 2016.

"More Hat Than Cattle", *The Economist*, 2 Jan. 2016. http://www.economist. com/news/finance-and-economics/21684811-seamless-regional-economic-bloc-just-around-corneras-always-more-hat/, accessed 12 Oct. 2016.

"Nan-fang Ts'ao-mu Chuang" [A Fourth-Century Flora of South-East Asia], trans. Li Hui-Lin. Hong Kong: Chinese University Press, 1979.

"National Accounts Main Aggregates Database", United Nations Statistics Division. http://unstats.un.org/unsd/snaama/dnllist.asp/, accessed 7 Sept. 2016.

"Opening Remarks, James A. Baker, III, Senate Foreign Relations Committee", United States Senate Committee on Foreign Relations, 12 May 2016. http:// www.foreign.senate.gov/imo/media/doc/051216_Baker_Testimony.pdf/, accessed 12 Oct. 2016.

"Oxfam Warns up to 1.5 Million in Danger if Aid Effort Cannot Reach Cyclone Victims", Oxfam America, 11 May 2008. https://www.oxfamamerica.org/press/oxfam-warns-up-to-15-million-in-danger-if-aid-effort-cannot-reach-cyclone-victims/, accessed 12 Oct. 2016.

"PHL Emerging as a Strong Software Development Hub", Team Asia, 26 Nov. 2012. http://www.teamasia.com/newsroom/read-client-news.aspx?id=407:phl-emerging-as-a-strong-software-development-hub, accessed 14 Oct. 2016.

"President Eisenhower's News Conference, 7 Apr. 1954", *The Pentagon Papers*, Gravel Edition, Vol. 1 (Boston: Beacon Press, 1971), pp. 597–8. https://www.mtholyoke.edu/acad/intrel/pentagon/ps11.htm, accessed 13 Oct. 2016.

"Puny Counter-Revolutionary Alliance", *Peking Review* 10, 3 (18 Aug. 1967): 40. https://www.marxists.org/subject/china/peking-review/1967/PR1967-34.pdf/, accessed 12 Oct. 2016.

"Remarks by H.E. Li Keqiang Premier of the State Council of the People's Republic of China at the 18th China-ASEAN Summit", Ministry of Foreign Affairs of the People's Republic of China, 22 Nov. 2015. http://www.fmprc.gov.cn/mfa_eng/zxxx_662805/t1317372.shtml, accessed 10 Oct. 2016.

"Remarks by President Obama at Opening Session of the U.S.-ASEAN Summit", White House, 15 Feb. 2016. https://www.whitehouse.gov/the-press-office/2016/02/15/remarks-president-obama-opening-session-us-asean-summit, accessed 12 Oct. 2016.

"Remarks by President Obama at the Cooperative Orthotic and Prosthetic Enterprise (COPE) Centre", White House, 7 Sept. 2016. https://www.whitehouse.gov/the-press-office/2016/09/07/remarks-president-obama-cooperative-orthotic-and-prosthetic-enterprise, accessed 12 Oct. 2016.

"Remarks by President Obama at Young Southeast Asian Leaders Initiative Town Hall, 11/14/14", White House, 14 Nov. 2014. https://www.whitehouse.gov/the-press-office/2014/11/14/remarks-president-obama-young-southeast-asian-leaders-initiative-town-ha/, accessed 12 Oct. 2016.

"Remarks by the President at the United States Military Academy Commencement Ceremony", White House, 28 May 2014. https://www.whitehouse.gov/the-press-office/2014/05/28/remarks-president-united-states-military-academy-commencement-ceremony/, accessed 12 Oct. 2016.

"Remarks by the President at the University of Indonesia in Jakarta, Indonesia", White House, 10 Nov. 2010. https://www.whitehouse.gov/the-press-office/2010/11/10/remarks-president-university-indonesia-jakarta-indonesia, accessed 12 Oct. 2016.

"Report to the National Security Council by the Executive Secretary (Lay)", *Foreign Relations of the United States, 1952–1954. East Asia and the Pacific (in two parts)*, Vol. 12, part 1, 25 June 1952. https://history.state.gov/historicaldocuments/frus1952-54v12p1/d36/, accessed 12 Oct. 2016.

"Singapore Is the Global City of Opportunity", Ministry of Communications and Information Singapore, 2005. http://www.mci.gov.sg/web/corp/press-room/categories/speeches/content/singapore-is-the-global-city-of-opportunity, accessed 12 Oct. 2016.

"Speech by Chairman of the Delegation of the People's Republic of China, Teng Hsiao-Ping, At the Special Session of the U.N. General Assembly". Beijing: Foreign Languages Press, 10 Apr. 1974. https://www.marxists.org/reference/archive/deng-xiaoping/1974/04/10.htm/, accessed 12 Oct. 2016.

"Speech by Chinese President Xi Jinping to Indonesian Parliament", ASEAN-China Centre, 2 Oct. 2013. http://www.asean-china-center.org/english/2013-10/03/c_133062675.htm, accessed 10 Oct. 2016.

"Speech by Prime Minister Lee Hsien Loong at the 19th Nikkei International Conference on the Future of Asia", Prime Minister's Office Singapore, 26 May 2013. http://www.pmo.gov.sg/mediacentre/speech-prime-minister-lee-hsien-loong-19th-nikkei-international-conference-future-asia/, accessed 12 Oct. 2016.

"Speech by Prime Minister Lee Kuan Yew to the National Press Club in Canberra, Australia, on 16 Apr 86", National Archives of Singapore, 16 Apr. 1986. http://www.nas.gov.sg/archivesonline/data/pdfdoc/lky19860416a.pdf/, accessed 12 Oct. 2016.

"Speech by Takeo Fukuda", *Contemporary Southeast Asia* 2, 1 (1980): 69–73.

"Statement by ASEAN Chair, Singapore's Minister for Foreign Affairs George Yeo in New York, September 27 2007", Embassy of the Republic of Singapore, Washington, DC. http://www.mfa.gov.sg/content/mfa/overseasmission/washington/newsroom/press_statements/2007/200709/press_200709_03.html, accessed 12 Oct. 2016.

"Text of 37th Singapore Lecture 'India's Singapore Story' by Prime Minister Narendra Modi during His Visit to Singapore", 23 Nov. 2013. https://www.iseas.edu.sg/images/event_highlights   /37thsingaporelecture/Textof37thSingaporeLecture.pdf, accessed 10 Oct. 2016.

"Thai Army Promises Elections in October 2015", *BBC News*, 28 June 2014. http://www.bbc.com/news/world-asia-28069578, accessed 1 Dec. 2016.

"The ASEAN Economic Community (AEC) 2015: A Guide to the Practical Benefits", Ministry of Trade and Industry Singapore. https://www.mti.gov.sg/MTIInsights/MTIImages/MTI%20AEC%202015%20Handbook.PDF, accessed 11 Oct. 2016.

"The South China Sea, Press Statement, Hillary Rodham Clinton, Secretary of State, Washington, DC", U.S. Department of State, 22 July 2011. http://www.state.gov/secretary/20092013clinton/rm   /2011/07/168989.htm/, accessed 12 Oct. 2016.

"The United States' Contribution to Regional Stability: Chuck Hagel", International Institute for Strategic Studies, IISS Shangri-La Dialogue: The Asia Security Summit, 31 May 2014. https://www.iiss.org/en/events/shangri%20la%20dialogue/archive/2014-c20c/plenary-1-d1ba/chuck-hagel-a9cb/, accessed 12 Oct. 2016.

"Too Much of a Good Thing", *The Economist*, 15 May 2014. http://www.economist.com/news/business/21602241-after-binge-aircraft-buying-and-airline-founding-it-time-sober-up-too-much-good, accessed 10 Oct. 2016.

"Trade (% of GDP)", World Bank. http://data.worldbank.org/indicator/NE.TRD.GNFS.ZS, accessed 14 Oct. 2016.

"Trade Statistics of Japan", Ministry of Finance. http://www.customs.go.jp/toukei/info/index_e.htm, accessed 11 July 2016.

"Transcript of Speech by the Prime Minister, Mr. Lee Kuan Yew, on 30th May, 1965, at the Delta Community Centre on the Occasion of its 4th Anniversary Celebrations", National Archives of Singapore, 30 May 1965. http://www.nas.gov.sg/archivesonline/data/pdfdoc/lky19650530a.pdf/, accessed 12 Oct. 2016."Vietnam", US Department of State. http://www.state.gov/documents/organization/229305.pdf, accessed 14 Oct. 2016.

"Vietnam: The End of the War. Broadcast by Malaysia's Minister of Home Affairs, Tan Sri M. Ghazali Shafie 6 May 1975", *Survival* 17, 4 (1975): 186–8.

"Vietnam's FDI Pledges Dip, but Actual Inflows Jump in 2015", *Reuters*, 29 Dec. 2015. http://www.reuters.com/article/vietnam-economy-fdi-idUSL3N14J1I120151230, accessed 14 Oct. 2016.

"World Bank Group President Jim Yong Kim Opening Remarks at the Vietnam 2035 Report Launching", World Bank, 23 Feb. 2016. http://www.worldbank.org/en/news/speech/2016/02/23/world-bank-group-president-jim-yong-kim-opening-remarks-at-the-vietnam-2035-report-launching, accessed 12 Oct. 2016.

"World Economic Outlook Database", International Monetary Fund. https://www.imf.org/external/data.htm, accessed 11 July 2016.

Abuza, Zachary. "The Smoldering Thai Insurgency", *CTC Sentinel*, 29 June 2015. https://www.ctc.usma.edu/posts/the-smoldering-thai-insurgency, accessed 10 Oct. 2016.

Acharya, Amitav. *Constructing a Security Community in Southeast Asia: ASEAN and the Problem of Regional Order*. London: Routledge, 2001.

————. "ASEAN at 40: Mid-Life Rejuvenation?" *Foreign Affairs*, 15 Aug. 2007. https://www.foreignaffairs.com/articles/asia/2007-08-15/asean-40-mid-life-rejuvenation/, accessed 12 Oct. 2016.

Agence France-Presse. "Indonesia Will Join Trans-Pacific Partnership, Jokowi Tells Obama", *The Guardian*, 27 Oct. 2015. https://www.theguardian.com/world/2015/oct/27/indonesia-will-join-trans-pacific-partnership-jokowi-tells-obama, accessed 13 Oct. 2016.

Allison, Laura. *The EU, ASEAN and Interregionalism: Regionalism Support and Norm Diffusion between the EU and ASEAN*. Houndmills: Palgrave, 2015.

Allison, Tony. "Myanmar Shows India the Road to Southeast Asia", *Asia Times*, 21 Feb. 2001. http://www.atimes.com/reports/CB21Ai01.html#top5, accessed 13 Oct. 2016.

Anderson, Benedict R. *Under Three Flags: Anarchism and the Anti-colonial Imagination*. London: Verso, 2005.

Andrade, Tonio. *The Gunpowder Age: China, Military Innovation, and the Rise of the West in World History*. Princeton: Princeton University Press, 2016.

Ang Cheng Guan. *Singapore, ASEAN and the Cambodian Conflict, 1978–1991*. Singapore: NUS Press, 2013.

Annan, Kofi A. and Kishore Mahbubani. "Rethinking Sanctions", *Project Syndicate*, 11 Jan. 2016. https://www.project-syndicate.org/onpoint/rethinking-economic-sanctions-by-kofi-a-annan-and-kishore-mahbubani-2016-01/, accessed 12 Oct. 2016.

Antonio, Rufino. "We, the People" (Letters to the Editor), *Manila Times*, 11 May 1972.

Arudou, Debito. "Tackle Embedded Racism before It Chokes Japan", *Japan Times*, 1 Nov. 2015. http://www.japantimes.co.jp/community/2015/11/01/issues/tackle-embedded-racism-chokes-japan/, accessed 12 Oct. 2016.

Auger, Timothy. *S.R. Nathan in Conversation*. Singapore: Editions Didier Millet, 2015.

Ba, Alice. *(Re)Negotiating East and Southeast Asia: Region, Regionalism, and the Association of Southeast Asian Nations*. Singapore: NUS Press, 2009.

Baker, Christopher John and Pasuk Phongpaichit. *A History of Thailand*. New York: Cambridge University Press, 2005.

Bastin, John and R. Roolvink, eds. *Malayan and Indonesian Studies: Essays Presented to Sir Richard Winstedt on his Eighty-fifth Birthday*. Bali: Clarendon, 1964.

Bayuni, Endy M. "SBY, the Military Strategist Besieged by War on Two Fronts", *Jakarta Post*, 25 Nov. 2009. http://www.thejakartapost.com/news/2009/11/25/sby-military-strategist-besieged-war-two-fronts.html, accessed 10 Oct. 2016.

Bellwood, Peter S., James J. Fox and D.T. Tryon. *The Austronesians: Historical and Comparative Perspectives*. Canberra: Dept. of Anthropology as Part of the Comparative Austronesian Project, Research School of Pacific and Asian Studies, Australian National University, 1995.

Berggruen, Nicolas and Nathan Gardels. "How the World's Most Powerful Leader Thinks", *Huffington Post*, 30 Sept. 2015.

Bremmer, Ian. "The New World of Business", *Fortune International*, 22 Jan. 2015. http://fortune.com/2015/01/22/the-new-world-of-business/, accessed 12 Oct. 2016.

Chachavalpongpun, Pavin and Moe Thuzar. *Myanmar: Life after Nargis*. Singapore: Institute of Southeast Asian Studies, 2009.

Chanda, Nayan. *Brother Enemy: The War after the War*. New York: Harcourt, 1986.

Chandra, Siddharth and Timothy Vogelsang. "Change and Involution in Sugar Production in Cultivation System Java, 1840–1870", *Journal of Economic History* 59, 4 (1998): 885–911.

Chochrane, Joe and Thomas Fuller. "Singapore, the Nation That Lee Kuan Yew Built, Questions Its Direction", *New York Times*, 24 Mar. 2015. http://

www.nytimes.com/2015/03/25/world/asia/singapore-the-nation-that-lee-built-questions-its-direction.html, accessed 12 Oct. 2016.

Chongkittavorn, Kavi. "Asean to Push Back New Admission to December", *The Nation* (Bangkok), 30 May 1997.

Christina, Bernadette. "Indonesia's Trade Minister Calls for TPP Membership in Two Years", *Reuters*, 9 Oct. 2015. http://www.reuters.com/article/us-trade-tpp-indonesia-idUSKCN0S312R20151009, accessed 13 Oct. 2016.

Citrinot, Luc. "ASEAN for ASEAN: Focus Will Be Given to Strengthening Intra-ASEAN Tourism", ASEAN Travel, 2016. http://asean.travel/2016/01/24/asean-for-asean-focus-will-be-given-to-strengthening-intra-asean-tourism/, accessed 10 Oct. 2016.

Clinton, William J. "Transcript of 'Global Challenges': A Public Address Given by Former US President William J. Clinton at Yale University on October 31, 2003", *YaleGlobal*, 31 Oct. 2003. http://yaleglobal.yale.edu/content/transcript-global-challenges, accessed 13 Oct. 2016.

Cœdès, George. *The Indianized States of Southeast Asia*. Honolulu: East-West Center Press, 1968.

Cohen, Matthew Isaac. "Introduction: Global Encounters in Southeast Asian Performing Arts", *Asian Theatre Journal* 31, 2 (2014): 353–68.

Cotterell, Arthur. *A History of Southeast Asia*. Singapore: Marshall Cavendish (Asia), 2014.

Country Studies/Area Handbook Series, Federal Research Division of the Library of Congress. http://countrystudies.us/, accessed 12 Oct. 2016.

Coxhead, Ian, ed. *Routledge Handbook of Southeast Asian Economics*. Abingdon: Routledge, 2015.

Croft-Cusworth, Catriona. "Beware ISIS' Threat to Indonesia", *National Interest*, 24 Mar. 2015. http://nationalinterest.org/blog/the-buzz/beware-isis-threat-indonesia-12472, accessed 13 Oct. 2016.

Dalrymple, William. "The Great & Beautiful Lost Kingdoms", *The New York Review of Books*, 21 May 2015. http://www.nybooks.com/articles/2015/05/21/great-and-beautiful-lost-kingdoms/, accessed 12 Oct. 2016.

Daquila, Teofilo C. *The Economies of Southeast Asia: Indonesia, Malaysia, Philippines, Singapore, and Thailand*. New York: Nova Publishers, 2005.

Das, Sanchita B. "What US-Asean Connect Means for the Region", *Straits Times*, 17 Mar. 2016. http://www.straitstimes.com/opinion/what-us-asean-connect-means-for-the-region, accessed 12 Oct. 2016.

de Miguel, Emilio. "Japan and Southeast Asia: From the Fukuda Doctrine to Abe's Five Principles", UNISCI Discussion Paper 32, May 2013. https://revistas.ucm.es/index.php/UNIS/article/viewFile/44792/42219/, accessed 12 Oct. 2016.

Development Co-operation Directorate (DCD-DAC). http://www.oecd.org/dac/, accessed 12 Oct. 2016.

Dilokwanich, Malinee. "A Study of Samkok: The First Thai Translation of a Chinese Novel", *Journal of the Siam Society* 73 (1985). 77–112.

Dobbs, S. *The Singapore River: A Social History, 1819–2002*. Singapore: Singapore University Press, 2003.

Easen, Nick. "In Asia, a Boom in Low-cost Flights", BBC, 2 Apr. 2012. http://www.bbc.com/travel/story/20120402-low-cost-flights-in-asia-booms, accessed 10 Oct. 2016.

Eisenman, Joshua, Eric Heginbotham and Derek Mitchell, eds. *China and the Developing World: Beijing's Strategy for the Twenty-First Century*. New York: M.E. Sharpe, 2007.

Expansión. "Myanmar: Human Development Index", Country Economy. http://countryeconomy.com/hdi/burma, accessed 12 Oct. 2016.

Fallows, James. "A Damaged Culture: A New Philippines?" *The Atlantic*, 1 Nov. 1987. http://www.theatlantic.com/technology/archive/1987/11/a-damaged-culture-a-new-philippines/7414/, accessed 13 Oct. 2016.

Fisher, Charles A. "Southeast Asia: The Balkans of the Orient? A Study in Continuity and Change", *Geography* 47, 4 (1962).

Fitzgerald, C.P. *The Southern Expansion of the Chinese People*. New York: Praeger, 1972.

Fukasaku, Kiichiro, Fukunari Kimura and Shujiro Urata, eds. *Asia & Europe: Beyond Competing Regionalism*. Eastbourne: Sussex Academic Press, 1998.

Fukuzawa Yukichi. "Datsu-A Ron", *Jiji-Shimpo*, 12 Mar. 1885, trans. Sinh Vinh, in *Fukuzawa Yukichi nenkan*, Vol. 11 (Tokyo: Fukuzawa Yukichi kyokai, 1984). Cited in "Fukuzawa Yukichi (1835–1901)", Nishikawa Shunsaku, *Prospects: The Quarterly Review of Comparative Education* 23, 3/4 (1993): 493–506.

Ganesan, N. *Bilateral Tensions in Post-Cold War ASEAN*. Singapore: Institute of Southeast Asian Studies, 1999.

Geertz, Clifford. *Islam Observed: Religious Development in Morocco and Indonesia*. Chicago: University of Chicago Press, 1971.

Giersch, Charles Patterson. *Asian Borderlands: The Transformation of Qing China's Yunnan Frontier*. Cambridge, MA, and London: Harvard University Press, 2006.

Goh Keng Swee, "A Holy Order to Scale New Heights: Dr. Goh Keng Swee's Last Major Speech before Retiring from Politics, 25 September 1984", in *Goh Keng Swee: A Legacy of Public Service*, ed. Emrys Chew and Chong Guan Kwa. Singapore: World Scientific, 2012.

_____. *The Economics of Modernization*. Singapore: Marshall Cavendish Editions, 2013.

Govaars, Ming. *Dutch Colonial Education: The Chinese Experience in Indonesia, 1900–1942*, trans. Lorre Lynn Trytten. Singapore: Chinese Heritage Centre, 2005.

Government of India. Ministry of Development of Northeastern Region. *Kaladan Multi-Modal Transit Transport Project*, 2014. http://www.mdoner.gov.in/content/introduction-1, accessed 12 Oct. 2016.

Guilmoto, Christophe Z. "The Tamil Migration Cycle, 1830–1950", *Economic and Political Weekly* (16–23 Jan. 1993): 111–20.

Haddad, William. "Japan, the Fukuda Doctrine, and ASEAN", *Contemporary Southeast Asia* 2, 1 (1980).

Hall, D.G.E. *A History of South-East Asia*. London: Macmillan, 1955.

Hall, Kenneth R. "Review: 'Borderless' Southeast Asia Historiography: New Scholarship on the Interactions between Southeast Asia and Its South Asian and Chinese Neighbours in the Pre-1500 Era", *Bijdragen tot de Taal-, Land- en Volkenkunde* 167, 4 (2011).

Hamilton, A. *A New Account of the East Indies*, Vol. 2. Edinburgh: John Mosman, 1727.

Harrison, Brian. *South-East Asia, a Short History*. London: Macmillan, 1963. 1st ed., 1954.

Hayipiyawong, N. "The Failure of Peace Negotiation Process between Government of Thailand and Revolution National Front (BRN) in Southern Thailand Conflict (Patani)". BA thesis, Universitas Muhammadiyah Yogyakarta, 2014. http://thesis.umy.ac.id/datapublik/t39343.pdf, accessed 12 Oct. 2016.

Higham, Charles. "The Long and Winding Road That Leads to Angkor", *Cambridge Archaeological Journal* 22, 2 (2012).

Hirschman, C. "The Meaning and Measurement of Ethnicity in Malaysia: An Analysis of Census Classifications", *Journal of Asian Studies* 46, 3 (1987): 555–82.

Htway, Thurein Hla. "Military Party Awards Major Projects to China", *Nikkei Asian Review*, 13 Jan. 2016. http://asia.nikkei.com/Business/Companies/Military-party-awards-major-projects-to-China, accessed 10 Oct. 2016.

Imagawa, Takeshi. "ASEAN-Japan Relations", *Keizaigaku-Ronsan* 30, 3 (May 1989): 121–42. http://civilisations.revues.org/1664?file=1/, accessed 12 Oct. 2016.

India ASEAN Trade and Investment Relations: Opportunities and Challenges. Delhi: Associated Chambers of Commerce and Industry of India, July 2016. http://www.assocham.org/upload/docs/ASEAN-STUDY.pdf/, accessed 29 Sept. 2016.

Ismail, Latifah. "Factors Influencing Gender Gap in Higher Education of Malaysia: A University of Malaya Sample". Faculty of Education, University of Malaya, 2014. https://umexpert.um.edu.my/file/publication/00000380_116971.pdf, accessed 10 Oct. 2016.

Jain, Ravindra K. *South Indians on the Plantation Frontier in Malaya*. New Haven and London: Yale University Press, 1970.

Jalil, Haikal. "Malaysia's Tertiary Education Not up to Par, Says Nurul Izzah", *Sun Daily*, 22 Feb. 2015. http://www.thesundaily.my/news/1335663, accessed 1 Dec. 2016.

_____. *Diplomacy: A Singapore Experience*. Singapore: Straits Times Press, 2011.

Japan External Trade Organisation, "East-Asia Economic Integration and the Roles of JETRO", Ministry of Foreign Affairs of Japan, http://www.mofa.

go.jp/region/asia-paci/cambodia/workshop0609/attach5.pdf, accessed 12 Oct. 2016.

Jayakumar, S. *Be at the Table or Be on the Menu: A Singapore Memoir*. Singapore: Straits Times Press, 2015.

Jin Kai. "Building 'A Bridge between China and Europe'", The *Diplomat*, 23 Apr. 2014. http://thediplomat.com/2014/04/building-a-bridge-between-china-and-europe/, accessed 12 Oct. 2016.

Jing Sun. *Japan and China as Charm Rivals: Soft Power in Regional Diplomacy*. Ann Arbor: University of Michigan Press, 2012.

Jones, Lee. *ASEAN, Sovereignty and Intervention in Southeast Asia*. Houndmills: Palgrave Macmillan, 2012.

Joseph, C. and J. Matthews, eds. *Equity, Opportunity and Education in Postcolonial Southeast Asia*. New York: Routledge, 2014.

Kausikan, Bilahari. "The Ages of ASEAN", in *The Inclusive Regionalist: A Festschrift Dedicated to Jusuf Wanandi*, ed. Hadi Soesastro and Clara Joewono. Jakarta: Centre for Strategic and International Studies, 2007.

_____. "Hard Truths and Wishful Hopes about the AEC", *Straits Times*, 2 Jan. 2016.

_____. "Standing up to and Getting Along with China", *Today*, 18 May 2016. http://www.todayonline.com/chinaindia/standing-and-getting-along-china/, accessed 12 Oct. 2016.

Keown, Damien. *A Dictionary of Buddhism*. Oxford: Oxford University Press, 2004.

Khoman, Thanat. "Which Road for Southeast Asia?" *Foreign Affairs* 42, 4 (1964).

_____. "ASEAN Conception and Evolution", ASEAN, 1 Sept. 1992. http://asean.org/?static_post=asean-conception-and-evolution-by-thanat-khoman/, accessed 12 Oct. 2016.

Khoo Boo Teik. *Paradoxes of Mahathirism: An Intellectual Biography of Mahathir Mohamad*. Kuala Lumpur: Oxford University Press, 1995.

Kim, Jim Yong. "Lessons from Vietnam in a Slowing Global Economy", *Straits Times*, 24 Feb. 2016. http://www.straitstimes.com/opinion/lessons-from-vietnam-in-a-slowing-global-economy, accessed 14 Oct. 2016.

Knight, Nick. *Understanding Australia's Neighbours: An Introduction to East and Southeast Asia*. New York: Cambridge University Press, 2011.

Koh, Tommy T.B., Rosario G. Manalo and Walter C.M. Woon. *The Making of the ASEAN Charter*. Singapore: World Scientific, 2009.

Kristof, Nicholas D. "China Sees Singapore as a Model for Progress", *New York Times*, 9 Aug. 1992. http://www.nytimes.com/1992/08/09/weekinreview/the-world-china-sees-singapore-as-a-model-for-progress.html/, accessed 12 Oct. 2016.

Lee, Cassey and Thee Kian Wie. "Southeast Asia: Indonesia and Malaysia", in *Routledge Handbook of the History of Global Economic Thought*, ed. Vincent Barnett. Abingdon: Routledge, 2014, pp. 306–14.

Lee Kuan Yew. "Speech by the Prime Minister, Mr. Lee Kuan Yew, at the Commonwealth Heads of Government Meeting in London on Wednesday, 8 June 1977: Changing Power Relations", National Archives of Singapore, 8 June 1977. http://www.nas.gov.sg/archivesonline/data/pdfdoc/lky19770608.pdf/, accessed 12 Oct. 2016.

_____. *From Third World to First: The Singapore Story, 1965–2000*, Vol. 2. Singapore: Marshall Cavendish, 2000.

Lim, Catherine. "An Open Letter to the Prime Minister", 7 June 2014. http://catherinelim.sg/2014/06/07/an-open-letter-to-the-prime-minster/, accessed 14 Oct. 2016.

Lim, Linda. "The Myth of US-China Economic Competition", *Straits Times*, 16 Dec. 2015. http://www.straitstimes.com/opinion/the-myth-of-us-china-economic-competition, accessed 13 Oct. 2016.

Lockard, Craig A. *Southeast Asia in World History*. Oxford: Oxford University Press, 2009.

Lopez, Greg. "Malaysia: A Simple Institutional Analysis", *Malaysia Today*, 22 Aug. 2011. http://www.malaysia-today.net/malaysia-a-simple-institutional-analysis/, accessed 13 Oct. 2016.

Lubis, Mila. "Indonesia Remains the 2nd Most Optimistic Country Globally", *Nielsen*, 30 May 2015. http://www.nielsen.com/id/en/press-room/2015/indonesia-remains-the-2nd-most-optimistic-country-globally.html/, accessed 12 Oct. 2016.

Luong, Dien. "Why Vietnam Loves the Trans-Pacific Partnership", *The Diplomat*, 16 Mar. 2016.

Macaranas, Bonifacio S. "Feudal Work Systems and Poverty: The Philippine Experience", International Labour and Employment Relations Association, 2009. http://www.ilera-directory.org/15thworldcongress/files/papers/Track_4/Poster/CS2T_2_MACARANAS.pdf, accessed 13 Oct. 2016.

MacKinnon, Ian and Mark Tran. "Brown Condemns 'Inhuman' Burma Leaders over Aid", *The Guardian*, 17 May 2008. https://www.theguardian.com/world/2008/may/17/cyclonenargis.burma2, accessed 12 Oct. 2016.

Mahathir bin Mohamad. "Look East Policy: The Challenges for Japan in a Globalized World", Ministry of Foreign Affairs of Japan, 12 Dec. 2002. http://www.mofa.go.jp/region/asia-paci/malaysia/pmv0212/speech.html/, accessed 12 Oct. 2016.

Mahbubani, Kishore. *Beyond the Age of Innocence: Rebuilding Trust between America and the World*. New York: Public Affairs, 2005.

_____. *The New Asian Hemisphere: The Irresistible Shift of Global Power to the East*. New York: Public Affairs, 2008.

_____. "Australia's Destiny in the Asian Century: Pain or No Pain?" *Australian National University*, 31 July 2012. https://asiapacific.anu.edu.au/researchschool/emerging_asia/papers/Mahbubani_final.pdf/, accessed 12 Oct. 2016.

_____. "Why Singapore Is the World's Most Successful Society", *Huffington Post*, 4 Aug. 2015. http://www.huffingtonpost.com/kishore-mahbubani/

singapore-world-successful-society_b_7934988.html, accessed 12 Oct. 2016.

_____. "Here's How the EU Should Start to Think Long-Term", *Europe's World*, 26 Nov. 2015. http://europesworld.org/2015/11/26/heres-how-the-eu-should-start-to-think-long-term/, accessed 12 Oct. 2016.

Mahbubani, Kishore and Lawrence H. Summers. "The Fusion of Civilizations", *Foreign Affairs*, May–June 2016.

Manguin, Pierre Yves, A. Mani and Geoff Wade. *Early Interactions between South and Southeast Asia: Reflections on Cross-cultural Exchange*. Singapore: Institute of Southeast Asian Studies, 2011.

Martynova, Elena S. "Strengthening of Cooperation between Russia and ASEAN: Rhetoric or Reality?" *Asian Politics & Policy* 6, 3 (2014): 397–412.

McCaskill, Don N. and Ken Kampe. *Development or Domestication? Indigenous Peoples of Southeast Asia*. Chiang Mai: Silkworm Books, 1997.

McDougall, Derek. *The International Politics of the New Asia Pacific*. Singapore: Institute of Southeast Asian Studies, 1997.

McEvedy, Colin and Richard Jones. *Atlas of World Population History*. Harmondsworth: Penguin, 1978.

Miksic, John N. *Historical Dictionaries of Ancient Civilizations and Historical Eras, No. 18*. Lanham: Scarecrow Press, 2007.

Morgan, David O. and Anthony Reid, eds. *The New Cambridge History of Islam*, Vol. 3: *The Eastern Islamic World, Eleventh to Eighteenth Centuries*. Cambridge: Cambridge University Press, 2010.

Muhammad Amin B., Mohammad Rahim K. and Geshina Ayu M.S. "A Trend Analysis of Violent Crimes in Malaysia", *Health and the Environment Journal* 5, 2 (2014).

Nair, Deepak. "A Strong Secretariat, a Strong ASEAN? A Re-evaluation". *ISEAS Perspective*, 2016. https://www.iseas.edu.sg/images/pdf/ISEAS_Perspective_2016_8.pdf, accessed 10 Oct. 2016.

Nandy, Ashis. *The Intimate Enemy: Loss and Recovery of Self under Colonialism*. New Delhi: Oxford University Press, 1988.

Nelson, Dean. "India to Open Super Highway to Burma and Thailand", *The Telegraph*, 29 May 2012. http://www.telegraph.co.uk/news/worldnews/asia/india/9297354/India-to-open-super-highway-to-Burma-and-Thailand.html, accessed 13 Oct. 2016.

Nichol, Jim. *Soviet Views of the Association of Southeast Asian Nations: An Examination of Unclassified Soviet Sources*. Washington, DC: Federal Research Division for the Library of Congress, 1985.

Nye, Joseph. *Peace in Parts: Integration and Conflict in Regional Organization*. Boston: Little, Brown, 1971.

Oberman, Raoul, Richard Dobbs, Arief Budiman, Fraser Thompson and Morten Rossé. "The Archipelago Economy: Unleashing Indonesia's Potential", McKinsey & Company. http://www.mckinsey.com/insights/asia-pacific/the_archipelago_economy, accessed 13 Oct. 2016.

Ooi Kee Beng. *In Lieu of Ideology: The Intellectual Biography of Goh Keng Swee.* Singapore: World Scientific, 2013.

O'Reilly, Dougald J.W. *Early Civilizations of Southeast Asia.* Lanham: AltaMira Press, 2007.

Ortuoste, Maria Consuelo C. "Internal and External Institutional Dynamics in Member-States and ASEAN: Tracing Creation, Change and Reciprocal Influences". PhD dissertation, Arizona State University, 2008. http://gradworks.umi.com/33/27/3327250.html, accessed 10 Oct. 2016.

Osborne, Milton E. *Southeast Asia: An Introductory History.* St Leonards: Allen & Unwin, 1997.

Overholt, William H. "The Rise and Fall of Ferdinand Marcos", *Asian Survey* 26, 11 (1986): 1137–63.

Page, John. "The East Asian Miracle", in *NBER Macroeconomics Annual 1994*, Vol. 9, ed. Stanley Fischer and Julio J. Rotemberg. Cambridge: MIT Press, 1994.

Pedrosa, Carmen Navarro. *Imelda Marcos: The Rise and Fall of One of the World's Most Powerful Women.* New York: St. Martin's Press, 1987.

Peffer, Nathaniel. "Regional Security in Southeast Asia", *International Organization* 8, 3 (1954): 311–5.

Pimpa, Nattavud. "Amazing Thailand: Organizational Culture in the Thai Public Sector", *International Business Research* 5, 11 (16 Oct. 2012). http://www.ccsenet.org/journal/index.php/ibr/article/view/21408/13905, accessed 12 Oct. 2016.

Pinker, Steven. *The Better Angels of Our Nature: Why Violence Has Declined.* New York: Viking, 2011.

Pires, Tomé. *Suma Oriental of Tomé Pires: An Account of the East, from the Red Sea to China, Written in Malacca and India in 1512–1515*, ed. and trans. Armando Cortesao. New Delhi: Asian Educational Services, 2005 (originally published by Hakluyt Society, 1944).

Pollock, Sheldon I. *The Language of the Gods in the World of Men: Sanskrit, Culture, and Power in Premodern India.* Berkeley: University of California Press, 2006.

Rajaratnam, S. "ASEAN: The Way Ahead", ASEAN, 1 Sept. 1992. http://asean.org/?static_post=asean-the-way-ahead-by-s-rajaratnam/, accessed 12 Oct. 2016.

Rannan-Eliya, Ravi P. "Achieving UHC with Limited Fiscal Resources: Lessons for Emerging Economies", Speech, Ministerial Meeting on Universal Health Coverage (UHC): The Post-2015 Challenge, Singapore, 2015. https://www.moh.gov.sg/content/dam/moh_web/PressRoom/Highlights/2015/Universal Health Coverage/Session 2 Slides 3 Rannan-Eliya.pdf, accessed 14 Oct. 2016.

Ravenhill, John. *APEC and the Construction of Pacific Rim Regionalism.* Cambridge: Cambridge University Press, 2011.

Reid, Anthony. *Southeast Asia in the Age of Commerce: 1450–1680.* New Haven: Yale University Press, 1988.

_____. *Charting the Shape of Early Modern Southeast Asia.* Chiang Mai: Silkworm Books, 2000.

_____. *Imperial Alchemy: Nationalism and Political Identity in Southeast Asia.* Cambridge: Cambridge University Press, 2010.

Ressa, Maria. "Indonesia's Tom Lembong: 'Let's Move Away from Playing Games'", *Rappler*, 20 Nov. 2015. http://www.rappler.com/thought-leaders/113434-indonesia-minister-tom-lembong-trade-politics, accessed 10 Oct. 2016.

Romero, Alex. "Duterte to Talk with China on Sea Dispute If ...", *Philstar*, 23 May 2016. http://www.philstar.com/headlines/2016/05/23/1586122/duterte-talk-china-sea-dispute-if.../, accessed 12 Oct. 2016.

Roth, Kenneth. "Rights Struggles of 2013", Human Rights Watch, 2014. https://www.hrw.org/world-report/2014/essays/rights-struggles-of-2013, accessed 13 Oct. 2016.

Roy, Sourav. "ASEAN: What's That and Who Cares? Certainly Not the Common Man in Asia", *Huffington Post*, 9 Oct. 2013. http://www.huffingtonpost.com/sourav-roy/asean-whats-that-and-who-cares_b_3894984.html, accessed 13 Oct. 2016.

Safire, William. "Essay; Singapore's Fear", *New York Times*, 20 July 1995. http://www.nytimes.com/1995/07/20/opinion/essay-singapore-s-fear.html, accessed 14 Oct. 2016.

_____. "Essay; The Dictator Speaks", *New York Times*, 15 Feb. 1999. http://www.nytimes.com/1999/02/15/opinion/essay-the-dictator-speaks.html, accessed 14 Oct. 2016.

Sakonhninhom, Malayvieng. "Flagships and Activities of ASEAN-ISIS", ASEAN Regional Forum, Mar. 2007. http://aseanregionalforum.asean.org/files/Archive/14th/ARF_Inter-sessional_Support_Group/Annex(34).pdf, accessed 10 Oct. 2016.

Schwarz, Adam. "Indonesia after Suharto", *Foreign Affairs*, July/Aug. 1997. https://www.foreignaffairs.com/articles/asia/1997-07-01/indonesia-after-suharto/, accessed 12 Oct. 2016.

Sen, Amartya. *The Argumentative Indian: Writings on Indian History, Culture, and Identity.* New York: Farrar, Straus and Giroux, 2005.

Severino, Rodolfo C. *Southeast Asia in Search of an ASEAN Community: Insights from the Former ASEAN Secretary-General.* Singapore: ISEAS Publishing, 2006.

Sjöholm, Fredrik. "Foreign Direct Investments in Southeast Asia". IFN Working Paper No. 987. Stockholm: Research Institute of Industrial Economics, 2013.

Sng, Jeffery and Pimpraphai Bisalputra. *Bencharong & Chinawares in the Court of Siam.* Bangkok: Chawpipope Osathanugrah, 2011.

_____. *A History of the Thai-Chinese.* Singapore: Editions Didier Millet, 2015.

Sridharan, Kripa and T.C.A. Srinivasa-Raghavan. *Regional Cooperation in South Asia and Southeast Asia.* Singapore: ISEAS, 2007.

Storey, Ian. "Thailand's Post-Coup Relations with China and America: More Beijing, Less Washington", *Trends in Southeast Asia* 20. Singapore: ISEAS–Yusof Ishak Institute, 2015.

Stuart-Fox, Martin. *A Short History of China and Southeast Asia: Tribute, Trade and Influence*. Crows Nest: Allen & Unwin, 2003.

Subrahmanyam, Sanjay. *The Career and Legend of Vasco Da Gama*. Cambridge: Cambridge University Press, 1997.

Sullivan, Michael. "Ask the Vietnamese about War, and They Think China, Not the U.S.", *NPR*, 1 May 2015. http://www.npr.org/sections/parallels/2015/05/01/402572349/ask-the-vietnamese-about-war-and-they-think-china-not-the-u-s/, accessed 12 Oct. 2016.

Suryadinata, Leo, ed. *Admiral Zheng He & Southeast Asia*. Singapore: Institute of Southeast Asian Studies, 2005.

Tagliacozzo, Eric. *Secret Trades, Porous Borders: Smuggling and States along a Southeast Asian Frontier, 1865–1915*. New Haven: Yale University Press, 2005.

Tan Sri Abdullah Ahmad. *Conversations with Tunku Abdul Rahman*. Singapore: Marshall Cavendish (Asia), 2016.

Tarling, Nicholas. *A Concise History of Southeast Asia*. New York: Praeger, 1966.

_____. ed. *The Cambridge History of Southeast Asia*, Vol. 1: *From Early Times to c. 1800*. Cambridge: Cambridge University Press, 1992.

_____. *The Cambridge History of Southeast Asia*, Vol. 2: *The Nineteenth and Twentieth Centuries*. Cambridge: Cambridge University Press, 1992.

Techakanont, Kriengkrai. "Thailand Automotive Parts Industry", in *Intermediate Goods Trade in East Asia: Economic Deepening through FTAs/EPAs, BRC Research Report No. 5*, ed. M. Kagami. Bangkok: Bangkok Research Centre, IDE-JETRO, 2011.

Termsak Chalermpalanupap. "In Defence of the ASEAN Charter", in *The Making of the ASEAN Charter*, ed. T. Koh, R.G. Manalo and W.C. Woon. Singapore: World Scientific, 2009, pp. 117–36.

Thayer, Philip Warren, ed., *Southeast Asia in the Coming World*. Baltimore: Johns Hopkins Press, 1971.

Theparat, Chatrudee. "Tokyo to Help with East-West Rail Link", *Bangkok Post*, 28 Jan. 2015. http://www.bangkokpost.com/news/general/460975/tokyo-to-help-with-east-west-rail-link/, accessed 12 Oct. 2016.

Trotman, Andrew. "Angela Merkel: Greece Should Never Have Been Allowed in the Euro", *The Telegraph*, 27 Aug. 2013. http://www.telegraph.co.uk/finance/financialcrisis/10269893/Angela-Merkel-Greece-should-never-have-been-allowed-in-the-euro.html/, accessed 12 Oct. 2016.

Tun Razak, "Our Destiny", *Straits Times*, 7 Aug. 1968. http://eresources.nlb.gov.sg/newspapers/Digitised/Article/straitstimes19680807-1.2.3.aspx/, accessed 12 Oct. 2016.

United Nations Conference on Trade and Development Statistics. http://unctadstat.unctad.org/, accessed 9 Apr. 2016.

van Leur, Jacob Cornelis. *Indonesian Trade and Society: Essays in Asian Social and Economic History.* The Hague: W. Van Horve, 1967.

Var, Veasna. "Cambodia Should Be Cautious When It Comes to Chinese Aid", *East Asia Forum*, 9 July 2016. http://www.eastasiaforum.org/2016/07/09/cambodia-should-be-cautious-when-it-comes-to-chinese-aid/, accessed 13 Oct. 2016.

Vines, Stephen. "Vietnam Joins ASEAN Grouping", *The Independent*, 29 July 1995. http://www.independent.co.uk/news/world/vietnam-joins-asean-grouping-1593712.html, accessed 14 Oct. 2016.

Viviano, Frank. "China's Great Armada, Admiral Zheng He", *National Geographic*, July 2005. http://ngm.nationalgeographic.com/features/world/asia/china/zheng-he-text/, accessed 12 Oct. 2016.

Walton, Gregory. "Sarcasm Gives Call Centres in Manila the Edge", *The Telegraph*, 9 Mar. 2015. http://www.telegraph.co.uk/news/newstopics/howaboutthat/11460424/Sarcasm-gives-call-centres-in-Manila-the-edge.html, accessed 13 Oct. 2016.

Wanandi, Jusuf. *Shades of Grey: A Political Memoir of Modern Indonesia 1965–1998.* Singapore: Equinox Publishing, 2012.

Wang Gungwu. "Ming Foreign Relations: Southeast Asia", in *The Cambridge History of China*, ed. Denis Twitchett. Cambridge: Cambridge University Press, 1998.

————, "Singapore's 'Chinese Dilemma' as China Rises", *Straits Times*, 1 June 2015.

Wang Gungwu and Ooi Kee Beng. *The Eurasian Core and Its Edges: Dialogues with Wang Gungwu on the History of the World.* Singapore: Institute of Southeast Asian Studies, 2014.

Weatherbee, Donald. *International Relations in Southeast Asia: The Struggle for Autonomy*, 2nd ed. Plymouth: Rowman & Littlefield, 2009.

Weidenbaum, Murray. *One-Armed Economist: On the Intersection of Business and Government.* New Brunswick and London: Transaction Publishers, 2005.

Weiss, Thomas G., D. Conor Seyle and Kelsey Coolidge. "The Rise of Non-State Actors in Global Governance: Opportunities and Limitations". One Earth Future Foundation, 2013. http://acuns.org/wp-content/uploads/2013/11/gg-weiss.pdf, accessed 13 Oct. 2016.

Wertheim, W.F. *Indonesian Society in Transition: A Study of Social Change.* The Hague: W. Van Hoeve, 1959.

Wichberg, E. *Early Chinese Economic Influence in the Philippines, 1850–1898.* Lawrence: Center for East Asian Studies, University of Kansas, 1962.

Wilkinson, R.J. "The Capture of Malacca, A.D. 1511", *Journal of the Straits Branch of the Royal Asiatic Society* 61 (1912): 71–6.

Wolf, Martin. "Donald Trump Embodies How Great Republics Meet Their End", *Financial Times*, 2 Mar. 2016. http://www.ft.com/cms/s/2/743d91b8-df8d-11e5-b67f-a61732c1d025.html#axzz4Kxj87a3R/, accessed 12 Oct. 2016.

Woon, Walter C.M. *The ASEAN Charter: A Commentary*. Singapore: NUS Press, 2015.

Wright, Robin. "How the Curse of Sykes-Picot Still Haunts the Middle East", *New Yorker*, 20 Apr. 2016. http://www.newyorker.com/news/news-desk/how-the-curse-of-sykes-picot-still-haunts-the-middle-east/, accessed 12 Oct. 2016.

Xi Jinping, "Promote Friendship between Our People and Work Together to Build a Bright Future", 7 Sept. 2013. http://www.fmprc.gov.cn/mfa_eng/wjdt_665385/zyjh_665391/t1078088.shtml, accessed 9 Nov. 2016.

Xuanzang, *The Great Tang Dynasty Record of the Western Regions*, trans. Li Rongxi. Berkeley: Numata Center for Buddhist Translation and Research, 1995.

Yegar, Moshe. *The Muslims of Burma: A Study of a Minority Group*. Wiesbaden: Otto Harrassowitz, 1972.

Yu, Sheng, Hsiao Chink Tang and Xu Xinpeng. "The Impact of ACFTA on People's Republic of China-ASEAN Trade: Estimates Based on an Extended Gravity Model for Component Trade", Asian Development Bank, July 2012. https://www.adb.org/contact/tang-hsiao-chink, accessed 12 Oct. 2016.

Zaccheus, Melody. "Five Things to Know about the New Indian Heritage Centre", *Straits Times*, 8 May 2015. http://www.straitstimes.com/singapore/five-things-to-know-about-the-new-indian-heritage-centre/, accessed 12 Oct. 2016.

Zakaria, Fareed. "America's Self-destructive Whites", *Washington Post*, 31 Dec. 2015. https://www.washingtonpost.com/opinions/americas-self-destructive-whites/2015/12/31/5017f958-afdc-11e5-9ab0-884d1cc4b33e_story.html/, accessed 12 Oct. 2016.

Zhao, Hong. "China–Myanmar Energy Cooperation and Its Regional Implications", *Journal of Current Southeast Asian Affairs* 30, 4 (2011): 89–109. http://journals.sub.uni-hamburg.de/giga/jsaa/article/view/ 502, accessed 14 Oct. 2016.

Zheng Bijian. "China's 'Peaceful Rise' to Great-Power Status", *Foreign Affairs*, Sept./Oct. 2005. https://www.foreignaffairs.com/articles/asia/2005-09-01/chinas-peaceful-rise-great-power-status/, accessed 12 Oct. 2016.

Zheng Yongnian and John Wong, eds. *Goh Keng Swee on China: Selected Essays*. Singapore: World Scientific, 2012.

Index

Acharya, Amitav, 101, 222
Act East Policy, 205
adat (customary law), 32
African Union, 178, 200
air travel, intra-ASEAN, 199, 223
Akbar, Emperor, 34
Albright, Madeleine, 87–9, 183
Angkor Thom, 24
Angkor Wat, 18, 24, 137
Anglo-Dutch Treaty of 1824, 38, 40
Anglo-Saxon media, portrayal of
    China in, 102–3, 107
Annan, Kofi, 117
annual ministerial meeting (AMM),
    74, 79, 87–8, 100
Antonio, Rufino D., 160
Aquino, Corazon, 85
Aquino III, Benigno, 110
Arab League, 138, 200
ASEAN-5 economies, 69
ASEAN-Australia relationship, 81–2
ASEAN Charter, 49, 57, 150, 180
    drafting of, 181
    High Level Task Force (HLTF),
        180–1
    improvements made in, 182
    institutional changes introduced
        by, 182
    launch of, 188
ASEAN Defence Ministers Meeting
    Plus, 93
ASEAN Economic Community
    (AEC), 155, 199, 208
ASEAN ecosystem of peace model
    domino theory of, 52–3
    fear of Communism and, 51–9
    geopolitical luck, 65–8
    market-oriented economic
        policies, 68–74
    regional networks, 74–5
    strong leaders, role of, 59–65

ASEAN-EU Programme for
    Regional Integration Support
    initiatives, 193–4
ASEAN Free Trade Area (AFTA),
    168, 187, 229
    implementation of, 49
ASEAN Institute of Strategic and
    International Studies (ASEAN-
    ISIS), 186, 194, 219–20
ASEAN Plus One, 74, 147
ASEAN Plus Six, 75, 183
ASEAN Plus Three, 75, 183
ASEAN Promotional Chapter of
    Tourism (APCT), 127
ASEAN Regional Forum (ARF), 75,
    88–9, 93, 168, 191
ASEAN Secretariat, 13–4, 79, 168,
    188–9, 194, 216, 226–30, 229–30
"The ASEAN Way" anthem, 155,
    207–8
Asia-Europe Meeting (ASEM), 75,
    168
Asia Pacific Economic Cooperation
    (APEC), 75, 101, 152, 185
Asia-Pacific region, geopolitical
    competition in, 201
Asia Pacific Roundtable (APR), 220
Asian Development Bank, 208
Asian Financial Crisis (1997–98), 34,
    49, 89–90, 99, 131, 145
Asian Infrastructure Investment
    Bank (AIIB), 191–2
Association of Southeast Asian
    Nations (ASEAN), 1–14, 128
    achievements of, 208–11
    admission of
        Myanmar, 77, 156, 158
        Vietnam, 59
    American-Chinese cooperation,
        76, 99
    Bali summit (1976), 54, 58

benefits of, 4
best practices of economic
    development, 68
Cold War divisions with Russia,
    58
contribution to long-term security
    and prosperity, 228
cultural diversity of, 59
founding of, 3
founding members of, 12, 49–50,
    65, 69, 74, 98, 172–3, 219
future of, 186
goals of, 208
great-power courtship of, 211
High Level Task Force (HLTF),
    180–1
on improving livelihoods of
    people, 209
India's entry as dialogue partner
    of, 78
institutionalization of, 180
joint communiqué in Phnom
    Penh, 77, 100, 143, 150, 180,
    191–2
leadership, 50, 187, 193, 195
    top-down and bottom-up, 194
model of peaceful cooperation, 51
Nobel Peace Prize for, 7, 207, 209
ongoing processes within, 212
partnership with Australia and
    New Zealand, 192–3
peace-generating efforts of, 75
people-to-people relationship in,
    179
phases of development of, 49
role in providing a neutral
    geopolitical platform, 101
as second-most successful
    regional organization, 6
size of the GDPs of ASEAN
    countries, 188–9
social and economic benefits, 211
SWOT analysis, *see* SWOT
    analysis, of ASEAN
Third World policies, 50
three bold recommendations,
    221–32

trade liberalization, 213
US-China rivalry, effect of, 95–6,
    102, 167, 190–1
value of, 211
Atisa monk, 22
Aung San Suu Kyi, 157–9, 214
Austronesian speakers, 17
Aziz, Rafidah, 155, 225

balance of power, 77
Bali, introduction of Islam in, 32
Balkans of Asia, 5, 48, 195, 209
bamboo network, 46
Bandaranaike, Sirimavo, 55
Bangkok Declaration (1967), 10, 187
baochuan, see treasure ships
"Berkeley Mafia" group of economic
    advisers, 71–2, 185
Berlin Wall, collapse of, 99
Bin Laden, Osama, 87
Border Roads Organisation (Indian
    Army), 203
Borobudur, Java, 18, 21–2
BP World Energy Outlook, 140
brain drain, 154
Brexit episode, 178, 197
Brooke, James, 139
Brunei, 31, 139–41
    middle-class population, 140
    modernization of, 140
    oil and gas revenues, 140
    relations with Singapore, 140
    Sultanate of, 139
    territorial dispute with Malaysia,
        141
    tourism, 141
Buddhism, 19, 20
    in Java, 21
    Kadampa school of, 22
    Mahayana Buddhism, 21
    in Sumatra, 22
Bunbongkarn, Suchit, 172
Bush, George W., 58, 79, 87, 94

call centres, 162
Cambodia, 141–3
    civil war, 141

closeness to China, 143
conflict with Thailand, 41, 179, 217
genocide, 141
history of, 142–3
Hun Sen's rule, 143
Sihanouk's life, story of, 142
Vietnamese invasion of, 49, 55–6, 64, 83, 99
  international opposition to, 64
capacity to pay, concept of, 189, 227
Carter, Jimmy, 87
Castro, Fidel, 67
Centre for Asia Pacific Aviation (CAPA), 223
Centre for Strategic and International Studies, Malaysia, 219
Chalermpalanupap, Termsak, 180
Chanda, Nayan, 108
Charlie Hebdo affair, 116
China, 49
  Anglo-Saxon media and, 102–3, 107
  Communist rule in, 52
  currency devaluation, 99
  emergence as a great power, 101
  friction with
    India, 101
    Japan, 101
  Han China, 21
  invasion of
    Myanmar, 108
    Vietnam, 55, 69, 108, 173
  military skirmishes with Soviet Union, 98
  Nine-Dash Line, 107, 111
  peaceful rise, policies of, 103–4
  policies for dealings with ASEAN, 77
  rapprochement with ASEAN, 129
  Shanghai Cooperation Organisation (SCO), 178, 198, 200
  South China Sea dispute, 77
    with Philippines, 96
    Scarborough Reef, 96

Second Thomas Shoal, 96
split with Soviet Union, 50, 55, 66
standoff with Vietnam over oil rig drilling, 208
Tiananmen incident (1989), 99
Zhenbao Island Incident (1969), 98
China-ASEAN relationship, 97–112, 205
  Agreement on Trade in Goods (2004), 100
  Agreement on Trade in Services (2007), 100
  annual ministerial meeting (AMM), 100
  with Cambodia, 110
  economic cooperation, 98
  on effort to return Pol Pot to power, 99
  free trade agreement (FTA), 99–100, 117
  Free Trade Area, 100, 105, 129
  growth of, 106
  history of, 97
  with Indonesia, 111
  Investment Agreement (2009), 100
  Joint Declaration, 98
  key factors in, 100–12
  with Laos, 110
  lowest point in, 100
  with Malaysia, 111
  Maritime Cooperation Fund, 106
  with Myanmar, 108
  phases of
    "falling in love" phase, 98–100
    initial phase of hostility, 97–8
  with Philippines, 110
  on South China Sea issue, 100, 110
  strategic partnership, 205
  with Thailand, 109
  Thucydides trap, 106
  travel between China and ASEAN countries, 106
  uncertainties surrounding, 100
  with Vietnam, 108–9
  on Vietnamese invasion of Cambodia, 99

Chinese Embassy, bombing of
(1999), 88
Chinese influences, in Southeast
Asia, 25–9, 43–5
benefits of two-way trade, 26
borderlands, 25
exaction of tributes, 25
history of, 25
incursions into Burma, 27
naval expedition sent to
Southeast Asia, 27
occupation of Vietnam, 27
One Belt One Road initiative, 28
payment of tributes, 27
seas and the monsoon trading
routes, 25
tribute trade, nature of, 26
Wudi, Emperor, 27
Cholas of Tanjore, 22
Rajendra, King, 24
rivalry with Srivijaya kingdom,
22, 24
tributary mission to China, 24
Christian societies, in Europe, 34
Christopher, Warren, 87
clash of civilizations, 8, 230–1
Clinton, Bill, 88, 197
Clinton, Hillary, 9, 95, 191
Coedés, George, 16
Cohen, Isaac, 224
Cold War, 4, 49–50, 57, 75, 76–8, 80,
173
Thailand's support for America
during, 90
US-ASEAN relationship during,
83–6
Common Era, 17
Communism
fear of, 51–9
in Indochina, 49
insurgency, 51
Sino-Soviet split of 1969, 50
Communist insurgencies of 1950s,
69
Communist Party
of China, 61
of Indonesia, 51

of Malaya, 51
of Thailand, 51
"community of twelve", 192–3
"Cool Biz" campaign, 135
corruption, 6, 61, 73, 120, 145, 166,
171, 174
Council of Europe, 58
admission of Russia into, 58
Crisis Group Asia, 215
Cultural Revolution, in China, 4
cybercrime, 93
Cyclone Nargis (2008), 214–5

da Gama, Vasco, 12, 35–6
Dalrymple, William, 18
de Albuquerque, Afonso, 36
de Miguel, Emilio, 131–2
death railway, construction of, 43
Deng Xiaoping, 55, 65–6, 101, 104,
106
Dutch Cultivation System, 47
Duterte, Rodrigo, 110, 162–4

East Asia Summit (EAS), 75, 80, 93,
140, 211
East-West trade routes, 31
Economic Cooperation
Organization, 200
Economic Research Institute for
ASEAN and East Asia, 225
Economist, The, 2, 102–3, 167, 208, 223
Edinburgh Fringe Festival, 225
Eisenhower, Dwight, 52
Eminent Persons group (EPG), 124,
126–7, 179, 194
EU-ASEAN relationship, 77, 112–21
administrative pragmatism, 118
on adopting ASEAN-X principle,
119
dialogue of equals, 116
differences over Myanmar, 114–5,
118
Grexit episode, 119
on method of cooperation and
collaboration, 120–1
policies of engagement with
Russia, 117–8

programme of scholarships, 116
and Syrian refugee crisis (2015),
113, 115
Eurasian Economic Union, 198, 200
European Commission, 114–5, 225
European Union (EU), 6, 178
Brexit episode, 178, 197
Grexit episode, 119, 120, 178
Eurovision contest, 225
Eurozone, 119–20
EU-Russian relationship, 79
on Ukraine, 79
Evans, Gareth, 183

Fisher, Charles, 5, 195
Food and Agriculture Organization
(FAO), 61, 145
foreign direct investment (FDI), 70,
175
"Four Tigers," 50, 68, 203
free market ecosystem, 69
free movement of people, 120
free trade agreement, 99–100, 113,
116, 117, 119, 124, 168, 172,
187, 229; *see also* Trans-Pacific
Partnership (TPP)
freedom of navigation, rights of, 92
Fukuda Doctrine, 129–30, 132, 134
Fukuda, Takeo, 129–31
Funan
domination of the trade
networks, 21
challenge to, 21
Hindu-Khmer empire of, 21
Indian and Chinese waves, 21
rise of, 20–1
trade with India and China, 21
tributes to China, 25

G8 countries, 58
Geertz, Clifford, 32–3
Georges-Picot, François, 40
global outsourcing business, 162
global trade, first great period of, 21
Goh Chok Tong, 64, 121, 166–8, 192,
194, 204
Goh Keng Swee, 10, 165–7

Gore, Al, 89, 152
great power policies, towards
ASEAN, 76–7
Australia, 81–2
China, 97–112
European Union, 77, 112–21
foreign direct investment (FDI),
80
geopolitics of, 78
India, 121–7
Japan, 127–36
key considerations for, 78
Russia, 80
trade relations, 80
United States, 79, 82–97
great power rivalry
America and China, 95–6, 102,
190–1
America and Soviet Union, 4,
49–50, 57, 75, 76–8, 80, 173
India and China, 190, 203
Japan and China, 190
Soviet Union and China, 50, 55,
66
Green Mekong Initiative (GMI), 202
Grexit episode, 119, 120, 178
Group of 77 (G77), 50, 70
Gulf Cooperation Council (GCC),
178, 200
Gulf oil spill, 94

Haddad, William, 130–1
Hagel, Charles, 95
Hamilton, Alexander, 39
Harrison, Brian, 36
high-speed train networks, 134
Hinduism, 19, 20
in Java, 21
Holbrooke, Richard, 83
Holy War, 32
between Christianity and Islam,
36
Hukbalahap insurgency, 52
Human Development Index, 140,
158
human rights violations, 91, 174

Ibrahim, Anwar, 89, 152
India-ASEAN relationship, 121–7
  on admission of India into
    ASEAN, 121–2
  Bollywood productions and,
    125–6
  Commemorative Summit held in
    New Delhi, 124
  cultural aspects of, 125
  on depicting scenes from the
    Hindu epics, 125
  dialogue partnership, 122
  economic aspects of, 124–5
  Eminent Persons group (EPG),
    124, 126–7
  on FDI inflows, 123
  Free Trade Area, 125
  on geopolitical rivalry between
    the US and China, 124
  Indian Heritage Centre, 126
  on Indian inclination towards
    Soviets, 123
  on India's soft power, 125
  under Modi administration, 124
  Open Skies agreement, 125
  with Singapore, 126
  socioeconomic development, 124
  three pillars of, 124
  trade figures, 122
  over Vietnamese invasion of
    Cambodia, 123
  Vision Statement, 124
Indian cultural influences, in
  Southeast Asia, 18–25
  Buddhist kingdom, in Sumatra,
    22
  Funan, rise of, 20–1
  Hindu legends, 33
  Hinduism and Buddhism, spread
    of, 20
  history of, 18
  impact on local Southeast Asian
    folk culture, 20
  Indianized states in Southeast
    Asia, 20
  Khmer inscriptions on, 20
  Mahabharata, depiction of scene
    from, 33

  maritime trade, 20
  monuments of Angkor Wat and
    Borobudur, 18
  mythology and folklore, 20
  political philosophy and literary
    aesthetic, 20
  rituals in royal courts, 19
  Sharia law, 32
  Srivijaya, kingdom of, 22
  Tagore's remarks on, 18
  traces of, 19
  travellers from India, 20
Indian Muslim traders, patronage
  of, 31
Indian National Army, 126
Indian Ocean tsunami (2004), 106,
  215
Indochina, *see* Vietnam
Indo-Myanmar Friendship Road,
  203
Indonesia, 144–8
  achievement of rice self-
    sufficiency, 61
  Asian Financial Crisis of 1997–98,
    34, 89
  challenges faced by, 146
  Chinese Indonesians, 45
  culture of tolerance, 34
  economic growth of, 60–1, 69, 145
  economic nationalism, 146
  Exclusive Economic Zone, 111
  foreign investments in, 71
  geography of, 144
  high-speed rail line, 202
  history of, 144
  Independence Monument,
    Jakarta, 33
  independence of, 45
  Majapahit, kingdom of, 144
  military training programmes
    with Singapore, 64
  pogroms, 46
  port polities, rise of, 20
  relations with US, 90
  religious tolerance, issue of, 146
  seafaring traders, 17
  Srivijaya, kingdom of, 22, 144

trade relations with India and
China, 17
violence of 1965, 34
Indonesia-Malaysia-Singapore
Growth Triangle, 64
Industrial Revolution, 35, 39, 44, 151
Initiative for ASEAN Integration
(IAI), 202
Inquisition (1478–1834), trials of, 35
Institute of Security and
International Studies (ISIS),
Thailand, 219
Institute of Southeast Asian Studies,
208
Institute of Strategic and
Development Studies (ISDS),
Philippines, 219
inter-ethnic violence, 34
intergovernmental organizations
(IGOs), 198, 225
International Court of Justice, 217
International Monetary Fund (IMF),
90, 132
international non-governmental
organizations (INGOs), 198
Islam, spread of, 30, 32
Islamic State in Iraq and Syria (ISIS),
8, 146

Japan
"Cool Biz" campaign, 135
investments in Thailand, 70–1
Meiji Restoration, 127
Plaza Accord of 1985, 71
relations with ASEAN, *see* Japan-
ASEAN relationship
Japan-ASEAN relationship, 127–36
ASEAN Cultural Fund, 131
"Cool Biz" campaign, 135
cultural and political divide, 128
economic aspects of, 130
in era of Western domination, 128
Fukuda Doctrine, 129–30, 132, 134
"heart-to-heart" understanding,
130, 133–4
on high-speed train networks, 134
industrial projects, 131

intraregional exchanges, 130
on Japan's failure to engage with
ASEAN, 130
Treaty of Amity and Cooperation,
129
Javanese culture
Hindu legends, 33
Islamic religion and Hindu
myths, 34
sculpture depicting scene from
Mahabharata, 33
shadow-puppet theatre (*wayang
kulit*), 33, 125
Jayakumar, S., 57, 89, 114–5, 129,
179–80, 188
Jayavarman VII, King, 24
Jim Yong Kim, 1, 210
Johor, Sultan of, 39

Kadampa school of Buddhism, 22
"kangani" system, 43
Kausikan, Bilahari, 3, 89, 109, 225
Khmer Rouge, 52, 55, 66, 142
Khoman, Thanat, 5, 9–10, 58, 172,
187
kingship, Hindu ideas of, 19
Kissinger, Henry, 98
Korean Armistice Agreement
(27 July 1953), 52
Korean peninsula, division of, 52
Kunming–Singapore railway, 134

Laos, 148–50
and ASEAN Charter, 150
chair of ASEAN, 150
communiqué with reference to
South China Sea, 150
economic progress, 149
energy exports to Thailand, 149
foreign policy, 150
and UN Charter of 1945, 150
Vietnam War, consequences of,
148–9
under Vietnamese domination,
149
Latin America, 6, 66, 70, 73, 104–5,
161, 209

Lay, James, 52
Lee Hsien Loong, 128, 221
Lee Kuan Yew, 54, 56, 62, 83, 118,
    139–40, 165–6, 187, 193
    visit to Washington, 83
Li Keqiang, 150, 205
Lim, Linda, 201
linguistic map, of Southeast Asia,
    16–7
"Look East" policy (Malaysia), 69

Macapagal-Arroyo, Gloria, 162
Mahabharata, depiction of scene
    from, 20, 33, 125
Mahathir Mohamad, 59, 63, 69, 89,
    111, 121, 151–2, 193
    non-*bumiputera* Malaysians, 154
    relations with US, 89
    territorial dispute with Brunei,
    141
    Trans-Pacific Partnership, 155
    United Malays National
        Organisation, 151
Mahbubani, Kishore, 50, 52–4, 56,
    63, 66, 68, 71, 83, 97
    "Australia's Destiny in the Asian
        Century: Pain or No Pain?" 81
    Beyond the Age of Innocence, 86,
        104–5
    "The Fusion of Civilizations",
        with Lawrence H. Summers,
        97, 230
    G77 ideology, 70
    Great Convergence, The, 197
Majapahit, kingdom of, 144
Majumdar, R.C., 16
Malaysia, 51, 150–5
    brain drain, 154
    diplomatic relations with China,
        99, 111
    economic growth of, 69, 154
    economic liberalization in, 155
    education sector, 154
    ethnic tensions in, 151
    foreign direct investment in, 70
    gross national product (GNP),
        151

Islamic Summit Conference, 152
"Look East" policy, 69
Malik, Adam, 10
Manila Pact (1964), 84
Manila Times, 160
Mao Zedong, 65, 142
Marcos, Ferdinand, 72, 161
    overthrow of, 161
maritime commerce, 17, 20, 92
Maritime Cooperation Fund, China-
    ASEAN, 106
Maritime Silk Road, 105–6, 164, 205
Marquez, Gabriel Garcia, 105
Martynova, Elena S., 80
Mawlood, Nawzad Hadi, 40
McGiffert, C., 26
McKinsey & Company, 229–30
Meiji Restoration, 127, 165–6
Melayu Patani nation, rights of, 195
Mercosur, 138, 178, 200
Merkel, Angela, 119–20
military coup, 171
Ming dynasty, 27
Mitchell, D., 26
Modi, Narendra, 124, 204
Moerdani, Benny, 61
mufakat, custom of, 2
Muslim Rohingyas, 195
    joint task force to assist, 195
Muslim wave, in Southeast Asia,
    29–35
    adoption of Islam by the rulers, 31
    attraction of Muslim teaching, 30
    in Bali, 32
    in Brunei, 31–2
    coexistence with Hindu myths, 34
    conversion to Islam, 31
    culture of tolerance, 34
    history of, 29
    Indian Muslim traders, patronage
        of, 31
    Javanese identity, 33
    pace of Islamization, 31
    reasons for success of Islam, 31
    spread of Islam, 30, 32
    Sufism, 30
musyawarah, custom of, 2

Myanmar, 155–9
  Aung San Suu Kyi, 157–9
  challenges faced by, 157
  China-India rivalry, effects of, 203
  Chinese invasion of, 108
  economic success, 158–9
  EU-ASEAN differences over,
    114–5, 118
  Human Development Index, 158
  Indo-Myanmar Friendship Road,
    203
  Kaladan Multi-modal Transit
    Transport Project, 203
  membership of ASEAN, 77, 156,
    158
  military rule, 155
  as multi-ethnic country, 158
  political transition, 158
  relations with China, 108
  self-imposed isolation, 156
  wars with China, 156
  Western isolation of, 110

Nair, Deepak, 229
Nandy, Ashis, 123
Nathan, S.R., 54–5, 60, 126, 179
New Order (1966–98), 45
Nine-Dash Line, 107, 111, 191
Nitisastro, Widjojo, 185
Nixon, Richard, 53
Nobel Peace Prize, 1, 7, 74, 157, 159,
  184, 207, 209, 232
Non-Aligned Movement (NAM),
  54–5, 66, 156
non-profit organizations, 229
North African Free Trade Area
  (NAFTA), 113
North Atlantic Treaty Organization
  (NATO), 87, 118
Nyan Win, 214, 216–7

Obama, Barack, 7, 83, 92–5, 140, 147,
  211, 221
oil rig drilling, China-Vietnam
  standoff over, 208
One Belt One Road initiative, 28

Open Skies agreement, between
  India and ASEAN, 125
Organization of American States
  (OAS), 60, 138, 178
Ortuoste, Maria, 219
Overholt, William, 73

Page, John, 72
Palembang port, 22
Pancasila, principles of, 34, 138, 144
Pangestu, Mari, 90, 225
Paris killings (2015), 116
peaceful rise, Chinese policies of,
  103–4
Peking Review, 65, 97
Permanent Court of Arbitration, the
  Hague, 110, 163
Pham, Van Dong, 55, 58
Philippine Software Industry
  Association, 162
Philippines, 159–64
  call centres, 162
  campaign to become 51st state of
    the United States, 160
  as centre of software
    development, 162
  cultural problem, 159
  dependence on American culture,
    160
  dispute with China on the South
    China Sea, 163
  economic growth of, 69
  Filipino-American communities,
    85
  foreign investments in, 71
  Hukbalahap insurgency, 52
  importance of ASEAN to, 164
  Latin American–style feudal
    system, 161
  People Power Revolution, 161
  political colonization of, 160
  relations with US, 85
  Spanish rule, 161
  US development assistance to, 85
  on Vietnamese occupation of
    Cambodia, 64
Pinker, Steven, 231

Pires, Tomé, 31
Plaza Accord (1985), 71, 129
Pol Pot, 67–8, 99, 141–2
  genocidal rule of, 47
  return to power, 99
  siding with China, 55
Pollock, Sheldon, 19
Portuguese-Spanish conflict, over
  Moluccas, 38
post-ministerial conference (PMC),
  74–5, 93, 220
Powell, Colin, 79
Prayuth, Chan-o-cha, 171
Preah Vihear temple, Cambodia-
  Thailand conflict over, 41, 179, 217
Project 2067 report, for ASEAN, 194
purchasing power parity (PPP), 170
Putin, Vladimir, 11, 80, 164

radical Islamism, emergence of, 8
Rahman, Tunku Abdul, 41, 45
Rajaratnam, S., 10–1, 53, 56, 59, 65,
  67, 165–6, 192, 202
Ramayana, 33, 125
Ramos, Narciso, 10
Razak, Abdul, 10, 53
Reagan, Ronald, 84
Red Sea–Suez route, opening of, 30
Red Shirt movement, 171, 217
Reid, Anthony, 16, 46
religious conversion, 31
religious tolerance, 146
Rice, Condoleezza, 78–9, 221
Roman empire, 21
Rómulo, Carlos, 64, 163
Roth, Kenneth, 157
rubber production, 42
  Indian immigrants for, 42–3
  Japanese invasion, impact of, 43
  "kangani" system for, 43
Rusk-Thanat Agreement (1962), 84
Russia, 80, *see also* Soviet Union
  admission to Council of Europe,
    58
  Asian strategy, 80
  Eurasian Economic Union, 198
  relations with ASEAN, 80

Saigon, fall of (30 April 1975), 53–4,
  69
Sakakibara, Eisuke, 131
sanitation facilities, access to, 210
Sanskrit cosmopolis, 19, 24
Sanskrit language
  Hindu ideas of, 19
  as sacred language of court and
    religious rituals, 19
  in Southeast Asia, 19
Savetsila, Siddhi, 59, 64–5
SBA Entrepreneurship Education,
  229
Scarborough Reef, 96, 110
Schwarz, Adam, 61, 145
seafaring traders, 17
seaports, along Straits of Malacca
  fortunes of, 22
  global trading patterns and, 22
  Palembang port, 22
  rise of Srivijaya and revival of, 22
Sen, Amartya, 34
Serat Menak, 33
Service Corps of Retired Executives
  (SCORE), 229
shadow-puppet theatre (*wayang
  kulit*), 33, 125
Shanghai Cooperation Organisation
  (SCO), 178, 198, 200
Shangri-La Dialogue (2014), 95–6
Sharia law, 32
Shultz, George, 83–4
Silk Road, 21, 28
  economic belt project, 28
  Maritime Silk Road, 106, 164
  revival of, 22
Singapore, 51, 165–8
  bilateral disputes with America,
    88
  Cooperative Programme funds,
    229
  Economic Development Board
    of, 70
  economic growth of, 69
  foreign direct investment in, 70
  free training courses to ASEAN
    Secretariat officials, 229

on India's admission into
ASEAN, 121–2
Kunming–Singapore railway, 134
living standards of people, 165
Meritocracy, Pragmatism and
Honesty (MPH) policy, 166
military training programmes
with Indonesia, 64
policy of equal payments, 228
political environment of, 167
political succession, 167–8
pro-foreign investment policies,
70
relations with
India, 126
United States, 84, 88
separation from Malaysia, 70, 165
Shangri-La Dialogue (2014), 95
training courses for ASEAN civil
servants, 229
US-China geopolitical rivalry,
impact of, 167
Singapore Institute of International
Affairs, 219
Singapore-Johor-Riau Growth
Triangle, 64
Sino-American geopolitical
competition, 95–6, 102, 190–1
Sino-Indian rivalry, 190, 203
Sino-Japanese rivalry, 190
Sino-Soviet split of 1969, 50, 55, 66
Sino-Vietnamese War (1979), 55, 69
social harmony, problems of, 34
social upliftment, 63
Song dynasty, 22
"sons of the soil," 43
South Asian Association of Regional
Cooperation (SAARC), 60, 178
South China Sea dispute
American policy on, 77
Anglo-Saxon media report on,
103
ASEAN-China relationship on,
100, 191
Chinese assertiveness on, 77, 96,
103
code of conduct on, 164

freedom of navigation, rights of,
92
Nine-Dash Line, 107, 111
between Philippines and China,
163
Scarborough Reef, 96
South Korea, 51, 68, 73, 89–90, 121–2,
161, 170, 175–6, 201, 204, 209
financial problems, 90
Southeast Asia
American economic engagement
in, 92
Chinese wave in, 25–9
connection with India and China,
18
cultural diversity of, 16
economic activity during
European colonial rule, 42
folk religion, 33
fundamental division of, 17
Indian wave in, 18–25
institutions of kingship and royal
courts, 19
land border with China, 25
linguistic map of, 16–7
maritime trade across Asia, 16
Muslim wave in, 29–35
natural resources of, 42
pace of Islamization across, 31
Sanskrit language, 19
seaports of, 22
spice trade with Europe, 35
Tagore's visit to, 18
waves of cultural influence, 15
Western wave in, 35–47
Southeast Asia Treaty Organization
(SEATO), 58
Southern African Development
Community, 200
Soviet Union, 49, 51, 66–7, 98
Cold War with United States, 4,
49–50, 57, 75, 76–8, 80, 173
collapse of, 80, 86, 173
military skirmishes with China, 98
Vietnam's alliance with, 55
Zhenbao Island Incident (1969),
98

spice trade, between Europe and
 Southeast Asia, 35
spices, search for, 35
Sridharan, Kripa, 194
Srinivasa-Raghavan, T.C.A., 194
Srivijaya, kingdom of, 144
 Buddhist temple, at
  Nagapattinam, 22
 challenge from Cholas of Tanjore,
  22, 24
 dominance of Southeast Asia, 22
 rise of, 22
 tributes to China, 24
Straits of Malacca, 17, 21
 commercial monopoly, 24
 rivalry between Srivijaya and
  Chola, 24
 seaports alongside, 22
Suez Canal, opening of, 42
Sufism, 30
Suharto, President, 33, 51, 59–60, 71,
 84, 111, 145, 184, 193, 222
 "Berkeley Mafia" group of
  economic advisers, 71–2
 coup attempt in 1965, 61
 friendship with Lee Kuan Yew, 62
 role in economic growth of
  Indonesia, 60–1
 social upliftment, 63
Sukarno, President, 41, 60, 144
 Pancasila, principles of, 34, 144
Suryavarman II, King, 24
Susanti, Dewi, 45
sustainable development, 202
SWOT analysis, of ASEAN, 178–206,
 218
 opportunities, 197–206
 strengths, 179–84
 threats, 190–6
 weaknesses, 184–90
Sykes, Mark, 40
Sykes-Picot Agreement (1916), 40
Sykes-Picot map, of Middle East,
 40–1
Syrian refugee crisis (2015), 8, 113,
 115

Ta Prohm temple, Angkor complex,
 18
Tagore, Rabindranath, 18
Tang dynasty, 22
Techakanont, K., 71
terrorist attacks, 8, 51, 91, 116
Thailand, 168–72
 Buddhist culture in, 71
 conflict with Cambodia, 41, 179,
  217
 diplomatic relations with China,
  99
 economic growth of, 69
 financial crisis, 89
 gross national product (GNP),
  170
  history of, 169–70
  influence of Indian culture on,
   169
 insurgency in, 195–6
 Japanese investment in, 70–1
 under junta rule, 196
 Manila Pact (1964), 84
 Melayu Patani nation, rights of,
  195
 military coup, 171
 People Power Party, 196
 policy towards Vietnamese
  occupation of Cambodia, 64
 political uncertainty, 186
 purchase of F-16 fighter-bombers,
  84
 purchasing power parity (PPP),
  170
 Red Shirts movement, 217
 relations with
  China, 90, 109
  US, 84, 90
 Rusk-Thanat Agreement (1962),
  84
 success in retaining its
  independence, 169
 support for America during the
  Cold War, 90
 war reserve weapons stockpile, 84
 Yellow Shirts movement, 171, 217
Tharoor, Shashi, 115

Third World society, 83
Thucydides trap, 106
Tiananmen incident (1989), 99
tolerance, culture of, 34
Track One cooperation, 219
"Track Two" (NGO) route, for
    ASEAN cooperation, 186, 194, 219
Trade and Investment Framework
    Agreement (TIFA), 91
trade liberalization, 119, 213
trading routes, seas and the
    monsoon, 25
Trans-Pacific Partnership (TPP), 155,
    174, 185, 201, 211
treasure ships, 28
Trump, Donald, 7–8, 11, 83, 94, 102,
    128, 164, 190, 230

UN Convention on the Law of the
    Sea (UNCLOS), 92
UN General Assembly, 51, 67, 213,
    215
UN Security Council, 78, 132
unemployment, rise in, 89–90
United Malays National
    Organisation, 151
United States, 51
    Cold War with Soviet Union, 4,
        49–50, 57, 75, 76–8, 80, 173
    defeat in Vietnam War, 83
    economic engagement in
        Southeast Asia, 92
    fight against international
        terrorism, 91
    Filipino-American communities,
        85
    great-power behaviour, 104
    policy of distancing from
        ASEAN, 78
    position on Vietnamese
        occupation of Cambodia, 68
    relations with Latin America,
        104–5
    support for ASEAN, 68
    Watergate political crisis (1972),
        53
"unity of Islam," 31

US-ASEAN Connect, 92
US-ASEAN relationship
    ASEAN-US Leaders' Meeting
        on Enhanced Partnership for
        Enduring Peace and Prosperity,
        92
    from asset to liability, 88
    benefits of, 84
    after Cold War, 86–91
    during Cold War, 83–6
    on Communist expansion, 83
    on cybercrime, 93
    in education sector, 85–6, 96–7
    on fight against terrorism, 91
    on human rights issues, 91
    with Indonesia, 90
    on intelligence collaboration, 91
    Joint Declaration on Cooperation
        to Combat International
        Terrorism (2002), 91
    Joint Vision Statement on
        Enhanced Partnership, 91
    with Malaysia, 89
    in matters of security, 92
    under Obama administration,
        92–4
    phases of, 82–97
        first phase, 83–6
        second phase, 86–91
        third phase, 91–7
    with Philippines, 85
    political relationship, 83
    principle to guide, 96
    pro-American orientation, 82
    security dialogue, 92
    with Singapore, 84
    on Sino-American geopolitical
        competition, 95–6
    summit meeting, 79
    Sunnylands summit, 92
    with Thailand, 84, 90
    Trade and Investment
        Framework Agreement (TIFA),
        91
    ups and downs in, 82
    on US Permanent Mission to
        ASEAN, 92

on Vietnam invasion of
    Cambodia, 83
US-ASEAN Summit, 79, 210–1

Vietnam, 172–6
    acquisition of Soviet-piloted MiG-
        23s, 84
    alliance with Soviet Union, 55
    Chinese invasion of, 55, 69, 108,
        173
    Communism in, 49, 52
    Communist victories in, 54
    decision to join ASEAN, 57
    economic prospects of, 175
    history of, 173
    invasion of Cambodia, 49, 55–6,
        64
        American position on, 67, 83
        ASEAN reaction on, 67
        Chinese position on, 67–8, 99
        Philippine position on, 64
        Soviet position on, 67
        Thai position on, 64
    mortality rate, 210
    opposition of ASEAN, 55
    relations with China, 108–9
    standoff over Chinese oil rig
        drilling, 208
    Trans-Pacific Partnership (TPP),
        174
    Vietnam War, 4, 7, 55, 80
        America's defeat in, 83
    withdrawal of Americans from,
        54

Wanandi, Jusuf, 61, 186, 219
Watergate political crisis (1972), 53
Weidenbaum, Murray, 46
Western wave, in Southeast Asia,
    35–47
    Anglo-Dutch Treaty of 1824, 38,
        40
    British, arrival of, 39
    British domination of Burma, 41

British-Dutch rivalry, 39
capture of Malacca by
    Portuguese, 36, 38
civilizing aspects of, 36
colonialism, issue of, 40
commercial war and religious
    crusade, 36
Dutch, arrival of, 38
European colonial rule, 42
first Europeans to arrive in
    Southeast Asia, 35
French, arrival of, 39
French domination of Indochina,
    41
goal of, 38
impact of, 35
Indian immigrants, arrival of,
    42–3
modernization of the region, 36
Portuguese, arrival of, 35
Portuguese-Spanish conflict over
    Moluccas, 38
search for spices, 35
Spanish colonization of the
    Philippines, 38
spice trade, 35
Sykes-Picot Agreement (1916), 40
violence against Moslems, 36
Wong Kan Seng, 59
World War II, 69, 128, 161
Wudi, Emperor, 27

Xi Jinping, 11, 28, 104–6, 204–5

Yang Jiechi, 191
Yellow Shirts movement, 171, 217
Yeo, George, 3, 129, 183, 212, 214
Yukichi, Fukuzawa, 127

Zhenbao Island Incident (1969), 98
Zheng, Bijian, 27–8, 31, 103
Zheng He, Admiral, 27–8, 31
Zhu Rongji, 99, 101